CHARLES A. RUUD is a member of the History Department at the University of Western Ontario.

Fighting Words conveys two meanings. The first is censorship, the ongoing fight against objectionable words and ideas waged by government through particular policies, statutes, and agencies. The other refers to words published legally which fight the limits on printed expression – the words of the writers, editors, and publishers who were bent on delivering themselves from the censorship measures imposed by the Russian autocracy.

Censorship took many forms in Imperial Russia. This study focuses on the main one: the governmental system which screened written works before or after publication to determine their acceptability.

Ruud shows that, during the nineteenth century, the Russian Imperial government came to grant far more extensive publishing freedom, governed by law, than most Westerners realize. It went a long way towards accepting liberal Western practices in dealing with an institution – the press – that had developed by copying Western precedents.

Ruud also reveals that the government, having modified its paternalistic role in 1865 by granting the press a position recognized in law, fell far short of implementing this reform and thus contributed to the growth of opposition to the Tsardom in the second half of the nineteenth century and the first few years of the twentieth.

CHARLES A. RUUD

Fighting Words:
Imperial Censorship and the
Russian Press, 1804–1906

UNIVERSITY OF TORONTO PRESS
Toronto Buffalo London

© University of Toronto Press 1982
Toronto Buffalo London
Printed in Canada

ISBN 0-8020-5565-6

To my parents and Julie

Canadian Cataloguing in Publication Data

Ruud, Charles A., 1933–
 Fighting words : imperial censorship and the
 Russian press, 1804–1906

 Bibliography: p.
 Includes index.
 ISBN 0-8020-5565-6

 1. Censorship – Soviet Union – History – 19th
 century. 2. Liberty of the press – Soviet Union –
 History – 19th century. I. Title.
 Z658.R9R88   363.3'1'0947   C81-095138-X

Contents

Preface

TRANSLITERATION

The Library of Congress system of transliteration has been followed, but with adjustments. Instead of the 'ii' ending that would occur in Russian surnames, I have adopted the Anglicized 'y'; 'Chernyshevskii' in the LC system is 'Chernyshevsky' in my text. I have also eliminated the apostrophe which serves to replace the Russian soft sign in the LC system; what would be 'Murav'ev' according to the LC system becomes 'Muraviev' in my text, and sometimes no letter replaces the apostrophe. Nor did I use the LC symbol for the Russian hard sign ('') or the soft 'e' (ё). I have, however, used these symbols in the bibliography.

I have standardized spelling to conform to modern orthography. 'Russkago' in the old style becomes 'Russkogo' in the new. Numerous titles of publications appear in the text as well as in the notes. In the text, I cite them in English translation with the transliterated Russian version in parentheses upon first mention.

CALENDAR

All Russian dates are in the Julian calendar, in effect in Russia until 1918. Dates in the Julian calendar were eleven days behind the western Gregorian calendar in the eighteenth century; twelve, in the nineteenth; and thirteen, in the twentieth.

ACKNOWLEDGMENTS

I have benefitted from the encouragement and example of many persons while writing this book, especially my teachers at Berkeley, Professors

Martin E. Malia and Nicholas V. Riasanovsky; K.A. Papmehl of the University of Western Ontario; Adam B. Ulam of Harvard University; and P.A. Zaionchkovsky of Moscow State University. The editorial work by Marjorie L. Ruud has been invaluable. Principal typists were Marion Dundas and Jacqueline Jones and I thank them for their patience and kindness.

I wish also to express my thanks to those who have supported this work financially: the Inter-University Committee on Travel Grants, the Canada Council, and the Dean of Social Science at the University of Western Ontario. I am grateful, as well, to the Russian Research Center at Harvard University, where I spent a year as a fellow.

This book has been published with the help of grants from the Social Science Federation of Canada, using funds provided by the Social Sciences and Humanities Research Council of Canada, and the Publications Fund of the University of Toronto Press. A grant from the J.B. Smallman Fund has also been provided by the University of Western Ontario.

FIGHTING WORDS: IMPERIAL CENSORSHIP
AND THE RUSSIAN PRESS, 1804–1906

Introduction

'Fighting Words,' the title of this study of approximately a century of censorship under the Russian emperors, serves to convey two meanings. The first is that of censorship, or the ongoing fight against objectionable words waged by the government through particular policies, statutes, and agencies. In its other meaning, my title refers to the words published legally by members of the press which served to fight the limits on printed expression. Under this rubric, 'fighting words' are those of the writers, editors, and publishers who comprised the unofficial (as opposed to the official, or governmental) press who were bent on delivering themselves from censorship measures imposed by the Russian autocracy.

Censorship took many forms in Imperial Russia. This study focuses on the main one: the governmental system which screened written works before or after publication to determine their acceptability. That system of censorship substantively began with the founding of the Chief Administration of Schools in the Ministry of Education in 1804 and lasted until November-April 1905–06. The administration's mandate set it apart from such specialized agencies as the ecclesiastical and foreign committees of censorship, which here receive only incidental discussion. Also such related matters as libel and defamation laws and the efforts of the Russian government to influence opinion in western Europe are given limited treatment. Nothing is said about censorship by the 'black office' (established to censor and monitor mail) or efforts to limit pornography.

Because this book is concerned with the censorship system and the unofficial press as 'institutions,' I have not examined in close detail the individual writers, editors, publishers, officials, or censors who play important roles or who receive mention because they are typical. I must leave to others to examine the effect censorship had on their careers, accomplishments, and intellectual and literary work, individually or collectively. Similarly, I do not deal with the impact of censorship or literature and journalism on the formation of a Russian 'mind.'

Censorship is an issue that arouses emotions: its practice produces an almost instinctive opposition. For this reason, those who use it often call it something else, as did the imperial officials who changed the name of their censoring agency to 'Chief Administration for Press Affairs' in 1865. I treat censorship as a policy question related to other policies of the autocracy, to changing circumstances, and to imperial politics. To be as objective as possible, I describe censorship in the neutral way another historian might, for example, view changing policies on taxation. Such a historian would probably not feel called upon to denounce taxes, though he might point to deficiencies in their application. In like fashion, I do not make a case against censorship.

Nor do I see censorship in Imperial Russia as a monolithic element in political and intellectual life. Policy on censorship changed a great deal over time; and, to make clear the evolution of policy, I have dealt with imperial censorship chronologically. There is a need to get the facts straight, to see them in the order in which they occurred, in order to see why and how the imperial government changed its policies and did so in the European pattern.

I would also have the reader keep in mind the continuous growth and development of the unofficial press in Russia. The conventional distinction between reigns in the nineteenth century which were 'liberal' and 'conservative' throws some light on censorship policy but means far less with respect to the expansion of publishing. The press made great strides during the 'conservative' reigns of both Nicholas I and Alexander III despite the sometimes harsh practices of both emperors. I explain the strides throughout the century and why the publishing industry managed to take them. I show that by the early twentieth century Russian writers and publishers commanded an audience which, though small by European standards, ensured them a strong measure of independence from the state.

That growth to independent authority took place over a single century (although it accelerated after 1865) within the framework of press controls established by the Russian autocratic government. At the start of the nineteenth century, having permitted private persons to own presses only a few years before, the Russian imperial government took steps to put relations between itself and writers for the press on a regular, predictable, but paternalistic basis through a hierarchical system of censors charged with enforcing certain publicly known regulations. Half a century later, the government realized the liabilities of preliminary censorship and, through the Statute of 1865, began to dismantle the administrative system for censorship and to involve the courts, which would rule whether or not published words were 'criminal.' For many reasons, imperial officials did not readily make the transition to the new order.

These developments in Russia all had European precedents. Every major European state initially had a system of preliminary censorship, whereby every legally published word was first read, considered, and approved by a censor. Each in its turn abandoned preliminary censorship and introduced both judicial and administrative controls over the press. England set aside preliminary censorship in 1695; France, in 1789 and again in 1814; Prussia, in 1850; and the German Empire, in 1874. Russia followed in 1905–06, after having eased the application of preliminary censorship forty years before. In each case, the ending of preliminary censorship brought with it the principles of what was understood in the nineteenth century as 'freedom of the press': the right of private individuals to publish whatever they chose subject to the law and the courts, but without pre-publication reading and approval by censors. No government, however, abandoned all administrative controls over the printed word, even when its state constitution provided for a free press.

In Imperial Russia, the reform of censorship in 1865 marked a watershed in government-press relations because it created entirely new conditions for publishing. (A translation of that entire statute appears as an appendix.) The word 'press' ceased to mean an enterprise dominated by the government wherein every word was assumed to have official approval; and, because the courts began to spell out in more detail the new relationship, writers, editors, publishers, and lawyers were able to improve even more rapidly the position of the press in Russian society in the second half of the nineteenth century.

Another reason why the Russian press flourished in the second half of the nineteenth century was that Russian publishers mechanized their operations, accumulated profits, and reached out to a widening audience. With the management of their enterprises more in their own hands following the censorship changes of 1865, these publishers could easily live with the remaining administrative controls on the printed word. Mass production made possible by printing technology imported from Europe, along with better systems of communication, extended even further the influence of the press. Confident in their demonstrated authority, publishers, journalists, and even printers organized the first pressure groups in Russia to demand freedom for the printed word.

This study makes clear the significant degree to which the press did influence government policy and the close attention paid by both the press and the government to consistency in the formation and enforcement of laws governing published words, especially in the half-century before 1905. For every measure the imperial government used in 'fighting words' it considered false, dangerous, or criminal, the press more and more regularly responded with 'fighting words' of its own – many of them arguments for freedom of the press.

1

The European pattern and
the beginnings of Russian censorship

Private presses came late to Imperial Russia and press controls came with them. Then, following the European pattern, Russia gradually freed the press from government tutelage – a process that spanned one hundred years and ended only in the early twentieth century.

Censorship – in its strictest definition, the formal pre-publication prohibition by a government of words it finds unacceptable – was only one among such other controls as licensing, official warnings, fines, committees of persuasion, prosecutions, and directives. The Russian autocracy was to use these means and others to keep published ideas within acceptable limits, and all fall within the province of censorship in its most general sense. All originated in western Europe (along with the modern press) and all eventually became part of the imperial system of controls. In emancipating the press in 1905–06 by subjecting it solely to the authority of the courts, Russia finally granted 'freedom of the press' as understood in Europe.

Imperial Russia's system of controls contrasts sharply with what followed in the Soviet Union. No organic connection exists between the two systems. Whereas censorship and the press in pre-revolutionary Russia fell within a European cultural framework, which gradually accommodated press freedom, the Soviet publishing system evolved sui generis after 1917 as a rejection of press freedom. Lenin began his famous *What Is to be Done?* with a contemptuous dismissal of 'freedom of criticism.' Such 'freedom' was merely a façade for concealing capitalist control of the press. Lenin organized a press subordinated to the Communist party, and Soviet constitutions have made that relationship law.

A few contrasts are instructive. The Soviet publishing industry and press are state-owned. The government controls all printing equipment and stocks of paper. Inasmuch as all publications must select information and interpret events from the viewpoint of the official ideology, a pervasive pre- and post-publication system of censorship exists in the USSR. Censors are fully a part of the modern Soviet publishing enterprise; even writers and editors have censorship functions.

Before the revolution, in contrast, a strong, independent publishing industry existed. The imperial government recognized in law the press's right to hold and express opinions of its own on a wide variety of issues. The state prescribed no official ideology after Nicholas I. Censors had no official part in the editorial operations of publishing houses and, after 1865, saw many books and periodicals only after they had reached the public. For these and other reasons, the press in Imperial Russia gained genuine rights and became much freer than westerners today generally realize – a point that has been made both by Alexander Solzhenitsyn and by Vladimir Nabokov.[1] Wrote Nabokov: 'Under the Tsars (despite the inept and barbarous character of their rule) a freedom-loving Russian had incomparably more possibility and means of expressing himself than at any time during Lenin's and Stalin's regime. He was protected by law. There were fearless and independent judges in Russia. The Russian *sud* [legal system] after the Alexander reforms was a magnificent institution, not only on paper. Periodicals of various tendencies and political parties of all possible kinds, legally or illegally, flourished and all parties were represented in the Dumas [legislative assemblies after 1905]. Public opinion was always liberal and progressive.'

As for the beginnings of censorship in Russia, private publishing got under way only during the reign of Catherine II (1762–96), and the empress became its prime censor. She had before her the nearly 400-year-long example of western state controls over private presses plus Russia's long-established paternalism towards the printed word. European monarchs and jurists had, in controlling the printed word, provided useful concepts: seditious libel, preliminary censorship, licensing – all of which Catherine and her successors were to define and apply as they saw fit. Only later did these administrative measures begin to give way. A review of European press controls shows this to have been the western experience as well.

I

England acquired printing presses in the fifteenth century, and from the start printers served private commerce as well as church and state. But as guardians of public order and morals, monarchs found it necessary to devise controls whenever printers exceeded acceptable limits.

Applying existing laws against heresy and libel was the monarch's first means of imposing post-publication, or punitive, censorship.[2] The infamous Star Chamber, begun in the same century as printing, dealt with the more critical cases of seditious libel because the king doubted that the common law courts would act with the necessary vigour.[3] Then, in June 1530, Henry VIII inaugurated preliminary censorship – the screening of works before publication by state agents (in this case, the bishops) – for new books in English 'concerning Holy Scripture'; but he lacked the means for enforcement.[4]

In November 1538 the Star Chamber extended preliminary censorship by requiring a licence for all works in English printed in the realm.[5] Successive regimes continued press controls, although what was proscribed changed. Edward VI banned 'papist' writings through his licensing system, Queen Mary forbade Protestant works, and Elizabeth once again reversed what was heresy in her injunctions of 1559. Under Elizabeth's Star Chamber decrees of 1566 and 1586, English church dogma became the measure of acceptability for expressed ideas.

Under Elizabeth, the state also centralized control over who could use the presses. The crown had chartered the Stationers' Company in London in 1557, and, except for the royally patented presses at Oxford and Cambridge, limited all printing within the realm to the company's members. In 1566, an order in council directed the wardens of the company to report any books 'against the force and meaning' of the laws and required the accused author to appear before the Queen's Commission in Causes Ecclesiastical.[6] Finally, under an ordinance of 1585, printers had to obtain all licences for books through the Stationers' Company.[7]

The Star Chamber had meanwhile come to treat insults against official persons as high crimes by borrowing grounds from Roman law and, under both the Tudors and Stuarts, prosecuted seditious libel as treason.[8] Treasonous words could draw such severe punishments as hanging, drawing and quartering, ear-cropping, nose-slitting, and imprisonment, or the lesser penalties of fines and pillorying.[9] Moreover, the Star Chamber disregarded whether words were true or had been conveyed to others. (In contrast, once the common law courts had begun in the sixteenth century to decide when words constituted personal libel, jurists accepted truth as a defense and ruled that words caused damage only if they reached a third party. Personal libel, of course, little concerned the state.)

By the end of the sixteenth century, the king had formidable means through the law to control what appeared in print; but the onset of religious and political factionalism caused many to disregard those laws. Dissenters in the seventeenth century, for example, issued an overwhelming tide of Calvinist tracts in full defiance of the Star Chamber decree of 1637 banning heretical works.[10] So, too, because unlicensed publishing continued unabated once the Calvinists had deposed Charles I and imposed their own censorship, John Milton was fully in step with the times in issuing two unlicensed tracts in 1643 and 1644: the first favoured divorce; the second was *Areopagitica*, favouring free speech for all but 'papists.'[11] (*Areopagitica* won little notice in its day, but its argument that truth emerges only in open battle with falsehood has proved to be the West's basic rationale for freedom of the press.) Again, when Cromwell purged Parliament of his enemies in 1657, those ejected could and did at once illegally publish their grievances.

With the Restoration under Charles II, censors once more served the king and gave particular attention to reimposing conformity to the Church of England. By default came the use of law courts alone to control publishing between 1679 and 1685, when Charles's dissolution of Parliament caused censorship to lapse. Suits for *scandalum magnatum* (libels against men in power) greatly increased in number, and, in 1680, the king's judges set up a surrogate form of censorship by banning government news in any publication but the official *London Gazette*.[12]

Although Parliament, under newly crowned James II, renewed the licensing act in 1685, the Revolution of 1688 brought changes which strongly affected censorship. Not only did Parliament limit the king's power and enlarge its own, but it also passed the Toleration Act (1689) which destroyed a basic justification for censorship: no longer was absolute authority over truth vested in a divinely right king and official church.

Preliminary censorship continued, however, until 1695, when Parliament ended a system it found more cumbersome than useful. In its place, common laws – those against criminal libel, personal or seditious – alone would govern the press. Thus did England become the first nation to grant 'liberty of the press,' or the right of citizens to have the legality of their words judged only after publication and solely by the judiciary. Public agreement followed that anyone responsible for 'improper, mischievous, or illegal' publications (in the words of Sir William Blackstone in his *Commentaries* of the mid 1700s) must 'take the consequences of his own temerity' in court.[13]

Thus far had press rights developed in England when Catherine II assumed the Russian throne in 1762, but what further evolved as British press policy to the end of the nineteenth century bears on this study. Agreement began to develop in England that writers have a right and even a duty to point out government errors, the argument used by Thomas Erskine to defend Tom Paine, tried in absentia in 1792 for alleged seditious libel in his *Rights of Man*.[14] But the jury convicted Paine, perhaps sharing the privately expressed views of the trial's initiator, Sir William Pitt, that 'Tom Paine was quite right ... [but] if I were to encourage Paine's influence, we should have a bloody revolution.'[15] For Pitt and Paine's jurors, seditious libel meant what it had meant since the time of Edward II: words, true or not, which could topple the established order. (Given a crisis, English courts could in the same way apply that principle today.)

Continuing fears of revolution prompted the Six Acts of 1819, which raised stamp duties on publications and expedited suits for seditious libel, many against radical writers. Once tensions had eased, the press in 1840 gained its strongest defence against libel – that of 'privilege' – accorded in the Parliamentary Papers Act. Under that act, anyone summarizing fairly a report by Parliament was immune from prosecution for libel. In addition, during the next twenty years, Parliament ended its advertising, paper, and stamp taxes, and the courts lessened the grounds for libel against 'public' persons. Through a legal precedent set in 1887, for example, English jurors could decide whether published words were fair in light of the values held by the writer, 'however prejudiced, exaggerated, or obstinate his views.'[16]

In its Law of Libel Amendment Act of 1888, Parliament extended press 'privilege' to include accurate reports of judicial processes, public meetings, and the like. But, in a retrenchment, it passed the Official Secrets Act in 1889 subjecting to criminal penalties any official instrumental in making classified documents public – a measure to limit press access to government information.[17]

Such were the dominant press controls in England before the twentieth century. In the 500 years of private publishing, preliminary censorship had lasted just over 150 years (1530–1695). Decentralization of authority and toleration in many spheres had gradually displaced the monolithic state, absolutist ruler, and one true church and had led to wider freedom for the press. The English experience would have its parallels in Russian imperial censorship policies, but the evolution of press controls in Russia was to follow continental precedents more closely.

II

Private printing in France, as in England, began in the fifteenth century when the existing laws on heresy and libel alone governed published words. Francis I in 1521 began preliminary censorship as a church function, and not until 1629 did an *ordonnance* by Louis XIII found the secular preliminary censorship system and identify its agents under the royal chancellor as *censeurs*. The government subjected the authors and printers of any uncensored works to prosecution and severe penalties.

A divinely right king and single true church still wielded power in France as the eighteenth century began, but the censorship each imposed became increasingly ineffective. At century's end, once the French Revolution had set aside king and royal censors alike, the Estates General granted citizens the right held by Englishmen since 1695: the freedom to speak, write, and print, barring 'abuse of the liberty in cases determined by law.'

This rejection of preliminary censorship jarred Catherine II of Russia and monarchs all across Europe. Over the next century – from the 1790s to the 1880s – successive French governments reimposed censorship or improvised strong post-publication controls. By then, just as in England, preliminary censorship had become morally reprehensible to the general public and, consequently, impracticable; but French officials insisted on retaining authority over what could appear in print. Their controls over a 'free' press became models for other European countries and for Russia as well.

As early as 1792–93, for example, the radical National Convention banned royalist publications and made death the penalty for anyone convicted of publishing against the convention. Preliminary censorship returned under Napoleon, along with mandatory oaths of loyalty for printers and booksellers. Although, with the restoration of the Bourbons, the Charter of 1814 promised press freedom, that very November Louis XVIII reimposed censorship – until the 'One-hundred Days' of Napoleon made him admit his error.[18]

With the press again free, a new law of 1819 made a criminal accomplice of anyone whose published works provoked a felony or misdemeanour, while a new administrative rule required deposits against possible fines from all political newspapers at rates aimed especially at the usually impoverished radical papers.[19] Lest a prosecution fail for lack of a defendant, the government required each paper to register its 'responsible editor' and required from him a signed copy of each issue at its distribution time.

During a suspension of the charter from 1820 to 1821, censorship returned. Although restoration of the charter freed the press once more, the chamber saw fit to broaden libel to include the vague new offense of inciting contempt against the government. In 1822 it imposed a warning system that empowered non-jury courts to suspend, temporarily or permanently, newspapers repeatedly warned by officials for having shown a tendency or orientation dangerous to the existing order.[20]

In 1827, Charles X reimposed censorship; but in 1830 – soon after he ruled that each paper must renew its license every three months – the Paris press helped rouse the citizens of the capital to send the last Bourbon ruler into exile.[21] Under Louis Philippe, a freed press faced harsh libel laws. Through a rash of prosecutions (520 from 1830 to 1834, with only 198 convictions), the government effectively harassed unfriendly papers. The republican *Tribune*, for example, chose to close in 1835 after fighting 111 law suits.[22]

Again in 1835, the government lengthened its list of seditious libels and reclassified some as treason, forbade mention of the king in political reporting, and compelled papers to print government statements. A propaganda office for the monarchy, the *Bureau de l'esprit publique*, issued articles and subsidized co-operative papers, primarily at election time.[23] The July Monarchy also covertly used the press agency Havas (founded by Charles Havas in 1835) to distribute pro-government articles to three hundred French newspapers and sought to rally public support through a short-lived government paper, *Epoque*.

These efforts by the government largely failed, and press agitation figured strongly in the Revolution of 1848; the editors of the two republican papers, *National* and *Réforme*, served in the eleven-man provisional government. But like every French government since the Revolution of 1789, the Second Republic was to use press controls. Initially, it ended most restrictions, and political publications of all kinds inundated Paris. Then came street disorders and the closure of papers by General Cavaignac. The National Assembly in turn resurrected many old press laws and, under President Louis Napoleon, further expanded the list of criminal libels. An official study showed that only sixteen of two hundred papers in forty-three prefectures supported the government, and, of the national papers, not a single privately owned paper did so.[24]

In 1852, a new press statute closely followed Napoleon's December *coup d'état* and his temporary suspension of opposition papers.[25] It empowered the minister of the interior rather than the courts to use the warning system of 1822 against papers whose tendency was dangerous – an administrative measure that the Russian Empire was to effect in 1862 and to include in its new press statute in 1865, just a year before Napoleon chose to abandon it. Under the Third Republic, the press again felt free to speak out. But, when all but 30 of 150 new papers proved oppositional, the republic imposed censorship in many parts of the country. Not until 1881 did it grant what liberals everywhere understood as freedom of the press: the right to circulate printed works subject only to the limits set for all citizens by the criminal code.[26] Frenchmen had enjoyed that freedom in only limited fashion since the 1789 revolution, but, from 1881 onward, realized it as a constant right.

Although belatedly, France had followed the English example of establishing by law a free, or uncensored, press. Initially, in France, as in England, absolutist press controls protected those in power from privately owned publications. Once the 1814 Charter had guaranteed press freedom, most French rulers were at least reluctant to use preliminary censorship. Instead, they devised restrictive, post-publication and administrative measures and a lengthening list of libels. Censorship protection for the church diminished following the Revolution. Still, when the Russian Empire wrote its principal nineteenth-century censorship statute in 1865, the French example of Napoleon III seemed the best way to protect the church and state from an increasingly critical periodical press.

Censorship elsewhere in Europe during the nineteenth century produced yet other examples of overlapping judicial and administrative measures. In Germany, following the 1848 uprisings, for example, the Federal Diet lifted the system of preliminary censorship it had legislated for the ten states twenty-nine years before but insisted on new forms of control.[27] Thus, although the constitution of 1850 guaranteed press freedom, the drafters of the Prussian press law of 1851 imposed such restraints as deposits against fines and registration of responsible editors. In 1863 the Diet roundly rejected the French warning system, doing so after Bismarck had persuaded the King of Prussia to proclaim it on his own authority.[28]

In 1874, three years after its founding, the German Empire committed itself to a free press but required the editors of general-interest periodicals to deliver one copy to the local police as each issue was circulated.[29] The police could confiscate any issue which, in its view, incited civil disobedience or class hatred or which offended the ruler of a German state. If the courts within five days upheld the seizure, the editor faced criminal prosecution; if not, the police released the issue. Germany had proclaimed the press fully responsible before the laws alone, but had imposed a form of preliminary censorship, as would Russia.

Following an earlier French example, the German government further offset its relatively liberal press law of 1874 by increasing prosecutions, usually under the law forbidding insult to the emperor, the chancellor, the state, and its institutions; and some 3,827 press-related trials took place between 1874 and 1890.[30] So, too, the Central Office for Press Affairs (founded in 1850) gave loyal journalists information and subsidies and published two newspapers.[31] In addition, once he had become chancellor in 1871, Bismarck used the Guelph Fund to buy support from journalists and papers, and gained control over the news dispatched by the Central Telegraph Agency (the Wolff Bureau) by giving it a monopoly on news transmission.[32] Finally, after 1878, Bismarck's anti-socialist legislation permitted the outright suppression of socialist publications.[33] By all these means, Germany hedged its constitutional guarantee of a free press.

Compared with Germany, Denmark in the nineteenth century enacted somewhat more liberal press laws; but Sweden, through its statute of 1812 and its several supplements, proved the most generous government in all of Europe.[34] Publications there reached the public without prior censorship and could then be confiscated solely by judicial officers, not the police, pending trial for specific crimes. Grounds for suit were libel and the undermining of the political and social order, abuse of religion or the honour of individuals, and obscenity. The fines for daily papers (seen to be more dangerous) were twice those against other publications. Alone on the continent, Sweden assigned specific official documents to the public arena and guaranteed press access to them. Editors could also consult a state-provided Liberty of the Press Committee about the legality of words as yet unpublished.

Throughout the 1800s, preliminary censorship ended in much of Europe, its decline paralleling that of absolutism in church and state. The abolition of censorship meant 'liberty of the press,' but governments granting that freedom repeatedly insisted on inspecting printed works just before or as they circulated to expedite their confiscation of dangerous or 'illegal' statements. Penalties and restraints through magistrates, jury courts, or mere administrators could follow; but the wide use of the judiciary meant, at least, as it had in England, that the press was gaining legal status and rights. But even as the position of the press improved, government officials remained basically intolerant to criticism by the press and stood ready to impose additional limits in times of crisis. The essentials of the European experience were duplicated in Imperial Russia.

III

As in the West, printing began in Russia under absolutist rulers who took for granted that the press must never challenge their authority nor that of the church. In Russia, however, private publishing and preliminary censorship began only in the late eighteenth century.

Not until the last half of the sixteenth century did the first press in all of Russia reach Moscow; the first book printed in Russia appeared in 1564. A second press soon operated in the capital and, later, in a monastery nearby. In the next one hundred years, printers used these two presses and a few new ones solely for the Russian Orthodox church. The first Russian emperor to make political use of printing was Peter I (1682–1725). He himself founded and supervised the first printed newspaper, the *Bulletin* (*Vedomosti*), begun in Moscow late in 1702.[35] It would, in time, describe the building of Russia's first fleet and factories, explain events and trade developments, publicize scientific advances in Europe, and print all imperial ukazes. In its columns, Peter described the prolonged war against Sweden (1700–21). The *Bulletin* kept its official character until the Russian Revolution closed it in 1917. (It lapsed in 1727, but the Academy of Sciences reopened it in 1728 as a twice-weekly paper and made it a daily after 1800.)

Another of Peter's innovations was the printing plant established under the Senate in 1719. A form of censorship soon followed: because secular works could undermine the church, Peter on 5 October 1720 forbade anyone to print 'both old and new books without having notified the ecclesiastical college and without having received its permission.'[36] Peter reaffirmed the church's censorship authority in his Ecclesiastical Statute of 1721, and, after creating the Holy Synod that same year, empowered the synod to examine all manuscripts to be circulated and to approve for sale all religious books and illustrations.[37]

To suppress ideas they opposed – whether spoken, written, or published – Peter and his successors used the articles forbidding lese-majesty and treason in the Code of the Tsar Alexis (1649). The Preobrazhensky Commission (Preobrazhenskii Prikaz), the police agency founded by Peter, could arrest anyone connected with a criminal utterance and subject him to such terrible punishments as physical torture. In the absence of private presses, Russia needed neither a separate censorship organization nor specific press laws.

Peter II (1727–30) continued preliminary censorship by the church. After transferring the Holy Synod press and all religious publishing to Moscow and dividing secular printing between the Senate (for ukazes) and the Academy of Sciences (for all else), he required synod approval of academy publications. Not until 1750, under the Empress Elizabeth (1741–61), did the academy win the right to censor its own works independently.[38] Moscow University, founded under Elizabeth, from the outset censored its own publications.

Private publishing on state presses first began in 1759 when A.P. Sumarokov contracted with the Academy of Sciences to print his *Industrious Bee* (*Trudoliubivaia Pchela*). But Sumarokov gave up the venture by year's end, complaining to a friend about the academy censor: 'Whatever he does not like he suppresses ... notwithstanding the fact that I am publishing in a private capacity and paying money for it.'[39] Also short-lived was the second unofficial journal, *Leisure Time Usefully Employed* (*Prazdnoe vremia v polzu upotreblennoe*), printed in 1759 and 1760 on the state press acquired by the Cadet Corps, which served both as leasor and censor. By the reign of Catherine the Great, the Russian state practised censorship but had not established a centralized system.

Catherine (1762–96) began her reign viewing the press as a means, and herself as an agent, of enlightenment. In her instructions of 1767 to the legislative commission drafting a new code of laws, Catherine called for 'great Care' in assessing published libels and stressed the 'Danger of *debasing* the human Mind by *Restraint* and *Oppression*; which can be productive of nothing but Ignorance.' She also insisted that words are treasonable only if they '*prepare* or *accompany* or *follow*' acts of treason and that to misinterpret words, often indiscreetly uttered, was to 'pervert the whole order of things.'[40] As chief censor during the first twenty years of her reign, Catherine readily undertook such tasks as assessing and correcting Sumarokov's comedy, 'The Grafter,' before its publication in 1768; and a year later she anonymously founded and then wrote for a satirical journal, *Miscellany* (*Vsiakaia Vsiachina*), aimed at persuading her subjects to improve their morals. In like spirit, she subsidized several historians whose works stimulated national pride.[41]

The state-church monopoly on printing continued, but the start of private publishing was anticipated in 1767 both by the Academy of Sciences and the police in separate memoranda to the legislative commission. In its submission, the academy urged that 'when private presses come into being, the university in Moscow and the academy in St Petersburg can issue permits for whatever will be printed there,' as could be done at 'other places where printing presses will be established and where there will be academies and universities.'[42] In its memorandum, the police offered to serve as censors, vowing to seize and destroy 'libelous writings or books creating temptation to human morals or life' and to punish their authors after referring them to the empress. Anyone challenging the 'law of God' would be dispatched to the 'highest ecclesiastical authority for punishment.'[43]

Special government approval for the first private press came four years later. In a ukaz early in 1771, Catherine permitted a foreigner, Johann Hartung of Mainz, Germany, to operate his own press to print books in languages other than Russian. She subjected his works to censorship by the Academy of Sciences, required his name on each publication, and forbade content opposing 'Christianity, the government, or common decency.' She allowed Johann Karl Schnorr to start a press under the same conditions the next year. In five more years, Catherine permitted Schnorr and Weitbrecht, another foreigner, to open a private printing plant in Moscow and there to publish both foreign and Russian books.[44] In her ukaz approving this shop, Catherine also required official approval for the reprinting of books, a censorship measure as well as a primitive form of copyright. Proof that another private press existed in 1778 is a government contract that year with a printer named Meier for the publication of ukazes.[45] Official presses apparently could not handle the growing volume of government publishing.

Finally, in 1783, Catherine by statute granted general approval for private presses.[46] Russia's Academy of Sciences in St Petersburg and university in Moscow would continue to censor works from their own presses; but the police would oversee the privately owned, or 'free,' printing plants and act as preliminary censors to bar any words against the 'laws of God and the state' or of a 'clearly seditious' nature. Private printing plants could open anywhere in the empire. The police were to treat them as they would any other factory or workshop and were merely to require their owners to register their locations.

By the end of Catherine's reign, private plants numbered twenty-six in the two capitals and eleven in the provinces. These plus the original state presses and new ones in the War Department, the Holy Synod in St Petersburg, and the Academy of Fine Arts produced nearly 9,000 different books under Catherine.

Among the first to become private printers under the 1783 statute was N.I. Novikov, who founded the Moscow Typographical Company in 1784. Novikov had begun publishing in 1769 by hiring the Academy of Sciences to print his unofficial journal, *Drone* (*Truten*), but Catherine's objections to Novikov's 'licence of language' had caused the empress to close *Drone* in 1770. Three more journals attempted by Novikov failed financially between 1770 and 1774. Becoming a Freemason in 1775, Novikov next directed his energies towards Masonic educational goals.[47] He published twenty-two issues of a weekly, *St Petersburg Scholarly Bulletin* (*Sanktpeterburgskie Uchenye Vedomosti*), in the first half of 1779. When, in 1780, he leased the presses of the University of Moscow under arrangements that were to last for nine years, Novikov became editor of *Moscow Bulletin* and introduced into its pages literary works and foreign news.[48]

Trouble with the empress recurred in the summer of 1784, when Catherine ordered Novikov to discontinue in *Moscow Bulletin* a history critical of the Jesuits, whom she favoured, and seized issues containing earlier instalments, despite their having passed the police censorship. In December 1785 Catherine detected 'much mischief' in Novikov's works and insisted that all presses be 'properly censored.'[49] Having in hand a list of 461 titles published by Novikov, she ordered the metropolitan of the Orthodox church in Moscow, Platon, and the military governor to assess them all. Of those he immediately read, Platon disapproved six; but, upon the empress's request that he interview the publisher, Platon found Novikov religiously sound.

Dissatisfied, Catherine that January directed the governor of Moscow to warn Novikov not to print 'works filled with the new schism [Masonry] aimed at misleading the ignorant and gathering them into their net.' Catherine next confiscated the six books Platon had disapproved and informed Moscow printers that 'strange philosophizing' could bring closures of printing plants and bookstores, legal proceedings, and further confiscations. In 1787, Catherine forbade the printing of any religious texts in secular plants and their sale in secular bookstores; and, early in 1789, she terminated Novikov's lease of Moscow University's press.[50]

Then came the increasingly alarming reports of the French Revolution and the appearance in St Petersburg in late May 1790 of a book Catherine found rampantly seditious. It was *A Journey from St. Petersburg to Moscow* by Alexander Radishchev, the head of the St Petersburg customs house and a decorated offspring of a gentry family.

As a young man, Radishchev had studied in Leipzig, and in 1773 he had, without incident, disavowed in print the absolute authority of the sovereign. He introduced a Russian translation of Mably's *Observations sur l'histoire de la Grèce*, printed on a government press, as follows: 'The injustice of the sovereign gives the people, who are his judges, the same or an even greater right over him than the law gives to judge criminals. The sovereign is the first citizen of the people's commonwealth.'[51] In 1779 Radishchev began his *Journey* and, ten years later, anonymously submitted it through a friend to the St Petersburg police censorship. According to Radishchev's later testimony, only at the end of 1789 (November, seemingly) did Police Chief Ryleev officially approve the work by affixing his signature. That Ryleev was unaware of what was in the book is likely, given these words by the contemporary publisher, Nicholas Selivanovsky: 'There was no censorship. Books were examined by the administration or the police chief; that is, they were presented but not read.'[52]

Because a printer he approached turned down the book, Radishchev bought his own press and legally set it up at home. With the help of subordinates in the customs house, he spent nearly six months printing 650 copies of the 456-page *Journey*. That May he released only thirty-one copies, all but six to St Petersburg booksellers.

Those few copies attracted increasing attention, for the book blamed a circle of sycophants for blinding Catherine to wrongs in her government, in the church, and in serfdom. Radishchev had exposed these wrongs, he later testified, to stimulate reforms. He inveighed, for example, against censorship. His book also included an 'Ode to Liberty,' in which Radishchev touched again on the rule of law governing crowned rulers: 'I consider you, Cromwell, a criminal, because, having power in your hands, you destroyed the citadel of freedom. But you have taught generation after generation how nations can avenge themselves; you had Charles executed by due process of law.'[53]

Having read at least part of Radishchev's *Journey*, Catherine, on 27 June, ordered a full-scale investigation. On 30 June the police arrested Radishchev and seized the copies of *Journey* remaining in his home, burning them shortly thereafter. By 7 July Catherine had closely scrutinized the book and pronounced the author 'infected and full of the French madness ... trying in every possible way to break down respect for authority and for the authorities.'[54] Yet another charge was that Radishchev had substantially changed the text approved by police censors.

In his deposition to the police, Radishchev admitted that he had been 'audacious' and asked for mercy. His attack on censorship had stemmed from wanting what was best for Russia and he had not sought to foment a rebellion. Rather, because attaining literary honours had been his first aim, he had written for a small audience and had done so anonymously to discover public reaction before identifying himself. Finally, what changes he had made in the censored manuscript were insignificant and he could remember only a few of them.[55]

That July, four judges of the St Petersburg Criminal Court sentenced Radishchev to death for lese-majesty, incitement to rebellion, and treason as defined in the Code of 1649 and the military statute (morskoi ustav). Following a review ordered by the empress, the Senate confirmed the lower court's decision and specified that Radishchev must suffer the knout, be sent in chains to Siberia for a period of penal labour, and then be beheaded.[56] In its review completed 19 August the Council of State agreed, but within two weeks Catherine had reduced the sentence to ten years' exile in Siberia. Radishchev was genuinely astonished at his fate. After all, Catherine had so far dealt rather tolerantly with Novikov – but he, too, was soon to suffer her wrath.

Towards the end of 1790 Catherine had named as military governor of Moscow A.A. Prozorovsky, a man who suspected that Novikov headed a masonic plot against the church and state. In April 1792 Prozorovsky found a pretext for arresting Novikov: the publisher had kept and even sold some of the books Platon had condemned. The empress ordered an investigation to find the grounds for trying Novikov, who soon occupied a cell in Schlusselburg fortress northeast of St Petersburg. Lengthy interrogations there provided no evidence of crimes, so Prozorovsky persuaded the empress to sentence Novikov without trial to fifteen more years of imprisonment for treasonable activities.[57]

The fates of Radishchev and Novikov warned writers and police censors alike to govern carefully what appeared in print, and Catherine had no more trouble with the press. Nonetheless, on 16 September 1796, as one of her last acts, the empress replaced her police censors with Russia's first agency to administer 'censorship,' a term officially used for the first time.[58] As a 'limitation on the freedom of publishing,' Catherine abolished the twenty-five-year-old 'free' printing industry, except for a few private presses especially approved by the state. Just as before the Statute of 1783, only through a government order could a private individual print a work or own a press.

Censorship offices to screen secular publications opened in Moscow and St Petersburg under the supervision of the Senate and, for imported works, in Riga, Odessa, and the Radzivillov customs office under the provincial governors. Each office included one censor from the Holy

Synod, another from the Academy of Sciences or the University of Moscow, and a third from the Senate; each was to bar anything 'against God's law, government orders, or common decency.' Postal officials were to burn any foreign journals in the mails found to violate those strictures. The Holy Synod alone continued to censor religious works.

When, less than two months later, Catherine died, Paul I (1796–1801) pardoned both Radishchev and Novikov; but he also immediately tightened censorship. Paul saw the French Revolution as an inevitable result of the Enlightenment and banned all sympathetic references to both. He named a special censorship committee under the State Council and ordered censors to refer to it any questionable publications.[59] Paul reviewed the minutes of this committee and often made rulings himself.

In 1799 Paul required censors to board ships with customs inspectors to examine written and printed material before it entered his realm, and he added censorship officers at Revel, Vyborg, Frederickshamn, and Archangel.[60] He also outlawed receiving an objectionable periodical by 'commercial traveller, courier, or post' and passing it on, and he penalized censors who failed to ban unacceptable publications.

Within months, Paul centralized all censorship in a single administration in St Petersburg which was to approve every book published in the empire, and decreed a ban on foreign books debauching 'faith, civil law, and morality.' At the same time, he forbade the selling of type by those given special permission to own private presses.[61] Paul opened the nineteenth century with strict, centralized controls on printing and publishing, but, partly because of those strictures, he was to rule for only another year.

From its very invention, the printing press in the West belonged to private printers and no western sovereign ever attempted to issue a general ban on private presses. Controls over the printed word in the West differed primarily with respect to whether censorship took place before or after publication. Limits on what was acceptable in print and the severity of punishments varied too, of course; but the fundamental acceptance of the press in private hands gave unofficial publishing a status soon legally defined and then gradually enlarged by law to include associated rights.

Russia's provincialism kept publishing outside the realm until the second half of the sixteenth century. The first few imported presses belonged to the church and state, who held absolute sway, and that monopoly on printing continued for two hundred years. Catherine permitted the first few private presses in the seventies and eighties and extended approval generally in 1783 as part of her efforts towards spreading enlightenment. Then the French Revolution made the empress cautious. Her severe punishments of Radishchev and Novikov were followed by the virtual elimination of private publishing before she died.

At a time when private publishing in the West had laid firm claim to its rights as a commercial enterprise and as an informational and cultural institution benefitting the state, all printers and publishers in Russia remained in servitude to the empire and in sufferance to the autocrat's whims. As the nineteenth century began, controls had grown even stricter under Paul, whose disenchantment with the West amounted to paranoia. But 1801 was to bring to power Alexander I, whose reign marked the beginning of imperial censorship as a centralized, educationally directed institution.

2

The early administrative system and the rise of mysticism, 1801–17

Having given tacit approval to the plot against the Emperor Paul I, Alexander succeeded his father on 12 March 1801, under a mandate to correct the conditions that had provoked the conspiracy. In particular, Alexander knew that he had to remove the draconian measures which had alienated the gentry, and the new emperor therefore made immediate changes in the use of censorship. But, because he did not know the further intentions of the plotters, he kept full control over publishing by restoring the 1796 regulations of Catherine II.

What was shortly to emerge between government and writers, however, was a harmony unmatched at any other time in the history of imperial censorship. The new emperor was to value and encourage publishing. His government was to open presses, promote advances in printing, subsidize books and journals, and produce the most liberal censorship statute ever to appear under the double-headed eagle of Imperial Russia. State universities and the Ministry of Public Education would become the principal censorship agencies; and relatively tolerant academics, many of them writers, would serve as censors, often in the role of avuncular advisors to the authors in their charge.

Writers already dotted the bureaucracy because most came from the nobility, who traditionally entered government service, and because few could earn a living in literature alone. So inspired a poet as Alexander Pushkin found early in life that a minor post in the Ministry of Foreign Affairs easily combined with his literary and social life. Nor did his verses against tyranny prevent his working for an absolutistic state.

Close ties and likemindedness among those who wrote and governed help explain the benignity of censorship when it officially began under Alexander I. The drafters of the Statute of 1804 saw writers and publishers as allies, not – as would their successors – as adversaries bent on evading whatever limits the state contrived.

I

Nothing in his past would have inclined Alexander I to favour a freer press. Little concerned with books, he was no champion of the printed word; and, although better versed in French than in Russian, he was not familiar with the classics of any language. Alexander's tutor, the Swiss republican Cezar LaHarpe, undoubtedly had praised constitutions and the rights of man, but he had also surely conveyed his belief that the Russian people were unready for a free press. As for the fledgling emperor's past experience with censorship, Alexander had sat on Paul's principal censorship committee and had taken part in banning several hundred books.[1]

Nineteen days after acceding to the throne, Alexander ended Paul's extraordinary restrictions on foreign books and works of music and returned to Catherine's 1796 system of censorship committees in the two capitals and in designated ports of entry.[2] Just a year later, he abolished those same committees and returned to Catherine's regulations of January 1783, with additions. He again allowed private persons to open printing plants merely by informing the police and to publish books in Russian and other languages;[3] but, instead of keeping the police as censors, Alexander used the directors of the public schools (under the civil governors) – an early indication that he regarded censorship as basically 'educational.' The academies, universities, government institutions, and the Holy Synod were to censor their own publications.

Meanwhile, finding the sweeping plans of his advisors persuasive, Alexander approved a major censorship reform by creating the Ministry of Public Education (along with other ministries) in September 1802 and making it responsible for a new, centralized censorship system for secular works. For the first time, censorship acquired the positive stamp of serving to raise cultural and educational levels. The next year, the emperor named a powerful steering committee, the Chief Administration of Schools, to counsel the minister of public education and to oversee censorship reform.[4]

Alexander intended to keep all matters of censorship firmly under the control of officials close to him. When LaHarpe deplored the naming of the dutiful but undistinguished Count P.V. Zavadovsky as the first minister of public education, Alexander replied that the Chief Administration of Schools was to run everything.[5] Two of its members – A.A. Czartoryski and N.N. Novosiltsev – belonged to his 'unofficial committee,' a group of close friends with whom Alexander met privately to plan the reforms of the first years of his reign.[6] Czartoryski, the emperor's Polish nobleman friend, was rector of the University of Vilna and vice-minister of foreign affairs; Novosiltsev was superintendent of the St Petersburg education district and president of the Academy of Sciences. Classed by the emperor as equally important on the Chief Administration were Senator M.N. Muraviev, vice-minister of public education and superintendent of the Moscow education district, and Major-General F.I. Klinger, superintendent of the Dorpat district and head of the Cadet Corps. Their intention was to transform Russian life by means of publishing and education, but not at the expense of the emperor's absolutist power.

Novosiltsev made the first proposal for censorship reform and based it on the 'free press' system in Denmark, which had ended preliminary censorship in 1771 but in 1799 had added counter measures to combat French ideas, forbidding any writer to blaspheme, advocate rebellion, spread false information about official policies, or conceal his identity.[7] Novosiltsev also favoured establishing a new government agency to decide whether to prosecute a press code violation. If the courts ruled that published works broke the law, the government would confiscate the works and punish those responsible. Books and periodicals would be judged by the courts *after* appearing in print rather than before, a radical change from the existing preliminary censorship system (which barred any appeals).

Two others on the Chief Administration, N.I. Fus and N.Ia. Ozeretskovsky, protested that Novosiltsev's plan would permit a dangerous work to circulate until an action could be brought against it and that confiscating a particular book merely heightened public interest in it.[8] Although some censors might prohibit good works, they conceded, the Russian system of preliminary censorship, properly used, should differ little in practice from Denmark's free system of publishing. Given these arguments, the Chief Administration voted to retain preliminary censorship and named I.I. Martynov, an official in the Ministry of Public Education, to draft the first 'Statute on the Censorship' issued by the Russian empire, which, with the recommendation of the Chief Administration, became law by imperial ukaz on 9 July 1804.[9]

Differing from all other pre-revolutionary statutes in the degree to which it encouraged publishing, the 1804 statute proved the most liberal press law of the imperial period.[10] It included forty-seven brief articles, all couched in very general language, for those around Alexander believed that reasonable men needed only a few guidelines. To the Ministry of Public Education fell full responsibility for secular publications, although the statute ill distinguished them from religious works. The three existing universities – Moscow, Dorpat, and Vilna – were to provide censors, a function also written into the charters of the new ones at Kazan and Kharkov; but, because St Petersburg had no university until 1819, a special censorship committee held sway in the capital. (In effect, the universities were to publish on their own presses whatever they pleased.[11]) Deans within each university served as the supervising censorship committee and faculty members were censors for the education district. Elsewhere, the civil governors drew censors from the schools of their districts.

Toleration was the prevailing tone of the statute. Each censor was to act quickly on articles intended for periodical publications. If he found passages contrary to God's law, the government, morals, or a citizen's personal honour, the censor was to explain his objections in directing the editor to make changes. Where passages were open to interpretation, he was to judge in the author's favour. Only the name of the printer, the place of publication, and the date had to appear on the publication; and a publisher did not have to re-submit a book to a censor for a second printing so long as no changes had been made.

Representative of the overall tone of the law is article twenty-two: 'A careful and reasonable investigation of any truth which relates to the faith, humanity, civil order, legislation, administration or any other area of government not only is not to be subjected to modest censorship strictures but also is to be permitted complete press freedom, which advances the cause of education.'[12] The lenient application of the law for the first few years of the reign confirms the great degree of toleration intended.

Writers who sought to undermine the church or state received general mention: 'If there is submitted to the censorship a manuscript full of ideas and expressions clearly repudiating the existence of God, inciting against the faith and the laws of the fatherland, insulting the supreme authority or completely opposed to the spirit of the social order and tranquillity, the committee will inform the government directly about such a manuscript in order to find the writer and to deal with him according to the law.'[13] Although the article provided grounds to indict an individual for mere *intent* to publish blasphemous or inflammatory words, the state, in fact, found no need to use that authority in the years immediately following 1804.

In designing the statute, the Chief Administration of Schools appears to have viewed journalistic rights in light of what Kant distinguished as the spheres of 'public' and 'private' reason.[14] That distinction made compatible, at least theoretically, absolutism and reasonable freedom to discuss public issues. Kant declared that a citizen must at all times obey his sovereign and the law; as a private man, he could believe whatever reason and conscience dictated and was then free to voice publicly his considered and informed views, even when they conflicted with his public duty. (No man of reason and conscience, conforming to the law, would, of course, encourage rebellion.) The drafters of the Statute of 1804 made similar assumptions about the press. Like Kant, they expected tensions in precisely defining the point at which criticism of the existing order became illegal, but such tensions within a just and rational legal order would advance knowledge and civic liberty.

II

Discussion of the new statute took place at a time when privately owned presses were few but increasing in numbers and when the influence of the state remained pervasive. In the year 1802 alone, four new printing plants opened in St Petersburg: those of Ponomarev, Breitkopf, E. Vilkovsky, and Schnorr. Within five years, four more began in the capital (including that of I.P. Glazunov), three more in Moscow, and one, only, outside the two major cities. Still, by 1807, Russia had only twelve private presses in the entire realm.[15]

By 1807, some fifty-four presses owned by the state served the empire, ten of them in St Petersburg and another eight in Moscow. A deliberate effort to found state printing plants had taken place during the first years of the reign, specifically to produce government documents.[16] To end the concentration of printing in the capitals, Alexander set about founding state presses in the provinces: in Riazan and Ufa in 1801, in Penza in 1803, in Ekaterinburg in 1804, in Petrozavodsk and Pskov and at newly founded Kharkov University in 1805. On 5 August 1807 the emperor issued a rescript ordering that each provincial administration have a printing plant. He also provided an annual allotment of 4,215 rubles for each state press, in addition to an outright grant of 20,310 rubles for improvements at each plant.[17]

At the beginning of the reign, only two newspapers, both named *Bulletin*, existed in Russia. The first, which the Academy of Sciences published, had been founded by Peter I in 1702. Moscow University had begun the second in the old capital in 1756, a year after its own start. The government used both as official outlets for ukazes, announcements, and court news. The editors added short news items culled from French, German, and English newspapers and provided what was called an 'unofficial' section, clearly ruled off, which contained articles by academics. These two newspapers provided from four to eight pages per issue and appeared bi-weekly.[18] Their subscription rate of ten rubles per year was less than half that charged by the monthly journals. (See table 1.)

Between 1801 and 1806, eighty-three new periodicals appeared in the Russian empire, although many survived barely a year or two.[19] Forty-two were literary journals offering prose, poetry, and plays by Russian and foreign writers. Eleven journals were produced under government patronage by such scholarly groups as the Free Russian Economic Society and the Society of Lovers of Learning, Science, and Art; and at least thirteen others provided general content. A striking success was N.M. Karamzin's *Messenger of Europe* (*Vestnik Evropy*, 1802–20) which featured European literature and politics and quickly acquired a subscription list of 1,200.

Only five periodicals were 'official,' or government-produced, although no sharp distinction existed between them and unofficial publications. With the shared aim of raising the general level of knowledge, both could and did discuss such affairs of state as the peasant question, constitutionalism, public courts, international affairs, and even freedom of the press – issues Catherine II and Paul I had regarded as the ruler's exclusive province.[20] Government officials, even censors, wrote for unofficial publications, which the state often subsidized.

One representative unofficial journal, the *Northern Messenger* (*Severnyi Vestnik*), for example, was begun in 1804 by Martynov, the principal drafter of the new censorship law of that year. A translator and teacher of the classics, Martynov drew support from the Free Society of the Lovers of Russian Literature and received a 3,000 ruble state subsidy (the equivalent of 120 subscriptions). *Messenger* consistently supported the government, even as it vigorously promoted western educational methods and learning; and it printed news of scholarly societies at home and abroad alongside translations of such westerners as Gibbon, Montesquieu, and Holbach. It quoted Sweden's king on the importance of a free press to an enlightened state and, through an anonymous article by N.N. Muraviev in 1805, upheld 'Great Britain's experience' as a glowing example for Russia of civic freedom, legal equality, regular judicial procedures, and popular education.[21] Then, towards the end of 1805,

Martynov announced that the loss of his government subsidy meant the insolvency of his journal, for it could not exist on subscriptions alone.[22]

Meanwhile, the government itself began a St Petersburg journal like Martynov's, an idea that originated in 1802 with M.N. Bakarevich of the Ministry of the Interior. Bakarevich favoured including historical material, state documents, and reports on civic and commercial affairs and put his plan into effect as editor of the *St Petersburg Journal*, begun in 1804 by the Ministry of the Interior.[23] Bakarevich also published European ideas – although to Bentham's 'On the Freedom of Publishing' he appended notes on the work's negative social consequences.[24] The *Journal* continued until 1809, when another Ministry of the Interior publication, the *Northern Post* [*Severnaia Pochta*, 1809–19] succeeded it. The initiators of the *Post* intended it to promote economic development and, 'to acquire the confidence of the public,' downplayed the paper's official status;[25] but they made no secret that the ministry published it and the vice-minister edited it. When, in its first three years, the *Post* attracted only a handful of subscribers, the minister of the interior increased circulation to 5,418 in the next two years by ordering local officials to sell subscriptions to subordinates throughout the provinces.[26]

Publishing in these early years of the reign suffered more from too few subscribers than too strict censorship, but limits by censors did exist. For example, after winning censorship approval in 1804 for a book on education which argued that the peasants could escape bondage only by gaining private property, I.P. Pnin failed in his request to print a second edition. In spelling out his reasons, as required, the censor objected to inflammatory words 'about the unfortunate state of the Russian peasants ... in the hands of some capricious pasha.' These words, continued the censor, could gather over Russia a 'black, fierce storm cloud' – a not unreasonable explanation considering official fear of a peasant uprising.[27] Another censorship technique was to stifle competition from unofficial publications by limiting their scope, as in narrowing to purely local topics the first weekly paper of Astrakhan, the *Eastern News* (*Vostochnye Izvestiia*, 1813–16), and turning down a proposed weekly in Tula on the grounds that the Moscow and St Petersburg *Bulletins* held the 'rights' for publishing domestic and foreign news.[28]

III

Yet, whatever their scope, whether official or unofficial, Russian periodicals in the first decade after the 1804 censorship statute attracted little general interest. Instead a public demand for religious works was evolving, a change welcomed by publisher A.F. Labzin, one of Russia's growing number of mystics and pietists. For Labzin, publishing was God's great means of spreading Christianity. Born in 1766, this zealous publicist entered the University of Moscow at the age of fourteen and there encountered a German Rosicrucian, Johann Gregor Schwarz, who influenced Labzin to reject the Enlightenment. Joining the circle around the Masonic publisher Nicholas Novikov, Labzin first published in Novikov's journal.[29] He subsequently served as a censor of foreign books until Paul banned them, and in 1800, he founded the important St Petersburg Masonic lodge, the Dying Sphinx, to which he dedicated himself for over twenty years. In 1805, he began to translate and publish the work of German mystics, especially H. Jung-Stilling. The next year he received permission to start *Messenger of Zion* (*Sionskii Vestnik*) from the superintendent of the St Petersburg education district, Nicholas Novosiltsev.

Novosiltsev's ruling was the first break in the church's absolute authority over religious publications. Two laws (those of 27 July 1787 and 9 February 1802) forbade private printing plants to publish religious works; and the Holy Synod, which could enforce its will through its censorship of all religious writings, disapproved lay commentary on spiritual matters. In approving *Messenger*, Novosiltsev ruled that article eight of the Statute of 1804 directing the Holy Synod to censor religious works applied only to sermons, catechisms, and theological works, and that *Messenger* rightly belonged under the secular censorship of the Ministry of Public Education.[30]

Labzin wrote, translated for, and edited the *Messenger* virtually without help,[31] and his radical articles on mysticism alarmed many. In July 1806, for example, he published a prophecy of Jung-Stilling that a new Lord would soon appear to capture the allegiance of mankind and, inferentially, displace Russian Orthodoxy. Moreover, by attacking rationalism, Labzin was winning the support of some Orthodox clergy. Highly-placed clerics and lay supporters consequently saw Labzin as dangerous.

A protest by the metropolitan of St Petersburg prompted Prince A.N. Golitsyn, the procurator of the Holy Synod, to oppose Labzin; and, ordered by the emperor to investigate the matter, Minister of Education Zavadovsky and Novosiltsev concluded that ministry censors should forbid Labzin's 'nonsense,' although they did not recommend shifting *Messenger* to ecclesiastical censorship. Labzin chose to close his journal rather than change its content, but he continued to publish translations of European mystics through private and even government-owned presses.[32]

Through growing hostilities and into open warfare with the French during the next seven years, gallomania and rationalism became the intellectual foes. S.N. Glinka's *Russian Messenger* (*Russkii Vestnik*, 1808 – 20 and 1824) took up the nationalistic attack on western influences by idealizing pre-Petrine Russian life. (Glinka won over 800 subscribers, half in the provinces.) *Son of the Fatherland* (*Syn Otechestva*, 1812–44), edited by N.I. Grech, published patriotic articles and defended Russian traditions. Similarly, M.I. Nevzorov's *Friend of Youth* (*Drug Iunoshestva*, 1807–15) denounced contemporary science and education, the encyclopedists, and the newer aesthetic views of the German philosophers.[33] Like Labzin a follower of Novikov and Masonry, Nevzorov was determined to combat rationalism and atheism, but he stressed nationalism rather than mysticism, very possibly as a consequence of Labzin's experience. He attracted merely 100 subscribers.

In the first years of the reign, Alexander's press policy had served to encourage western-oriented, reasoned discussions and translations which would help improve the Russian state. Thus Novosiltsev could readily condemn the mysticism of Labzin's *Messenger of Zion* as 'nonsense' in 1806. At the same time, the start of hostilities with France in 1805 had already turned censorship authorities against French thinkers and ideas, just as it had persuaded the emperor to establish the committee of 5 September 1805, to guard against internal subversion by the French in Russia. A succeeding committee, that of 13 January 1807, added to its mandate the ferreting out of dangerous books and acquired the authority to issue orders and instructions to other government agencies, including the censorship administration.[34]

As the French crisis deepened, the government established, in December 1811, a new Ministry of Police (modelled, ironically, on the French system under Joseph Fouché) to centralize all security functions in the empire, and thereby brought the police back into censorship. The police were to approve new printing plants, theatre productions, and public posters, and one office of the ministry's chancellery for secret political investigations (Fouché had a similar secret section) was to make certain that all works published and sold in the empire had received censorship approval.[35] Because that section was also to discover any works wrongly approved by the censor, the police began to supervise civil censorship for the first time.

Count Alexei K. Razumovsky, minister of public education from 1810 to 1816, strongly objected to the Committee of Ministers about police intrusion into censorship, but he encountered a formidable opponent in the first minister of police, A.D. Balashov.[36] Within a year, Napoleon's march towards Moscow caused Alexander to assign Balashov to other duties; and, with the defeat of Napoleon in 1813, the need for strict censorship ended. In two more years Balashov's successor as minister of police, Count Sergei K. Viazmintov, bid for the transfer of all censorship to his ministry and failed. Increasingly unpopular for its inefficiency and abuse of power, the police ministry ended in November 1819 and its powers were largely absorbed by the Ministry of the Interior.

IV

Napoleon's march to Moscow had convinced many Russians that human powers alone could not turn back the diabolic invasion from the West. The Bible became their guide, as it already was for the many men of high standing within the Masonic movement. In St Petersburg, in December 1812, the founding of the Russian Bible Society added to the swell of religious feeling, a development soon strongly to affect censorship.

First president of the Bible Society was none other than the procurator of the Holy Synod, Prince Alexander Golitsyn. The scion of an old and distinguished Russian family, Golitsyn had been an early intimate of Alexander, and, in Czartoryski's view 'did not seem to possess any talent but that of amusing people.'[37] Lacking in training, inclination, and religious grounding, Golitsyn was justly surprised when the emperor in 1803 made him procurator, or government supervisor of church administration. Then piety engulfed Golitsyn and, according to a contemporary, 'completely unprepared, he began to discuss theology.'[38] For his part, Alexander responded to Golitsyn's growing interest in religion by giving him an additional, though largely inconsequential, post in 1810 as the head of the Department of Foreign Confessions.

In becoming Bible Society president, Golitsyn aligned himself with a group acceptable to the Orthodox church. Many high-ranking clergy belonged, as did lower clergymen, Orthodox laymen, Masons, sectarians, and mystics of all shades.[39] The society's objective was to publish the Bible in many languages and distribute it within and without Russia. From St Petersburg evolved a network of local chapters and correspondents in every province.

Although its English counterpart gave aid, the Russian Bible Society benefitted most from the patronage of Alexander I; for within two months of its founding, the emperor enrolled as a member. He did so at the urgings of Golitsyn, who credited the Bible for his firm faith during the French occupation of Moscow and who loaned his own copy to the emperor for solace and strength. Alexander made clear his strong support by giving the society large sums of money and buildings in St Petersburg and Moscow to house printing plants and offices and by purchasing Bibles for distribution to the army and religious institutions (the Bible until then had been almost exclusively in the hands of the church and the well-to-do). Given such support, the society in its first decade produced 104 editions in 26 languages totalling 507,000 copies, most of them published in St Petersburg, Moscow, and the Baltic provinces. Of great importance, the Bible Society produced the first modern Russian translation without a parallel Old Church Slavonic text in 1822–23.[40]

What bound together individuals of widely divergent spiritual views – and what initially saved the society from rebuke from any quarter, the church included – was the consensus that private reading of the Bible benefitted mankind. But the stress on private scriptural interpretations by the zealous mystics who valued the dictates of the 'inner light' over those of the church was to create frictions.

A relatively generous censorship policy resumed in the years after the war, and pietistic and mystical publishing flourished under the censorship of the Ministry of Public Education. Reformist and nationalistic publishing were also important. There were, on the one hand, the translations of the German mystics which Labzin continued to publish and, on the other, descriptions of the American and English constitutions. In 1815, by granting the Poles a constitutional charter, Alexander encouraged hopes for a similar reform at home, and the next year a journal openly argued that a 'constitution' could never be more than a 'paper statute' unless protected by the representatives of the people – a very western argument.[41]

Discontent with the permissiveness of post-war censorship had caused Minister Viazmintov to request in 1815 that his police assume control over the censorship system from the Ministry of Public Education. As president of the Russian Academy, Admiral A.S. Shishkov had testified before the State Council in 1815 to block Viazmintov's plan but had joined in criticizing censorship practices. He attacked toleration of essays on the Enlightenment and indirectly scored pietistic works. What was needed, Shishkov argued, was a single, independent censorship agency that would rigorously ban all words that might mislead undiscriminating readers. That one agency, moreover, would censor all writings, whether sacred or secular.

Those then advocating 'freedom of thought,' continued Shishkov, feared an effective censorship by honest and able officials; and he agreed with Viazmintov that censors no longer had sound standards. Only a detailed set of rules would control publishing and prevent 'bad, impudent, corrupting, ignorant, and idle works.'[42] As a leading linguistic conservative, Shishkov was also concerned about preserving the traditional ecclesiastical and literary language based on Greek and Slavonic antecedents. For the time being, the State Council demurred on making any changes in censorship, but, within the next decade, Shishkov himself was to formulate and implement the sort of rules he had advocated.

As for the emperor, both mysticism and a sense of divine mission underlay his design for the Holy Alliance in 1815 and his support at home for mystics, pietists, and their works (he subsidized at least two pietistic books). Alexander also made membership in the Bible Society politically important, for he favoured as his officials men publicly committed to Christ. Prominent among such appointees was the Bible Society president, Golitsyn, who became minister of public education and overseer of censorship in 1816 without relinquishing his positions as procurator of the Holy Synod and head of the Department of Foreign Confessions. The officials serving under him, almost to a man, also belonged to the Bible Society.

That same year, Golitsyn resurrected the journal he had disapproved and Novosiltsev had labelled 'nonsense' in 1806.[43] In approaching its editor, Labzin, Golitsyn confessed his error ten years before in condemning *Messenger of Zion*; he had since come into the light, and, with imperial approval he urged Labzin to reopen his journal as the unofficial organ of the Bible Society. To show his good will, Golitsyn secured for Labzin a decoration – an order of St Vladimir, second class. He also permitted Labzin to undergo civil censorship, not that of the Holy Synod, although he denied Labzin's request for no censorship at all. The emperor gave the *Messenger* a subsidy of 15,000 rubles and became a sponsoring subscriber, as did his brother, the Grand Duke Constantine Pavlovich, and all the theological academies of the empire.[44]

Thus honoured, subsidized, and sponsored, Labzin undertook his journal once again, justly assuming he was a religious spokesman for the autocracy. He had, in effect, received official sanction for all that he printed in his privately owned plant; and there he chose to publish little more than his own writings and translations of other mystics.

Golitsyn had recruited and patronized Labzin as part of his mission to ensure that 'Christian piety would always be the basis of true education.'[45] No one yet openly questioned that intention, for it was, first of all, the emperor's, and the sincerity of his belief set Alexander above reproach. The targets for those convinced that the mystical bent of the administration would cause dire consequences were rather to be Golit-syn and his censorship policies. For a time, however, Golitsyn stood unchallenged as Alexander's agent for spiritualizing the nation and, on 24 October 1817 Alexander underscored that authority by making Golit-syn Minister of Spiritual Affairs and Public Education.

This unprecedented administrative amalgam of religion and education suggested a greater authority for Golitsyn at the expense of the Orthodox church. Then, a month later, when Prince P.S. Meshchersky succeeded Golitsyn as procurator of the Holy Synod, that office, until then directly under the emperor, was made subordinate to the minister of spiritual affairs and public education – as was the Department of Foreign Confes-sions. But of greatest concern to church officials and supporters was the continued overseeing of published works with mystical content by Golit-syn's censorship administration. Within a year, Golitsyn was to interfere directly in ecclesiastical censorship to defend the 'inner church' from criticism by Orthodox clergy, a move which was to consolidate the growing opposition against him. The church would soon show its con-siderable political power and talent for manoeuvre.

Meanwhile, paralleling Russian interest in the ideas of the Enlighten-ment and then of mysticism and pietism, the government and the pub-lishing trade turned to the West for new printing technology. The government, bent on advancing education, had promoted publishing since early in the reign, and its own printing establishments had become technological leaders.

To accommodate the expanding system of schools, the Ministry of Public Education opened its own plant in 1817 to publish school books, having bought eleven Paris-made oak presses from a private owner in Moscow. (The ministry also spent 35,000 rubles to buy thirteen serf-printers to operate the presses.) Both the general staff and the navy modernized their printing plants, in large part to publish educational materials on military subjects. The general staff sent three printers to Paris for training, and their Paris-trained master engraver, E.I. Koshkin, won membership in the Academy of Arts.[46]

To manufacture its own paper and to print documents and banknotes, the government in 1817–18 invested heavily in its Department for the Manufacture of Government Paper. From the West came machines to make paper – including the first horizontal paper-making machine, which produced paper in rolls – and the latest enumerating machines.

The Russian Bible Society meanwhile acquired western rapid-printing machines for its ambitious projects.[47] Although it produced its first 5,000

Bibles on the presses of the Holy Synod in Moscow, the society next hired a London printer, Thomas Ruth (Rutt), to manage its new plant in St Petersburg. In 1818, the society received as a gift from its American inventor a 'Columbia' iron hand-press made in Philadelphia, which was soon to be in wide use in England and France. Admiring St Petersburg printers urged its local manufacture, and, by the early twenties, iron presses from the Alexandrovsk machine works in the capital were rapidly displacing the slower wooden models. Even more important to the society were its two flat-bed cylinder machines which printed from stereotype plates, a fairly recent English innovation by Edward Cooper. Within several years, the Alexandrovsk plant was making the first cylinder press in Russia. (In the next reign, Nicholas I would close the Bible Society, but its modern equipment would pass to the Holy Synod. Most of its nearly one hundred printers would move to private shops in St Petersburg, carrying with them the advanced technological knowledge that would further a modest publishing revolution in the capital in the 1830s.)

In summary, by introducing the Statute of 1804 and placing censorship under the new Ministry of Public Education, Alexander I had forged good relations between his government and the private publishing industry. Because he thought much like an eighteenth-century enlightened despot, the emperor used censorship and the press to advance knowledge. He staffed his censorship organization with easy-going university academics who were also writers. Only when the French loomed as enemies did the government tighten censorship through the intervention of the Ministry of the Police. For the most part, censorship was benign and loose; and Prince Golitsyn took advantage of this state of affairs.

3

Golitsyn's fall and the decline of mysticism, 1817–25

During the last years of the reign of Alexander I, Golitsyn's use of the press as chief censor caused the church to fight back and to change censorship radically. In its campaign to regain control over all printed commentary on sacred matters, the church tried to portray published books as a threat to the very foundations of the Russian state. Allied to churchmen were officials already strongly opposed to the lax generosity made possible to writers by the Statute of 1804.

Alexander's close, liberal advisors had designed and implemented that statute to spread enlightenment, but the emperor's new subordinates after 1815 had veered to promoting radical religious ideas from the West. Partly because Alexander let authority slip from his hands, Golitsyn assumed that his policy was approved by the acquiescent emperor. Nor could the press resist; not until the next reign would editors and publishers have either the desire or the capacity to do so.

Instead the church entered the lists to topple Golitsyn, and several clerics and their allies in government proved to be resourceful political combatants. Because so much was at stake in the conflict, involving both religious convictions and political power, the struggle transformed official thinking about the printed word.

I

The shared zeal of Alexander and Golitsyn that had led to their altering the education ministry in 1817 colours their correspondence of the year before. One letter by Golitsyn refers to the 'cross of 1812' (Napoleon's invasion) which had 'prepared you, sire, for this auspicious state, that the Holy Spirit might work through you,' and recalls Alexander's successes in France and at the Congress of Vienna. 'And now the time has come,' Golitsyn continued, 'when the Lord wishes to reign on the earth, when he wishes the powerful to bow down before Him.' In his reply of twenty pages, Alexander concurred: 'My only help is in the Lord. I have completely abandoned myself to His guidance.'[1]

Golitsyn placed spiritual considerations above the Statute of 1804 in governing the press. For example, he used his office to scold the editor of *Ladies' Journal* (*Damskii Zhurnal*) for dwelling excessively on the comforts of life; and, in 1819, he banned a Lutheran catechism for reflecting a false religion of 'reason and the heart.'[2] Those appointed by Golitsyn to the Chief Administration of Schools, the agency which had effected the energetic censorship reforms of the pre-war period, favoured his policies. They included M.L. Magnitsky, superintendent of the Kazan education district; D.P. Runich, superintendent of the St Petersburg district; A.S. Sturdza, a foreign ministry official; Filaret, rector of the St Petersburg Ecclesiastical Academy and later metropolitan of Moscow; Innokenty, rector of the St Petersburg Theological Seminary and an ecclesiastical censor; and Prince P.S. Meshchersky, procurator of the Holy Synod.[3] All of them had joined the Bible Society. Innokenty and Filaret supervised printing of the society's books, and the directors of Golitsyn's two ministry departments – V.M. Popov for popular education and A.I. Turgenev for ecclesiastical affairs – both held important offices in the St Petersburg branch.

Given all these evangelical-bureaucratic ties, Labzin – spokesman for the mystical wing of Russian pietism – bid for a senate appointment.[4] He had to settle for the vice-presidency of the Russian Academy of Fine Arts; but his resulting prestige, his unique position in religious publishing as editor of the revived *Messenger of Zion*, and his growing influence among the clergy offended the church. In 1818, his radical religious views stirred direct opposition, for Labzin had come to extol inner feelings as man's best approach to God. Despite his earlier enthusiasm for the Bible Society, he now gave a secondary role to scripture and to the church as well. The supporters of orthodoxy found this doctrine a serious threat.

Two members of the Chief Administration whose first loyalty lay with the Russian Orthodox church explained this threat to Golitsyn – first Innokenty, the St Petersburg rector, and then Sturdza, fully armed with offending issues of the *Messenger*. Golitsyn reluctantly conceded but argued the impossibility of restraining a publisher already so favoured by the government. Sturdza replied that the ministry need only inform

Labzin that his religious writing must henceforth undergo ecclesiastical censorship in accordance with article eight of the 1804 statute. Accordingly, Golitsyn wrote to the Metropolitan Michael that the *Messenger of Zion* belonged under ecclesiastical censorship and, without advance notice to Labzin, informed the St Petersburg military governor that the Holy Synod was to supervise Labzin's printing plant. 'And so I became *hors de loi* ...,' wrote Labzin bitterly, recognizing the abrupt new arrangement as a denunciation.[5]

As in 1806, rather than submit to ecclesiastical censorship, Labzin closed his journal. By this retreat, he avoided condemnation and won from Alexander 3,000 rubles for travel and a sustenance allowance of 3,000 rubles annually – more than he had earned as a publisher. (As for his subsequent life, Labzin returned to the capital after some months and there imprudently criticized the proposed honorary membership in the Academy of Fine Arts of three leading political figures, among them Count A.A. Arakcheev, the emperor's principal lieutenant. Punishment for this insubordination was severe: exile for Labzin and his wife to a tiny Tartar village in Simbirsk province for several months. In May 1823, with the assistance of Golitsyn, Labzin secured a partial reprieve, a pension, and permission to live in the town of Simbirsk. Two years later he died.)[6]

By seeming to undermine Orthodoxy, Labzin cut himself off from Alexander and Golitsyn. He had also put the Bible Society in question, for churchmen had begun to link Labzin with the spread of Bibles to a wider circle of readers and with the lessened authority of the church over scriptural interpretation.

Although he had pleased the defenders of the church by closing *Messenger of Zion*, Golitsyn made no other changes in what the pietists published. His work, he felt, served God and, as he told one of his opponents, met the wishes of the emperor.[7] Six months later disagreement intensified over a book approved by the ecclesiastical censorship which Golitsyn, in turn, banned.

II

Innokenty, Labzin's critic, was the church censor involved, and the issue once again was whether mysticism undermined Russian Orthodoxy. His conviction that it did had caused Innokenty, earlier in 1818, to criticize the civil censorship authority's approval of a Russian translation of Jung-Stilling's *Victorious Conscience*. It next prompted him to approve a book designed as an attack on *Messenger of Zion* and dedicated to the fight against heresy.[8] The first printing of six hundred copies of that book, *Conversations on the Grave of a Little Girl on the Immortal Soul* by E. Stanevich, was ready for distribution under a permit from Innokenty when Golitsyn intervened, on 22 December 1818. Golitsyn had the permit withdrawn because the book placed the 'external church' (a euphemism for the Russian Orthodox church) above the 'inner church.' 'This division is incomprehensible to Christianity,' Golitsyn told the Church Schools Commission, the body overseeing clerical censorship, on which he sat. The emperor was displeased, he said, and the commission must prevent any further mistakes of this kind. For his part, Innokenty suffered a virtual banishment arranged by Golitsyn: appointment as bishop of Orenburg, a city in the southeast of European Russia.[9] When Innokenty died there nine months later, the resentment against Golitsyn intensified.

A Holy Synod committee appointed in February 1819 had in the meantime begun to draft a statute that would restore the censorship of religious works to the church.[10] As drafted, the statute required the Holy Synod to screen all works referring to the Holy Scriptures, Christian principles, the history of Christianity, and to the Russian Orthodox church. In March 1820 the Holy Synod approved the proposed statute but did not submit it to the emperor. Apparently it chose to await a parallel proposal for change in civil censorship by a committee named that spring by the Chief Administration of Schools.

Chairing that committee was a one-time believer in the Bible Society who had turned against Golitsyn – Michael Magnitsky. (Notably, when Golitsyn had recommended that Magnitsky become superintendent of the Kazan education district, Alexander had agreed only after warning Golitsyn that Magnitsky would eventually turn upon him.)[11] That June the committee began deliberations which were to drag on during the next three years of mounting enmity against Golitsyn. A concerted campaign against mysticism and Golitsyn had begun in which, as Sturdza writes, 'the Orthodox *druzhina* [corps] under the banner of the Holy Synod industriously worked against Golitsyn and quietly undermined the Ministry of Spiritual Affairs and Public Education.'[12]

Just a month after Magnitsky and the civil censorship committee had begun its work, there arrived in St Petersburg the unwitting instrument of Golitsyn's ultimate defeat as minister and patron of mysticism. He was Jacob Gosner, nominally a Catholic priest, but in fact a persuasive advocate of pietistic religious enthusiasms. Golitsyn showed Gosner much attention, and the German became a director of the St Petersburg branch of the Bible Society. Gosner and another Catholic priest, Ignatius Lindle of the Bavarian Bible Society, attracted followers; and, although some who 'wept, and fell on their knees,' were sincere converts, recalled Grech, others were officials bent on pleasing.[13]

Meanwhile, the successful Spanish revolution in March and that of Naples in July ended all talk of constitutions by the emperor. Alexander had lost patience with the ungrateful Poles and reneged on his promises to them. In turn, when Alexander saw revolutionary overtones in the October 1820 protest against harsh discipline by the Semenovsky regiment, the military unit which had deposed Paul I, Golitsyn that same month closed a constitutionally directed weekly, *Spirit of the Journals* (*Dukh Zhurnalov*), for inciting discontent against the government.[14]

Golitsyn's opponents levelled against the mystics the same charge of stirring anti-government feelings. One opponent was A.A. Arakcheev, the emperor's right-hand man from about 1815 (he headed the Ministry of War during the war with Napoleon and, from 1817, the military colonies). Arakcheev regarded Golitsyn both as a liability to the throne and a rival for influence; and when Michael, the metropolitan of St Petersburg, died on 24 March 1821, Arakcheev was instrumental, according to Sturdza, in appointing as successor an effective ally against Golitsyn – Serafim, metropolitan of Moscow from March 1819 until July 1821 and a critic of the Bible Society.[15]

Michael's death ended a three-month illness which, according to Moroshkin, an Orthodox priest, began on 23 December 1820, when the metropolitan clashed bitterly with Golitsyn at a meeting of the Holy Synod. Many blamed Golitsyn for Michael's death. Two weeks before he died, Michael sent the emperor a letter condemning Golitsyn's activites. Moroshkin says that the circumstances enabled Arakcheev to press successfully for Serafim's appointment, which he describes as 'the beginning of the fall of Golitsyn.'[16]

Arakcheev may also have weakened support for Golitsyn by arranging the transfer to Moscow of Golitsyn's staunch ally, Filaret, to succeed Serafim. Filaret, who believed God's word to be sufficiently clear for all men, helped translate the Bible into Russian, and he had served the St Petersburg Bible Society while a member of the Holy Synod. He had remained in the capital near the emperor and Golitsyn despite appointments to Tver in 1819 and to Iaroslavl in 1820, and his removal to Moscow deprived Golitsyn of a valued supporter.

(Another target of those uneasy about mysticism was the Masonic Order; and in this same year, 1821, the Masonic grand master of the

Astrea Lodge, Koshelev, advised the emperor that a growing spirit of rebellion and an absence of principles characterized many within his ranks.[17] In other words, mysticism might be fostering rebellion.)

Aside from Arakcheev, the most effective of Golitsyn's foes was an ascetic, hawk-eyed monk, Photius. The 'martyred' Innokenty had been his spiritual advisor at the Theological Academy, and Photius was among those who implicated Golitsyn in Innokenty's death. A fervent and persuasive cleric, he had a knack for conveying intense religious devotion. Photius held that the 'inner-church movement,' Golitsyn's great cause, portended the coming of anti-Christ. As Satan's agents, the mystics and pietists would destroy the traditional church and, with it, the authority of the throne – a warning Photius gave the emperor in June 1822, during an audience arranged by the unsuspecting Golitsyn (whom Photius had met and impressed a month earlier). Within two months, on 1 August, Alexander issued a ukaz closing the Masonic lodges; and that same month Photius became archimandrite of St George monastery in Novgorod.[18]

III

While the campaign against Golitsyn and mysticism grew, censorship remained restrictive and moralistic – contrary to the 1804 statute. For example, the St Petersburg Censorship Committee rejected Michael A. Bestuzhev's application to found a literary journal in 1823 on the grounds that it had too much work and that Bestuzhev lacked experience.[19] Further evidence was the banning the year before of a translation of Sir Walter Scott's 'On the Eve of St John,' a lyrical ballad about love and revenge in medieval Scotland. When the translator of that poem, V.A. Zhukovsky, reminded Golitsyn that a censor had to base a rejection on the Statute of 1804 and demanded specifics on what was 'contrary to morality, religion, and the good purposes of the government,' Golitsyn complied by having three censors list their objections. One faulted Zhukovsky's use of the old Russian word for monk, 'chernets' ('black-garbed'), which would cause readers to think of the black-robed monastics of the Russian church. The censors also charged that Zhukovsky had obscured Scott's delicate treatment of 'illicit love' and the repentance of the murderous baron and his unfaithful wife.[20] Only after Zhukovsky had made such adjustments as changing the title to 'Duncan's Eve' did Golitsyn approve the altered translation in November 1822.

The processing of Zhukovsky's appeal came as the Magnitsky committee was completing its draft of a statute to replace that of 1804.[21] Assuming as he did that many writers sought to subvert the existing order, Magnitsky framed the new rules to combat 'tricks and subterfuges.' He proposed forbidding passages which questioned revealed religious truths; weakened respect for authority; advanced sectarianism, magic, cabalistics, or Freemasonry; or explained the mysteries of faith through reason or intuition. Because the censor's prime role was to defend the church and state from hostile ideas, said Magnitsky, the censor could ban 'translated novels and voluptuous poems' for reasons of style.[22] And, although the proposed statute permitted a writer to appeal a censorship decision, no longer would the law give the writer the benefit of the doubt about his intentions. Magnitsky favoured the system already practised under Golitsyn, but with one major difference: he provided grounds for proscribing the pietists and mystics whom Golitsyn patronized.

With its completion in May 1823, the Magnitsky proposal went forward to the Chief Administration and then to a subcommittee which was to harmonize it with the proposed clerical censorship statute prepared three years earlier. That August the emperor received both proposals but, preoccupied with the presentiment of his own death and the problem of succession, he took no action.

Frustrated in their effort to restore church authority over religious publishing through a new statute, church supporters instead began a concerted effort to topple Golitsyn. To bolster their ranks, Arakcheev summoned Photius to the capital;[23] and these two joined others to use a book by the German mystic Gosner to unseat Golitsyn as minister.

Photius saw his call to St Petersburg as another step in his seven-year campaign against 'secret societies.' About himself, he wrote: 'In 1824, on February 1, the beggar Photius was summoned to St Petersburg for activities on behalf of the church, faith, and salvation of the tsar and fatherland. He arrived and began to act against the heretic and freethinker Gosner – his sects, all the heresies, schisms, and plots, under the guise of religion spread through books – and in every way possible to expose Prince Golitsyn and denounce him to the tsar. Photius acted quietly.'[24]

Gosner's book, *The Spirit of the Life and Teaching of Jesus Christ in the New Testament, Vol. I: a Commentary on the Gospel of Matthew*, had earlier been published in the original German in St Petersburg. Inspired by its contents, O.M. Briskorn, a retired military engineer, had arranged to have the book published in Russian by P.Kh. Bezak and his cousin, Nicholas Grech, but he had died in 1823 before completing the translation.[25] Among several who carried the project forward was Golitsyn's director of the Department of Public Education, V.M. Popov, who helped correct the manuscript. Another follower of Gosner, the censor Biriukov, gave the translation official approval.

Having learned that the Russian version of the *Commentary* was imminent, the opponents of Golitsyn, led by Arakcheev and Magnitsky, determined in February 1824 to secure proofs of the book, show them to Alexander, and thereby discredit Golitsyn. Grech says that in March 1824 'a baptized Jew and known spy, Platonov,' approached him for such proofs, which Grech refused, and then failed in his attempt to obtain them through bribing plant apprentices.[26]

The plotters next discovered that one of the translators had sent proofs of the book to a doctor friend, to whom they dispatched another agent, Stepanov, to beg for spiritual counsel. As hoped, the doctor gave some of the proofs of Gosner's book to Stepanov, who passed them on to Magnitsky, Arakcheev, Shishkov, and the metropolitan Serafim. Serafim agreed to deliver the pages to the emperor personally and to explain their implications.[27] On 17 April Serafim visited Alexander to emphasize to him that the book opposed Orthodoxy, the autocracy, and all Christian confessions (although, in the later opinion of an expert, the book was no better or worse than works by mystics already in print). Three days later, Photius met secretly for three hours with Alexander, through arrangements probably made by Arakcheev, to denounce further the mystics and their publications.[28]

Golitsyn sought out Photius on 23 April, and the monk then demanded that the minister ban the publication of mystical books. 'It is already too late to stop it,' Golitsyn responded. 'It is not I but the Emperor who is at fault.' According to his version of the events, Photius decided that day never to see Golitsyn again. However, two days later Golitsyn again precipitated a meeting and insisted he could do nothing about mystical publishing. As the finale to this stormy meeting Photius anathematized Golitsyn.[29]

Photius informed the emperor of the clash, and on the same day Alexander asked the Committee of Ministers to examine the Gosner book. He also ordered Golitsyn to begin discussions with Serafim on a program for the censoring of religious books and then to report to the committee. The Committee of Ministers in turn assigned the analysis of the Gosner book to Admiral Shishkov, president of the Russian Academy, and V.S. Lanskoy, the minister of the interior.

In a letter of 29 April Photius pressed further, calling for an end to the dual ministry, the Bible Society, and the revolutionary movement fomented by the mystics.[30] He demanded a restoration of the Holy Synod to its former authority and the expulsion of Gosner from Russia. Golitsyn, he said, was at the centre of a plot to subvert the realm which involved other government officials, as well as censors; and he singled out the censor Timovsky and the publisher Grech as key figures.

Golitsyn's dismissal came the next month. The minister had become a political liability, for his continuation as chief censor would further alienate the church, one of the strongest bulwarks of the throne. On 15 May Alexander abolished the Ministry of Spiritual Affairs and Public Education and appointed as his new minister of public education a man opposed to the mystics, Admiral Shishkov. (Magnitsky had vainly hoped for the appointment.) Shishkov's authority included heading the Department of Foreign Confessions; but once again the Holy Synod, through its procurator, was to deal directly with the emperor. That summer Photius would write, 'Our minister is now only Jesus Christ,' and credit Arakcheev with the church's liberation. Alexander did not disband the Bible Society, but Golitsyn gave up the presidency. Serafim, the metropolitan of St Petersburg, succeeded him, and on 29 May he ruled that only Orthodox clergy could distribute scripture.[31]

To demonstrate his disbelief that Golitsyn was plotting against the church and state, Alexander appointed his former minister as head of the Post Office Department and as a member of the State Council. Golitsyn had served faithfully, he knew, and had deflected opposition from the emperor. The affinity of the two men stood fast, and Golitsyn was to remain close to the imperial family even after Alexander's death the next year, in November 1825.

IV

Shortly after he became minister of public education on 20 May 1824, Shishkov completed his report on the Gosner book. He argued that the work incited against Orthodoxy and the throne through its guileful presentation of mystical doctrines and specious commentaries on the scriptures. To counter such falsehoods, a new supervising censorship committee should watch over publishing and over teaching in the schools and universities.[32] Shishkov also urged that charges be laid against V.M. Popov, Golitsyn's director of the Department of Public Education, for abetting the publication of a criminal book. On this last point, Alexander reluctantly agreed. He advised the Committee of Ministers to order a trial of Popov (as a state official) before the Senate and trials before the lower courts for the censors involved and for Bezak and Grech, the owners of the printing plant. The emperor expelled Gosner and ordered his book burned.[33]

Shishkov particularly wanted official condemnation of Popov, an active member of the Bible Society from its founding. Popov had served as secretary of the society, locally and nationally, and had travelled to England, Shishkov noted ominously, for the purpose of visiting English Methodists. An official of the Ministry of the Interior until 1817, Popov had become director of the Department of Public Education when Golitsyn became minister. One contemporary described Popov as a 'gentle fanatic, a quiet simple man who, however, in the name of faith could be moved to villainy.'[34] (Popov was later to join one of the most bizarre of mystical circles, that of Madame Tatarinova; an investigation of that sect, prompted by complaints of his two daughters that Popov was coercing them to join it, led to his being sent to a monastery in Kazan in 1840, where he died two years later.)

In these first days as minister, Shishkov saw the Gosner book and the complaints of Photius as the prime reasons for his coming to office.[35] He therefore saw a tightening of censorship and a decisive condemnation of mysticism as axiomatic, but he badly miscalculated what he could accomplish. The general mood of the government at the time Golitsyn stepped down so little suggested a crack-down, in fact, that Pushkin initially thought that Shishkov would liberalize censorship.[36]

In his second audience with the emperor, on 31 May, Shishkov argued for a program of ten principles for reforming censorship, ignoring the proposals of the church and of Magnitsky submitted to the emperor nearly a year before. Shishkov sought to start over and advocated buying and destroying all volumes that a newly appointed censorship committee would find unacceptable. Those subversive books remaining in private hands would be neutralized by the new books approved by his censors.[37]

On 20 May the Committee of Ministers heard Shishkov's report on the Gosner book and, showing little enthusiasm, decided on trials for Popov, the censors, and the publishers involved. Shishkov returned to the emperor on 26 July to urge a law like Catherine's of 1787 requiring all books of religious content to be printed on the presses of the Holy Synod. Alexander gave him polite attention but no response. Shishkov's frustrations over the 'coldness and indifference' he was meeting about changes in censorship practices were growing, for even members of the Holy Synod took no interest, satisfied as they were with their triumph over

Golitsyn.[38] Shishkov was to show his bitter disappointment through his memoirs, a document that would cause Nikitenko, a censor in the next reign, to remark: 'It is evident that Alexander listened patiently to all the pompous reports of his minister, gave no objection to them, as though agreeing, and shelved them.' Nikitenko further deduced that Shishkov was an 'honest man' but that Alexander 'stood immeasurably higher ... intellectually' and 'understood better than Shishkov that it was impossible to stop the trend of the time by repressive measures.'[39] It was more likely that Alexander would not condemn the mystics because he was with them in spirit.

Popov's trial in May 1825 was also to exasperate Shishkov. Again, Alexander was a stumbling block, for he had let the senators know that he opposed a conviction. Keen public interest in the trial made the outcome all the more crucial to Shishkov. 'The city is preoccupied with one subject, the Popov affair,' wrote Michael Speransky to Arakcheev on 25 May.[40]

The charges against Popov were threefold: (1) that he had helped edit the Gosner book; (2) that he had wrongly influenced the censorship process to approve it; and (3) that he had declared to police that both Gosner and his books embodied the Christian spirit. Absent was the charge that Popov had translated several chapters of the book, as both Grech and Shishkov claimed.[41]

Popov's defender in the Senate, Sen. Ivan M. Muraviev-Apostol, focused on the issue of criminality, contending that Popov had every right as director of the Department of Public Education to endorse a manuscript. Nor had Popov committed a criminal act in correcting the work. 'That which is not prohibited,' said the senator, 'cannot be judged.' Senator Sumarokov, as chief prosecutor, argued the seditious nature of Popov's acts: 'To print dangerous principles to shake the faith is the height of criminality.'[42]

Sensing that Popov would go free, Shishkov wrote Arakcheev on 16 May that the Senate majority was 'trampling not only on the law but on right reason.' The not-guilty verdict that followed caused Shishkov to label Popov's acquittal by the senators a 'very real assault on church, throne, and fatherland.' In contrast, the emperor summoned Muraviev-Apostol to hear all that had happened and thanked him, without expressing an opinion.[43]

Undaunted, Shishkov convinced the State Council to review the Senate's verdict and to admit a statement from him. In it Shishkov argued that only a stern action against a known advocate of Gosner's works could effectively repudiate all such subversive literature. The council responded in November by upholding the Senate acquittal.

Meanwhile, on 1 September, Alexander had gone to Taganrog. On 19 November Shishkov sent a last appeal to him there, never answered, against Popov. December brought Nicholas's accession, and the Decembrist revolt; and, within two months, Shishkov was urging Nicholas to reopen the Popov case and this time name both Popov and Golitsyn as collaborators of Gosner. Shishkov blamed all three for causing the Decembrist uprising by having spread 'false ideas about the *inner church* (that is, no church at all), popular freedom and equality of classes, constitutions, the destruction of emperors, and the shedding of human blood for future well-being.'[44]

Disregarding Shishkov's charges, Nicholas named Golitsyn to his committee investigating Decembrism and in 1826 awarded him a decoration for his work. Popov continued to serve Golitsyn as a member of the council of the Post Office Department, an arrangement Alexander I had made.[45] The proceedings against the censors and publishers of the Gosner book continued in the lower courts until 1828, but ended in acquittals as well.

Clerics largely ignored these trials, for they were satisfied that Shishkov had ended mystical publishing and had preserved what Serafim called the 'well-being of the church.'[46] Sixty books of mystical content had been published from 1813 to 1824, and that deplorable outpouring had been stopped.

In most of that same nine-year period Golitsyn had presided over the Bible Society. As successor to Golitsyn in the presidency of the society, Serafim had continued his campaign against its activities. On 16 September 1824 he advised Filaret to stop articles praising the society like the one in the August *Moscow Bulletin*. In a letter to Alexander on 28 December Serafim blamed the society for the mystical ideas in secular and ecclesiastical schools and urged its abolition.[47]

Once Nicholas had become emperor a year later, sympathy from the throne for the Bible Society ended. On 12 April 1826 Nicholas issued a ukaz ordering the society to halt its activities; and, having evidently given the matter some study, he issued a second ukaz on 15 July ending the organization.[48] At the same time Nicholas rejected another of his brother's 'favourites,' Arakcheev, who was to fall on hard times in the new reign.

The church had emerged the victor in an out-and-out political struggle over censorship – a struggle that is not surprising in view of the close connection between religion and politics everywhere in Europe early in the nineteenth century. What happened in Russia had links to what Stendahl described in France in *The Red and the Black*. Events in both countries had persuaded men of the church that the true faith could be preserved only in the political arena.

V

Arguments against mysticism and Golitsyn's censorship policies appear in a memorandum which was written, apparently, between the dates of Nicholas's two ukazes on the Bible Society.[49] The document stresses the power of subversive publications.

Since the time of Peter the Great, the memorandum began, Europeans who feared the great strength of Russia had plotted to undermine it by implanting in Russia beliefs alien to Orthodoxy and by supporting Russian sectarians and schismatics. Following the Napoleonic War, this source continues, the plotters maliciously spread the idea that Alexander I, who had already saved Europe from Napoleon, must save Europe from irreligion – just as, through a secret council of the Illuminati, they promoted the false doctrine of religious unity among all peoples. One dire result inside Russia was the blanket approval of privately printed mystical books by the secular censorship authority, for Golitsyn and many censors had fallen under the sway of the plotters' lies.

Russia's enemies had also organized sects, secret societies, and Masonic lodges to advance their purposes, argued the memorandum; and the lodges had grown enormously after the war, when Russian soldiers returned from Europe favourably impressed by Masonry. Furthering the Bible Society was also said to be part of the plan, for the translation and wide distribution of the Bible weakened the authority of the church and promoted dissent.

Undoubtedly the memorandum originated in Shishkov's Ministry of Public Education, for it named Golitsyn as a principal instrument of the plotters. It closed by praising Shishkov and Serafim for preventing the 'toppling' of the altar and throne in Russia. In all, the exaggerated tone, the over-drawn connections between disparate events, and the assertion of conspiracy by the mystics made the memorandum unconvincing. Nicholas had received a much clearer message from the Decembrist revolt. By 1825 the mystical movement of the post-Napoleonic-War period under Alexander, with all its consequences for censorship, had spent itself and was to give way under Nicholas to the exaltation of Orthodoxy and nationalism.

Unlike his brother, Nicholas would prevent the emergence of a head-strong minister like Golitsyn. The personal governmental arm of the emperor – His Majesty's Own Chancellery – would serve to keep the ministries in check. One section, the Third, was to watch over censorship.

But the misgivings about the evils inherent in publishing that emerged in the later years of the reign of Alexander I were to continue under Nicholas. The legacy of Golitsyn, Magnitsky, and Shishkov was the view that printed words could promote dangerous falsehoods as well as truth – and, moreover, could do so subtly and insidiously, an assumption that the 1804 statute, in effect throughout the reign, had specifically excluded. Magnitsky had therefore insisted in his proposed reformed censorship statute that the intentions of an author and the actual impact his words would have on other minds were what mattered. Shishkov was to take this same stand in drafting the Statute of 1826.

4

Nicholas I's censorship innovations, 1825–32

A Russianizer and fervent nationalist, a man who could not stomach the acidic Gallican spirit of the eighteenth century – this was the first chief censor under Nicholas I. He was Admiral A.S. Shishkov, the minister of public education inherited from Alexander I. A long-time critic of linguistic borrowings by modern writers and of foreignisms of any kind, Shishkov was finally to realize his dream of dictating both style and content to Russian authors through his all-encompassing Statute of 1826.

But the excesses of Shishkov dismayed those under Nicholas who easily perceived the influence of writers in Russia. The emperor, intent on having strict and swift means to stop dissent readily at hand, responded to Shishkov's efforts by issuing the much more liberal Statute of 1828, while covertly giving powers to the Third Section, or secret political police, to deal with disloyal writers. Then came the shock of revolutions in the West and the granting of yet further authority over the press to the Third Section, which viewed the printed word as a threatening element in the body politic.

I

Nicholas I easily crushed the ill-planned Decembrist insurrection which disrupted St Petersburg the day of his accession, 14 December 1825, and then spent the next half-year investigating its causes. During that uncertain period Shishkov drafted his repressive censorship proposals. To replace the imprecise 1804 statute, a mere 47 articles in all, Shishkov proposed 230 articles – most of them written by his deputy, P. Shirinsky-Shikhmatov, who used as a model Magnitsky's stillborn statute of the previous reign. In May 1826 Nicholas pondered the draft and required Shishkov to answer criticism of it by journalist F.V. Bulgarin. Then, more concerned with other matters, the emperor approved the new statute on 10 June without making changes or consulting anyone else.[1]

Shishkov had made clear his aims: to ensure that printed works 'have a useful or at least not-dangerous orientation for the welfare of the fatherland' and 'to direct public opinion into agreeing with the present political circumstances and views of the government.'[2] Toward those ends, Shishkov bent every effort to replace literary- and education-minded censors with professional censors of the kind common in Europe since Napoleon.

By ruling that no censor could hold any other position, Shishkov rid himself of the censors provided by the universities since 1804. Four full-time censorship committees took their place: the Main Censorship Committee in St Petersburg (a chairman and six censors) plus lesser, three-man committees in Moscow, Dorpat, and Vilna. In addition, whereas the minister of public education and his Chief Administration of the Schools had previously run the censorship system, Shishkov named a Supreme Committee comprised of the ministers of foreign affairs and of the interior, as well as of public education. Their administrative arm was the Chancellery, whose director sat with the Supreme Committee to form the Chief Administration of Censorship.[3]

Shishkov's censorship rules put the interest of the existing order first. They banned 'metaphysical discussion of natural, civic, or judicial rights' and forbade historical works which reported favourably on challenges to ruling authority anywhere. Writers could no longer defend or even describe Christian dissent, nor could they put forward materialistic theories of behaviour. Besides assuming the worst about ambiguous passages, censors were to correct any violations of 'the rules and purity of the Russian language.' Punishment for published violations was to fall not merely on the censor, as under the 1804 statute, but also on the author; and the publisher of a banned journal could never start another. No manuscript could go to press until every ministry concerned had cleared references to its affairs.

Shishkov left under the civil censorship 'general discussion' about God and Christianity because 'every enlightened Christian and censors especially' knew what was permissible on such topics.[4] Where doubts arose, he ruled, church censors would be consulted. The church, still awaiting approval by Nicholas of its draft for a new ecclesiastical censorship law, could accept these rules because it trusted Shishkov.

Elsewhere, dismay was widespread over what many called a 'cast-iron statute.' The State Council, the emperor's highest advisory body, viewed as impossible the statute's attempt to 'communicate to the literature of the entire country a single orientation.' M.Ia. Von Vock, the director of the chancellery of the Third Section, wrote to his chief A.Kh. Benckendorff, then in Moscow for the coronation, that writers expected the new statute to 'close their mouths' and that 'society echoes their dissatisfaction.'[5]

When, only a month after signing Shishkov's statute, Nicholas conveyed the likelihood of reforms in his coronation manifesto of 13 July, the emperor must have regretted having just taken so public a stand for strict censorship. A way out lay in the committee he had meanwhile named to draft rules for foreign publications (not covered by Shishkov), and he readily agreed with the committee's request to reconsider the entire 1826 law. The committee, which included Benckendorff and Minister of Foreign Affairs K.V. Nesselrode, asked Shishkov to appear before it late in 1826;[6] after objecting to Nicholas about such a summons, Shishkov declined. As he later recalled, he saw the committee 'in clear opposition to me, or rather to my principles on free publishing.' The minister said that he would send someone in his place and reply to any proposals the committee might make.

Over a year passed, and then, said Shishkov, 'suddenly a ukaz came out which established a new censorship statute in place of the old one.'[7] (More precisely, well before the ukaz of 22 April 1828, to which Shishkov referred, the State Council had commended the proposed statute for approximating censorship's 'true meaning.') The very day after Nicholas signed the ukaz making the statute law, the 74-year-old Shishkov resigned, pleading ill health and advancing years. His abrupt departure was his protest against a new statute drafted behind his back with the assent of his autocratic master.

Shishkov's successor, Prince Karl A. Lieven, brought the image of a moderate but pliable official to the Ministry of Public Education and the censorship authority. An Estonian of noble birth, Lieven had been an adjutant to Potemkin, a court favourite, under Catherine II and the dutiful governor of Archangel under Paul I. More recently, as superintendent of the Dorpat education district, he had shown a progressive outlook by founding medical, theological, pedagogical, and professional institutes at Dorpat University.[8]

On 17 May the Senate published the new censorship statute. A new law and a new minister seemed to repudiate Shishkov and his policy.

That law, however, gave only the appearance of reform because, as will be shown, the emperor coupled it with a secret system of press controls.

The Statute of 1828 banned whatever endangered the faith, the throne, or the good morals and personal honour of the citizenry – the same strictures that Catherine II had set. Censors were not, however, to read meanings into texts nor to alter passages without the author's approval. Ministers could no longer screen all references to their administrative affairs, and authors no longer shared liability for illegal published content with the censors who had approved it.[9]

Universities were again to provide censors, a return to the system of 1804. One committee, under the superintendent of the education district, was to serve each university city: St Petersburg, Moscow, Vilna, Dorpat, Kharkov, and Kazan. The cities of Riga, Revel, Mitau, and Odessa were each to have one censor, with provisions for others as required.[10] Under the minister of public education, a new Chief Administration of the Censorship replaced the Supreme Committee as the central supervising agency. Its six members were the presidents of the imperial Academies of Science, Fine Art, and the Study of the Russian Language; the assistant minister of public education; and representatives from the ministries of the interior and foreign affairs.

The Statute of 1828 created for the first time a separate Foreign Censorship Committee responsible to the Chief Administration. With headquarters in St Petersburg and subordinate censors in Riga, Vilna, and Odessa, this committee screened books imported by booksellers and by libraries, government bureaus, and individuals. (Yet another committee in the Post Office Department – later to be called the 'Black Office' – censored foreign periodicals arriving by mail.) For the guidance of the customs inspectors, the Foreign Committee published monthly *The Alphabetical List of Books Forbidden by the Foreign Censorship*. This bulletin listed about 150 titles each month, until the 1848 revolutions in the West caused the commitee to ban about 600 titles monthly.[11]

II

On the same day he signed the Statute of 1828, Nicholas also approved Imperial Russia's first copyright law, a measure that had had to await the development of the concept of private property in the late eighteenth century and the growth of private printing and authorship early in the nineteenth century. To end the literary piracy then common, the law gave a writer ownership rights over all his works; and should a writer not make specific bequests, his heirs acquired and held for twenty-five years exclusive rights over what he had written. To make the copyright system work, the censorship office kept records of manuscripts and authors, while the courts decided all disputes.[12]

With the 1828 copyright law, Russia belatedly followed western Europe in recognizing literary property. (Venice had led the way in the sixteenth century and England followed in the eighteenth.) For the first time, a writer in Russia could secure his livelihood by bargaining with publishers over the format and financial returns for his work. As well, publishers could secure the exclusive rights to works and undertake large and expensive publishing projects without fear of facing pirated editions. By safeguarding the profits of both writers and publishers, the 1828 copyright law helped cause a steady, profit-centred growth in the publishing industry during the reign of Nicholas.

As a case in point, Russia's first great publishing success came in 1829 when publisher A.F. Smirdin paid Faddei Bulgarin 2,000 rubles for exclusive rights to his *Ivan Vyzhigin*, a picaresque, moralizing novel which was to set a record for sales.[13] Not without irony, literary critic V.G. Belinsky responded by saluting the arrival of a new great stage in Russian literature – the 'Smirdin phase,' when commercial worth of a manuscript outweighed its literary merit.[14]

The contrast between the promise of the new censorship statute and the controls actually effected was sharp. In his memoirs, the conservative writer and editor S.N. Glinka (who became a censor on 1 October 1827) observed that 'from the beginning of the existing censorship never had there been such a free, such a favourable statute for human thought as the 1828 Statute seemed,' but then concluded, 'With sorrow, I repeat the word "seemed."'[15] Looking back, Glinka well knew that censorship after 1828 had acquired bit by bit nearly all the strictures of Shishkov's 'cast-iron' law.

Prince V.F. Odoevsky, a drafter of the Statute of 1828, similarly labelled the law a generous one but blamed the government for distorting it. Censorship, admitted Odoevsky, is the 'most difficult' administrative problem of all; rather than detailing and searching out every possible infraction, however, it should follow the broad guidelines of serving the faith, the throne, morality, and the honour of citizens – precisely what the 1828 statute required. Strict censorship merely caused the press to convey ideas obliquely, 'and no police can stop all the stratagems of ... talented writers.' And, because tricks heighten readers' interest, strict controls 'produce the opposite of the desired results.'[16] For these reasons – ones commonly heard in the censorship debates of the nineteenth century – he and his fellow committeemen, said Odoevsky, had drafted the 1828 statute to end Shishkov's rigid censorship.

Nicholas held, however, that the new law was insufficient in itself; for, at the very outset of the new censorship system (that is, on 25 April, when the 1828 statute had been signed but not yet published) he established secret police powers over the press. Thus, just as he was about to show the public a liberalized censorship, Nicholas armed himself with covert powers over the printed word to meet any contingency. He gave those powers to the Third Section, or political police, one of several sections he had created in His Majesty's Own Chancellery to strengthen his personal control over the government. The duties of these sections overlapped those of the regular ministries; and the Third Section, founded to provide Nicholas 'information on all events,' was to be the watchdog in censorship affairs and to interfere in them when it saw fit.[17]

The one open censorship responsibility of the Third Section, that of approving or disapproving theatrical productions as actually staged, Benckendorff had helped draft into the 1828 statute. He was undoubtedly instrumental in the secret directive of 25 April 1828 as well. Under that directive, censors became secret agents of the Third Section, to whom they were to report any manuscripts 'inclined to the spread of atheism or which reflect in the artist or writer violations of the obligations of loyal subjects.'[18] Where justified, the Third Section was to establish surveillance over an author to uncover possible charges against him. Merely by submitting a manuscript to the censor, then, any author might face charges from the Third Section or, more likely, an 'interview,' a favourite means of reminding loyal subjects of their duties. One must add, however, that the police mainly confined their use of the 25 April directive to such crisis periods as those of the French and Belgian revolutions in 1830, the Polish rebellion in 1831, and the cataclysm of 1848.

Another reason why the year 1828 did not usher in liberal censorship was the restored authority of the Holy Synod over all writings broadly classifiable as religious. That mandate came when Nicholas on 22 April approved (but did not decree, as he had the companion civil censorship statute) a new ecclesiastical censorship law. Its publication on 28 June followed Senate approval.[19]

Churchmen at last achieved what had eluded them since the outpouring of mystical writings that passed through the civil censorship office under Golitsyn: authority for the Holy Synod to ban books it found irreligious no matter where published or by whom. Seven subject categories in the ecclesiastical censorship law of 1828 covered every book that could possibly be labelled 'religious.' Also included for synod review were classical texts used in church schools 'on whatever subject.' Ecclesiastical censorship committees were to serve St Petersburg, Moscow, Kiev, and Kazan under the direction of church academies, and only academy teachers locally appointed and confirmed by the Holy Synod could be censors.

Once again the Holy Synod enjoyed the powerful position in publishing it had held before the war with Napoleon. In the twenty-seven years yet remaining under Nicholas, its influence on publishing was to prove mainly obscurantist.

III

For the first three years under the Statute of 1828, writers had a largely sympathetic ally in the upper echelons of the Third Section in Von Vock, the chancellery director, whose letter to Benckendorff criticizing Shishkov's statute was quoted earlier. Until his death from cholera in 1831 in the midst of the Polish rebellion, Von Vock moved freely among writers in the salons of St Petersburg as their intimate and friend.

But even as he cultivated literary personalities on their home ground, Von Vock cautioned his government about the power of the press in its capacity to influence 'public opinion,' a force that European officials had taken especially seriously since the French Revolution. Von Vock undoubtedly drew on the thinking of western police officials about how governments could best prevent dangerous ideas from taking hold in the minds of the people. As early as 1808, for example, Metternich, then ambassador to France, had warned Vienna that Napoleon was manipulating the press of Europe in order to shape public opinion useful to him.[20]

Almost certainly familiar to Von Vock were the ideas of Joseph Fouché, minister of police under Napoleon (and, later, Louis XVIII), whose authority included control of the press. Fouché, for example, feared the 'previously unknown pressure of public opinion' – a reference to the tendency towards independent judgment by broad segments of the people whose unquestioning support heads of state and government officials had largely taken for granted. Fouché also described religion, the moral code, and repressive measures by the state as no longer sufficient to keep subjects obedient. No less deplorable was the growing power of the press to heighten and spread disaffection. The problem lay in how to control journalists without provoking them to write and agitate even more strongly against the government, a dilemma specifically noted under Louis Philippe by his chief minister, François Guizot, who favoured using state resources to get words into print to bolster the government.[21]

In the Russian context, Von Vock believed that the government could not manage public opinion but could take measures to blunt its extremes.[22] That view fit not only the spirit of tolerant supervision implied by the new Statute of 1828 but also the fact that censors had then to screen only a handful of publications read by a small audience within and akin to the St Petersburg social circles where Von Vock moved so familiarly. However, as he analysed public opinion in reports to the emperor over the next several years, Von Vock came to see that changes in Russian public opinion required more government interference in press affairs.

Von Vock assessed public opinion at length in the first of four annual reports by the Third Section to the emperor from 1827 through 1830.[23] (The editor of these documents, A. Sergeev, has concluded that Von Vock wrote these reports signed by Benckendorff.) While praising the emperor and insisting that most of his subjects fervently supported him, Von Vock candidly assessed those sections of public opinion critical of Nicholas or his policies. He identified groups – labelling them as 'liberals,' 'patriots,' 'the press,' and the like – and summarized their positions. He cited the issues of greatest public concern and showed how the enemies of the emperor distorted them.

For Von Vock, public opinion in 1827 had become articulate and the government had to listen to it. He implied that sections of the population had legitimate complaints, knowing, as he surely did, that the emperor had reached the same conclusion in reviewing the Decembrist revolt.[24] The autocracy, he further implied, most influenced public opinion by how it governed Russia, not by how it censored the press, and he hinted that the emperor should move towards freeing the serfs.

The bases of public opinion had shifted since the time of Catherine the Great, when court society had dictated public opinion, Von Vock continued. That group was now completely isolated. A level lower, 'higher society' had divided into the contented and the discontented. The former looked to Count Michael Speransky and Count Victor Kochubei for leadership and were completely loyal. The latter were Russian patriots located in Moscow who looked to Admiral N.S. Mordvinov; they criticized the new reign and resented the 'Germans' at court.

Central to public opinion was the staunchly loyal middle class (*srednii klass*) – the 'soul of the empire' – with its city-dwelling landowners, non-serving gentry, merchants of the first three guilds, educated persons, and men of letters. A strong, favourable influence on this group, said Von Vock, was the daily *Northern Bee* (*Severnaia Pchela*) of Faddei Bulgarin and N.I. Grech. Yet another loyal segment were the soldiers, although some officers clung to the views of Pestel, the executed Decembrist rebel. The *chinovniki*, or civil servants, Von Vock dismissed as self-serving obstructionists.

Among the disaffected were the younger generation, those from seventeen to twenty-five, who dreamed of constitutionalism and who represented a 'gangrenous part' of society. Also restless were the peasants and lower clergy. The former resented their long-standing bondage as serfs and the latter suffered from lack of means and education. To counter such discontent, Von Vock urged the emperor to grant 'certain privileges and rewards' to sympathetic writers in the unofficial press.[25] Although earlier rulers had subsidized journals, Von Vock was advocating payments to individuals as part of a systematic campaign to influence public opinion.

In his second report, on public opinion during 1828, Von Vock cited war with Turkey as a principal issue. That war was neither popular nor understood in Russia.[26] Following the war, 'demagogic intrigues' had begun among youths of good birth and army officers, especially in Moscow, and unnamed 'liberals' were trying to sway the young to their views.

Von Vock's next report concerned 1829 and the bad effect of the ministries and chief departments on public opinion. It labelled Minister of Public Education Lieven as incompetent, especially at a time when those agitating for political reforms had joined 'those who wish to publish newspapers.' (In September 1829 Nicholas required printers to send the Third Section copies of all papers, journals, and miscellanies.)[27] Because the printed word could and did shape public opinion, Von Vock again advised Nicholas to hire writers to put the best light on the government, as European rulers were doing.

In his final report, for 1830, Von Vock blamed strong censorship measures for causing anti-government feeling. The arrest of three St Petersburg writers early in the year had, he said, angered many among the middle class, the segment of public opinion most important to the crown.[28] Turning to the rebellion in Poland, Von Vock castigated the 'liberals' who favoured restoring the Polish constitution; and to them he linked Pushkin, whose verses stirred dreams of a constitutional order in Russia. Certain influential journalists in St Petersburg and Moscow, said Von Vock, also sought to undermine the autocracy.[29]

Taken as a whole, the four reports advocate judicious government action, both in overseeing the press and in governing generally, as the best means for shaping favourable public opinion. By viewing public opinion as a distinct and palpable force, they also reflect the new government sensitivity, in the aftermath of Decembrism, to what the public was thinking. Finally, these assessments enabled the Third Section to formulate and implement a censorship policy, the lines of which emerged in the early thirties as follows: to enlist journalists to write on behalf of the government, to repress 'subversive' journalists before they could serve dissenting groups or win a following, and to discern which topics were being used by enemies of the state to foment discontent in order that pro-government writers could counteract their effect.

IV

Minister of Public Education Lieven had meanwhile determined to administer censorship under the Statute of 1828 to the letter of the law. Conflicts with fellow ministers followed. E.F. Kankrin, the minister of finance, for example, complained to the Committee of Ministers in January 1830 that the press had falsely reported a doubling of tariffs on imported silk and that a pre-publication screening by his ministry would have prevented the mistake. Lieven reminded Kankrin that the new statute made no provision for screening but invited him to publish a correction, to which Kankrin archly replied that such rebuttals only undermine public confidence in the government. As complaints like Kankrin's multiplied, Nicholas I himself granted administrators preliminary censorship authority, thus altering the Statute of 1828.[30]

Events in 1830 also affected the reformed law. During July, in France, a revolutionary crowd forced Charles X from the throne. Nicholas I only grudgingly recognized Louis Philippe's new government after seriously pondering armed intervention. In November the Belgians expelled the Dutch to make way for their own king, and William I of Orange appealed to Nicholas for armed assistance; but although Nicholas again vainly tried to prod help from the monarchs of Prussia and Austria, the emperor had his hands full as the so-called Congress Poland began a rebellion against Russian rule in November 1830. At the same time, Nicholas faced a cholera epidemic and mutinies in the military colonies and among the military in Sevastopol.[31]

In the midst of these troubles, Benckendorff, in November 1830, summoned to his office Baron A.A. Delvig, the editor of the *Literary Gazette* (*Literaturnaia Gazeta*), for an explanation of why that journal, whose distinguished contributors included Pushkin, Viazemsky, and Zhukovsky, had taken on a 'liberal' character. Benckendorff particularly disapproved Delvig's having published a poem by Casimir Delavigne honouring those who died in Paris during the events of July 1830. Delvig explained that he had chosen the poem for its literary merit. (He had, in fact, says his cousin A.I. Delvig, simply used it to fill a 'hole' in the columns at the back of the *Gazette*.)[32]

Delvig reminded Benckendorff that the censor alone was liable for what appeared in the *Literary Gazette* and, 'on the basis of the law, the publisher does not answer for an article approved by the censorship.' Benckendorff shot back that laws did not concern anyone, like himself, 'in charge.' On 8 November Benckendorff informed the Chief Administration of the Censorship that Delvig had committed an offense unpardonable for a 'man entrusted with a journal.'[33] Lieven offered to close the journal, but Benckendorff settled for removing Delvig from the editorship. The censor was reprimanded because the Delavigne poem had destroyed the effect of articles placed by Benckendorff in the *Northern Bee* to calm the Russian people after the Paris uprising.

When Delvig died the following January, diarist A.V. Nikitenko stated that 'the public blames Benckendorff.' Benckendorff's handling of Delvig, combined with other arbitrary acts on the part of censorship officials, had already caused Nikitenko (whose own role in censorship will be discussed later) to consider the effort to liberalize censorship as ended. He designated 1830 as a turning point, writing on 30 December that during the year, 'the censorship regulations [of 1828] have been quite overturned ... [and] the laws are violated by the very persons who wrote them ...'[34]

Meanwhile, Benckendorff had formally objected to the provision in the Statute of 1828 placing blame for unacceptable published material solely on the censor who had approved it. On 6 January 1831 the Third Section proposed that authors again share responsibility, as they had under the law of 1826, with their names to be known to the censor. Although the Chief Administration replied that such a provision would contradict article forty-seven of the 1828 statute, Lieven helpfully suggested that a secret circular to censors could circumvent the article without changing the law in the public's eyes.[35]

Nicholas then summoned Count Nesselrode, Adjutant General Vasilchikov, Minister of Justice D.V. Dashkov, and Benckendorff (none from the censorship administration) to decide how best to effect the Third Section's recommendation; and that committee adopted Lieven's suggestion. Their report, approved by the emperor on 28 March, ruled that the author of atheistic or seditious works who 'can be shown to have intentionally published them must be handed over to justice on the basis of the general laws, despite censorship approval given to him.'[36] The committee named the Third Section to decide what publications were seditious or atheistic and required editors to name the authors they published. (Previously editors could publish unsigned works but might later have to identify the author.) Through these provisions, the committee and emperor opened the way to post-publication harassment of writers by the Third Section.

The committee's plan became the secret directive of 28 March 1831, giving the police jurisdiction over authors of dangerous published words and imposing a form of post-publication censorship. Along with the secret directive of 25 April 1828, it underscores the two-faced policy effected under the 'liberal' statute of 1828.

Another official ready to tighten the 1828 law was Lieven's successor-to-be, S.S. Uvarov, then president of the Academy of Sciences and its representative on the Chief Administration. He argued that periodicals could and did attack the government while adhering strictly to the law. By overviewing several issues of a publication, one could sense their 'orientation'; but the existing statute provided no defense, he argued, against the dangerous trend apparent in a journal like the *Moscow Telegraph* (*Moskovskii Telegraf*) of Nicholas Polevoi.[37] Uvarov called for post-publication measures to fill that gap.

For its part, the Third Section exercised its authority over published materials arbitrarily. On the one hand, the small staff made hasty, safe decisions; on the other, Benckendorff himself lacked sophistication in literary matters and, as a Baltic German, had imperfectly mastered Russian. Bullish in manner, he sought to frighten writers and editors into good behaviour, often altering the regulations through personal fiat and bypassing regular channels to discipline censors, editors, and writers. Writers or censors learned that their best protection from penalty lay in works clearly supporting the government – and even these could be misinterpreted.

V

One publisher and writer who tailored his journalism to suit Benckendorff was F.V. Bulgarin, co-owner, with N.I. Grech, of the paper praised by Von Vock, the *Northern Bee*.[38] As mentioned earlier, Bulgarin won his very substantial readership among those whom the Third Section saw as the government's main support, the middle class.

Born into an ardently patriotic Polish family in western Russia in 1789, Bulgarin at first adopted the anti-Russian beliefs of his parents; but, upon attending a Russian military academy, he embraced Orthodoxy and Russian nationalism. Once in the Russian army, Bulgarin fought against the French in 1807 and the Swedes the following year, only to be discharged in 1811 for bad behaviour. Journeying to Warsaw, he joined the Polish army to fight for Napoleon and rose to the rank of captain. In 1814, he was captured by the Russians, but, like many Poles in the French service, won a pardon from Alexander I. Then, after taking up residence in St Petersburg, Bulgarin set about to prove himself wholly Russian. His mastery of the Russian language served him well as a novelist and journalist, and in 1825 he founded the *Northern Bee* with Grech, who was then still involved in the Popov affair.

Bulgarin's memorandum reached the emperor, who, in turn, sent it to brists in 1826. Because his time in the French army was the reason given for that arrest, Bulgarin, on 12 May 1826, wrote the official in charge of the investigation, A.N. Potapov, chief of the army general staff, to say that his French soldiering tortured his conscience and that he wished to place his 'information and experience' at the disposal of the emperor. Several days later, about three weeks before Nicholas signed Shishkov's censorship statute, Bulgarin forwarded to Potapov a memorandum, 'On Censorship in Russia and Publishing in General,' which criticized government policy. Bulgarin also urged the government to hire friendly journalists to enhance its public image and indicated his readiness to perform 'literary services.'[39]

Bulgarin's memorandum reached the emperor who, in turn, sent it to Shishkov for a reply. (The memorandum bore no signature, for Bulgarin said his words contradicted the proposed censorship law and he did not want his identity known to the minister.) Shishkov promptly and successfully disputed Bulgarin's arguments, insisting, for example, that proposed government policies could never be discussed by the press because that right belonged exclusively to the Russian government.[40]

Six months later, in November, Benckendorff recommended to the Senate that Bulgarin receive a salaried post at the eighth rank, but without duties, under Minister of Education Shishkov. He endorsed Bulgarin as a man of firm principles who had blunted the influence of wrong-thinking 'youth and certain smart alecks.'[41] Moreover, his being a Pole made him an asset. Bulgarin got the post. Five years later, in December 1831, when Benckendorff endorsed Bulgarin's request for an extended sick leave at a higher rank, Prince Lieven, then education minister, refused to agree because he found no evidence that Bulgarin had done any work in his ministry. Bulgarin consequently resigned and ceased to be on the government payroll until 1844, when he became a member of the Imperial Commission on Stud Farming at a higher rank.[42]

Only grudgingly tolerant of Bulgarin, Nicholas chose in January 1830 to send both Bulgarin and Grech to the St Petersburg guardhouse for the *Bee*'s attack on Zagoskin's naturalistic novel, *Yury Miloslavsky*; and, at a ball in the early thirties, the emperor asked Pushkin to recite twice a stinging epigram he had written about Bulgarin. The emperor once said he distrusted Bulgarin and, as late as 1840, claimed never to have met him. Five years later, he refused Bulgarin's request for 25,000 rubles to help publish two books, one an encomium of the first two decades of Nicholas's rule.[43]

Ever the self-promoter, Bulgarin claimed he had the emperor's personal patronage when Benckendorff, rather, was his benefactor. Upon Benckendorff's recommendatons, for example, Bulgarin in 1830 received two jewelled rings from Nicholas for two historical novels: *Dmitry the Pretender* and *Ivan Vyzhigin*. Benckendorff also held up the publication of Pushkin's *Boris Godunov* so that Bulgarin's *Dmitry* could appear first and then approved Bulgarin's request to list Nicholas among the subscribers to *Vyzhigin*.

Given that support, Bulgarin freely sought to influence censorship decisions affecting him and his paper. Thus, in 1830, the Chief Administration of the Censorship acted on Bulgarin's behalf in banning accounts of the notorious French police spy Eugène François Vidocq because of a widely held understanding that references to Vidocq lampooned Bulgarin. Pushkin had established that parallel in a satirical piece in the *Literary Gazette*, taking revenge for Bulgarin's supposed theft of ideas for *Dmitry the Pretender* from *Boris Godunov*.[44]

Meanwhile *Northern Bee* thrived as the first popular newspaper in private hands, gaining a circulation of 7,000 in the thirties, dropping sharply in the forties, but reaching 10,000 during the Crimean War in the mid-fifties. Bulgarin himself remained the object of scorn for such literary aristocrats as Pushkin and Viazemsky and such journalistic radicals as Belinsky and Kraevsky; for what made his paper popular with the loyal middle-class landlords, merchants, and minor bureaucrats was its gossip, its ill-concealed attacks on notable literary personalities, and its light and vulgar fiction – all overlaid with patriotism and 'pacifistic sentiments.'[45]

Besides prospering through sensationalism, the *Bee* enjoyed the singular advantage of having in its censor-approved 'program' the right to publish 'political information.' Thus Bulgarin could print foreign and domestic news and could introduce its readers to the *feuilleton*, the critical review of literature and events which had originated on the front page of French dailies. Bulgarin was permitted to do so because he was the ideal publisher in the eyes of the prime shaper of press policy during the opening years of the reign of Nicholas I – the head of the Third Section, Benckendorff.

The emperor in these same years had proved inept with respect to censorship and press policy. He had little time for writers or for literature, and his indifference influenced his laws and directives. He bungled in approving the 'cast-iron' statute of Shishkov and then had permitted the writing of a new censorship statute behind his minister's back. In turn, he had negated the new, more tolerant statute by involving the Third Section in censorship and giving Benckendorff greater authority than the minister of public education over the press.

This turn towards two kinds of press controls, however, had set the course for censorship policy during the remaining years of Nicholas's reign. The Ministry of Public Education would continue to conduct the regular system of preliminary censorship, while the Third Section, or political police, would provide an irregular system of surveillance and contingency controls.

The irregular system was the government's response to revolutionary events in the West and to the growing awareness that public opinion had political implications. Von Vock was the first Russian official to attempt a comprehensive analysis of public opinion, but his argument that political consequences could result from the press's interpretation of events was one already voiced and acted upon by officials in the West. Following such precedents, Nicholas I directed Benckendorff to engage in covert activities against the press similar to those already used by the heads of the police of Napoleon and Louis XVIII. He likewise began venturing into behind-the-scenes recruitment of 'private' authors to write on behalf of the government.

5

Censorship and the new journalism, 1832–48

Certain that he should prescribe what Russians could read, Nicholas I dominated the printed word through his censors, his secret police, and, after 1832, his personal involvement in press matters. Besides setting such limits as tone and the number of periodicals and permissible topics, he directed his Ministry of Public Education to instill 'official nationality' nationwide and had agents hired to build favourable opinion about Russia in western Europe. Although he could not realize the dream of every autocrat – spontaneous praise from most writers – Nicholas did keep the press at home manageable. Readerships remained small by European standards, a daily press hardly existed, and book publishing grew only slightly each year.

What readers wanted was nonetheless figuring more and more in Russian publishing. That mysterious chemical brew of rapport between writers and readers began to bubble in Russia in the 1830s, the very time when the great literary critic Belinsky hailed the start of Russian journalism – writings for the public-at-large rather than for a learned few. And, as they developed a sense of audience, Russian editors and writers courted followings, knowing full well that popular periodicals and authors were harder for the government to control.

I

In January 1832 the emperor personally intervened in the censorship process in reaction to an article, 'The Nineteenth Century,' published that month in a new journal, *The European* (*Evropeets*), by editor Ivan Kireevsky, a mild and scholarly man of literary and philosophical interests. Kireevsky had returned the previous year from Germany determined to enlighten Russians about the humanistic culture of western Europe.

Kireevsky wrote his article as literary criticism and to establish in the first issue his ideological position: that Russia must learn from Europe.[1] He argued that a new European cultural synthesis was displacing the old conflict between reason and romanticism. Philosophy, science, literature, and religion were turning to practical concerns that grew out of economic and social changes. Coming into prominence, for example, were the literary tastes of the 'half-educated' masses, whose raw enthusiasms Kireevsky welcomed. Because the resulting European culture was both humane and universal, as Russia's was not, Russia must borrow from the West.

Nicholas I disagreed and condemned Kireevsky for a purely political diatribe. Benckendorff branded Kireevsky 'wrong-thinking' and 'untrustworthy' and accused him of conveying 'secret intentions' through allusory language: 'activity of the mind' really meant 'revolution,' just as 'skillfully contrived middle ground' referred to constitutionalism.[2]

To be sure, Kireevsky had no revolutionary motives, but neither had he portrayed Russia as self-sufficient and morally superior, the image Nicholas insisted upon. Although the censorship authority had already approved the third (March) issue, Benckendorff closed *The European* that February (no more than fifty had subscribed). In addition, Benckendorff – not the minister of public education – issued the orders barring Kireevsky from journalism and placing him under police supervision, and then reprimanded the censor, S.T. Aksakov. Benckendorff used the powers set forth in the secret directive of 28 March 1831, which made action against a writer possible even though the censor had approved that writer's published work.

Kireevsky escaped administrative exile only because of an appeal by his poet friend, V.A. Zhukovsky. Zhukovsky argued in vain, however, that the government had wrongly impugned Kireevsky's honour, the very issue he had raised in 1822 regarding his own treatment by a censor. 'Why is it,' he asked, 'that he who destroys someone else's honour has the right to be believed, and the one whose honour is destroyed is without ... means to defend his most valuable possession, his good name?'[3] Zhukovsky was railing against the dilemma of all persons censored and punished for criminal 'motives' who cannot plead their cases before a court of law. In Kireevsky's case, the authorities did not so much as answer Zhukovsky's appeal.

When Zhukovsky and others could not convince Kireevsky to write directly in his own defense to the emperor, Peter Chaadaev, who was acquainted with the head of the Third Section, wrote a letter to Benckendorff that went forward over Kireevsky's name. In it he argued that Kireevsky had merely wanted to help Russia modernize in order to abolish serfdom.[4] The authorities paid no heed. Rather, the episode brought Nicholas more directly into censorship matters. To guard against any other publications like *The European*, Nicholas announced that no new journal could begin to publish without his approval, a responsibility he preempted from the minister of public education and kept for the rest of his life.

Also in the wake of Kireevsky's misadventure, Vice-minister of Public Education S.S. Uvarov took strong exception to the European ideas infiltrating Russian universities. In his report about a visit to the University of Moscow in 1832, he proposed 'Orthodoxy, autocracy, and nationality' as 'intellectual dams' against the destructive ideas of the West.[5] On 21 March 1833 Nicholas I empowered Uvarov to apply that ideology to censorship and education by naming him minister. The imperial government thereby began what was to be known as 'official nationality' – the doctrine of the absolute superiority of the Russian church, state, and people – and would use censorship to instil it.

Once he was minister of public education, Uvarov informed censors that he intended not only to enforce censorship rules strictly (the Statute of 1828 plus directives) but also to improve the 'tone and exposition' of published works. Because, said Uvarov, the 'taste for reading and literary activity, which earlier was confined to the upper middle classes, is now spreading *even* further,' he ordered the close scrutiny of proposals for inexpensive periodicals designed to appeal to a mass audience.[6]

Similarly, Nicholas issued a blanket interdiction in March 1834 against any Russian versions of the so-called 'penny magazines' that provided cheap, trifling, but also educational, reading in many European countries. Unbending in his refusal to approve applications for several new journals in the thirties, despite their backing by the Chief Administration of the Censorship, Nicholas rejected the application in September 1836 by Prince Odoevsky and others to launch *Russian Miscellany*.[7]

Given Nicholas's attitude, censors became more cautious. Unlike Lieven, Uvarov freely acted against censor-approved publications if they struck him as offensive. He especially disliked a review of Walter Scott's *Life of Napoleon Bonaparte* in May 1833, finding it slighting to Russians and their government; and he asked Nicholas to close the offending journal, the *Moscow Telegraph* of N.P. Polevoi. Explained Uvarov: 'I gave the most detailed suggestions to the editors of the journals and received from them solemn promises to rectify the false and impertinent inclinations of their periodical publications' – a promise Polevoi had failed to keep. In a reply describing the article as 'more stupid for its contradictions than unfavourable,' the emperor asked Uvarov to tell Polevoi 'not to write any nonsense or his journal will be closed.'[8]

Within a year, Uvarov had persuaded the emperor that Polevoi was publishing 'nonsense.' In March 1834 *Telegraph* criticized a play that Nicholas had admired (N.V. Kukolnik's 'The Hand of the Almighty Saved the Motherland'). The minister admitted to a subordinate that the review was a useful pretext to close a journal he found to be revolutionary. Furthermore, he continued, 'the rights of the Russian citizenry do not include the right to communicate in writing with the people ... a privilege the government can give and take away when it wants.' On 3 April Nicholas finally agreed to close *Telegraph*, basing his decision on pages of incriminating quotations gathered by Uvarov.[9]

Two years later, in 1836, the *Moscow Telescope* (*Moskovskii Teleskop*) of N.I. Nadezhdin, another duly censored journal, suffered closure for contradicting Uvarov's policy of 'official nationality.' At issue was an outspoken essay: the 'Philosophical Letter' of Peter Chaadaev, which had circulated clandestinely in manuscript since 1830. The letter contended that Russia as a nation had contributed nothing to the world because of the restrictions imposed upon it by the Eastern church – a position similar to that of Kireevsky four years before. Nadezhdin may have concluded that the appearance six months earlier, on 19 April, of Gogol's criticism of the Russian provincial bureaucracy in the 'Inspector General' had portended a relaxation of censorship. But Gogol's lampoon against bureaucracy was one thing; Chaadaev's profoundly gloomy survey of the Russian national past was another.[10]

Nicholas banned *Telescope* and sent Nadezhdin into exile, a punishment harsher than either Kireevsky or Polevoi had suffered. He then placed Chaadaev under police surveillance disguised as medical care by declaring him insane, a calculated slander against the author. The guilty censor, A.V. Boldyrev, lost his posts as censor and as rector of Moscow University, as well as his pension rights.[11]

Even the liberal writers condemned the publication of the letter, using largely nationalistic arguments. Prince P.A. Viazemsky wrote directly to Uvarov to protest that the censorship authority should not tolerate 'negative' comment about Russia and its past, stressing that Pushkin had pressed him to write his criticism.[12]

II

Russian officials' sensitivity to western political and social thought had its match in their concern over what westerners thought and said about Russia. One painful outburst came when European periodicals of all persuasions roundly condemned Nicholas's suppression of the Polish rebellion. In France the Polish affair had proved to be the great turning point in attitudes towards Russia, wrote a Russian agent later, and virtually all parties had united against the empire.[13] Polish émigrés in Europe had their own anti-Russian press, and all these critics distressed Russian officialdom.

Increasingly aware of how such criticism seeped into Russia and how it also undermined Russia's credit rating on the world market, imperial officials determined to counteract such attacks at their source. Probably early in the 1830s, Benckendorff sent as his agent to Germany a certain Baron Schweitzer. Schweitzer's 'struggle with the journals' there left hardly any traces in the records but proved successful, at least in the opinion of Prince Klemens von Metternich, the Austrian chancellor.[14] Yet another Third Section agent was Charles Durand, whose subsidized French-language *Journal de Francfort* opposed the extremist 'liberal' ideas of the French press from 1833 to 1839.

Third Section efforts to influence public opinion abroad began in piecemeal fashion, and Benckendorff often hired operatives as they offered their services; but a small network of agents that prefigured the more complex operations by later Okhrana agents did emerge. As private citizens, writers, or mere correspondents for the Ministry of Public Education, these agents bribed and subsidized journalists and private journals abroad and issued or authored publications of their own.

Benckendorff's principal agent in Paris, which became the centre of Third Section activity, was Yakov N. Tolstoy (1791–1867), the author of an 1835 book praising Field Marshal Ivan F. Paskevich, who had suppressed the Polish rebellion. In 1837, to use his own words, Tolstoy assumed in the Russian government 'a unique position, not defined by any table of ranks.' He became a 'correspondent of the Ministry of Public Education in Paris' but secretly served 'on special assignment to the Third Section.' His task was to 'defend Russia in the journals and refute articles against her.' Tolstoy also hoped to explain the Polish crisis, show the political and economic progress of the empire, sway the French towards an alliance with Russia, and convince Europeans that 'revolution is the scourge of humanity.' Quoting Frederick the Great, Tolstoy said he needed three things: 'money, money, and money.'[15]

Service as a foreign propagandist appealed to yet another Russian journalist: N.I. Grech, whose publishing partner, Bulgarin, had been something of a pioneer in manipulating opinion at home on behalf of the autocracy. Having moved his family abroad, Grech in 1840 issued a book in Germany to deny that he, Bulgarin, or O.I. Senkovsky, another prominent publisher, had ever served as agents of the Russian government. On 31 July 1843 Grech proposed to the Third Section that he become just that.[16] He offered to publish a pamphlet to refute an attack on the Russian government which had appeared in Paris that year: *Russie en 1839*, an account by the Marquis de Custine of how he had travelled to Russia to find justification for absolutism only to return to France a convinced parliamentarian.

Nicholas approved the plan, and that October Grech wrote to the Third Section: 'How I would like to be our agent and mover of public opinion in France and Germany.' He had approached, he said, the French playwright Hippolyte Auger (a soldier in the Russian army from 1814 to 1817, according to Grech) about writing a vaudeville production entitled 'Voyage en Russie,' to be produced in the French capital to 'mock Custine before all Paris.' The government chose to finance only the pamphlet, which appeared first in German and then in French in 1844 in Paris.[17] A Belgian edition soon followed. When a Frankfurt paper charged that the Russian government had backed the pamphlet, Benckendorff concluded that only Grech could have provided the many details cited in the charge. Grech consequently fell from favour.

Though its efforts had met only limited success, the Third Section had geared itself to influence both domestic and foreign opinion. The July Revolution and the Polish rebellion had made Nicholas uneasy, and he favoured every means possible to make 'official nationality' prevail. The secret police, with covert methods, more and more became his means.

III

Given the vagaries of censorship policy and of the readers' market, publishing in the thirties in Imperial Russia could be risky. Bulgarin and Grech stand out for their marked success, and so does another who underwrote a completely new venture in Russian journalism. He was A.F. Smirdin, the first large-scale publisher and bookseller in Russia.

At first a bookshop clerk, Smirdin in time acquired his own store and printing plant and then, in 1833, an expanded store combined with a lending library on Nevskii Prospekt in St Petersburg. There he provided a variety of services to entice customers and won credit for having the first 'European' bookstore in Russia. In his salesroom or second-floor reading room and subscriber library, patrons could find any Russian book – just as, for prescribed fees, they could borrow or subscribe to any Russian periodical. Smirdin also followed the European practice of publishing thick catalogues of company holdings compiled by a professional bibliographer.[18]

In expanding his publishing after 1833, Smirdin took full advantage of the nationalist policies of Uvarov – both the government's restrictions on foreign publications and its favouritism to all things Russian. In addition, improved printing techniques enabled him to publish works especially attractive to Russian readers. Only in the previous decade had Russian paper companies copied European techniques to make the thin, smooth paper necessary for sharp printing impressions. Next, in the late twenties, Russian type founders had greatly improved the design, variety, and consistency of printing type – an effort pioneered by the printing plant of the Army General Staff. Type-founder and designer E. Revilon established his firm in the capital in 1830 and, with the patronage and design collaboration of the Glazunov publishing house, won much of the trade in type that had been with Europe.[19]

The Glazunov firm, begun under Catherine II and renewed under Alexander I, was the first sizeable native publishing house in Russia in private hands. It served as a channel for the latest western printing methods. Its head in the thirties was Ilia Petrovich, son of the founder. He had studied with the famous French printing firm of Didot and, upon returning home, had instructed his own artists to design Russian typefaces using the Didot international proportioning system. Another typographical leader was Smirdin's rival, A.A. Pliushar, who also sent his son to Paris to study with Didot.

Besides his emphasis on innovative typography, Smirdin made good use of illustrations (although Pliushar probably excelled him in lithography).[20] Finally, by paying generous authors' fees, maintaining high printing standards, and promoting wide circulation of works through low prices, Smirdin attracted both the top literary talents of his day – including Pushkin, Gogol, Zhukovsky, and Krylov – and young, aspiring writers. Through all these means, Smirdin successfully promoted book-buying among that group of middle-class Russians that Von Vock had described as the 'soul of the empire.'

Aware of trends in European journalism, Smirdin in January 1834 launched Russia's leading journal of the thirties, his *Library for Readers* (*Biblioteka dlia Chteniia*). Its editor, O.I. Senkovsky, earned the unheard-of salary of 15,000 rubles a year.[21] Senkovsky, who in 1822 had been the youngest professor at the University of St Petersburg, craved attention and made himself a public figure of sorts through his sallies in *Library* against writers. During his fourteen years as editor to 1848, *Library* reached its peak readership of 7,000 in 1837. Although it had less than half that number in the late forties, *Library* won the largest circulation of any journal during the reign of Nicholas I. Like many editors and writers of the period, Senkovsky had served as a censor (1828–33) and knew well the limits imposed by official nationality, a doctrine he favoured.

Senkovsky, Grech, and Bulgarin became the dominating 'triumvirate' of Russian journalism in the thirties. Veering away from pre-Nicholaevan publishing standards, all three used in varied, sensationalized writings to sell their periodicals to middle-class readers, and thereby reaped the scorn of serious intellectuals. (Only initially did Senkovsky attract works from Russia's best writers.) Yet Senkovsky deserves credit for giving Russian readers, so taken with French publications, a journal similar to two attractive Parisian periodicals – the *Revue encyclopédique* and the *Encyclopédie nouvelle* edited by Pierre Leroux – but without their radical content. Under his meticulous management, *Library* set new Russian standards in format and production details and was probably the first Russian periodical to meet deadlines. It not only appeared on the same prescribed day each month but also paid its contributors promptly and, another 'first,' on an established scale.[22]

Commonly referred to as a 'thick' journal, *Library* had an imposing format. A typical issue numbered around three hundred pages and offered seven sections in this order: Russian literature, foreign literature, science and art, industry and agriculture, criticism, literary chronicle, and miscellany. Provincial landowners far from bookstores, libraries, and newspapers found in it a full month of reading, including serialized books from Russia and Europe and the miscellany's popularized summary of world events. Just this appeal to provincial readers, said Belinsky, ensured *Library*'s success: 'Imagine a family of steppe landowners that reads everything it lays its hands on from cover to cover; it still does not succeed in reading to the last page ... and already another issue has arrived, so thick, so rich, so indiscreet, so loquacious.'[23]

In 1835, only a year after starting *Library*, Smirdin bought controlling interest in *Northern Bee*, Russia's first popular newspaper in private hands (it had appeared thrice-weekly until 1831 and thereafter daily).[24] With the *Bee*'s record of prosperity, Bulgarin and Grech commanded a high price from Smirdin. Just three years later, Smirdin bought the nationalist journal, *Son of the Fatherland* (*Syn Otechestva*).

Then in the late thirties came a slump in the publishing market caused by an economic depression following crop failures. Sales of books dropped sharply, and Smirdin found himself overcommitted and short on funds. Competition had also increased during the expanding market of the thirties, as former employees of publishing houses had begun their own firms.[25] No longer could Smirdin rely on selling large editions quickly to underwrite further ventures. Nor could he halt the decline of his three periodicals, as others laid claim to readers by offering less frivolous content.

Determined to recover through a bold stroke, Smirdin borrowed money for an enormous project: the publication over a ten-year period (1846-56) of the *Complete Collection of the Works of Russian Authors* (thirty-five writers in seventy one-ruble volumes). The first several volumes sold well, but not well enough to prevent Smirdin from cancelling the series. Showing his sympathy, Nicholas I gave Smirdin permission to conduct lotteries to sell backlogs of books. But this innovation also failed.[26] As the publisher's business declined in the forties and fifties, so did his health; and Smirdin died in 1857.

In the final analysis, Belinsky assessed Smirdin positively for having ended the time when 'books were dearer than silver and gold.' Smirdin's had been the 'noble passion for bookselling in the European sense of the word,' wrote Belinsky, even though it had 'served to endanger his personal advantage and ... his commercial position.'[27]

In retrospect, Smirdin's start in bookselling and publishing came in the years described by D.S. Mirsky as the beginnings of Russian journalism. 'Despite severe pressures from the censorship, the journalists of the decade [1825-34] and the two following made a plucky stand for independence, if not in political, at least in general cultural questions,' writes Mirsky. 'And it was owing to their efforts that public opinion began to take shape.'[28]

Journalists could also win both money and acclaim, and, as everywhere in Europe, journalism attracted a wide range of middle-class men seeking status and influence. As more and more earned livings by their pens, editors no longer had to rely on writers who also held government posts and official outlooks; and Russian journalists in turn began to see themselves as shapers of public opinion like their counterparts in western Europe.[29]

Not only Smirdin but writers and publishers as a whole benefitted from Nicholas's strict limits on foreign literature and the number of periodicals and from the new copyright system. The financially stronger and literarily venturesome journals of the thirties proved a transition to the leaders of the forties – *Notes of the Fatherland* (*Otechestvennye Zapiski*) and the revived *Contemporary* (*Sovremennik*), both of which began publicizing values at odds with official nationality. And, once such periodicals won substantial, loyal readerships, the government, to its discomfort, found itself less ready to dictate content or withdraw rights to publish.

The independent tendencies of journalists also grew out of the brashness that is a common tool of their trade. Controversy and sensationalism have always sold periodicals, and among the readiest to take risks to catch readers' attention were a number of social outsiders. The Poles Bulgarin and Senkovsky, for example, capitalized on their adopted Russian nationalism and their flamboyance to succeed in journalism. Nicholas Polevoi, son of a mere tradesman, similarly prospered with his *Moscow Telegraph* until his bid for public acclaim crossed limits acceptable to the government and led to the *Telegraph*'s closure. Nicholas Nadezhdin, of humble provincial origins, chose journalism over the priesthood and then lost his *Moscow Telescope* by startling both the public and the government with Chaadaev's 'Philosophical Letter.'[30] Even Smirdin, son of a Moscow merchant, practised a kind of excessive daring in his ambitious publishing ventures.

IV

All this rivalry for readers led not only to a great variety in published work but also to a new mission among certain writers to raise literary standards and the social conscience of literate Russians. Thus Alexander Pushkin set his sights on publishing a journal on the level of the great ones in Europe. When, in 1831, he approached the Third Section about his plan, Pushkin was sophisticated enough to pledge his loyalty and to request police endorsement of his proposal before it went to Nicholas. That same year, Pushkin formally submitted his proposal to the emperor. In it he praised the state for making publishing a sound commercial venture: 'The protection of ... [literary] property and the censorship statute are among the most important blessings of the current reign.' But, continued Pushkin, unless the government approved still more periodicals, Bulgarin alone would set publishing standards: 'For the renewal of balance in literature, we [Pushkin and like-minded writers] need a journal of the same kind as the *Northern Bee*, that is, a journal in which political and foreign news can be printed.'[31]

Not until 1836, with imperial approval, did Pushkin launch his soon-important *Contemporary*, but he did not gain permission to include political news. In the first issue N.V. Gogol condemned Senkovsky and his kind of journalism, which appealed to the 'limited reader' who takes 'everything as pure truth.'[32] Among the journals in general, Gogol continued, petty in-fighting obsessed the reviewers, who practised the literary sneer at the expense of analysis and thought. Critics ought rather to aspire to a level of expression equal to creative writing.

Exempt from Gogol's scorn was a young literary critic whose reviews in *Moscow Telescope* in the previous three years had also won Pushkin's respect. He was Vissarion Belinsky, the son of an army doctor, who was to ruffle the relative calm in government-press relations. Belinsky wrote mainly for two journals whose publishers agreed that the reading public was ready for more than mere diversion. They were able to explore new, even sensitive, ideas because (as the emperor eventually realized) the censors tended to be complacent or sympathetic. In many cases the censors had vested interests in the journals and chose to help widen published discussion. Thus was Belinsky to use literary criticism as a vehicle for serious questions about the existing order.

Belinsky first appeared in print in the *Moscow Telescope* in 1834, and his writings then had no political overtones. When Uvarov banned *Telescope* in the fall of 1836 for publishing Chaadaev's 'Letter,' Belinsky undertook the study of Hegelian philosophy and sought to explain it as editor in 1838 of the short-lived and under-subscribed *Moscow Observer* (*Moskovskii Nabliudatel*, 1835–9).

In 1839 Belinsky moved to St Petersburg to join the staff of *Notes of the Fatherland*, a defunct journal revived that year by A.A. Kraevsky to challenge journalistic mediocrity. Belinsky's criticism during the next two years justified the autocracy as compatible with Hegelian rationality; but, having gradually come to deplore social conditions in Russia, Belinsky abandoned Hegelian abstractions for humanistic values. By infusing his work with indignation and a sense of moral imperative, he won a large readership, even though the censors cut out much of what he wrote. Westernizer historian T.N. Granovsky felt that censorship probably even benefitted Belinsky by imposing a special discipline on him.[33]

Notes of the Fatherland itself was a synthesis of the literary journal of Alexander I's reign and the more widely read and topically varied periodicals of the reign of Nicholas I. *Notes* departmentalized its coverage and coupled the critic's reviews with articles on science, industry, the economy, and household management, plus a chronicle of current world events. In addition, it published five annual reviews of Russian literature by Belinsky (two more appeared in *Contemporary* after Belinsky moved there in 1846). The journal proved to be the publishing success of the decade, its subscription list growing from 1,250 in 1839 to 4,000 in 1847.

From the start, Kraevsky attracted the best younger writers; and, when he ended 1839 with a deficit, a number generously sent him their manuscripts as gifts. Once *Notes* again made a profit and these same writers sought pay for subsequent works, the parsimonious Kraevsky gained a reputation as a sharp-pencilled businessman. His critic, I.I. Panaev, later satirized Kraevsky's agreement to restore payments as a 'triumph' of talent and labour over 'entrepreneurialism.' Critics of Kraevsky also faulted him for seeking the company of businessmen and officials and for not committing his journal to a clear, unwavering intellectual position, a stand much prized by the intellectuals of the forties. (Kraevsky practised an unoffensive even-handedness, argues Starchevsky, to keep his subscribers loyal.) The many complaints about Kraevsky actually emphasize a characteristic of his journalism: he ran *Notes* along western lines, practising economic management and providing catholic content.[34]

To Kraevsky's credit, *Notes* emphasized social and cultural progress rather than official nationality. Several articles on slavery in the United States and the French colonies, for example, indirectly raised the issue of serfdom in Russia. *Notes* introduced its readers to George Sand and the new European sensibility, to scientific advances, to the thought of European socialists, and, through philosophical articles by Alexander Herzen, to immediate social concerns.[35]

Belinsky at first felt that Kraevsky, whom he praised extravagantly, shared his zeal to improve society through the printed word. 'Journalism in our time is everything,' Belinsky told his friend and collaborator V.P. Botkin. 'Pushkin, Goethe, and even Hegel himself were journalists. The journal is a pulpit and who can be angry at this?'[36] But, in time, money problems arose, and Kraevsky often delayed payment to Belinsky because the latter's social criticism frayed relations with censorship authorities.

When he chose in 1846 to join the *Contemporary*, then controlled by I.I. Panaev and N.A. Nekrasov, Belinsky correctly assessed his own popularity but wrongly assumed that the Russian reading public was too small to support two serious, thick journals. In 1847 he urged Botkin to defect to *Contemporary* because 'the necessary condition for the success of one journal is the fall of the other.'[37] To be sure, the circulation of *Contemporary* had leaped from 223 in 1846 to 2,000 in 1847 and was to reach 3,100 in 1848; but, to Belinsky's surprise, *Notes* retained many of its writers, discovered a new and successful critic, the poet V.N. Maikov, and for a time held a substantial lead in subscribers.

Without eclipsing the popular publications of the triumvirate, two intellectual journals had won strong authority in the forties. The government had no wish to see such publications multiply. When the historian Granovsky requested permission in 1844 with a group of other pro-western intellectuals to found a journal, Uvarov finally replied several months later with a cryptic 'not necessary.'[38]

The success of *Notes* and *Contemporary*, despite Uvarov's policies and those of the Third Section, resulted from several circumstances. First, both had established themselves financially and journalistically in the decade before 1848, a time of reasonably benign censorship controls. Second, both took care to skirt delicate political subjects. Third, lacking truly mass audiences, both journals appeared to the government to be read only by intellectuals.

During these years when he helped further the new literary journalism, Belinsky also championed the westernizer position in debate with the slavophiles over Russia's heritage and future. In this sense, both *Notes* and *Contemporary* were westernizer journals. Their editors and writers held that Russia should heed and absorb western cultural values.

In contrast, the men who would later be known as slavophiles had begun to coalesce as an intellectual group in the mid-forties, arguing that Russia's ills stemmed from the slavish worship of European ideas since Peter the Great. Because they were to seek personal liberties and a new communal spirit under the autocrat, these Russians served official nationality no better than did the westernizers. Lacking prestigious followers and appearing untrustworthy and bizarre to officialdom, they would prove especially vulnerable to censorship; and, although their ideas mark a very important stage in Russian intellectual history, the slavophiles were never able to publish a truly successful periodical of their own.

This group first entered journalism through a journal begun by Michael Pogodin, an historian of Russia at Moscow University. Because the emperor had stopped approving new journals in the mid-thirties. Pogodin enlisted the help of several officials, including Minister of Public Education Uvarov, to win Nicholas's permission in 1837 to launch the *Muscovite* (*Moskvitianin*). Named to honour the true centre of Russian patriotism, it was to voice Russian nationalism and Orthodoxy in the old capital (served then by only one journal, the *Observer*). When the *Muscovite* finally appeared in 1841, Uvarov pronounced it a 'model' of the best in journalism, while Pogodin claimed a favourable response from 'higher circles' in St Petersburg.[39]

As publisher, Pogodin made much of the values of old Muscovy. Calling editorial salaries a 'pernicious demand of our century,' he found his translators and proof-readers among the seminarians who frequented his editorial offices, assigned the journal's 'Spiritual Eloquence' section to various local ecclesiastics, and assembled his best section by printing old Russian documents.[40] The disappointing end product, on cheap paper, suffered from typographical errors, an indifferent publishing schedule, and faulty distribution.

In 1845, with fewer than 300 subscribers, Pogodin sought to perk up his ailing journal by turning it over to the Moscow slavophiles, whose views he felt he shared. Ivan Kireevsky, realigned in his thinking since the closing of the *European*, became editor, only to depart over ideological and managerial differences after three issues.[41] His successor, A.E. Studitsky, a local professor but not a slavophile, managed to publish only two issues of the monthly journal in 1846 and three in 1847, as subscriptions fell to 200. In the final analysis, then, the *Muscovite* under Pogodin (it revived briefly under others in the fifties) mattered very little journalistically but stands as an example of the many periodicals which failed from inept editorship and outdated methods even as publishing markets expanded.

IV

As already mentioned, government censors often made decisions to assist journalists. Because many had full-time positions in the publishing world or at the universities, the leading Moscow and St Petersburg censors served only part-time and with a certain division of interests, a condition common since the start of Russian censorship in 1804 and periodically resisted by the government. Typical of such censors were A.L. Krylov (1789–1853), P.A. Korsakov (1790–1844), and A.N. Ochkin (1791–1865). The first was a censor from 1841 to 1853 while he taught statistics at St Petersburg University and published articles in various journals. Korsakov, a writer and translator, was a censor in St Petersburg from 1835 to 1844 and during that time edited *Lighthouse* (*Maiak*, 1840–45), a pro-government journal, and wrote for *Daguerreotype* (*Dagerotip*,

1842), a literary and theatrical journal. Ochkin, a St Petersburg censor from 1841 to 1848, edited the semi-official *St Petersburg Bulletin* and contributed to *Library for Readers* and the *Journal of Useful Information* (*Zhurnal Obshchepoleznykh Svedenii*, 1833–38, 1847–59), an agricultural bulletin. Many such censors saw themselves as go-betweens who could best serve the cause of enlightenment by giving aid to publications they favoured.

The experiences of censor A.V. Nikitenko (1804–77) show the difficulties faced by the literary-minded official charged with banning words objectionable to the autocrat. Like Belinsky, Nikitenko saw private journalism as a counterweight to official nationality. Although his literary tastes had developed during the era of Pushkin, he recognized that journalism was becoming the main outlet for younger writers, and he wanted it to preserve the values he had learned during the great age of poetry.

In April 1833, two years after becoming a professor of Russian literature and language at St Petersburg University, Nikitenko became a censor. Besides welcoming the added income, Nikitenko took censorship seriously; for, he said, he would strive to 'reconcile the irreconcilable: to satisfy the demands of government, of writers, and of one's inner feeling.' Ruefully he added: 'The censor is considered the natural enemy of writers – and essentially this is not a mistake.'[42]

Conscientious though he was, Nikitenko spent eight days in the guardhouse in 1834 and a night in 1842 for approving material that alarmed high officials. The first offense involved a translation of Victor Hugo's 'To a Pretty Girl,' in which the author swore that were he God he would surrender all he had for one kiss from his beloved. When the metropolitan of Moscow and Novgorod, Serafim, protested this sacrilege, Nicholas ordered Nikitenko confined.[43]

Nikitenko had close ties with the literary community and took pride in what he could do for writers. Two important victories resulted from his arguments before the Main Censorship Committee: the publication of Gogol's *Mirgorod* in 1835 and of *Dead Souls* in 1842. Nikitenko declined to censor Pushkin, probably because his verses offered censors too many pitfalls.[44]

While a censor, Nikitenko served from 1840 to 1841 as editor of *Son of the Fatherland*. In December 1846 he accepted the editorship of *Contemporary*, an outside responsibility approved by Uvarov, the minister of public education. When a dispute with the publishers erupted, Nikitenko began to have second thoughts about his position: 'They [Panaev and

Nekrasov] evidently hoped to find in me a blind instrument and wanted to act independently under the cover of my name. I will not agree to this.'[45] Nikitenko persevered and *Contemporary* prospered, in part because Belinsky's talent as a literary critic reached full flower at this same time.

But the relative calm in government-press relations was about to be shattered by the events of 1848 in Europe, and one of the first reactions of the government would be to tighten censorship and forbid censors to serve as editors and writers for periodicals. In the meantime, however, imperial censors like Nikitenko had done much to bring about the new literary journalism of the forties.

In 1832, the outset of the period discussed in this chapter, Ivan Kireevsky argued that Europe was developing a more humane, practical, and universal culture based on a synthesis of reason and romanticism. Russia, he said, must learn from Europe. Nicholas I and his officials disagreed and deliberately tried to prevent the growth in Russia of a many-sided public opinion like that already evident in Europe. The emperor refused applications for new journals, closed several unacceptable periodicals during the 1830s, and rejected the idea of any Russian versions of the 'penny papers.' Those few who did read journals and newspapers should find there the ideas of Orthodoxy, autocracy, and nationality, Nicholas maintained. To a great extent Nicholas succeeded in his goals, and did so by protecting pro-government publishing from competition.

But the social and cultural changes that Kireevsky had favoured in 1832 were to a large extent occurring in Russia – among them the growth and advancement of publishing along European lines. The publisher Smirdin, a beneficiary of Nicholas's policies, not only utilized the latest western printing technology and sold books like a European, but also owned a popular journal which copied the format of a leading Parisian periodical. The loyalists Smirdin, Grech, Bulgarin, and Senkovsky, by greatly expanding publishing and journalism in the thirties, had in turn prepared the way for the westernizing journals of the forties.

6

A system under siege, 1848–55

After the European revolutions of 1848, Nicholas I lost faith in the persuasive powers of official nationality as a component in his censorship system. He reacted fearfully and defensively against the press, ordering censors to forbid anything conceivably dangerous to the realm and subjecting a maturing press to petty whims and capricious standards. Ignoring counsels of moderation, the emperor undercut Minister of Public Education Uvarov and forced him from office; he then appointed as chief censor a man whose ideas he had found too extreme twenty-five years earlier.

Many writers and censors saw the clumsy 'terror' unleashed by Nicholas as a temporary aberration, and time proved them correct. Those involved in journalism – the major innovation in publishing under Nicholas – and in literature meanwhile continued to serve a new readership that was exercising choice and thereby influencing editors and publishers. Although this atypical period of censorship by a government unhinged by apprehension largely ruled out initiatives from the press, one striking exception stands out: some writers explored the peasant question and brought forward a topic that would occupy the press for the rest of the century and beyond.

I

Cabled news about revolution in France reached St Petersburg on 22 February 1848. Even though events in Paris were separated from St Petersburg by great distances and vast social and political differences, high officials immediately feared for the autocracy. Those who had favoured censorship changes moved quickly. Prince A.F. Orlov, head of the Third Section, prepared recommendations on the crisis and personally presented them to the emperor on 23 February. To give his full time to state security, he repeated a request first made four years before that the Third Section be relieved of post-publication censorship duties. Orlov criticized censorship permissiveness for making his agency's follow-up work necessary at all.

Having repeatedly heard complaints about *Contemporary* and *Notes of the Fatherland*, Orlov reported that he had scrutinized the journals himself. He agreed with those who ranked them the best in the empire. While both tended towards radicalism, neither was publishing ideas that he considered criminal. Having no political goals, said Orlov, Belinsky and his followers did not deliberately preach 'communism' and wrote in westernized fashion merely to create interest. But because 'they can sow in the younger generation ideas about political questions and communism,' Orlov urged stricter censorship of their journals.[1]

Baron Modest Korf, a member of the Second (legal) Section of His Majesty's Own Chancellery, was equally quick to give Nicholas advice. He had hesitated earlier, he wrote in his memorandum, lest he be considered an informer, but he could no longer delay pointing out that Uvarov's 'sickly condition, perhaps even some surfeiting or satiation, had significantly weakened his authority and the direction of [his] ministry.' According to Nikitenko, Korf coveted Uvarov's post and wrote accordingly. K.S. Veselovsky, a member of the academy and a political economist, also blamed stark ambition for Korf's submission. Since fortune 'does not always know herself on whom to bestow her caresses, [Korf] was not averse to helping her, having told himself that the time was ripe.'[2]

Korf presented his memorandum to Nicholas through the Grand Duke, the future Alexander II, on 24 February, the day of Orlov's own audience with the emperor. In it, Korf differed from Uvarov on how the censorship authority should deal with the West. Uvarov had intended that Russian ideas, or official nationality, saturate publications to cause readers to reject western ideas. Korf, on the other hand, stressed that censorship had to ensure that the Russian press correctly interpreted information and ideas from the West. If facts about western revolutions 'become general knowledge,' said Korf, 'then ought they not at least to be offered to readers in the vivid colours of the contempt they deserve?'[3] Korf proposed that loyal, articulate censors replace the many under Uvarov who were poorly trained and indifferent or who had close ties with the press; that cuts be made in each censor's excessive workload of

900 pages every two weeks; and that only a single periodical release foreign news, which others could then reprint.

On 27 February Nicholas I responded to the advice of Orlov and Korf by creating a committee under the chairmanship of Prince A.S. Menshikov 'to provide me with proof where it finds dereliction of the censorship and its command, the Ministry of Public Education, and which journals have departed from their programs.' Semevsky says the committee was Korf's idea. Korf in 1855 credited Orlov.[4]

The hostility of the group was clear to Uvarov from the outset, for the appointees included Korf and L.V. Dubbelt of the Third Section, both committed beforehand to ending the status quo, and A.G. Stroganov, whose brother had denounced Uvarov to the emperor after being fired in 1847 from heading the Moscow education district. (Two others were D.P. Buturlin, director of the Imperial Public Library, and P.I. Degai, a jurist and doctor of laws.) The historian Michael Pogodin wrote to S.P. Shevyrev: 'Uvarov told Granovsky that the entire Ministry of Education is in danger ... not to mention literature.'[5]

The Menshikov committee completed its investigation during March and filed a report on 2 April that was especially critical of *Contemporary* and *Notes of the Fatherland*. The editors of both journals, said the committee, must be warned that they would be punished and their journals closed if they continued to advance 'reprehensible' and 'ambiguous' ideas. Their 'doubtful spirit' and veiled allusions appeared a deliberate attempt to insinuate radical ideas among their readers.[6] The Menshikov report also recommended that a permanent group oversee censorship and improve the quality of censors and that a new censorship statute be written.

On the very date of the report, Nicholas named the 'Committee for Supreme Supervision over the Spirit and Orientation of Private Publications in Russia,' commonly referred to by its founding date (2 April, 1848) or by the name of its chairman (Buturlin). The three-man body, which included Korf and Degai, proved to be a smaller version of the Menshikov committee authorized to carry out its own proposals. The Buturlin committee at once forbade censors to have ties with the press or outside work of any kind. It told Uvarov to warn his censors against passages copied from foreign works and banned any commentary on 'economic reforms' – a reference to serfdom. Finally, it set aside the article in the Statute of 1828 which gave the benefit of the doubt to authors by requiring censors to approve only what was explicitly clear and acceptable.

As for the drafting of a new censorship statute, the emperor delegated this task to Uvarov. The minister in turn appointed an in-house committee which included I.I. Davydov, the director of the St Petersburg Pedagogical Academy; E.E. Komovsky, director of the Department of Education; N.I. Burt (Berte), vice-director of the Department of Education; and an official of that department, Dukhshinsky.[7] Because this committee represented a viewpoint and political aim wholly different from the Buturlin committee, conflicts were certain to arise. On balance, however, the Buturlin committee had already caused Uvarov's censorship to become more abrupt and intolerant, a reflection of the increasing concern among higher officials over the revolutionary tide in Europe which had swept on from Paris to engulf even Vienna and Berlin.

Another who regarded censorship as crucial in this threatening period was an heir to the liberal tradition of Pushkin in literature and politics – Prince P.A. Viazemsky, a minor figure in Uvarov's ministry but an important one in the world of letters. In April he composed and presented his views 'On Censorship' to the emperor. Although Buturlin passed the submission to Uvarov with the notation that Nicholas had found it to contain much of value, the emperor appears to have ignored it completely.[8]

Most notable was Viazemsky's recommendation for a new censorship agency directly responsible to the emperor and under an official he trusted who was both 'political' and 'governmental' in talent and experience. To legitimize itself, the censorship authority should cease to quibble over words and concentrate on the sense of a publication. Social change had created new problems, he wrote, especially in broadening the readership of periodicals to include the emerging 'middle class,' a group generally resentful because it despaired of moving higher. To counter that discontent, the government needed a means to 'direct literature and to fertilize the field it works' – that is, it should copy France by publishing books and a daily newspaper to advance its own viewpoint and by channelling information to friendly writers.[9] Lastly, Viazemsky urged the government to rethink its outmoded attitudes towards society, surely alluding to serfdom.

Viazemsky, like Von Vock and Kireevsky earlier in the reign, linked the growth of journalism with the spread of reading to new groups whose vague discontent and hunger for information made them welcome a more diverse and readable press. They wanted more coverage of events in Europe. Much like Uvarov, Viazemsky favoured responding with the more sophisticated techniques of western governments to deal with public opinion as a force in its own right.

II

Nicholas and his government, however, were in no mood to follow Viazemsky's advice. Rather, the emperor's deepening wariness and intolerance quickly spread through the bureaucracy. The press, in turn, provided a ready target for officials determined to act decisively. As part of this official reaction and in response to the Menshikov report and the emperor's instructions, Uvarov wrote editors Kraevsky and Nikitenko on 6 April that ideas in their journals were 'to a high degree criminal.' Each was to 'conform to the views of the government' or suffer the consequences.[10] Both Nikitenko and Kraevsky at once saw good reason to make clear their loyalty.

In a letter to Orlov a few days later, Nikitenko vowed that his was 'a heart devoted to the great sovereign.' He wrote that he had become editor in the first place to publish works 'consistent with the existing order'; but, because of inexperience, he had failed to distinguish between the gifted young on his staff who were ill-intentioned and those who could profit from mature guidance to grow in loyalty to the state. After showing Nikitenko's letter to the emperor, Orlov wrote on it, 'The sovereign responded that [Nikitenko] should show his feelings in the matter.'[11] Within days, Nikitenko resigned as editor of *Contemporary*, a move he would have had to make in any case to remain a censor.

During an interview with an official of the Third Section, M.M. Popov, on 11 April, Kraevsky took the approach of pledging to make his journal an 'organ of the government.' A month later he wrote to Dubbelt of the Third Section explaining that European issues had penetrated his *Notes of the Fatherland* because the censorship authority had forbidden comment on Russia's relations with western Europe. He continued: 'Little by little, my collaborators, for the most part young people, attracted by this orientation, frequently carried me along and blunted my attention so that I permitted much that ... could cause dangerous consequences in readers' thinking.' Kraevsky then asked the Third Section to permit him to publish an article, 'Russia and Europe at the Present Minute.' That duly-approved article spoke in these terms: 'In one half [Europe] there is anarchy with all its horrible consequences; in the other [Russia], peace and calm with all their benefits.'[12]

Yet another publisher, Bulgarin, approached the Third Section to prove his loyalty. He did so in a letter of 6 April linking Nikitenko, the 'most dangerous man' in Russia, with a hanged Decembrist and a 'party of Communists.' And he charged Kraevsky not only with having some 130,000 rubles in annual income at his disposal but also with having influenced censorship 'completely' as its 'veritable director-in-chief.'[13] Apparently Bulgarin hoped to win favour as an informer, but his denunciations were outlandish. Having made their own adjustments to the government's new attitude, Kraevsky continued his publishing activities and Nikitenko his work as a censor.

To correct the misconduct of both journalists and censors, the emperor had turned to trusted officials on the Buturlin committee, whom he directed to discover infractions in works already in print. As Nicholas told Korf: 'since I cannot read all the productions of our literature, you will be able to do so for me and to convey to me your impressions, so that my dereliction in this matter will end'. Such delegation of authority, especially to a covert committee responsible solely to the emperor, typified the style of rule of Nicholas I. Only the ministers and the Chief Administration of the Censorship were to know about the Buturlin committee, Korf told Uvarov.[14]

In his own assessment of the committee, Korf saw that this anomaly in the administrative structure only heightened Nicholas's system of 'dual censorship' and created distinct problems. The regular civil censors continued to read each book, journal, and newspaper twice (a practice required by the emperor, said Uvarov). The Third Section continued to exercise some, although lessened, influence over the censorship process; and the Buturlin committee, like righteously stern headmasters, quietly began to search out violations that had slipped past the censors into print. One editor recalled that he himself knew very little about the committee, but he had come to realize that the censors responsible for his journal lived in dread of it.[15]

Charged with eradicating anything dangerous, the committee ranged widely over literature, even that from the provinces, to verify its credo that subversion lurked everywhere. Nikitenko found life in Russia's publishing world surrealistic. 'Panicky fear took possession of minds ... terror gripped everyone who thought and wrote ... [and] secret denunciations and spying complicated matters still more.' Slavophile Ivan Kireevsky, who already knew the caprices of the censorship authorities first-hand, decided that the 'terror' would eventually subside. He cautioned Pogodin in 1848 against protesting the new policy: 'It is not a great misfortune if literature is suppressed for two or three years. It will live again.' Rather, the government 'ought to be assured that at the present minute we are all ready to sacrifice our second-degree interests in order to save Russia from rebellion and useless war.'[16]

Despite his gloom, Nikitenko remained at his post and helped writers avoid the pitfalls of the time of panic; like Kireevsky, he understood that the fear would pass. He therefore wrote on 15 June to F.A. Koni, the editor of the theatrical publication *Pantheon* (*Panteon*), that he should delay publishing P.G. Obodovsky's play, *Bogdan Khmelnitsky*. 'I doubt that it could be approved. It is about a rebellion of people, *although in favour of Russia* – but ... there are persons, scenes, that are very delicate for the present. You as an experienced editor understand all this without additional explanation.'[17]

Uvarov found himself repeatedly at odds with the Buturlin committee in a struggle for precedent. Perhaps Nicholas I had hoped that the dissimilar agencies would check and balance one another, as had the collegial system under Peter I. Instead they clashed, one severe difference stemming from an article ordered by Uvarov and printed in *Contemporary* in March 1849. I.I. Davydov, a member of the committee to draft a new censorship statute, had written the piece to argue that the universities were loyally promoting official nationality and should not be closed, as rumours suggested they might. The Buturlin committee, unaware of the source of the article, ordered Uvarov to inform the author, the editor, and the censor involved that the government viewed the article with 'dissatisfaction'; its 'appeal to public opinion' about an official issue was 'intolerable in our social structure.'[18]

As was his custom, Nicholas asked the identity of the person responsible for the article, and Uvarov named himself. He defended his decision and criticized the Buturlin committee: 'On the one hand, the ministry, shaped by its own structure and directed by the instructions of its superiors, carries responsibility openly and legally and acts in a defined area. On the other hand, the committee, which stands outside the ministry, removed from contact with it, reaches a conclusion not based on any preliminary information which, with imperial approval, becomes a command. Bewilderment and conflict have been and will be inevitable.' When Nicholas offered no solution, Uvarov decided to insulate himself from the committee by proposing to reorganize censorship within his ministry.[19] He also favoured new regulations in line with the policies of the Buturlin committee. In April, one month after the Davydov controversy had made very clear the gulf between the minister and the Buturlin committee, Uvarov presented these plans to the State Council in his ministry's draft for a new statute.

All censorship functions, both domestic and foreign, were to merge in a single department within the Ministry of Public Education under a director responsible to the minister through a new Council of the Ministry. The minister would deal only with high policy decisions. Local censorship committees would disband, and all censors would serve under the new department. Their numbers would increase and expenditures would rise from 40,500 rubles annually to 67,000, largely because the Foreign Censorship Committee would henceforth examine a shipment of books volume by volume rather than review the invoiced titles (it had screened 90,000 volumes for import into Russia in 1828 and over 400,000 in 1848). Censors were to judge both the literal meaning of a book or article and its likely impact on public opinion. Censor and author alike would be responsible if unacceptable words appeared in print.

The Buturlin committee (perhaps because, as Lemke argues, it saw its existence threatened) objected that the draft, like the Statute of 1826, wrongly revealed 'all the conditions and intentions of the government.'[20] The committee preferred continuing the less specific Statute of 1828, which gave the government more latitude in controlling the press. Apparently in agreement, the State Council rejected the proposed statute.

Uvarov had badly misread the political climate in 1849 or little cared about keeping a post he had held fifteen years. Either way, his failure to reform the censorship system was a major reason for his departure from office within six months, on 20 October. The censorship system, dominated by the Buturlin committee, remained intact, and the committee's major critic had stepped aside. Uvarov had sought in vain to convince the emperor to do more to explain his policies to the public.

III

Prince Platon A. Shirinsky-Shikhmatov, who succeeded Uvarov as minister of public education, well-suited the Buturlin committee, for he had drafted the 'cast-iron' statute of Admiral Shishkov at the beginning of the reign and still feared subversion of the government through alien ideas. Shikhmatov appointed his own 'eyes' to discover any irregularities in published periodicals and, in 1850, ruled that books for the common people must be 'penetrated with the living spirit of the Orthodox church

and with loyalty to the throne, state, and social order. He upheld a censor who rejected a proposal to reprint the correspondence of Catherine II
with Voltaire because of its many 'indiscretions and witticisms' and
absence of 'religious convictions' and next sought to determine if notes
in musical compositions could 'conceal evil intentions.'[21]

No less alert was the Third Section, and, in July 1852, Dubbelt
informed Shikhmatov that a 'society of slavophiles' in Moscow intended
to 'revolutionize' Russian literature by exploring their own 'indigenous
and popular subjects.' Given that advice, Shikhmatov examined the
slavophiles' *Moscow Miscellany*, published two months earlier with
censorship approval, and found fault with its strident descriptions of
narodnost (meaning, roughly, 'national spirit and character'). In praising
the peasant commune, for example, Constantine Aksakov came close to
advocating democracy. When, in a second volume submitted for censorship in January 1853, Aksakov extolled the equality and brotherhood among heroic warriors of Prince Vladimir at tenth-century feasts,
Dubbelt successfully advised rejecting the entire book: 'I find that the
Moscow slavophiles confuse their devotion to Russia with principles
that cannot be allowed in a monarchical state and clearly undermine the
current order.'[22]

Two months later, Shikhmatov imposed special censorship restrictions
on the principal slavophile writers. Henceforth they had to submit all
their manuscripts to the Chief Administration of the Censorship in St
Petersburg, a restriction that lasted until the next reign.

Prince V.V. Lvov, the censor who had approved the first *Miscellany*,
had meanwhile lost his post over a far more distinguished work.[23] It was
Ivan Turgenev's *Sportsman's Sketches*, published in August 1852. By
showing peasants as ordinary human beings in thrall to a barbaric system, *Sketches* helped stir public support for emancipation and, some say,
influenced Alexander II himself. This series of imaginative observations
by a hunter wandering the countryside had its start in *Contemporary* in
1847, when Panaev published 'Khor and Kalinich.' So favourable was
reader response that Turgenev provided twenty more sketches in the
next three years, although he noticeably tempered his words about landlords and officials after a warning to *Contemporary* from the censors in
1848.

Early in 1852 Turgenev decided to issue his published sketches plus
one more as a book and to publish it in Moscow, where censors seemed
less strict. First he asked Prince Lvov, a fellow writer, to review the work

as a friend. After Lvov had suggested minor changes, the manuscript went to the Moscow Censorship Committee on 28 February and, within days, won approval. The responsible censor was Lvov.

The death of Gogol on 21 February had, at this same time, prompted Turgenev to write a short eulogy for a local paper; but the St Petersburg Censorship Committee, under instructions to bar mention of this satirist disliked by Nicholas, forbade the piece. Turgenev then sent it to the *Moscow Bulletin*, where it appeared, approved by Moscow censors, on 13 March. Upon learning of this manoeuvre, an angry Nicholas sent Turgenev to the guardhouse from mid-April to mid-May and then confined him indefinitely to his estate at Spasskoe.[24]

As for *Sketches*, a copy went forward in May to the St Petersburg Censorship Committee – the usual practice for a new work – and that committee undertook an investigation, finally completed on the day in early August when sale of the book began in Moscow. In his report, E.E. Volkov deplored Turgenev's having 'poeticized' peasants while depicting landowners as 'vulgar savages,' priests as sycophants, and officials as bribe-takers. All in all, concluded Volkov, the book gave him an 'unpleasant feeling.'

Several factors weighed against Turgenev. Merging his short pieces as a single work had heightened their implicit criticism of serfdom, just as, in book form, they would attract more attention than through their intermittent appearance in a serious journal. In turn, closeness to the throne made censors in St Petersburg particularly strict, especially when an author under review had recently been rusticated by Nicholas.

Reporting to Nicholas on 12 August, Shikhmatov condemned *Sportsman's Sketches*, by then on sale in St Petersburg, for caricaturing the gentry. The emperor agreed to the firing of Lvov and continued Turgenev's confinement at Spasskoe for what proved to be another fifteen months. Within six months, all copies of *Sketches* had been sold, but reprinting had to await the next reign, as did the reinstatement of Lvov as a censor – that hapless official having been found to be a slavophile.

Shikhmatov, by all accounts suffering from the pressures of a job he did not want, died in office in May 1853. Vice-minister A.S. Norov took command and made no changes in censorship practice. Norov consequently reprimanded V.N. Beketov, said to be the most liberal and humane censor of his time, for approving 'Mumu,' a story Turgenev had written in the guardhouse, printed in the March 1854 issue of *Contemporary*. This tale about a lady's treatment of her household serfs, ruled Norov, could 'easily lead readers of the lower classes to censure the existing relationship between serfs and owners, which, as one of our state institutions, cannot be subject to discussion by private persons ...'[25]

Norov became minister that April, and, in the fall, fired the two censors responsible for the appearance of V. Likhachev's 'The Dreamer' in the *Muscovite*, because references to 'inequalities' between the rich and the poor might appear to be criticism of serfdom. In the wake of the firings, Nikitenko deplored that censorship responsibilities had wrought a 'panicky fear' in Norov. Undoubtedly the Buturlin committee kept Norov on edge; in December 1854 he proposed its abolition and the expansion of the regular censorship system in the ministry, an echo of Uvarov's request five years earlier. Nicholas instead added Norov to the Buturlin committee so that he could work from within to modify its excessive demands.[26]

Change would come only with the death of Nicholas, as was shown in the fate of the complete works of Gogol. An effort to publish them began in December 1853 and included an unsuccessful appeal to Nicholas by the Grand Duke Constantine. Nicholas died in February 1855, and Alexander II gave his blessing to the project the following May. V.I. Nazimov, a member of the Chief Administration of the Censorship (which, along with the Third Section, had endorsed the project), described Gogol's works as outstanding moral documents: 'One involuntarily feels aversion to that which is indecent and reprehensible, and the good and the true triumph over them.'[27]

Sensitivity on the peasant question continued to influence censorship, however, as the experience of F.M. Tolstoy shows.[28] During the fall of 1855, Tolstoy submitted his story, 'Morgun,' to the St Petersburg Censorship Committee, only to have two censors object that it focused on the mistreatment of a deserving serf. Such a plot could cause the reader to favour the 'flattening' of social differences and dramatized problems that were strictly the business of the government. Despite Tolstoy's offer to make changes, the Chief Administration of the Censorship rejected the story outright. In turn, Vice-minister Viazemsky assured Tolstoy that the government did not doubt the 'purity' of his intentions but simply could not permit in print anything that might provoke class tensions.

Change came fairly quickly under Alexander with respect to coverage of the Crimean War (1853–55). Under Nicholas, no unofficial periodicals had correspondents at the front; the War Ministry's *Russian War Veteran* (*Russkii Invalid*) printed official reports and the Naval Ministry's *Naval Miscellany* (*Morskoi Sbornik*), had reports from correspondents, which the *Northern Bee* and the semi-official *St Petersburg Bulletin* alone could reprint.[29] (Nekrasov blamed *Contemporary*'s loss of 600 subscribers in 1854 on his being denied permission to print anything about the war. The claim was likely accurate inasmuch as *Bee*'s subscription list meanwhile increased by 5,000.[30]) Early in the new reign, in contrast, *Contemporary* began a series of fictional stories from the front by a young artillery officer, Count Leo Tolstoy, whose earlier stories of his childhood and youth had already won acclaim. Tolstoy's first story, the warmly patriotic 'Sevastopol in December,' passed censorship in May 1855, three months after Alexander II's accession, and appeared the next month. Following its publication, the new emperor ordered that the story be translated into French for wider distribution and that the army command make certain no harm befell Tolstoy.

Also in June, Norov approached the minister of war about permitting at least some war coverage in *Contemporary* and *Notes of the Fatherland*. Agreement resulted, and both journals published their first war news that August, the month Sevastopol fell. Then came Tolstoy's 'Sevastopol in May,' published in September, which showed the war's senseless brutality. The censor agreed to pass the story only with changes, and it was already in type when additional changes were ordered. Panaev found the story so badly mutilated that he wished to withdraw it, but the censorship authority insisted on its publication. In complying, Panaev omitted Tolstoy's initials, which, he said, he could no longer justify.[31]

IV

Compared with publishing in western Europe, the volume of works printed in Imperial Russia during the first half of the nineteenth century is modest. But by the close of Nicholas's reign, to provide one comparison, the circulations of the leading Russian journals were not widely at variance with the leading intellectual reviews in the West.[32] Only by the second quarter of the nineteenth century had Russian publishing begun to free itself from the tutelage of the state and to base itself on a commercial market, a development that would bring a large degree of independence to private publishing by the 1840s.

According to admittedly scant publishing figures, from 1801 to 1805 the average annual output of books and periodicals was 385 titles (260 in Russian and 125 in other languages, mainly German). By 1825, that average had increased to 583 titles, but only 323 were in Russian (a 63 per cent increase), with 260 in other languages (a 103 per cent increase).[33]

Under Nicholas I the Ministry of Public Education began to compile figures which differentiated between periodicals (which the censorship authority viewed with greatest concern) and books, and to publish summaries in its *Journal*. Except for the government's launching forty-four provincial bulletins (*vedomosti*) in 1851, the number of periodicals varies remarkably little each year from 1833 to 1855 – a clear result of Nicholas's determination to limit numbers. Thus there were 54 in 1833 and, including the 44 bulletins, 104 in 1855. (See table 2.)

In 1837, the *Journal* began to publish more detailed figures on book publishing alone. The aggregate book production in the empire that year was 1,147 titles. (See table 3.) That level dropped off from time to time but not appreciably; the lowest number before the end of the reign was 878 titles in 1841. The number of titles tells less about quantity than does the number of signatures (each is 16 pages). (See table 4.) Thus, although the 878 books published in 1841 represented a decline of 150 titles from the year before, the pages within their covers were insignificantly fewer (8,477 signatures in 1840 and 8,316 in 1841). In contrast, the drop of 118 titles from 1849 to 1850 (1,113 to 995) at the height of the 'censorship terror' coincides with roughly a 17 per cent drop in the number of signatures published (from 8,186 to 6,799). Overall, figures for the reign of Nicholas I reveal a slight decline in the number of signatures published annually (from 10,659 in 1833 to 9,961 in 1855), despite an increase in population.

With respect to periodicals, scattered sources show that during the 'terror' both *Contemporary* and *Notes of the Fatherland* substantially held their own. *Notes* had a circulation of 1,250 in 1839 (its first year under Kraevsky), increased its subscribers to 3,000 in 1843, and peaked at 4,000 in 1847. *Contemporary* began a new life under Nekrasov and Panaev in 1847 with 2,000 subscribers. Led by Belinsky and under the editorship of Nikitenko, the journal attracted a readership of 3,100 in 1848. Both journals suffered drops in subscriptions in 1849: *Contemporary* lost 700 and *Notes* lost 500. Both had recovered by the end of the reign, although *Notes* had lost ground to its rival. (By 1852, *Contemporary* reached 3,400 subscribers, a jump of 1,000 over a three-year period and well above the financial break-even point of 2,700. Although those numbers fell off again in 1854, *Contemporary*'s circulation had climbed back to 2,849 by the end of the reign.)[34]

Library for Readers, the leading popular journal, had begun a downward slide even before the 'terror' as a result of competition from the more progressive journals and neglect by its editor. From the mid-forties, Senkovsky began spending more of his time outside St Petersburg, and he became ill in the late forties. From its strong circulation of 7,000 in the thirties, *Library* had dropped to 3,000 subscribers in 1847 and 2,100 in 1849 (the figures for 1850 are unavailable).[35]

An opposite case is that of the *Muscovite*. Having had no more than 400 subscribers at any time in the forties, the journal gained a new lease on life in 1850 with a change in editors under A.A. Grigoriev and a shift of emphasis from nationalism to literary and cultural concerns. The subscription list reached 550 that year and doubled to 1,100 in 1851.[36] A reversal came in 1853, when the *Muscovite* lost most of its young writers, and the journal closed permanently in 1856.

However much the Buturlin committee served to stop the spread of radical ideas, Nicholas I would have preferred using a positive program to instill pro-government ideas and win favourable public opinion about the autocracy. Nicholas's paternalism, however, presented an insoluble dilemma: how was the government to influence the increasing numbers of readers of the new middle class, who had come to value European-type journalism, by means of an unofficial press that was growing more independent in outlook. The Buturlin committee, in disagreement with Uvarov, rejected the idea that the government could deliberately engage in journalism to explain or justify itself. Nicholas shared that absolutist position and favoured manipulation or intimidation of the unofficial press to maintain at least the appearance of its spontaneous support.

When Nicholas died, a new kind of autocrat assumed the throne. Under Alexander II, the imperial government was to enter upon the 'era of great reforms' but without having learned to explain itself to its people. To compound the problems of orderly reform, the unofficial press had by 1855 become a diversified, self-supporting, and restive social institution.

7

Confused steps towards reform, 1855–61

Abruptly thrust into power in February 1855, and burdened with the Crimean campaign and peace talks a year later, Alexander II gave only incidental attention to censorship during the first two years of his reign. He focused next on freeing the serfs and invited his landowners to take the initiative. Their reluctance, along with the enormous implications of emancipation, led the emperor in January 1858 to permit the press to discuss the peasant question and, in turn, reform issues generally. He directed his minister of public education to prepare a new censorship statute incorporating this change. Broad dissatisfaction with existing press policy, however, had much to do with the ensuing delays in censorship reform.

Alexander II's style of rule also contributed to confusion over press policy. The emperor, as far as one can tell from the record, issued only vague guidelines to his subordinates about dealing with the press. He seems initially to have thought that journalists would universally respond to an easing of restrictions by showering spontaneous printed praise on the tsar and his policies; he soon learned otherwise.

There was, furthermore, no agreement among Alexander's subordinates that the press should have greater freedom. Some, of course, believed that the government had no choice but to grant the press more scope; but many others interfered at every opportunity to prevent liberalization. Each of Alexander's 'great reforms' was to depend on the driving will of a few dedicated officials who managed to hold the support of the monarch while they pushed towards their goal. Reform of censorship in the early years of the reign stood still for lack of any such champion.

Confusion over censorship policy led to complications. On the one hand, writers became more outspoken and censors less strict as they sensed Alexander's desire to court the press and win its invaluable support for his reforms. On the other hand, dissent in the press seemed linked to the mounting rebellion of the student generation. By 1861 the need to establish press controls appropriate to the new reign was unmistakable.

I

Alexander inherited the monolithic censorship structure of Nicholas I and, with it, the Statute of 1828, supplemented since its writing by a mass of often contradictory directives. His chief censor was Minister of Public Education A.S. Norov, under whom served, in line of command, the Chief Administration of the Censorship in St Petersburg, the superintendents of the education districts, the local censorship committees, and the censors.

At the outset of the reign, Norov mistakenly predicted that the emperor would soon call for changes in censorship policy,[1] and accordingly relaxed the existing rules. In May, as already shown, the censorship authority allowed war news in *Contemporary* and *Notes of the Fatherland* and approved the publication of Gogol's works. Within a year, Alexander himself took steps to ease censorship restrictions. On 6 December 1855 he abolished the Buturlin committee, so closely associated with the 'censorship terror' begun in 1848. In addition, disregarding Nicholas's ban on published criticism of government affairs, Alexander permitted the journals of the naval and war ministries, *Naval Miscellany* and *Military Miscellany (Voennyi Sbornik)*, to describe how officials had abused their positions.

(Both journals had as their aim preparing the officer corps to lead a modernized military in a reformed Russia; both also proved to be indicative of advanced thinking within the government. The Grand Duke Constantine, who headed the Naval Ministry, placed his close associate A.V. Golovnin [later minister of public education] in charge of *Naval Miscellany*. And the head of the Ministry of War planning staff, D.A. Miliutin [later minister of war], chose as editors of *Military Miscellany* early in 1858 two known advocates of change who would found the first populist revolutionary organization, Land and Liberty, only three years later. They were N.G. Chernyshevsky, whose *Contemporary* article, as will shortly be shown, caused a stir among the censors in April 1858; and N.N. Obruchev, a military officer. Together they urged teaching common soldiers to read, an appeal which led to government approval of *Soldiers' Conversation* [*Soldatskaia Beseda*, 1858–67], a journal for enlisted men.[2])

Past strictures on new periodicals also fell, with eight approved in 1855; the overall total of 104 in 1855 rose to 230 by 1860 and 378 by 1872. (See tables 2, 7.) Notable among the new unofficial journals were Michael Katkov's *Russian Messenger* (*Russkii Vestnik*) and the slavophiles' *Russian Conversation* (*Russkaia Beseda*), both begun in Moscow in 1856 with permission to print commentary on broad contemporary issues.[3] In approving *Conversation*, Alexander lifted Nicholas's special strictures on the slavophiles.

The first proposal for a new censorship statute originated with Nikitenko, who submitted a project to Minister Norov in mid-summer 1855.[4] Not until January 1858 did Norov offer his own recommendations to the Council of Ministers, and by then the emperor had himself abruptly changed censorship policy by permitting the press to discuss the peasant question. That step was the first in a series of expedient improvisations that seriously clouded censorship policy.

Serfdom as an institution was clearly one of the most sensitive issues in the empire and had been a forbidden topic since the days of Radishchev. Even a censorship moderate like P.A. Viazemsky, the vice-minister of public education, stood opposed in 1856 to exploration of the peasant question: 'Expression of private views on it and its discussion in the press are hardly literary business and especially not journalistic; the question by its very nature and conditions is primarily a government matter which requires in its time solution by the highest authority.' Among the few who scored the folly of enforced silence was K.D. Kavelin, a professor and legal scholar whose proposals in 1855 for ending serfdom had had wide circulation in manuscript form among his peers. Kavelin linked serfdom 'with the juridical, administrative, economic, financial, and agricultural structure of our life and, therefore, the abolition of this right obviously demands close preliminary discussion from all viewpoints.'[5]

Alexander II seems to have taken Kavelin's point that emancipation required 'preliminary discussion.' He was soon to invite the gentry to begin discussing the matter, an unprecedented gesture to the landowners. Before long, seeking additional support, the emperor would open the peasant issue to the periodical press. To help achieve emancipation, he chose to liberalize censorship.

In assuming the role of a reformer, Alexander perhaps responded, in part, to an undated, anonymous memorandum preserved in the archives of the Committee of Ministers for 1859. As quoted by historian S.M. Seredonin, the note counselled that the period after the Crimean War imposed special demands on the emperor because the disastrous war had discredited the monarchy. The 'first steps' of the new emperor would 'define opinion' about him. As head of the reform movement, the writer argued, Alexander would keep political initiative in his own hands.[6]

Whether or not the Crimean defeat during his first year as emperor – also the year of Kavelin's proposals – helped to convince Alexander that serfdom was a national liability, the emperor's announcement of the Treaty of Paris in March 1856 implied that emancipation was imminent. Concluding with a promise of reform, Alexander envisioned for every Russian the 'fruits of honest labour under the shelter of laws equally just to all, equally protective of all.' Vague though they were, these words sparked rumours that the emperor planned to free the twenty million private serfs who comprised about one-third of the empire's population.

To clarify the situation, the governor-general of Moscow, Count A.A. Zakrevsky, asked the emperor to explain his intentions to the Moscow marshals of the gentry. Alexander did so on 30 March by informing his surprised listeners: 'Even you understand that the existing order of ownership of souls cannot continue unchanged.' Alexander had taken the initiative, but, at the same time, he promised not to decree the terms of liberation. What he sought were proposals from the gentry: 'It is better to begin to abolish serfdom from above than to await that time when it will begin to abolish itself from below. I ask you to consider the best way to bring it about. Take my words to the gentry for discussion.'[7]

The disquieting news of the emperor's remarks spread informally; accordingly, on 10 April, S.S. Lanskoy, the minister of the interior, dispatched a circular to provincial governors and marshals to ease fears among the gentry of severe blows to their position and holdings. The government, he wrote, was determined to uphold landed interests and the 'legal order.'[8] Lanskoy had as his aim the 'calming of passions' among the gentry and committed the government to nothing more than keeping the peace.

In a move crucial to his next manoeuvre, the emperor in these early months of 1856 appointed as governor-general over three Lithuanian provinces (Vilna, Kovno, and Grodno) his old military instructor, V.I. Nazimov. Nazimov met Alexander in Brest-Litovsk in May and there offered to promote interest in the liberation of the serfs among his gentry. Two months later, Alexander directed his appeal for initiatives to the marshals of the gentry assembled for his August coronation. When

Lanskoy and A. Levshin, the vice-minister of the interior, spoke to the gentry, they found almost universal reluctance, except for the marshals under Nazimov. Of greater importance, however, was the fact that Nazimov privately agreed to return home and, through discussions, induce the Lithuanian gentry to request permission to 'liberate' their serfs as an example for gentry elsewhere.[9]

Nowhere did the Russian gentry themselves initiate plans for emancipation. Alexander, after all, had asked them to subordinate self-interest to the needs of the state. Not even a generous financial settlement, if there were one, could satisfactorily compensate their losses.

II

Awaiting proposals from the gentry, Alexander, in January 1857, set in motion more traditional means of forming policy by naming the 'last secret committee on the peasant question.'[10] Late in December, Lanskoy had urged Alexander to select and name publicly a committee to draft general principles, lest secrecy bury the issue.[11] Alexander ignored this counsel and proceeded to name as committee members eleven officials who, for the most part, lacked both sympathy for emancipation and knowledge about the peasant question.[12] They included President of the State Council A.F. Orlov as chairman. Thus did the emperor involve high-ranking bureaucrats in a project he knew they did not favour (just as he hoped to recruit the reluctant gentry); their writing the government program would ensure its acceptance by the State Council. (Any proposals the staff of the Ministry of the Interior alone might have drafted for Alexander would have fared badly with the State Council, a likelihood Levshin himself remarked upon.[13] Instead, Minister of the Interior Lanskoy was to propose plans favoured by Alexander before the secret committee as one of its members.)

At Alexander's direction, the committee was to derive 'principles' for granting gradual freedom to the peasants. All the members, Alexander stressed at the first meeting on 3 January, must keep their deliberations 'in the greatest secrecy.'[14] He had no intention of promoting a public debate.

Three journals nonetheless touched on the peasant question in the early months of 1857.[15] First *Economic Directory* (*Ekonomicheskii Ukazatel*), a journal favouring classical economic doctrines, argued that the lands of the village commune should be divided among the peasants because the 'more landowners we have' the less likely was social 'disruption.' In refutation, N.G. Chernyshevsky in *Contemporary* argued that the commune protected peasants from falling into debt to the owners of great estates. Once freed from the 'patriarchal system [serfdom],' he continued, peasants would secure through the commune at least minimum subsistence. Finally, the *Landowners' Gazette* (*Zemlevladelcheskaia Gazeta*) contended that peasants lacked sufficient ability to handle their own affairs and would always remain poor. That March Minister of Education Norov admitted to Alexander that a 'theoretical' debate on the peasant question was in print, and the emperor directed him to bar such discussions.[16]

In June, discouraged by the committee's lack of progress, Alexander told the Russian ambassador to France that he was determined to push ahead. 'It ought to be completed,' he said, '... [but] I have no one who can help me in this important work.' Alexander then pointedly directed the committee to reach 'general conclusions on how to approach this matter.' Shortly thereafter, on 26 July, Lanskoy offered the committee his ministry's plan, the terms of which were much like those finally evolved: landlords would give serfs freedom without receiving compensation and would give them access to land which they would purchase over a transition period.[17] The committee took no interest in the proposal.

Returning briefly to the capital in July before journeying to Stuttgart to meet Napoleon III, and still finding no final report, Alexander named a new committee member – his brother, the Grand Duke Constantine, a known partisan of reform. The committee's agreement on principles on 14 August may well have resulted from Constantine's presence and his arguments, for his close associate, A.V. Golovnin, credits the Grand Duke with convincing the group to draft a general plan. But even the most conservative member of the committee could endorse that plan, set forth in their report of 18 August. It proposed three lengthy stages before all serfs would become free men. Alexander expressed gratitude to the committee despite their having proposed, in effect, to postpone emancipation.[18] What the emperor yet wanted was the plan Lanskoy had put before the secret committee in July, but he needed a new means to further it.

Shortly after Alexander returned to St Petersburg in October, Nazimov arrived with a request from the Lithuanian gentry for permission to open discussions on the peasant question, and the emperor once again seized the initiative. Identifying the request as a spontaneous expression of the willingness of landowners to liberate the serfs, Alexander summoned the secret committee to prepare an immediate official response.

(More precisely, the Lithuanian gentry had asked to discuss the liberation of serfs without land and had gone that far only because of prodding by Nazimov. They spoke of a 'new order' and 'settlement' rather than 'liberation,' and thus their celebrated initiative essentially sought to ensure that the 'free' peasants would remain as workers on the estates.)

Acting under the instructions of the secret committee, Lanskoy gave Vice-Minister Levshin three days in which to draft the government's answer, and, although he complied, Levshin strongly disapproved of the haste. He recalled in 1860, 'I had never encountered a situation where such an important question was resolved with such rapidity.'[19]

III

In formulating the resulting order, the rescript to Nazimov, Levshin and his aides drew on the Ministry of the Interior program favoured by Alexander. Thus the rescript outlined a measure of economic independence for the peasants: each freed family was to purchase its house and garden plot during a transitional period and secure the use of field land in order to earn its livelihood and meet its payment obligations.[20] The rescript also affirmed the property rights in land and the traditional administrative and police powers of the gentry, but, in assigning even limited purchasable property to the peasants, it overruled the landless liberation favoured by the Lithuanian gentry.

Through the rescript, Alexander set forward for the first time specific principles for emancipation. He fully agreed, the rescript announced, with having the gentry under Nazimov embark on 'projects with respect to the organization and improvement of the existence of the bonded serfs'; and he approved their forming committees for this purpose.[21]

Lanskoy more precisely defined the general terms of the rescript of 20 November in supplemental instructions the next day. Whereas the rescript spoke of 'improving the conditions' of serfs, the instructions spoke directly of 'liberation' and the 'abolition of serf bondage.' Moreover, Lanskoy set a timetable: the three Lithuanian committees were to submit proposals within six months and the general committee, within one year; the transitional phase to full personal freedom was not to exceed twelve years.[22]

Alexander and Lanskoy had made the secret committee and the Lithuanian gentry accomplices to action they opposed. The committee at once ordered the circulation of the rescript and instructions to provincial governors throughout the empire to show that these directions concerned Lithuania alone. But, when he dispatched the documents on 24 November Lanskoy attached a circular of 'information' to the governors, 'in case the gentry of the provinces entrusted to you should show a similar desire' to free their serfs. The committee sought too late to stop this escalation of the program for emancipation, and Levshin deplored the circular as another rash act: 'The committees of Kovno, Grodno, and Vilna had not spoken about the inevitability of liberation and, consequently, the minister should not have said in a circular to the whole empire that *the committees recognized the necessity of liberating* the peasants from serf dependence.'[23]

In December Lanskoy used a request from Petersburg province to alter inventory rules (governing landlords' authority over their serfs) as a pretext to send a rescript to St Petersburg Governor-General P.N. Ignatiev, but this time the secret committee decisively intervened to prevent Lanskoy's duplicating the Lithuanian rescript and instructions. At the committee's insistence, neither the rescript of 5 December nor its instructions mentioned 'liberation.' The freeing of serfs was implicit, to be sure, but the instructions to Ignatiev, unlike those to Nazimov, required each peasant to purchase his personal freedom, a provision Lanskoy did not favour.

The secret committee then moved to publish both rescripts, but only the instructions to Ignatiev, in the official section of the *Journal* of the Ministry of the Interior. Explaining their proposal to the emperor on 5 December, the date of the second rescript and instructions, the committee argued that the instructions to Nazimov 'include expressions which might cause unpleasant rumours,' while the instructions to Ignatiev 'are written cautiously enough to be printed.'[24] The conservative majority of the committee wanted to establish as official policy that serfs must buy their freedom.

Alexander approved publishing the two rescripts and the instructions to Ignatiev; but on 8 December, nine days before the *Journal* appeared, Lanskoy sent to the marshals of the gentry the rescript and instructions to Ignatiev with a circular stressing that not only this new set of documents but also the rescript and instructions to Nazimov contained government guidelines.[25] On 10 December, making a point that the two sets of instructions differed, Lanskoy requested the marshals to report their gentry's reaction, apparently to learn which principles they preferred.

In this same period, the secret committee won approval for the unofficial press to reprint both rescripts and the conservative instructions to Ignatiev, but without comment. Minister of Education Norov so instructed his censors on 15 December, two days before these documents appeared in the Ministry of the Interior's *Journal*, explaining that their wide circulation would encourage other gentry to organize their own committees.[26]

Within a month, the gentry of Nizhnii Novgorod and of Moscow asked to form committees, and by mid-January the government had approved the publication in the unofficial press of the rescript to each group. This limited response from the gentry was disappointing, but it made all the more welcome the warm applause for the government's efforts from another quarter – the press.

Forbidden to praise the rescripts in print, some 180 writers instead hailed them at a banquet on 28 December in Moscow by raising their glasses before a portrait of the emperor. An account of the celebration in *Russian Messenger* made clear that Alexander had won the backing of the press community for his reform policy.[27]

In St Petersburg, Lanskoy meanwhile continued his campaign for publicizing the emancipation issues. On 3 January 1858 he pressed the secret committee to allow articles in the *Journal* of the Ministry of the Interior to 'familiarize the public with the new future order of things and to answer complaints of landlords and questions which merit special attention.' He also urged some criticism of proposals. The committee balked at any criticism, arguing that the principles of the rescripts were 'immutable'; but, at Constantine's urgings, the committee won the emperor's approval for 'articles in the spirit of the government' not only in the *Journal* but in 'all the journals.'[28]

The next day, 4 January, State Secretary V.P. Butkov, secretary to the committee, asked Norov to produce the existing censorship regulations governing published references to serfdom. Replied the minister: 'The censorship statute includes no rules which directly bear on the peasant class in Russia.'[29] To fill that void, the emperor and the committee immediately collaborated on general guidelines for censors; and these rules constituted the most significant change in censorship policy thus far under Alexander. The emperor, reversing his position of a year earlier, now saw public discussion as a prerequisite to reform, especially as it could prod the gentry to co-operate in emancipation.

On 16 January, Norov, acting under the emperor's instructions, issued the new rules for printed commentary on the peasant question. Henceforth, censors were to ban articles 'analyzing, discussing, and criticizing' the principles of the rescripts and instructions, but were to permit 'all purely scholarly books and articles which analyze and discuss economic questions about the current and future arrangements for the landlords' peasants.'[30] Although the ban on criticism of the rescripts' principles upheld the secret committee's stand that these were immutable, permission to discuss 'future arrangements' was to give censors sufficient grounds to approve articles favouring liberation and redemption principles not in the rescripts. Such discussion is precisely what Lanskoy had proposed in vain to the committee for his ministry's *Journal*.

The same day he issued his directive, Norov asked the Council of Ministers to support the drafting of a new censorship statute by his ministry. Norov's timing must have been purposeful: he saw the opening of the emancipation discussion as an appropriate time to broach censorship reform. But, according to Nikitenko, Norov suffered a humiliating defeat, for when he recommended easing censorship, Minister of Justice Panin and others denounced expanded discussion in the press as foolhardy.[31] This confrontation could not have pleased Alexander, for it revealed that a number of his ministers opposed his forthcoming policy change for censorship practices.

IV

Exactly one week later, Alexander convened the Committee of Ministers, a body much larger than the Council of Ministers, and announced there that he intended a positive discussion in the press of public issues generally, not just emancipation. Alexander anticipated that an informed public would support the throne, even as he expected the press to further the reformist aims of the government.[32] He was ordering the minister of public education to prepare, accordingly, a new censorship statute; that order went forward two days later, on 25 January.[33] In addition, each ministry was to name a special censorship representative to the St Petersburg Censorship Committee to weigh all proposed articles touching its affairs. This measure followed logically from the government's previous extension of press limits on the peasant question; censors would have to guard against writers presuming too much.

Perhaps because his minister had ineptly taken the initiative, Alexander asked Norov to submit his resignation. It came 16 March and was followed immediately by that of Viazemsky, his vice-minister. By then the committee to draft a new statute had set to work; and at its first meeting, on 6 February, Viazemsky had given what proved to be his final official statement. The 'government recognizes the usefulness and legality' of the press in providing moral and intellectual enlightenment, he said; and the new press law should permit 'that new freedom which the government recognizes as possible.'[34]

The press was already showing its daring, and censors who favoured broader discussion were abetting it. In January 1858 N.F. (von) Kruze, who had become a censor in 1855, had approved the *Russian Messenger*'s account of the writers' banquet praising the emperor, an impropriety in the eyes of several officials because of its implied commentary on the peasant question; and that April Kruze was himself honoured at a testimonial dinner given by St Petersburg writers, who again used this means to praise a reformer. What Kruze extolled as 'cautious toleration' to his superiors, journalists recognized as a commitment to less severe censorship.

In December 1858 Kruze was fired by the new minister of public education, E.P. Kovalevsky, for approving what Nikitenko described as liberal articles in Michael Katkov's *Russian Messenger*. Thereupon Katkov and others spearheaded a subscription campaign to thank Kruze for his past efforts – 'an important precedent,' Katkov wrote to Pogodin. The government thought so, too, and secretly instructed the University of Moscow to stop this demonstration of largess, but to no avail.[35]

This stiffening resolve among writers and sympathetic censors to expand discussion in the press immediately confronted Kovalevsky, then, when he became minister of public education on 23 March, 1858.[36] Although Kovalevsky had been very successful in furthering university autonomy during two previous years as superintendent of the Moscow education district, once he was minister and was faced with the insubordination of writers, censors, and students and the criticism of fellow officials, Kovalevsky seemed at a loss to accomplish the reform of education and censorship commissioned by Alexander. Keeping the newly enlarged discussions of public affairs within acceptable limits proved a difficult challenge in itself.

As he had told his Committee of Ministers in January 1858, Alexander expected the press to respond to broader limits by supporting the state (censorship regulations, after all, forbade anything not in the 'spirit of the government'); and, almost as one, writers endorsed the pending emancipation. Chernyshevsky, however, objected to features of the plan. He consequently wrote an article, 'On the Conditions of Peasant Life,' and, as editor, printed the first part in *Contemporary* in February. In it he warmly praised the emperor but criticized the *obrok* and *barshchina* (forms of rent for field land) stipulated in the rescript to Nazimov. No great outcry resulted, for the emperor had opened such discussions only the month before. Part two of Chernyshevsky's article appeared in April, based largely on the *Zapiska* written in 1855 by K.D. Kavelin, the liberal professor who had since become tutor to Alexander's son. Suggesting that landowners generally opposed the reform, Chernyshevsky called on the advocates of liberation to unite behind Kavelin's proposals, which included both serf redemption of field land and local self-government in place of the administrative powers of the gentry – ideas counter to the content of the rescripts.[37]

Many officials at once strongly objected to the April article, and Chernyshevsky seems to have been surprised. His archive contains two unpublished responses from him pointing out that the article stressed the importance of liberating peasants with land, a position shared by the emperor, who understood that anything else would bring a peasant rebellion. What seems most likely in this situation is that Chernyshevsky's 'indiscretion' focused the anger of officials opposed to relaxing censorship.[38]

State Secretary Butkov, presumably instructed by the emperor or the secret committee, informed newly named Minister Kovalevsky that the press had violated Norov's January directive. Kovalevsky, in turn, castigated his censors. Following an airing of the issue in the Council of Ministers, the censor who had approved Chernyshevsky's April text – no less than the chairman of the St Petersburg Censorship Committee, Prince Shcherbatov – received a reprimand.[39]

The Main Committee on Peasant Affairs, which in January had succeeded the secret committee when the peasant question became 'public,' spoke for the emperor on 22 April by banning discussion in the press about 'future arrangements for the peasants.'[40] Yet, contrary to the rescripts, the committee itself within the next year was to choose the very arrangements Chernyshevsky favoured.

The Emancipation Statute of 1861 did in several ways accord with what the unofficial press had favoured but the gentry had opposed – acquisition by peasants of field land, abolition of the landowners' administrative powers, and rejection of the *obrok* and the *barshchina* as a means of redemption. Thus Ivaniukov, the principal student of the press in 1858, credits discussion in the press with having influenced the reform. But the measures supported by the press, after all, suited Alexander, and he had opened discussion to help shape a liberal reform. His goal was met, he felt, when, in late 1858, Gen. Ia.I. Rostovtsev of the main committee proposed redemption of field land and civil rights for peasants, elimination of landlord administrative powers, and a short period of obligation. The emperor agreed and thereby quietly overturned the 'immutable' principles of the rescripts and instructions.[41]

By discussing the peasant question and related reform issues, the press definitely bolstered its strength; circulation figures climbed and the number of periodicals increased. *Contemporary*, in particular, added significantly to its readership in 1858 and 1859. In fact, preventing such widely read journals from promoting changes the government opposed soon became a priority for the censorship authority.

V

On 7 April, just before the second part of Chernyshevsky's article appeared, Kovalevsky told Nikitenko that the emperor wanted the reform of censorship to limit discussion without limiting thought – presumably to forbid 'negative spirit' or politicizing but to allow a wide range of topics. In his diary Nikitenko ruminated about the great difficulties involved in guaranteeing 'freedom of thought,' but concluded that tht government had realized 'that it is more useful and less dangerous to co-operate with the press than to war with it.' At Kovalevsky's direction, Nikitenko began drafting proposals for a new statute and completed them, with a memorandum to Alexander, by 3 September. Kovalevsky approved the proposals but, in his preoccupation with student unrest, failed to act on them. Then, on 5 October, when Nikitenko met with F.M. Tiutchev, head of the Foreign Censorship Committee, to explore how best to move the draft forward, Tiutchev gave the surprising news that he, Kovalevsky, Dolgorukov (head of the Third Section), and A.E. Timashev (also of the Third Section) comprised a committee chaired by Foreign Minister Gorchakov to consider the French censorship system for Russia.[42]

During the next week, Kovalevsky informed Nikitenko that the Gorchakov committee had decided that a committee to use moral persuasion should be named to help keep the press in line, and, when Nikitenko labelled that plan a 'pure dream,' Kovalevsky agreed. On 12 October, apparently having consulted Alexander, the minister asked Nikitenko to shorten the proposed statute for submission to the State Council.[43]

That December, with Alexander's support, Gorchakov won assent from both the Committee of Ministers and the State Council for the formation of a committee of persuasion to influence the press. Operating outside the Ministry of Education, this new Committee on Press Affairs was to convince journalists to discuss public questions 'from the viewpoint of the government.'[44] It was also to design an official newspaper to rally support for the autocracy and to counteract Alexander Herzen's *Bell (Kolokol)*, then being smuggled into Russia from London. Such a committee was a Russian version of the press bureau which other European governments had been using for years to influence public opinion. The July monarchy in France, for example, had established the *Bureau de l'esprit publique*; and, in Prussia, the Ministry of the Interior had opened the Prussian Central Office for Press Affairs in 1850.

Kovalevsky had been away when the Committee on Press Affairs won approval, and he threatened to resign upon learning of it. Instead he nominated as members three trusted associates – Nikitenko, Viazemsky, and Tiutchev. The emperor by-passed all three in favour of Count A.E. Adlerberg, son of the minister of the imperial court, as chairman; Vice-minister of Public Education N.A. Mukhanov, a friend of Gorchakov; and Timashev, the Third Section official on Gorchakov's committee.[45]

As the Committee on Press Affairs was being organized in January, 1859, Ivan Aksakov, the contentious slavophile, published his first issue of *Sail (Parus)*. P.I. Kapnist, a censor, and the Moscow Censorship Committee approved two articles later condemned by the ministry, in one of which Aksakov wailed: 'When, my God, will it be possible, in keeping with the demands of conscience, not to use cunning, not to fabricate allegorical phrases, but to speak one's opinion directly and simply in public?' Approved by Kapnist for the second issue, a week later, was 'The Past Year in Russian History,' in which historian Michael Pogodin praised Russian passivity in foreign affairs.[46]

Protests followed both articles, and among the irate were the members of the Committee on Press Affairs, one of whom favoured exile for Aksakov.[47] Kovalevsky could do no less than close the journal, the first such closure of the reign. Demoting Kapnist to a 'more suitable' post, Kovalevsky ruled that Aksakov had 'used maliciously' his right to publish, that Pogodin had 'caustically degraded' foreign policy, and that the censorship committee had grossly neglected its duty. To add to Kovalevsky's troubles, on 22 January the main committee objected to a proposal in the *St Petersburg Bulletin* that the gentry be granted the use of state lands as compensation for freeing their serfs. Because the censorship representative from the Ministry of the Interior had not approved these words on the impending reform as required, the main committee pre-empted censorship power over all discussions of the peasant question, another slap at Kovalevsky's administration.[48]

Two days later Alexander publicly announced the Committee on Press Affairs. He instructed periodicals to publish all articles signed by the committee and authorized its members to write and to commission articles for periodicals, to approve anything prepared by the ministries for publication, and to instruct censors. Members were also to enlist ministers to answer criticism in the foreign press through dispatches sent out from the Ministry of Foreign Affairs. To all these efforts, Moscow editor Michael Katkov at once retorted in print: 'Let the hired rhetoricians repeat whatever they want in their journals. No one takes their word as an expression of public opinion.'[49]

Censor-approved words like these of Katkov were just what the committee intended to stop, and, to that end, the group gained the power to forbid printing plants to release any publications which it found objectionable. Katkov's outspokenness had, at the same time, helped convince Alexander that public suspicion had tarnished the press committee's image, and by March he favoured adding to it an official respected by the press, Nikitenko.[50] When the committee finally acquiesced to his being a voting member, Nikitenko reluctantly agreed to serve, only to find himself at odds with his colleagues. Of some comfort was an admission by Alexander that he, too, disapproved some of the committee's methods.

In March 1859 the Main Committee on Peasant Affairs forwarded their principles for emancipation to the editing commissions who were to write the statute. The main committee, which continued to screen all press discussion on the peasant question, had already virtually ended press debate on the issue.

Alexander made clear, however, that the press still had leave to discuss other reform issues. A censorship circular on 3 April quoted him as saying that the Council of Ministers found press reports of 'irregularities and abuses' in government to be 'useful,' as were articles on the value of *glasnost* (publicizing law enforcement through open trials) proposed in the judicial reform. All the same, Alexander insisted, facts must be correct and words must uphold the 'true aims and purposes of the government.'[51]

In evaluating the public discussion of emancipation, A.G. Troinitsky, head of the Chief Administration of the Censorship, expressed views much like those of Alexander. Troinitsky credited the discussion with spreading among the educated ('especially in the landlord class') two essential ideas: that serfdom must end and the peasants must be assured a land allotment. Least satisfactory, despite the caution of the censors, were those writings that had 'abused and irritated landlords and incited dissatisfaction in peasants.'[52]

For Adlerberg, chairman of the Committee on Press Affairs, however, writers merely spread rumours in print, and none of Nikitenko's argument about the usefulness of the press could sway him. After a crucial committee meeting in June, Nikitenko lost heart. The four members did agree in principle in July on the projected government journal, but that September the committee admitted its ineffectualness by asking to merge with the Chief Administration of the Censorship. In its final report of 26 October 1859, the committee conceded that it was 'incompatible' with the preliminary censorship authority; but, if it had failed to stop press excesses, so had the censors. Partly at fault, continued the report (and here the hand of Nikitenko shows), was the absence of clear rules. The Statute of 1828 still in effect was badly out-dated.[53]

Meanwhile, Nikitenko's draft for the new censorship statute had been rejected by the State Council only a few days earlier. Notably, the council opposed the very provision the emperor had called for in directing Kovalevsky to draft a new statute: permitting the press to discuss state issues. Some members had scored the attempt to define more precisely what could appear in print; others had wanted to add new administrative measures because, said one, 'no matter what the laws and statutes, their success depends on correct and attentive supervision.'[54]

The State Council must have voted as it did believing that Alexander had had second thoughts about granting greater leeway to the press. Kovalevsky, in any case, at this point made clear that he had had enough of censorship. Only a month before he had told Nikitenko: 'I will oppose with all my strength any attempt to separate [censorship] from the Ministry of Public Education because this would have oppressive consequences for literature.'[55] Now Kovalevsky himself asked the Council of Ministers to make the censorship authority an independent agency whose head would oversee the drafting of the new statute. The demands of this office overtaxed a single minister, argued Kovalevsky, and the superintendents of the education districts had too little time for censorship along with their other duties.

VI

Ending a confused year for censorship, the Council of Ministers on 12 November 1859 approved the merger of the Committee on Press Affairs with the Chief Administration and the separation of the entire censorship apparatus from the Ministry of Public Education. Censorship had become the 'plaything of the fates,' wrote Nikitenko.

To head the proposed independent censorship agency Alexander named Baron M.A. Korf. Because the press had cause to distrust him as a former member of the Buturlin committee of 1848, Korf chose at once to speak out as a friend of writers and publishers, thereby incurring the distrust of many officials. In promising writers that he would 'establish a liberal system,' Korf raised false hopes, noted Nikitenko, who accurately predicted his downfall.[56]

By the end of November, Korf had named A.G. Troinitsky as his assistant – evidence that he intended to have a liberal administration. A brief ukaz drafted by Korf for Alexander to issue on 1 January 1860 explained that the new agency would absorb the Foreign Censorship Committee and the ministries' liaison censors, while the Procurator of the Holy Synod would continue to censor ecclesiastical literature, and the governors to oversee the press in the provinces. Korf also planned to increase the budget for censorship, but, upon requesting 200,000 rubles to buy a building whose refurbishing would cost yet more, he received directions from the emperor to use the old quarters of the Pedagogical Institute. Korf balked and Alexander permitted him to resign. As Troinitsky tells the story, besides Korf's 'unhappy idea' of purchasing new quarters, 'strong opposition at high levels rose against the very principle of the new agency, and, at the last minute, Baron Korf parted from the sovereign.'[57]

Alexander reinstated the Chief Administration of the Censorship in the Ministry of Public Education on 14 January 1860, and ten days later the members of the defunct Committee on Press Affairs joined its ranks.[58] Kovalevsky once more assumed authority over censorship, but the minister had made his point that his pressing involvement in educational reform gave him no time to draft a new censorship statute. The sixteen months Kovalevsky would yet serve as minister consequently proved to be a holding period in censorship policy.

One portent of things to come, however, was the directive Alexander had issued on 23 December 1859, forbidding the press to comment on the gentry's right to discuss certain issues in their assemblies.[59] Here was an early indication that the bias of the press against landowners on the emancipation issue might be giving way to an opposite but even less satisfactory stand: support by the press for gentry 'rights.' Two articulate groups, the gentry and the press, could unite against the government. The government was equally uneasy about unrest among university students and the involvement in it of the press. Alexander wanted a reform of education at once.

Early in his reign, Alexander had freed the universities from the supervision of the governor-generals and named known liberals in their places as superintendents of the education districts. Student debates, meetings, and publications followed. For example, the St Petersburg superintendent, Prince Shcherbatov, assumed responsibility for censoring the students' *Messenger of Free Opinion* and the *Bell*, the latter named for Herzen's émigré paper.[60]

With the ending of the Crimean War, a rush of students swelled university enrolments, and even women attended lectures. By 1858, such problems as outmoded laboratories and libraries made greater autonomy in the universities imperative, and Alexander directed Kovalevsky to draft a statute for education reform. The student disorders in 1859 – already noted for having kept Kovalevsky from acting on the proposal for censorship reform drafted by Nikitenko – caused Alexander again to insist on changes in education. But when Kovalevsky finally presented proposals in 1860, objections from the influential educator N.I. Pirogov forced the ministry to rewrite the project. Not until 1864 would a new statute appear.

Despite the impasse in censorship and educational reform, the year 1861 brought with it the Emancipation Statute and its profound changes for Russia. That January, Alexander told the State Council that 'I am not forgetting and will not forget that the beginning of [emancipation] was on the initiative of the gentry itself, and I am happy that it has fallen to me to testify to this fact before posterity.'[61] On 19 February he decreed the Emancipation Statute law and a public announcement followed twelve days later. Given the uncertainties of the transition under way, Kovalevsky at this time banned a speech arranged at the University of St Petersburg by historian N.I. Kostomarov to honour slavophile Constantine Aksakov. Students staged an angry demonstration.

An impatient emperor ordered Kovalevsky to halt further outbreaks, but Kovalevsky responded that strong measures would only provoke graver discontent. Dissatisfied, Alexander appointed a committee to study the situation and propose remedies, causing Nikitenko to predict the minister's resignation, which came during April.[62] To succeed Kovalevsky, Alexander named Admiral E.V. Putiatin, a militant ready to impose strict control on students and writers alike, and Putiatin began at once to frame regulations for the universities.

As the new minister set to work, a new contributor to a radically inclined journal begun in 1859, *Russian Word* (*Russkoe Slovo*), presumed to speak for students. He was Dmitry Pisarev, and in his journal that May he advocated a break from 'those stale things, that decayed furniture, called general authority.' Alluding to serfdom, he condemned a 'whole world ... created of habits, customs, means of thinking, prejudices, moral cowardice, and degeneracy on the soil of idleness.'[63] Pisarev did not condemn the authority of the state (no censor would have approved such words) but neither did he condemn students' demonstrations.

Once summer holidays had begun, Putiatin published his new rules for the universities. He abolished students organizations and financial support for those in need. He also restricted attendance at university lectures by auditors, whom he saw as agitators. Then, in late August, just as the students began to return, a revolutionary manifesto printed by the clandestine Free Russian Press, entitled 'To the Younger Generation,' appeared in the capital. Its authors sought to channel student discontent into political action, but neither students nor officials took the manifesto seriously.

That fall, when students staged their first protests against the new rules, Putiatin abruptly closed St Petersburg University and announced that he would resume classes only for those who promised to obey the rules. He did so on 11 October. The next day, when police interrupted an illegal student meeting to make arrests and a second group of students intervened, the police arrested three hundred of them. Most students boycotted classes.

The police linked the student disturbances with the appearance at this time of three issues of a clandestinely printed pamphlet, 'The Great Russian.' In addition, the apparent sympathy of *Contemporary* and the *Russian Word* for student complaints caused the Chief Administration of the Censorship under Putiatin to consider seriously closing both journals. Suspecting Chernyshevsky of complicity in the unrest, the Third Section on 2 October had begun charting the writer's every movement and contact with students.[64]

No less concerned than Putiatin about these apparent threats to the social order was P.A. Valuev, minister of the interior and director of the local police since April. Alexander had made him minister, Valuev was later to recall, to handle emancipation and its immense problems in a 'conciliatory way.'[65] (A former governor-general of Courland, he had most recently headed two departments in the Ministry of State Domains, the agency that supervised imperial lands and serfs.) Valuev was to play a giant role in censorship affairs in the next decades.

That November Putiatin proposed two major changes in censorship practice, having very likely had Valuev as behind-the-scenes advisor. The changes involved transferring all censorship authority to the Ministry of the Interior and adopting a new system of control – post-publication, or punitive, rather than preliminary censorship.[66] The government would remove responsibility for printed content from the censors and place it all on editors and writers. Putiatin and Valuev at once publicly announced that a four-man commission from the two ministries would receive and consider unofficial proposals regarding censorship.

Of several such submissions, the most notable came from a group of editors and publishers who convened in Moscow before the end of November. This group forwarded to the government what may be called the first 'professional' statement by Russian journalists. Included among the editors from St Petersburg and Moscow were representatives of *Contemporary*, *Russian Word*, *Notes of the Fatherland*, *Moscow Bulletin*, *Russian War Veteran*, *Day*, *Dawn* (*Zaria*), *Our Times* (*Nashe Vremia*), and *Century* (*Vek*). Their *Zapiska* urged an end to preliminary censorship because caprice and whim made it arbitrary, and similarly opposed censorship by outside agencies and ministries and any secret instructions for censors. It proposed press representatives on the Chief Administration of the Censorship and an appeals procedure for rejected manuscripts. Because legitimate criticism benefitted rather than hurt the political order, the editors concluded, an 'open and candid relationship between the government and literature is necessary.'[67]

In sharp contrast to this statement was Nikitenko's devastating critique of the press for the Chief Administration of the Censorship this same month. That critique, which probably helped bring about the suspension of both journals in the next year, found *Contemporary* and *Russian Word* engaged in a sustained attack on the political, social, intellectual, and religious values of Russian society. These publications used extremism to attract and 'bedazzle' the public, said Nikitenko. Most ominously, the young 'get notions about the unlimited freedom of man' and 'about the primacy of satisfying feelings and interests before all morality.'[68]

In the next month, December, Putiatin closed beleaguered St Petersburg University for the rest of the school year; and, almost at once, Alexander asked him to step down as minister of public education. He named to the vacated post a man closely associated with the Grand Duke Constantine and his view that broad consultation should precede policy changes. He was A.V. Golovnin, Constantine's assistant in the reform of the Naval Ministry. Alexander had apparently concluded that repressive measures were only aggravating student and press dissatisfaction.

In its own evaluations in February 1862, the joint commission from the Ministries of Education and the Interior divided on what to do with the censorship issue. As Valuev's representatives, V.Ia. Fuchs and P.I. Fridberg favoured transferring censorship to the Ministry of the Interior and introducing the 'punitive system.'[69] Both representatives from the Ministry of Education – A.A. Burt and P.I. Iankevich – favoured, as did Golovnin, keeping censorship in their ministry, continuing the preliminary system for all but official and academic works, and introducing judicial controls.[70] This stand-off between the two ministries again introduced bureaucratic rivalry into the contentious censorship issue.

So far, the principal changes in imperial press controls under Alexander had occurred in the first years of the reign to help carry out the liberation of the serfs. The emperor had soon learned that the secret methods of governing used by Nicholas I ill suited the reform at hand. Interwoven as it was with other social, economic, and institutional issues, emancipation required discussion in the press. In January 1858 Alexander had opened the discussion of the peasant question – a move unprecedented in the history of the Russian state – and then announced that he would permit comment on other political issues as well.

An inadequately prepared censorship system, lacking relevant rules or precedents, thereupon faced in 1858 and 1859 an airing of public issues familiar only in advanced western nations. Because some censors permitted far more latitude than their superiors approved, the government responded with a series of measures designed to tighten censorship and assert control over the press. A period of unrelieved confusion had left its mark when A.V. Golovnin stepped in as minister of public education, intent on trying certain western ways of dealing with the press.

8

The dilemmas of liberal censorship, 1862–63

By naming a protégé of the Grand Duke Constantine to succeed Putiatin, Alexander II suggested a liberal course for censorship policy – an impression his new minister of public education, A.V. Golovnin, worked hard to reinforce. No minister so personally cultivated the press or so earnestly solicited its opinions; but, because circumstances dictated that Golovnin also hold firm against press offenses, a dualistic policy resulted. To complicate further the plans of Golovnin, P.A. Valuev, the minister of the interior, aggressively vied for control of censorship in 1862.

Despite his conviction that historical progress dictated the press's becoming a liberal institution in its own right, Golovnin found himself unable to follow through on his plan to write an appropriately modern press statute. Yet his failure to reform the law should not overshadow two major accomplishments of his year as chief censor of the Russian empire: the government's granting the press wider scope to discuss public issues and permitting new commercial advantages. Both developments encouraged a more widely circulated Russian daily press.

I

The reputation of Golovnin as a liberal rested largely on his long association with the Grand Duke Constantine, Alexander's brother, who had pressed forward the peasant reform and, earlier, the reform of the Naval Ministry.[1] From 1855 to 1859, Golovnin had served Constantine as overseer and censor of the Naval Ministry's publication, *Naval Miscellany*, a voice favouring extensive reforms after the Crimean War; and he agreed with the Grand Duke that those affected should be both consulted and kept informed about changes in policy.

Once he had become minister of public education in December 1861, Golovnin confidently set about committing himself publicly to censorship reform, and in January he invited the press to submit its views. In response, a group of St Petersburg journalists met in the Chess Club on 14 January and unanimously advocated the introduction of post-publication, or punitive, censorship governed by the judicial process. These same journalists sent Golovnin at least four briefs which were to appear, along with comments from censors and censorship officials, in the *Opinions of Various Persons on the Censorship*, a volume printed on the orders of Golovnin.[2]

One brief, 'Memorandum of the Editors of the Journal *Contemporary*' (written by Nicholas Chernyshevsky), was a shrewd appeal for change that praised the progressive historical role of the Russian autocracy and pointed to the contributions made by *Contemporary* to peasant reform. While granting the need for some form of censorship, the editors – none named – hoped for a certain measure of reform under Golovnin and seemed to believe that support from the press would strengthen his hand.[3] Russian writers favoured reforms, they said, but recognized that 'only the government has the power to accomplish anything significant.' Moreover, observance by the government of its own regulations would best convince the press to follow the rules.[4] The editors followed up their brief with two articles critical of the censorship system in the March issue of *Contemporary* – both censor-approved, of course.[5]

The second major brief in *Opinions of Various Persons* emphasized needed institutional changes in the censorship system, and, in complementing the submission from *Contemporary*, suggested a division of labour for maximum effect. Signed by nine publications (no individuals were named), this brief also insisted that the government hold to its 'chosen road' of changing the old order, and gave first priority to ending preliminary censorship.[6]

Under the preferred *karatelnyi* system of punitive, or post-publication, controls, wrote the editors, 'a prosecutor for the government presents a complaint only after something has appeared in the press.' But the 'existing court with its written procedures, innumerable chancellery documents, and absence both of oral defense and defense attorneys' was 'still more absurd' than censorship. An overhaul of the judicial system would have to precede censorship reform.

Because private individuals and officials would have the right to sue members of the press, the editors proposed creating a censorship investigation committee to permit only 'significant' complaints to proceed to trial. The committe would include an equal number from the press and the government. The authors of this second brief asked the government to make such a committee work, again echoing the *Contemporary* brief that the government best engenders respect for the law by itself having 'confidence in the law it has established.'[7]

Two briefs from an influential segment of the press had made the same point, although with restraint: because the legal order rightly held precedence, the government not only had to write consistent laws and impartially enforce them, but also had to be ruled by them. Arguing that only a legalist and reformist autocracy would hold the loyalty of the press and the people, these Russian journalists called upon the government to subordinate itself to a new legal order lest it lose all authority.

What these words surely alluded to was the historic decline of absolutism which had occurred in the West and now threatened the Russian state. These Russian journalists were gently reminding their government that it needed their loyalty, especially at a time when Russian newspapers were winning larger readerships that cut across traditional class lines.

Strictures on newspapers to mid-century had made the 'thick' journal, read mainly by the middle class, dominant among periodicals. Throughout his reign, Nicholas had allowed only three dailies of general interest: two were official (the Academy of Sciences' *St Petersburg Bulletin* and the Ministry of War's *Russian War Veteran*) and one, the *Northern Bee*, was in private hands (it alone of the unofficial periodicals boasted a 'political' section which could print foreign news). Nicholas approved only six new dailies, all aimed at special interest groups, in the final decade of his reign.[8]

In contrast, Alexander II permitted sixty new dailies in the first ten years he ruled and granted political sections to many (although none to papers costing under seven rubles per year). In the first year of his reign, the extension of the telegraph to Warsaw from the West had connected the Russian empire with the European news network, and wired dispatches had shortly begun to flow into the Ministry of Foreign Affairs in St Petersburg. The ministry screened what could appear in official periodicals and permitted privileged papers to reprint the items. In the early sixties Russian papers became prosperous enough to buy news independently relayed from the West, even as the more affluent papers won permission to buy foreign reports from the Russian Telegraph Agency, a new government bureau. (All telegraph news was censored.)

Expanded coverage along with the sale of papers on the streets and in railway stations – previously banned – gave rise to the Russian 'common reader'[9] who wanted a variety of easily understood material. Tailored to his liking was the daily's column of foreign items, each condensed to a few lines. Even the more sophisticated reader began to favour news dailies over literary publications, so that, for example, the last attempted literary weekly, *Rumour* (*Molva*), appeared only a few months in 1857.

During Golovnin's tenure as minister of public education, the government in 1862 gave another unprecedented boost to newspapers by allowing unofficial dailies to print commercial advertisements and thereby lower subcription fees. This same year A.V. Starchevsky was to transform *Son of the Fatherland* from a weekly into a daily that soon reached 20,000 readers, 13,000 of them in the provinces. At six rubles a year, it was the first cheap daily. In the next year A.A. Kraevsky also was to launch an unofficial daily, *Voice* (*Golos*) – albeit aided by government subsidies – and was to circulate 10,000 copies by the close of the sixties. *Moscow Bulletin* shifted to daily status in this same decade and was leased in 1863 by Michael Katkov, who doubled its circulation to 12,000 in two years by capitalizing on nationalistic feelings during the Polish rebellion. (Not until 1900 would a Russian newspaper, equipped with high-speed presses, achieve the circulations of hundreds of thousands that some English papers had reached in the first half of the century.)[10]

Editors courted readers through such features as the 'leading article,' or front-page editorial on current issues, and through the *feuilleton*, a column of diverting commentary on topics ranging from world affairs to fashion. A.S. Suvorin's Sunday *feuilletons* almost by themselves kept the *St Petersburg Bulletin* prosperous, while Katkov's front-page 'leaders' earned for him the popular sobriquet 'thunderer.'[11]

Of the flurry of low-cost weekly newspapers for the lower classes, one of the most successful was the *Russian Gazette* (*Russkaia Gazeta*), which cost under four rubles a year. Unique in its appeal was the *Wrapping Leaflet* (*Uvertochnyi Listok* 1860), printed on large sheets of sturdy paper meant for use by shopkeepers as store wrappings. Such weeklies, because they were meant for common readers, avoided sensitive issues and, on the whole, had few censorship problems.

Three St Petersburg dailies started by radical staff members of the journal *Contemporary* met a different fate. They were *Sketches* (*Ocherki* 1863), *Contemporary Word* (*Sovremennoe Slovo* 1862–63), and *Popular Chronicle* (*Narodnaia Letopis* 1865). All three soon succumbed to closure by the censorship authority, while *Contemporary* itself continued – except for a suspension in 1862. The government found the radical dailies less tolerable not only because they reached more people among the masses than did the more costly and intellectual *Contemporary*, but also because they lacked the prestige and loyal following won by *Contemporary* over many years.

What is most noteworthy, however, is the start of a steady shift to a greater proportion of daily and weekly periodicals for the general public in the overall number of periodicals in Russia, a change that had long since happened in the West.[12] That shift was under way, then, when Golovnin became minister of public education and solicited the briefs on what changes should take place in censorship policy.

These briefs may or may not have reached the eyes of Minister of the Interior Valuev, but in intimating the need for an independent press under a new legal order they would have displeased him just as much as similar proposals from the gentry in these same early months of 1862. In 1861, during his first year as minister, Valuev had asserted to the emperor that administrative and police powers must be used to silence all challenges to absolutism – even when such challenges originated among the very gentry he had been appointed to appease in the aftermath of the emancipation.

When, in December 1861, about one-fifth of the gentry at the Tula Congress, led by V.P. Minin, had petitioned the emperor for a 'commission of gentry from all provinces for the purpose of formulating new legislative projects to correct grievances over the emancipation,' Valuev had immediately responded that these petitioners had exceeded their rightful role. He informed the provincial governor that hopes among the gentry of formulating national policies were 'groundless and unsuitable.'[13]

In its assembly convened on 6 January, the gentry of Moscow boldly went even further in endorsing an 'extensive widening of the electoral principle in government service' as well as a 'public discussion in the press of questions which touch on reform in all areas.' Valuev this time gave notice that the government would not tolerate such insubordination by framing two warnings that gentry assemblies must forego illegal discussion, that is, discussions with constitutionalist implications. The first warning came in an unsigned article published on 17 January in the fledgling ministry daily, the *Northern Post* (*Severnaia Pochta*), founded by Valuev that very month to voice government policies. The other was a letter to provincial marshals of the gentry. Because the St Petersburg assembly convened on 16 January, Valuev apparently regarded his article and letter as urgently necessary, and he worked all night on 15 January to compose them.[14]

In his article, Valuev warned the gentry against speaking without full information or 'correct evaluation' of government policies. Alluding to 'new forms of organization' in the prevailing 'transitional era' and anticipating the *zemstvo* (local government) reform of 1864, Valuev explained that local government would be the bailiwick of the gentry, and in this area the gentry would be 'the chief collaborators of the government in completing the peasant reform and in developing a new administrative order granting great latitude in local government.' Valuev also reassured the many gentry who saw emancipation as a devastating blow to their position that 'the government will not hesitate to give them the help they deserve.'[15]

Marshal of Tsarskoe Selo *uezd* (district), A.P. Platonov, nonetheless urged fellow landowners in the St Petersburg assembly to petition the emperor for a 'general popular representative assembly in the empire.'[16] The members prudently dropped the proposal, and nothing ever came of it.

Anticipating trouble next from the Tver gentry convening on 1 February, Valuev directed a member, A.B. Lobanov-Rostovsky, to convey to his fellows an official warning against improper demands.[17] The assembly defiantly framed a resolution calling for a national convention elected by all the people, autonomous public courts, and full publicity in all areas of government. In turn, the Tver gentry renounced their class privileges, and thirteen arbiters of the peace (local gentry appointed to help implement emancipation) announced that they would henceforth be guided by the resolutions of the gentry assembly.[18]

To crush such defiance, Alexander on 12 February directed Valuev to meet with Minister of Justice V.I. Panin and plan the government's response. In his diary Valuev recorded how that very evening, after meeting Panin and V.A. Dolgorukov, head of the Third Section, he framed recommendations for a possible emergency. He considered the most serious possibilities: 'Disorders might break out. All the arbiters of the peace might resign simultaneously ... and the governor has shown that he does not know what is going on in the province. Therefore, the chief instigators must be arrested, taken to St Petersburg fortress, and subjected to the judgment of the Senate.'[19]

Valuev in turn gave broad authority to an adjutant general on the scene, who was to command, if necessary, units of the army stationed in

Tver, to arrest persons 'indirectly' involved with the thirteen arbiters, to overrule the local governor, to remove and replace local officials, and, 'in case of extreme necessity,' to replace all the arbiters of the peace.[20] Although the severest measures proved unnecessary, the thirteen arbiters of the peace were arrested.

Defiance required stern repression, but Valuev also saw the need for meeting at least part way the gentry's demands for a greater role in the central government. On 23 February, he urged the emperor to reform the State Council to include a congress, consisting of delegates elected by *zemstvos* and appointed by the government, which would advise on national affairs. A single idea had taken hold in Russia, argued Valuev: 'In all European countries various estates are given some degree of participation in the business of legislation or general administration of the state; and if this so everywhere, then it should also be the case with us.'[21]

Apparently encouraged by Alexander, Valuev within the next twelve months drafted his proposal. His defense of it before the State Council in April 1863, although unsuccessful, underscores the limited participation he wanted: 'This measure preserves fully [the emperor's] legislative and administrative power, and at the same time creates a central institution that would resemble representation of the country.'[22]

II

Just as Golovnin sought to win the support of the press by consulting its members on press policy, so Valuev sought to ensure the allegiance of the gentry by giving that class a consultative voice in national policies. When the press gave attention and support to the initiatives of the gentry for direct participation during these first months of 1862, Valuev strongly disapproved; a ban against such discussion was added in March to Golovnin's proposals for new censorship regulations.

Meanwhile, in mid-February, Chernyshevsky, the *Contemporary* editor who had been under police surveillance since the previous October, submitted for censorship an article lauding the gentry. Comprised of five 'letters' dated from 5 through 16 February, Chernyshevsky's 'Letters Without an Address' underwent review later in the month and failed to pass.[23]

Although phrased euphemistically, 'Letters' praises the initiatives of the gentry and seems to endorse a popular assembly to legislate reforms. In favouring 'general legislation' and administrative, court, and press reforms, wrote Chernyshevsky, the gentry spoke for all classes and did so, 'not because they have a stronger desire than other classes, but only because the gentry currently has the organization through which to express its views.' He referred also to the 'weaknesses of the current order which the gentry is seeking to eliminate.'[24] Chernyshevsky shared these goals, and his 'Letters' raised a possibility the government could not permit: an alliance between radical journalists and the liberal gentry.

On 25 February, Golovnin discussed his censorship proposals with the emperor, and then defended them before the Council of Ministers on 1 March.[25] The government, he argued, must win support from journalists by being consistently judicious; and, so reasoning, Golovnin made the same proposal Putiatin had made: preliminary censorship must end. But, whereas Putiatin had argued that preliminary censorship no longer protected the government, Golovnin stressed that it needlessly antagonized the press.

Golovnin felt very strongly that a judicious but firm censorship policy was crucial to the well-being of the autocracy. His plan, he recalled later, was 'to formulate a new statute on publishing to be enacted when the judicial reform became effective and, prior to that, to introduce temporary measures which would provide more severity for everything important and essential and, at the same time, give all possible relief to literature.'[26] In his third month as minister, Golovnin set after that goal by making proposals which had full support from the emperor. Valuev's bid to consolidate all censorship authority in his ministry had been premature.

Proof that Golovnin wielded authority was his success in abolishing the Chief Administration of the Censorship to gain direct control over the censorship committees – one of his proposals enacted by the Council of Ministers on 10 March.[27] That same day, by appointing a close friend and ally, V.A. Tsee, to head the St Petersburg Censorship Committee and to serve as second-in-command of censorship, Golovnin made his personal stamp indelible. (Golovnin and Tsee had discovered their like-mindedness as fellow students in the 1830s and their long correspondence reveals their shared belief that Russia should modernize but avoid the extremes of democracy.)

Another of Golovnin's proposals approved on 10 March yielded power to Valuev, however, by authorizing the Ministry of the Interior not only to discover violations of censorship regulations in printed works that had reached the public but also to recommend penalties for the censors and publishers responsible; this was a role similar to that of the Third Section in the previous reign. Besides receiving some of the resources of the abolished Chief Administration, Valuev immediately hired thirteen assistants for his new post-publication role and, on 16 March, created the Council of the Ministry of the Interior for Publishing Affairs.[28]

Two other proposals by Golovnin became part of the March 10 regulations: the freeing of official and academic publications from preliminary censorship and the abolition of special departmental censorships. But the Council of Ministers refused to give Golovnin authority to free individual periodicals that he found trustworthy.

The ukaz of 10 March enacting the new regulations went beyond Golovnin's proposals in its ban on any words implying that gentry assemblies had the right to discuss 'general state affairs and questions.' It also required the minister of the interior in the capital and the governors in the provinces to screen any news to be published about gentry assemblies – a measure surely urged by Valuev. Still other sections prohibited any criticism of the landed class, the emancipation act, the army, or state finances; references to class tensions; and discussion of full citizenship rights for Jews.[29]

Soon after their appearance, the March 10 regulations were described in *Day* (*Den*) by editor Ivan Aksakov as a measure to 'strengthen preliminary censorship by means of punitive censorship, only dividing censorship responsibilities between the two ministries.'[30] Golovnin had other intentions: a gradual transition to post-publication controls effected solely by the courts. As a first step, the minister had already appointed a Commission for the Revising, Altering, and Supplementing of the Regulations on Press Affairs, and it, too, was announced on 10 March.

Nine days later Golovnin instructed this group, chaired by Prince D.A. Obolensky, to draft rules which would release more publications from preliminary censorship but subject them to new restraints. Golovnin favoured the French system of meting out warnings which, if repeated, became grounds for suspending or closing an objectionable periodical. He also asked the commission to require printing plants to 'present for inspection any publication printed without preliminary censorship' before its circulation – a surrogate form of preliminary censorship. Golovnin wanted to use these administrative 'transitional measures' until the new courts came into being in two or three years and for an indefinite period thereafter. The new courts would need time to learn to handle press offenses and to deal with the 'fevered mind' of anyone foolishly bent on the 'role of martyr.'[31]

Golovnin had already prepared and printed materials for the commission: foreign press legislation, the history of Russian censorship, relevant past regulations, and *Opinions of Various Persons on the Censorship*. The official announcement of the commission on 10 March had asked for submissions from the public, and the minister now urged the commission itself to stimulate useful discussion about reforming censorship. Golovnin directly asked one member, K. Veselovsky, to write for publication about his area of expertise – French, Belgian, Prussian, and German press laws. Believing that Golovnin would 'provoke a newspaper polemic,' Veselovsky demurred and suffered what he termed the loss of the minister's 'confidence.'[32]

Another commission member opposed to consultation was Major General V.V. Sturmer, whom Golovnin had reluctantly appointed to the St Petersburg Censorship Committee in February at the request of the minister of war, and probably just as reluctantly had appointed to the commission. The stand of members A. Voronov, of the Chief Administration of Schools, and I. Andreevsky, professor of police law at St Petersburg University, is unclear; but the one other member, Tsee, wholeheartedly approved soliciting opinion. Thus, while Sturmer found Tsee's St Petersburg Censorship Committee meetings 'simply indecent, for writers are invited and they impudently demand an accounting from censors,' Tsee took pride that May in telling Alexander of his nearly daily consultations with the press.[33]

Nikitenko had mixed feelings about the direction of censorship under Golovnin. He was pleased that, through the March regulations, 'Golovnin has captured [the] essence of censorship for himself and its obscure, disadvantageous side is left to Valuev'; but he frowned on the minister's courting the press.[34] With Golovnin's backing, for example, Tsee was offering to read works before editors submitted them for censorship, recommending subjects for articles, and agreeing to the exposure of wrongdoing within and without the government so long as writers refrained from extreme language.

One journal candidly assessed such manoeuvres as 'orchestration' by printing a cartoon of a baton-wielding Tsee conducting the editors of journals and papers. But the very appearance of the critical cartoon shows that Golovnin and Tsee favoured a certain amount of contrary opinion in print.

Valuev took exception to such permissiveness and told Golovnin so. Golovnin nonetheless forged ahead with his program for exposing rather than burying controversy. Accordingly, that April, he convinced the emperor to lift the ban on any printed mention of Alexander Herzen. The emperor approved for publication in *Our Times* (*Nashe Vremia*) Boris Chicherin's critical 'Letter to Herzen' which had appeared in *Bell* in

1858; and he agreed to circulating through Russian bookstores an anti-Herzen pamphlet proposed by the metropolitan of Moscow, written by a censor, paid for by a landowner, and published in Berlin three years earlier.[35] (Some 3,000 copies of that pamphlet had been languishing in the warehouse of the St Petersburg Censorship Committee.)

III

Alexander's agreement to permit writers to attack Herzen by name may partly have evolved from the arrest in mid-April of a student, P. Zaichnevsky, who had been secretly lithographing anti-government pamphlets since 1859. But that arrest had also pointed to a laxity in the policing of presses, a duty of the Ministry of the Interior since 10 March. When Valuev had at this time requested and received from Golovnin his records, incomplete though they were, on existing printing plants, Valuev's police traced 150 such establishments and found only 96 of them properly authorized.

Then, on 1 May, appeared a seditious revolutionary pamphlet, 'Young Russia,' written in jail and smuggled to a clandestine printer by Zaichnevsky. It argued that only armed rebellion could accomplish what liberals and socialists sought by peaceful means. National and provincial elective assemblies and publicly owned factories would be the result.

Lest more such leaflets appear, the political police began a round-up of suspected subversives. When Golovnin made no immediate move to tighten censorship, Alexander gave him notice to do so. New rules, approved by the Council of Ministers on 12 May and slanted towards giving more power to Interior, soon emerged.[36] Through them Golovnin effected at once an administrative measure he had asked the Obolensky commission to include in the new censorship statute: the ministers of education and the interior would together suspend for up to eight months any periodical having a 'dangerous orientation.' The new rules also severely restricted criticism of the government and, in any criticism censors did approve, forbade the naming of any official. No criticism of 'administrative abuses or shortcomings' could appear in publications which charged six rubles or less for an annual subscription or in books of up to 160 pages; no official could submit an article for publication without government approval; and editors had to identify the authors of articles published anonymously if the censorship so demanded.

Not long after these restrictive measures, Alexander granted the concession, mentioned earlier, that all privately owned and governmental periodicals were to have the right to publish private advertisements, a privilege until then reserved for the *Bulletin* of St Petersburg and of Moscow and for the police dailies of those two cities. (A year later the minister of the interior would gain the authority to prohibit such advertisements for periods of from two to eight months in publications which violated the May 12 rules.)[37]

In a circular to his censorship committees about the new rules, Golovnin made the unusual admission that the emperor had requested the May 12 regulations on the advice of the minister of the interior. Of special concern, he said, were certain journals in which 'everything that the government does is systematically vilified ... [with] the clear aim of provoking discontent.' In two other statements that May, Golovnin alluded to insurrection. To Alexander he argued that the immediate task was to anticipate issues that might lead to revolution and to 'soften' them well in advance, that is, to air contentious problems and to deal with them. To Constantine he spoke more bluntly: 'Our only role consists of a struggle with the impending revolution. Only a blind man can fail to see its approach.'[38]

Still committed to open debate, Golovnin personally approved for publication an article by D. Shcheglov criticizing the regulations of 12 May as vague and subject to abuse. In reply to a sharp complaint from Valuev, Golovnin identified himself as the responsible censor and upheld the legality of the article, no matter how disagreeable the argument. Golovnin further informed Valuev that a censor-approved refutation had already appeared in print.[39] Airing and answering a complaint in print best suited Golovnin, but not Valuev.

Meanwhile, on 14 May, Alexander had approved new temporary regulations proposed by Valuev for the supervision of presses.[40] Again administrative controls which Golovnin had directed the Obolensky commission to draft came immediately into effect. These emergency rules required each printshop operator to be licensed and to keep a book in which to record all publications and all censorship rulings. Anyone who imported, manufactured, traded, or sold printing equipment also had to keep records of transactions and obtain a license. Civil police under the Ministry of the Interior were to inspect all printing-related establishments and cite violations; the criminal courts were to decide the penalties.

Just as he shared the sense of crisis prompting these new regulations of 12 and 14 May, Golovnin had also come to agree that *Contemporary* and *Russian Word* heightened the threat of revolution. Following the very serious St Petersburg fires, blamed on revolutionaries, during the last week of May, Golovnin on 4 June announced to the emperor his intention of taking measures against the two radical journals. Three days later he urged the Council of Ministers to recommend closing them permanently and, evidently hoping to placate his liberal constituency, at the same time proposed reopening St Petersburg University in the fall. The council disagreed and Valuev gloated: 'The vacillations of Golovnin created an unfavourable impression on those present, including the sovereign. He wanted complete closure of the journals by imperial order. I insisted on an eight-month suspension because this measure was within his and my own power. He proposed to open the university and then explained that he would be happy if he did not [open it].'[41]

The ministers suspended the two journals for eight months on 19 June. The same day, in a letter to Nekrasov, Chernyshevsky reported that only the day before Golovnin had advised him 'to consider [*Contemporary*] closed and to liquidate its affairs.' Despite that seemingly strong warning, Chernyshevsky assessed the suspension of his journal and of *Russian Word* as having come 'without any especially new violations on their part, as a consequence of the general conclusion that their orientation is unacceptable.' Their suspensions were merely 'part of the general series of events which began after the first fires when the idea seized the government that the state of affairs demanded strong repressive measures.'[42]

Just three weeks later, on 8 July, the Third Section ended nine months' surveillance of Chernyshevsky and found an excuse to arrest him. On the strength of a letter from Herzen to N.A. Serno-Solovevich offering to publish *Contemporary* abroad, the government accused Chernyshevsky of illegal connections with an émigré group. The severity of the late-May fires and the resulting widespread fear of anarchy very likely gave the government the justification it had for some time wanted to remove Chernyshevsky from the scene. If Chernyshevsky's testimony is trustworthy, Golovnin had earlier sought to accomplish the same end by offering the outspoken writer a passport to go abroad, an offer Chernyshevsky had refused.[43]

Golovnin had next to face a violation of the rules of 12 May by Ivan Aksakov, the troublesome but patriotic editor of *Day*. Aksakov's offense was twice refusing Alexander's request, through the Moscow Censorship Committee, for the name of the author of an anonymous article mentioning disorders in the Baltic region. Golovnin took the conciliatory position that Aksakov would in the future have to reveal authors' names.

'This is not enough,' fumed the emperor. 'Tell him that he should at once fulfil my will. All obligations in the law are the same for all editors and, in the event that he does not comply, deprive him of his right of editorship.'[44] When Aksakov would not bend and even invited arrest, Golovnin suspended *Day* from the end of June until 1 September and barred Aksakov from its editorship through 1862.

All these clashes made more credible the blanket indictment against the press expressed to Alexander on 22 June by Valuev: 'Our press is of one piece in its opposition to the government.' Valuev's assessment directly refuted Golovnin's stand that most Russian writers benefitted the state, a stand the minister of public education supported by a daily digest from the press prepared for the emperor.[45] Both ministers exaggerated as each vied throughout 1862 to gain from the emperor control of the press.

Of benefit to Golovnin was the rash of published attacks on Herzen. When Katkov independently published his derogatory 'Remarks for the Publisher of *Bell*' in his *Russian Messenger* in July, Golovnin instigated the reprinting of the article in *Son of the Fatherland*. Golovnin duly informed Alexander and pointed to *Son*'s impressive circulation of 19,000. Still other papers – *Northern Bee*, *Journal de St Petersbourg*, and *Home Talk* (*Domashniaia Beseda*) – reprinted the article; and Tsee later met Katkov in Moscow to express the minister's confidence in him, a clumsy gesture that very likely irritated Katkov.[46]

Golovnin permitted Iury Samarin, an intimate slavophile ally of Aksakov, to fill in as responsible editor for *Day* from September through December, while forbidding Aksakov to be the editor 'in reality,' as Samarin insisted in a letter of 12 July. Golovnin's pointed response to Samarin, which the emperor approved, condemned Aksakov for having incited discontent against the government by depicting the *zemstvo* and the government as moral opposites. Such deviousness Golovnin would not tolerate, although he would permit the press to expose wrongs and to express the hopes of the people. Still, the minister was characteristically conciliatory: he agreed that Aksakov would be Samarin's 'chief collaborator' and could 'sometimes' independently submit articles for censorship.[47]

Meanwhile Golovnin discharged the censor responsible for *Day*, N. Giliarov-Platonov. Pleading human considerations, the chairman of the Moscow Censorship Committee tried to dissuade Golovnin, but the minister insisted that Giliarov, a slavophile himself, had been overly lenient with Aksakov. Golovnin also pointed out that no censor could write for a journal, as Giliarov did for Katkov's *Russian Messenger*. In August, Golovnin transferred two of his 'best' censors, Rakhmaninoff and de Robert, to Moscow, where Rakhmaninoff assumed responsibility for *Day* and was to elicit loud complaints of heavy-handedness from Aksakov. In October, Golovnin sent Tsee to Moscow to stress further that the censorship committee must enforce stricter limits.[48]

Golovnin's stand against the three publications suspended in June fit into his long-term plans for censorship reform. All three editors' demands for change only angered officials and undermined Golovnin's efforts to establish a new judicial system of controls. He made that very point in refusing a request by the editor of the official *War Veteran* to publish petitions from Finland seeking a new monetary system, abolition of censorship there, and a distinctive Finnish flag. Each censorship 'mistake,' he stressed, 'will leave its mark on the new statute.'[49]

In August, Golovnin gave another reason for shaping a congenial press. He stressed to Tsee the need 'to improve our credit in Europe' through articles in unofficial periodicals on such stabilizing measures as the naming of investigating commissions, the closing of the Sunday Schools and Chess Clubs, and the suspending of *Contemporary* and *Russian Word*. To Alexander Golovnin explained that the unofficial press could well persuade Europe that Russia was rapidly developing her intellectual and material forces and enjoying strong popular support.[50] At the same time, he argued that the unofficial press could ring true only if it expressed some criticism of the existing order.

IV

During the crisis months of April and May and on through the summer, the Obolensky commission had proceeded with drafting proposals for the new censorship statute. In mid-September, Golovnin informed Obolensky that Alexander wished to present those proposals to the Council of Ministers in December and learned that the commission hoped to complete its work by the end of October.[51] It missed that goal by a month, and the delay coincided with growing evidence of unrest in Poland during what proved to be the prelude to the uprising there in 1863.

Golovnin had fielded criticism of his policies all year, but by December he had lost the emperor's full backing. For example, when Gorchakov, the foreign minister, in November blamed political cartoons lampooning statesmen of friendly powers for harming Russia's foreign relations, Golovnin sent Alexander a letter arguing that 'caricatures' showed political maturity and distracted Russian readers from 'internal events'; the emperor merely noted on the letter's margin: 'the opposite of that everywhere.'[52]

Mounting disapproval of Golovnin culminated in the draft proposals completed by the Obolensky commission by the end of November. Apparently taking Golovnin by surprise, the commission recommended the transfer of all censorship authority to the Ministry of the Interior. Even Golovnin's right-hand man, Tsee, agreed to that transfer; for when Golovnin in December drafted a report to the emperor arguing that Public Education could best administer preliminary censorship, Tsee scrawled a note on the back which said in part, 'I came to the conclusion that the Ministry of Public Education ought not to keep censorship.'[53]

The Obolensky report in nearly every other respect complied with Golovnin's March directives to the commission, and the commissioners apparently agreed that a free press should evolve in Russia as it had in Europe. They recommended an end to preliminary censorship for all official and academic publications (confirming an accomplished fact), as well as for all books over 320 pages and certain journals approved by the minister of the interior (the report assigned all authority to Valuev). Granting responsibility to all the press had to await the new court system and other liberal institutions, argued the commission. 'Full freedom of the press, in the sense in which it is understood in the principal states of Europe, has developed gradually and alongside other free institutions as a seemingly necessary accompaniment ... and any attempt to violate this connection by separate liberal reforms seems bankrupt.'[54]

As for the transfer of censorship powers, the commission contended that only the Ministry of the Interior could provide the 'unity' and 'independence that censorship had lacked for twenty years.'[55] The report criticized the existing division of authority and argued that an earlier experience in shared authority – that by the 1859 Committee on Press Affairs and the Ministry of Public Education's censorship administration – had failed. In so saying, the commission rejected Golovnin's argument in March that the division of censorship between the two ministries rightly separated preliminary censorship, with its educational goals, from the enforcement of printing-press and bookselling regulations.

Although Golovnin had read three hundred pages of the still-incomplete report in November and had promised Obolensky that he would endorse the finished draft, the minister must not have known about the transfer proposal until he received the full report in early December.[56]

He suggested as much when he said that the commission had 'independently' reached its conclusions and he therefore had the right to disapprove their draft. By that stand, Golovnin hoped to prevent the transfer of censorship authority to Interior.

On 10 December Golovnin reported to the emperor that the Obolensky proposals were an exaggerated response to the events of 1862 and were unsuitable for calmer times. Censorship by the Ministry of the Interior would only inflame relations between the government and loyal journalists.[57] The Ministry of Public Education, rather, could best conduct relations with the press.

One proof of Golovnin's arguments was a compilation of articles he published in 1862 to show that, under his administration, press support for the government had increased. This was the *Short Outline* (*Kratkoe Obozrenie*), about which Lemke remarks: 'Golovnin tried [in it] to underline the gratitude of literature and journalism and draw off the thunder repeatedly let loose against both not only by Valuev but also by many other high bureaucrats, especially Panin and Chevkin.'[58] The minister sent this publication to Alexander on 9 December.

Although the *Short Outline* appeared anonymously under the imprint of the ministry, this internal document was the work of a single editor – P.I. Kapnist, who earlier had won the gratitude of the press for his flexibility as a censor. Kapnist included some material from *Contemporary* but more from such moderate, pro-government papers as Usov's *Northern Bee*. In his own commentary, Kapnist praised the press for providing an alert and expanding reading public with information on a broad range of affairs. Journalists, he said, regularly gave proper credit to the throne for advances, and the positive guidance of censorship had virtually eliminated so pernicious a subject as 'communism,' as well as corrosive polemics on the peasant question, the gentry, and the principles of monarchy.[59]

On 14 December Golovnin sent Alexander another argument against the transfer of censorship powers – a report by his vice-minister, Baron A.P. Nikolai. Alexander found it useful but doubted that the Council of Ministers would reject the Obolensky commission proposals. Unfortunately for Golovnin, Ivan Aksakov somehow obtained a copy of the Obolensky report and criticized it in *Day* on 22 December. His objection to granting too much power over the press to the Minister of the Interior could not have helped Golovnin.[60]

Obolensky pointedly rebutted the Nikolai report and protested to the emperor and then to Valuev on 25 December that Golovnin had out-

rageously betrayed the commission.[61] Alexander thereupon counselled
Golovnin that he could best serve the throne by giving up his authority
over censorship in order to concentrate on educational reform. Because
he could gracefully bow to an imperial request and still oppose the
report, Golovnin finally agreed to divest his ministry of censorship
powers. In January 1863 Golovnin himself proposed to transfer the
entire censorship apparatus and the work of the Obolensky commission
to the Ministry of the Interior,[62] although he hoped to continue to
influence publishing by issuing books for peasants and placing articles in
the unofficial press. The transfer took place in March.

Writing later in his memoirs, Golovnin concluded that outside events
had done much to defeat his liberal policies in 1862: 'If everything had
remained calm, if there had not been embarrassing outbursts from journalism, from the student youth, if there had not been criminal attempts
at revolutionary propaganda, and finally, the open rebellion of the Poles
at that very time when previously unheard-of compromises and concessions had been granted [under Golovnin's mentor, the viceroy of Poland,
the Grand Duke Constantine] – [my] administration in the Ministry of
Public Education would have continued and would have attained some
results on the road to freedom, latitude, and legality.'[63]

Golovnin, the moderate, saw himself caught between the millstones of
radical dissent and official counter-measures. But to many he appeared
too idealistic and insufficiently hard-headed, as did his principal supporter, the Grand Duke, whose compromising ways many officials
(Valuev included) blamed as a cause of unrest in Poland. Full-scale
insurrection broke out there in January 1863. Both for Golovnin and for
Constantine, the events of 1862 had proved unmanageable.

Another of Golovnin's disappointments was the defection of Tsee. Late
in December, Golovnin attempted to persuade Tsee to stay with his
ministry should its censorship authority be transferred, contending that
Tsee did not share Valuev's political views. If Tsee would accept a position on the Chief Administration of Schools, Golovnin promised that his
old friend could travel to the cities of Russia on inspection tours of universities and secondary schools and maintain contact with local writers.
The Ministry of Public Education, vowed Golovnin, 'will always have
good relations with writers.'[64]

Tsee instead chose to remain chairman of the St Petersburg Censorship
Committee and seemingly allied himself with Valuev's policies. Even
before the transfer, for example, three of Tsee's censors in February
favoured a bid by D.F. Shcheglov to comment somewhat favourably

about Herzen in a review of press remarks about the émigré critic in *Library for Readers*. The best answer to public scepticism about the spontaneity of the press attacks on Herzen, argued Shcheglov, 'is an article showing that it is possible to speak favourably about Herzen at a time when he does not deserve it.' In a letter to Tsee, Shcheglov said that his journal wanted to repudiate dangerous ideas, but, unless it granted some justice to Herzen's views, *Library* would lose credibility. 'We are not a government journal and we cannot turn ourselves into government agents.' Although the argument coincided with the stand of both Golovnin and Tsee in 1862, Tsee refused Shcheglov's request. All the same, Tsee lost his post in April when Valuev fired him over the publication in Dostoevsky's *Time* of a controversial article on the Polish question.[65]

Golovnin had become minister of public education in December 1861 because Alexander had decided to try a more liberal approach to censorship. Sections of the press welcomed Golovnin's overtures, but those journalists bent on bringing about radical changes assumed that Alexander II and his minister were yielding to social pressures beyond their control. Events from late February onward in turn caused many officials to link radical writings and incipient political activity, whether by the liberal gentry or the revolutionaries. Capitalizing on the misgivings of Alexander II about Golovnin's handling of censorship issues as the internal crisis mounted, Valuev won his campaign to transfer all censorship authority to his ministry. As 1863 began, a minister who saw the press as a disruptive force in an absolutist state assumed responsibility for a new censorship statute. Valuev, moreover, was prepared to deal more firmly with the radicals.

9

The reform of 6 April 1865

Views on what role the legal unofficial press should play under an absolutist government came forward often as the Obolensky commission completed its second draft of proposals for a new censorship statute in 1863. Some imperial officials saw forthright journalists as informants about the public mood; others linked 'freedom of expression' with the success of such 'free institutions' as the impending new courts. Opinions like these implied a willingness to yield new latitude to journalists and writers, and reflected a mood of confidence and sense of a 'coming of age' that buoyed the government in 1863 and 1864 and tended to promote a bona fide reform of censorship practices.

Restraints came from those who saw risks in granting too much freedom to the press – among them, Minister of the Interior Valuev. While he recognized that the press must have a broader role in Imperial Russia, Valuev deeply distrusted journalists. To prevent them from manipulating concessions from the government to promote dangerous political ideas, he intended to secure effective means to limit periodicals that obeyed the letter but not the spirit of the law. Valuev favoured, finally, the administrative controls then in use in France – the warning system that would enable the government to grant a large measure of press freedom while reserving expeditious means to strike at 'dangerously oriented' publications.

I

To the immense satisfaction of the government, press opinion strongly supported the repression of the Polish insurrection in 1863. Particularly notable were the nationalistic articles of Aksakov's *Day* and Katkov's daily *Moscow Bulletin* and monthly *Russian Messenger*. These publications renounced rebellion and opposed any compromise with the Poles, as did broad sections of the general population.[1] Alexander had hoped to stir just such spontaneous support through his reforms; and, given this surge of positive opinion in 1863, he and many officials saw the political threat from the radical journals diminish to manageable proportions. Ivan Goncharov, the novelist, who had become a member of the new Council of the Ministry of the Interior for Publishing Affairs in March 1862, was one such official. He argued that the inherently rational public, after hearing all views, would remain staunchly loyal to the emperor. Goncharov saw full exposure of the ideas of the radical press as the best means of discrediting them.

While nationalistic indignation over the Polish insurrection remained high, Goncharov assessed censorship practices during 1863 for fellow council members. He urged toleration for the 'continual [but] for the most part, minor violations of the censorship rules' by *Day*'s staff, which stemmed 'partly from passion, partly from a visionary desire to realize its favourite ideas of Slavic nationality, and partly from youthful impetuosity.' (Goncharov well knew that Aksakov's patriotism, so welcome on the Polish issue, frequently led to demands for civil liberties, including freedom of the press, that infuriated officials from the emperor on down.) In turn, Goncharov advocated calculated tolerance for *Contemporary*, which, with censorship approval, had published during March, April, and May 1863, the novel written by Chernyshevsky in prison, *What Is To Be Done?*, a nihilistic attack on traditional values. Such a work should appear, argued Goncharov, because it effectively turned most readers against nihilism and exposed the 'absurdity of [Chernyshevsky's] ideas.'[2]

Dissatisfaction with Goncharov's liberalism was to surface in a memorandum by a council colleague, O.A. Przhetslavsky, late in 1864, even though the primary target was editor Michael Katkov.[3] Przhetslavsky argued that an absolute monarch cannot tolerate a disquieting novel like Chernyshevsky's; nor should the emperor, he continued, permit an editor to parlay strong support for government policies into a virtually invulnerable journalistic position, as had Katkov. Whenever he chose, Katkov could independently challenge the autocracy's rightful domination over public opinion.

Przhetslavsky found proof for his charges in Katkov's attacks on Golovnin. Initially, in 1862 and 1863, Katkov had criticized the policies of the Grand Duke Constantine as viceroy of Poland. In response,

Golovnin had supplied materials to Baron F.I. Firks (a Belgian agent of the Ministry of Finance who wrote under the pseudonym N.K. Schedo-Ferroti) for a pamphlet published in Brussels to defend the Grand Duke. Firks's pamphlet also attacked Katkov for 'cultivating nationalistic vanity and plumbing the nasty instincts of the literary plebeians.' Golovnin secured 1,000 copies of the pamphlet, 'Que veut-on de Pologne?' and, in the fall of 1864, had his ministry distribute them to educational institutions.[4] Upon learning of Golovnin's manoeuvre, Katkov early that September wrote an article charging Golovnin with 'duplicity.' He also accused the minister of opportunism; for, some months before, Golovnin had, he said, urged him to publish a pamphlet of his articles which completely opposed Firks's views on the Polish question. Katkov told of Golovnin's offer to buy 12,000 of the proposed pamphlets for distribution to educational institutions, an offer Katkov said he refused.[5]

On 10 September the Council for Publishing Affairs discussed Katkov's attack. The next day, on behalf of the emperor, State Secretary Butkov wrote Golovnin to ask if the charges were true, and Golovnin sent a full account of his actions to the State Council. On 19 September, Alexander informed Golovnin that Firks's pamphlet failed to reflect the 'views of the government.' When Golovnin apologized and offered his resignation, however, Alexander told him to keep his place.[6]

These events lay behind the November 15 memorandum by Przhetslavsky labelling Katkov's influence an 'anomaly in the general order of our state.' Valuev, agreeing with Przhetslavsky, invited Katkov to St Petersburg, hoping to persuade the editor to practice restraint. When Valuev alluded to the possible loss of the right to publish, Katkov responded that he would rather give up journalism than yield to threats.[7]

Before the year ended, Valuev took part in a review by the Committee of Ministers of a petition from officials at Moscow University requesting the right to assume censorship authority over Katkov's *Moscow Bulletin*. The committee declined to make this exception to regular procedures but used the opportunity to praise Katkov's paper for its patriotism and 'very important services.' Among the champions of Katkov were Minister of War Miliutin and Minister of Foreign Affairs Gorchakov.[8] The committee as a whole advised Valuev to ease his censorship of *Moscow Bulletin*. Similarly, the assembly of Moscow gentry, on 5 January 1865, endorsed the work of Katkov and his co-editor, Leontiev.

On 14 January the Council for Publishing Affairs finally considered the memorandum from Przhetslavsky and rejected his proposal that Katkov be disciplined. Goncharov voted with the majority and, in filing the opinion required of each council member, warmly praised Katkov's contributions. Vigorous expressions of opinion, he argued, benefitted the Russian autocracy, which had rightly encouraged debate on the judicial, peasant, and educational reforms.[9]

As 1865 began, Goncharov's remarks represented a majority opinion that the government need not over-react to publications outspoken in a good cause. At the same time, Katkov's successes rested on the journalistic strategy first exploited by Bulgarin under Nicholas: the editor or journalist who strongly approved in print the policies and philosophy of the government could command special favour from the censors.

II

Meanwhile Valuev had proceeded with censorship reform, having secured the transfer of its administration from the Ministry of Public Education to his own Ministry of the Interior. Well aware that all ministers of public education under Alexander had come to grief over censorship, Valuev faulted Golovnin, in particular, for having been so naïvely solicitous to journalists, initially even to the most radical ones. Alexander had muddled policy, as well, by broadening discussion and then irritably narrowing it when commentaries went beyond the bounds he intended but had not defined. Most recently, the emperor had permitted an editor he valued – Katkov – to set a bad example by exceeding the limits Valuev intended to enforce. In Valuev's view, the government should in no way mislead journalists to presume too much.

By the fall of 1864, Valuev had in hand his draft of the proposed statute that would, he felt, equip him to control the press satisfactorily. In the debate that would lead to ratification, Valuev had essentially three aims: (1) to show the need for administrative weapons against radical elements in the press; (2) to ensure himself, as minister of the interior, full authority over those administrative measures; and (3) to insist on enough liberal concessions to justify labelling the new statute a reform.

The proposed statute was primarily the work of the 'second' Obolensky commission. The 'first' commission had written a draft for Golovnin; the second commission under the same chairman but with new members had begun writing a draft for Valuev in March 1863.

Obolensky had told his second commission at the outset of its work that the new statute would have to dismantle preliminary censorship by freeing specific categories of publications in stages and spelling out the 'prosecuting legislation and ... police rules' to govern them. What resulted was their draft of May 1863. It proposed freeing all monthly journals in Moscow and St Petersburg and only those dailies and weeklies approved by the minister of the interior.[10] To counteract any 'dangerous orientation' in freed publications, the draft proposed administrative penalties borrowed from the French, a system imposed in part in 1862 by Golovnin and Valuev. Periodicals charged under that French warning system could suffer fines, suspensions, or even closure.

The commission in turn proposed freedom for all books over twenty signatures (320 pages) and for those already exempt from censorship (government publications, scholarly studies by the universities and academies, and works in Greek and Latin). It left somewhat ambiguous who was to initiate judicial prosecution against persons whose printed works violated imperial law, but the commission favoured the creation in Moscow and St Petersburg of special criminal courts with juries (as an interim measure until the new courts designed by the judicial reform were functioning).[11]

While recommending its proposals as 'transitional' and 'temporary,' the commission assumed that the new statute would continue in effect well beyond the creation of the first new courts in the two capitals in 1866 (no time had been set for transforming the courts elsewhere). The commission also expected revisions in the statute once the new courts began to try cases involving the press.

With a group of advisors, including Obolensky, Valuev himself made minor adjustments in the commission's proposals in October 1863. Then he circulated the project for comment from officials and members of the State Council in advance of formal deliberations. Golovnin sent the earliest written response on 7 December 1863. The minister of education, from whom Valuev had wrested censorship authority, merely reviewed his own earlier efforts towards improving press policy. 'The end in view,' he emphasized, 'consisted in gradually introducing a broad measure of freedom of the printed word when offenses would be punished by the courts and more and more arbitrariness would be eliminated from the censorship.'[12]

Baron M.A. Korf, as head of the Second (legal) Section of his Majesty's Own Chancellery, also responded. In his commentary, dated 7 February 1864, Korf opposed the statute altogether. Once created, the new courts could alone oversee the press; for, Korf argued, emancipation had proved that Russia could move rapidly to reform without social upheaval. Like other modern states, Russia needed freedom of opinion: 'Legislative and normal administrative activity require a constant infusion of information for their successful outcome ... but this assistance can come only from a free press, openly expressing the real thoughts and feelings of society.' As for the project circulated by Valuev, Korf preferred freeing all books of ten or more printed signatures, or one-third of the books published in Russia (the draft set a minimum of twenty signatures, or one-seventh of published books). He also opposed requiring periodicals to submit deposits against possible fines and disagreed that the minister of the interior should have final authority in censorship matters.[13]

D.N. Zamiatnin, the minister of justice, similarly expressed his disapproval of any censorship statute on 13 March. He argued that the code being formulated by the Ministry of Justice comprehended all the crimes which persons using the printed word or any other means might commit. The government, he continued, should end preliminary censorship and subject to judicial prosecution all persons whose words violated the criminal code.[14] Zamiatnin also opposed interim courts, arguing that they had been proposed by administrators wholly unqualified in matters of law.

A month later, on 9 April, former Minister of Justice V.N. Panin succeeded Korf as head of the Second Section. Under Panin's supervision, the Second Section discussed the Obolensky proposals from 25 May to 18 June. In his commentary, dated 19 September, Panin disagreed with Korf by favouring the dual system of administrative and legal controls proposed by Valuev. Further, he held that deposits against possible fines under the warning system were necessary.[15]

III

When Valuev officially submitted the Obolensky project to the State Council on 17 November 1864 (three days before the announcement of the judicial reform), the commentaries attached included those of Golovnin, Korf, Zamiatnin, and Panin. Valuev also appended his own commentary, mostly in answer to Korf. The minister opposed freeing more books from preliminary censorship and insisted on deposits. While agreeing in principle with many of Korf's arguments, Valuev called for gradual liberation and transitional administrative measures.[16]

That Valuev, in the name of reform, intended even more rigorous press controls emerges from his budgetary requests submitted with the Obolensky project to the State Council that November. Assuming that the project would become law, Valuev asked to add eight more to his seventy-seven-man senior censorship staff. He also wanted the head of the new Chief Administration of Press Affairs to have a high service rank. Reviewing past costs, Valuev listed the 1860 censorship budget at 163,640 rubles, and that of 1863 at 187,740 rubles (including 11,800 rubles for supervising printing plants). For 1865, he requested 219,500 rubles plus funds for printing plant supervision. The workload of the censorship system justified the increases, said Valuev, for periodicals had increased from 251 to 301 in a few years, with 70 of these publishing 'political' sections. Finally, to soften the blow to the treasury, Valuev proposed a new stamp tax on periodicals.[17]

Having made his requests, Valuev could only await the decision of the State Council. Before it acted, the council's Department of Laws was to evaluate the Obolensky draft and recommend any changes favoured by a majority, and the council's Combined Departments on the State Economy and Laws was to recommend action on the budgetary proposals.

Just two days before the Department of Laws began deliberations, Zamiatnin made a last-ditch appeal for ending censorship altogether when the new courts came into being. In a statement of 14 January 1865, he again argued that transitional courts could not handle press cases. Rather, reformed courts and a press acting on its own responsibility would support each other and should emerge simultaneously. Zamiatnin objected to more in the proposed statute than the interim courts, however. He again disapproved the 'mixing of police and judicial powers, which had been recognized as dangerous and due for abolition'; and he specifically opposed the commission's assigning independent authority to the police to impose penalties on printing plants, bookstores, and the like for violations of procedural laws.[18] Because the circuit court would review appeals challenging police enforcement of those laws, the police would in effect be quasi-judicial officers.

Zamiatnin also opposed raising the educational and property qualifications for jurors in cases concerning printed words. That move by the commission, as their recorded discussions showed, said Zamiatnin, was made to provide a conservative check on judges, who were expected to be from social groups 'where progressive elements are concentrated.' Brusquely professing to have more faith in judges than did the commission, Zamiatnin conceded that jurors should have at least a secondary education to qualify them to serve in cases involving the press.[19]

On 16, 20, 21, and 23 January came the first phase of the review of the proposed statute by the Department of Laws. On the third day, Valuev lamented in his diary: 'The same as yesterday: the improbably pseudo-liberal aspirations of almost all members to disarm the government against the press. Golovnin and Korf spoke about newspapers as though they were the *Iliad*. I alone support the project.' Only two days later the department voted on its proposed changes in the project as a whole, and a dramatic shift in opinion had taken place. In Valuev's words on 23 January: 'The main thing won despite the composition of the meeting and various attempts to introduce real changes in the project.'[20]

The 'real changes' were proposals to limit Valuev's power. Nikitenko, who favoured such changes, noted with despair that the department had at first undertaken to 'limit the unlimited authority of the minister of the interior by correcting many deficiencies in the project only to end with full agreement on it.' Nikitenko strongly blamed Korf for repudiating – just when is not clear – his counter-proposals of the previous February. According to Nikitenko, Norov had also presented a memorandum, prepared with Nikitenko's help, much along the lines of Korf's February submission; but Valuev had triumphed.[21]

A strong voice against the role set forth for Valuev in the project was that of Miliutin, the minister of war. While objecting that he and other ministers had no role in censorship matters whatever, Miliutin mainly argued for establishing censorship policy through 'collegiality,' or decision making by a council presiding over censorship functions. (He had in mind the new Council of the Chief Administration of Press Affairs to be named under the statute – the successor to the Council of the Ministry of the Interior for Publishing Affairs, which had merely advised Valuev.) In addition, Miliutin objected that the project did not clearly differentiate offenses subject to prosecution from those subject to administrative penalties. If the performance of the courts displeased the minister of the interior, the project empowered him to use administrative measures instead, however arbitrarily.[22]

With respect to warnings, fines, and suspensions (but not closures), Korf, Golovnin, and Zamiatnin – surprisingly enough – joined Valuev and four others (F.P. Litke, Dolgorukov, N.I. Bakhtin, and Butkov) in upholding the project. Decisiveness, they argued, required vesting responsibility for this area in a single person, the minister. A collegial system would lead to disputes between the minister and the council which higher authorities would have to arbitrate.[23]

The project also gave the minister of the interior, through a vaguely worded paragraph, what Valuev interpreted as sole authority to initiate court cases for press crimes. Zamiatnin opposed this interpretation as an infringement on his own powers; and Panin, as head of the Second Section, agreed in a submission to the State Council: 'A court which produces sentences only on the crimes which are specified by a certain branch of the administration stops being a direct enforcer of the law.'[24] On this crucial question of jurisdiction, Zamiatnin failed to sway a majority on the council to recommend a change.

The department favoured few changes in the proposed statute, but the most significant one was transferring closure power from the minister of the interior to the First Department of the Senate. It also deleted penalty-imposing powers for the police and substituted existing courts for the proposed special interim courts. Thus could Valuev exult on 23 January that 'the various attempts to introduce real changes into the project' had failed.[25] The department was to meet again in March, however, before sending the project to the General Assembly.

IV

In February, the Combined Departments on the State Economy and Laws of the State Council reviewed Valuev's budgetary requests. Given the low state of the treasury (which was prompting efforts to sell Alaska), the combined departments favoured an allocation of only 189,710 rubles for 1865, salaries at 1860 levels for censors, and a lesser rank than requested for the head of the Chief Administration. Nor did the department favour a stamp tax. Valuev had wanted it both to offset censorship costs and to discourage radically-inclined publications (the tax would increase subscription costs). Both Reutern, the minister of finance, and I. Tolstoy, the head of the Post Office, had earlier told Valuev they opposed such a tax.[26]

On 10 and 13 March the Department of Laws met for final action on the proposed censorship statute. The minority who had favoured 'collegiality' in January, led by Miliutin, had lined up three more supporters and, with them, passed the recommendation that the minister share authority with the Council of the Chief Administration of Press Affairs to decide when to warn, fine, or suspend periodicals and when to initiate judicial prosecution. The Committee of Ministers would settle disputes.[27]

Miliutin had also swung sufficient votes in this session to win approval for his unsuccessful January proposal to free from preliminary censorship in the two capitals all books having ten, rather than twenty, signatures. Very significantly, however, the department at the same time recommended including the surrogate form of preliminary censorship proposed to the Obolensky commission by Golovnin in March 1862 requiring that censors inspect all books and journals freed from preliminary censorship during a brief pre-circulation waiting period and that they inspect each newspaper issue as its circulation began. (This transitional measure, which did become part of the new statute, gave the government a means to discover blatantly unacceptable works before or as they reached the public. It differed from preliminary censorship in that material would come before the censors in printed, not manuscript, form.) To clarify the precise length of books to be freed from censorship, the department defined a signature as sixteen pages in octavo. With respect to the freeing of periodicals in the two capitals, a majority wanted all of them (not just dailies and weeklies) to obtain permission to publish from the Minister of the Interior.[28]

Two weeks later, on 24 March, the conservatively-minded General Assembly of the State Council considered the changes proposed by its two subcommittees. In debating the proposals from its Department of Laws, the Assembly rejected the one most odious to Valuev: that the minister share his censorship authority. It did so by placing the Chief Administration (composed of its head and council) 'under the higher supervision of the minister.' A jubilant Valuev recorded that, after the first vote had gone his way, the 'opposition gave up, feeling that all was lost,' so that the 'other votes' showed significant majorities on my side.[29]

The 'other votes' included the budget cuts by the Combined Departments on the State Economy and Laws. The General Assembly rejected economizing and granted Valuev his full request, stipulating that he return in three years with new proposals. That same day Valuev told Troinitsky, his deputy, 'Everything has passed: the warning without the vote [of the council], 28–11; the [increase in] staff, 28–11, the rank of the head [of the Chief Administration], 24–14.'[30]

Each step of the way, the administrative-judicial measures favoured by Valuev had undergone full discussion and debate, and the minister had won almost all that he wanted from a strong majority of the state's highest consultative body. (His only major losses were the freeing of books of ten or more rather than twenty or more signatures and the vesting of authority to close periodicals in the Senate rather than the minister – changes included in the statute when it was voted upon and passed as a whole.) Of little concern to him were the concessions to Zamiatnin – the ommission of interim courts and special qualifications for jurors in press cases.

During debates, critics had pointed to the power of the minister of the interior to limit or even eliminate the judiciary's authority over press crimes, so that no one listening could mistake the 'temporary' statute of

1865 as an all-out reform. The best the many reformist officials could hope for was a period of good relations between the government and the press that would justify a new statute making the courts wholly responsible for keeping printed content lawful. In fact, the 'temporary' Statute of 1865 was to stand until 1905.

Journalists also widely aired their opinions about the new censorship laws both during their formulation and after the new statute had been publicly announced. Golovnin had invited commentary early in 1862, and an informed press discussion had continued even after Valuev had become responsible for censorship in 1863. Almost unanimously, the press opposed the administrative penalties identified with the French Second Empire, the system proposed by the Obolensky commission and finally confirmed as a part of the Statute of 1865. Pisarev in *Russian Word*, Chernyshevsky in *Contemporary*, the Dostoevskys in *Time*, Aksakov in *Day*, V.D. Skariatin in *Notes of the Fatherland*, and Katkov in *Moscow Bulletin* – all had declared the warning system of Louis Napoleon unsuitable for Russia.[31]

Among the writers who disingenuously opposed administrative controls by arguing that the press did not shape public opinion were Chernyshevsky and writers for *Time* and *Moscow Bulletin*. Such others as Pisarev, Aksakov, D. Puzanov, and Skariatin held that free discussion positively channelled ideas and stirred what Aksakov called 'social creativity.' Some counselled the government that it must grant a free press to promote citizen participation in public life and a wider culture because, inevitably, Russia would have to modernize along European lines.[32]

Opinions on the role of jurists included calls for special courts (Aksakov), use of the regular courts alone to oversee the press (*Time* and Skariatin), and the writing of moderately restrictive laws to equip the courts to act alone (Katkov, Zarin, Nelishchev).[33] At least two writers alluded to the failure of the existing censorship system to satisfy the government (Shcheglov and Zarin) and one openly held that the new legislation might prove a setback for the press. *Contemporary* writers urged that legal responsibility for a periodical fall solely on the publisher and that illegal commentary in print be grounds for prosecution only if it had reached the public.[34]

V

The Council of State issued the Statute of 1865 in a ukaz dated 6 April, published 15 April, and designated effected on 1 September. Accompanying that document was a personal decree of the emperor freeing from preliminary censorship on 1 September those publications eligible under the new regulations.[35]

The new regulations included five sections. The first assigned all censorship matters, except ecclesiastical, to the Chief Administration of Press Affairs in the Ministry of the Interior, described the hierarchy of officials and committees, and assigned responsibilities to each. Section two defined periodical publications and the procedures they must follow in order to function, required copies of all publications from printing plants, and outlined administrative penalties. Section three laid down rules for printing plants and bookstores. Procedures for initiating court cases against published works appeared in section four; and here, too, the government set forth 'crimes' which persons could commit only by means of making words public in print or on stage. Finally, section five detailed the rules for plays and required preliminary censorship of all those to be performed or published.

All parts of the statute which the courts would enforce were to become articles of the criminal code then being updated (the revised code would appear in 1866). In the meantime, several press cases would go forward in the courts, and the prosecutor would necessarily cite the alleged wrong-doings as violations of specific articles in the censorship statute.

This new statute, having first been secretly called for in 1858 by the emperor himself to permit press discussion of government policy, had come to include a cut-back in preliminary censorship and the introduction of the courts as joint-overseers of the press. It had emerged, finally, as the most methodically-prepared, broadly discussed, comprehensive, and centralizing press law in the history of the state.

'Western' both in content and in the mode of its drafting, the censorship statute of 1865 also owed much to the judicial reform of 1864, which is usually regarded as the most European of the great reforms. Not only did the judicial reform announce a new legal order – one in which the press could reasonably expect to share – but it also indirectly expanded press coverage of government affairs by opening certain trials to the public. Moreover, the fact that the legal reformers favoured publicity (glasnost) about trials helped justify granting a continued discussion of official questions under the new censorship statute.

Although the government's tolerance level for political discussions had risen and fallen time and again in the half century since the first censorship statute of 1804, the law of 1865 was to permit many within the ranks of the press to discuss official and social issues on their own responsibility. (The debate on the statute had concerned the extent of the discussion, not whether it would take place.) Relief from the petty bother of preliminary censorship meant, for most, the boon of publishing more expeditiously. For the few who would use their new freedom to publish writings unacceptable to the state, administrative and judicial penalties awaited.

Assessing the statute as a whole, Ivan Aksakov welcomed it with 'true gratitude.'[36] He took the government at its word that it intended to give the press the advantage as far as possible and that the temporary regulations were a transition to measures granting even more freedom. Ironically, among those relatively few journalists who were to suffer administrative penalties in the final half of the sixties, Aksakov would be the editor most frequently and most severely punished.

10

The first year of
the reformed system, 1865–66

In administering the Statute of 1865, Minister of the Interior Valuev sought to counteract the encouragement given to writers and publishers by their newly-extended and untested 'legal' rights. One drawback of his having to rely largely on post-publication measures, however, was that outspoken journalists thrived on testing limits in full view of the public; another was that the government had far less latitude in warning or suspending a journal for its 'dangerous orientation' when its contents were widely known.

Court cases heightened the government's accountability and vulnerability, for the accused journalist enjoyed an open court in which to defend himself, while his allegedly criminal work remained free to circulate, except in extraordinary circumstances, pending the court's decision. Publication of the court proceedings themselves had also become legal. Yet another issue was whether to try staff members of an offending periodical for violating the law or to issue them an administrative warning. To the dismay of the Ministry of Justice, the censorship administration alone made the distinction.

I

The Statute of 1865 had created entirely new conditions for publishing in Imperial Russia, for it granted for the first time an element of press freedom. But even as it shifted some authority over the press to the courts, it gave very strong powers to censors, who could interfere in the publishing and distribution processes as a means of fighting radical periodicals. Thus had Russia both eased and tightened controls over the press in the same legislative act. And it had done so by copying from the West not only freedom of the press but also certain counter-measures to check what the government viewed as abuses of that freedom.

Eight days before the new law took effect, Valuev confidentially instructed his censors about their new duties. According to his guidelines of 23 August, censors who found published words which clearly violated criminal law were to forward them to a superior for possible prosecution in the courts. Censors were also to assess the orientation of each publication, the motives of its writers, and the probable response of its readers. 'Distinctly repetitive' patterns of writing which hinted at radical ideas justified a warning. Six days later, Valuev similarly explained to Minister of Justice Zamiatnin that censors would use warnings against periodicals whose words were dangerous but fell short of violating criminal law. His aim was the 'elimination of those organs whose orientation proves to be immediately dangerous.'[1]

Writing in May 1865 about the new law, Nikitenko had rightly speculated that Valuev had an 'enormous plan' to use 'freedom' to keep the press in line: 'Publishers were somewhat freed from responsibility under [the censor's] shield. Now this is not so. There is no censorship [for freed periodicals]. Over the heads of writers and editors hangs a sword of Damocles in the form of two warnings and a third, which is followed by closing. This sword is in the hand of the minister; he wields it when it pleases him, and he will not have to explain his action.' Nikitenko sympathized with those journalists in St Petersburg who had taken the 'reasonable position' of preferring to remain under preliminary censorship (the statute gave them a choice) and deplored that Valuev could close a periodical for so undefined an offense as a 'dangerous orientation.' (A writer for Valuev's daily paper, the *Northern Post*, was to admit editorially in 1867: 'Since there is no possibility of even approximately defining dangerous orientation, it is more appropriate, open, and fitting not to mask the law in an artificial form of definitiveness.')[2]

The publications targeted by Valuev were few in number, however, given the more than three hundred periodicals printed in the Russian Empire in the second half of the nineteenth century. To be precise, in 1865 and 1866, Valuev issued sixteen warnings to six publications (two journals and four newspapers). Similarly, the thirty-two additional warnings in the next thirty-eight months went to only two journals and eleven newspapers. (See table 5.) The particulars of those warnings and their allusive charges strongly suggest that Valuev first decided which periodicals were dangerous and then devised grounds to act against them.

Backed by the Council of the Chief Administration of Press Affairs (the successor to the old Council of the Ministry of the Interior for Publishing Affairs), Valuev issued the first warning under the new statute to the *St Petersburg Bulletin* two days after an article on 18 September suggested that, by mortgaging state property, the government had raised doubts that it could honour its five per cent bank notes. The warning cited the *Bulletin* for undermining public confidence in government paper.[3] Although 'undermining confidence in the government' was grounds for prosecution, the council probably doubted that the evidence – the article itself – could support a conviction in court.

Two months later came the next warning, issued to *Contemporary* on 10 November for several articles in August and September. Among them were 'New Times,' which seemed to advocate free love, and 'Notes of a Contemporary,' which suggested that capitalist exploiters had kept workers from sharing the wealth they created.[4] Four of the six members of the council saw grounds for a court case, but Valuev decided to issue a warning.

Ivan Goncharov, whose favourable survey of Russian publishing in 1863 has already been discussed, was one member fairly often at odds with Valuev. When Valuev advocated a warning for *Day*'s first issue after the statute took effect, for example, Goncharov successfully argued that an article criticizing the rigid stratification and great differences in wealth among monasteries was accurate and therefore conformed with the new statute. (All concern about *Day* was shortly to end, however, for Aksakov announced he would cease publication at the close of 1865.) During November, Goncharov vainly opposed a second warning to *Contemporary* for its October issue, arguing that the Chief Administration should wait for 'more tangible evidence.' The warning issued on 4 December condemned 'sympathetic remarks' on the fall of thrones and altars, and the ridicule of religion and law in an article linking Orthodoxy with the decaying culture of Byzantium.[5]

Three days before, on 1 December, the editor and publisher of the newspaper *Voice*, A.A. Kraevsky, had received his first warning for eight articles published over seven issues. Whereas the two warnings to *Contemporary* had detailed its errors, the warning to *Voice* merely generalized that its writers had improperly judged and censured governmental measures and officials and had manifested sympathy for persons who provoke the government.[6]

In this same final month of 1865, the St Petersburg Censorship Committee recommended a first warning to *Russian Word* for content in the

October issue, including Dmitry Pisarev's review of Chernyshevsky's *What Is To Be Done?* The editors, agreed Goncharov, cumulatively conveyed their intention of undermining public tranquility and morality.[7] A warning went forward on 20 December.

When a colleague called for a second warning to *Russian Word* in January 1866, based on an article by Pisarev in the November issue, Goncharov convinced the council to favour a court case. Pressed by Valuev, the council then reversed itself and agreed that, because Pisarev 'discusses Christianity in such a way that it is difficult to apply directly any article of the law, it is recognized as more convenient to give *Russian Word* a warning.' Valuev issued that warning on 8 January, condemning Pisarev's 'indirect attempt to give expression to the ideas of communism.' After seeing the journal's January issue, the council voted for a third warning for *Russian Word* – the final step to a temporary suspension. Several articles taken together, agreed Goncharov, showed that the editors sought to present themselves as 'ultra-liberal progressives.' On 16 February Valuev suspended *Russian Word* for five months.[8]

In these first months under the new statute, Valuev, in consultation with the council, initiated court cases as well. Because the statute set forth only the vague provision that the Chief Administration of Press Affairs was to initiate prosecutions 'when this was not done by subordinate authorities,' the emperor, at Valuev's request, had confirmed that sole authority rested with the Chief Administration (which the statute had placed 'under the higher supervision of the minister'). Therefore, on 29 August, 1865, two days before the new statute took effect, Valuev informed Minister of Justice Zamiatnin that the censorship administration in the Ministry of the Interior was to guide the procuracy of the Ministry of Justice (the prosecutor of all court cases) in government suits about printed works. The emperor, Valuev continued, had empowered the minister of justice to resolve any conflict between the administration and the procuracy or to refer the dispute to the Committee of Ministers.[9]

Until the new courts under the judicial reform came into being, prosecutions went forward in 'special sessions' of the old criminal courts, as the statute stipulated. Moreover, judicial procedures for press cases – very generally described in the statute – were to be formulated precisely only after the organization of the new courts.[10] Court cases in the interim proved to be something of a muddle. Those that did go forward, however, help explain why, within five years, the government virtually abandoned the courts as a means of curbing radical publications.

II

P.A. Bibikov, a retired army officer who prepared a small collection entitled *Critical Studies (1859–1865)* in an edition of 1,500 copies in St Petersburg in September 1865, was the subject of the first censorship trial. The publisher, I. Glazunov, submitted a copy to the St Petersburg Censorship Committee for the three-day pre-distribution holding period required under the new statute. The committee found objectionable material which would lead to a court case against Bibikov and permitted the book to circulate. Then, probably because pre-trial investigative procedures were as yet unwritten, the committee enlisted the police as investigators. The police stopped the sale of the book, searched Bibikov's apartment, and reported their findings to the prosecutor for the case, the procurator of the St Petersburg Criminal Court.[11]

The censorship committee charged Bibikov with promoting 'crude materialism' and 'undermining the doctrines of the Christian faith, distorting the principles of marriage and of the supreme authority, and, at the same time, advocating enthusiastically the dangerous doctrine of socialism.'[12] The prosecutor narrowed the charge to violation of the article in the April 6 statute prohibiting printed censure of the principles of the 'family with intent to undermine or weaken its foundations' (sec. 4, art. 9, para. 3, which set a fine of up to three hundred rubles or six weeks' imprisonment).

Bibikov's trial put in practice a principle central to the judicial reform but wholly new to the Russian courts, that of publicity (*glasnost*) through open trials. Admitting spectators to the court room, wrote the drafters of the judicial reform, would impel judges to pronounce just verdicts and would increase public confidence in the judicial system. As a 'very real instrument against dangerous ideas,' a sentence in open court provided 'healthy criticism' of illegal acts and public humiliation of criminal agents. Only under prescribed circumstances could a judge close a trial. He could do so under the Code of Civil Procedure by accepting a petition to that effect from both sides (articles 66, 326) or by classifying a case as prejudicial to religion, public order, and morality (article 325). The Code of Criminal Procedure also provided causes for trials in camera: offenses against the sanctity of religion; crimes against morality; crimes against the honour and chastity of women; and crimes of immoral behaviour, unnatural vices, and pandering (article 620).[13]

The judicial reform extended the principle of publicity to the accused, as well, who gained the right in open trial to defend himself publicly.[14] In

November 1865, therefore, Bibikov presented a statement to the court arguing that he had confined the discussion in his book to the legal aspects of marriage, a subject within the law.[15] The panel of judges rejected this defense and sentenced Bibikov to seven days in the guardhouse, but it also ruled the search of Bibikov's apartment and the presentence seizure of his book by the police illegal (confiscation authority rested solely with the Chief Administration, who could order it only in extraordinary cases after initiating a prosecution following publication). Finally, finding the argument of the book too weak to mislead any reader, the court neither banned nor purged *Critical Studies* (penalties within its power).

In the second, and last, case against the press under the old criminal court system, the Chief Administration in mid-December pressed charges against editor A.A. Kraevsky and one of his writers for an article in the December 9 issue of *Voice*. The offensive article, written by Ivan A. Ostrikov, a student at the St Petersburg Theological Academy, blamed 'unthinking followers of Orthodoxy' – a phrase inserted by Kraevsky – for depriving Old Believers in Vitebsk of their places of worship despite the 'Emperor's declaration of freedom of worship for the schismatics.[16] The state charged Kraevsky and Ostrikov with intending to undermine confidence in imperial laws and institutions and having thereby violated the Statute of 1865 (sec. 4, art. 9, para. 1, which became article 1035 of the 1866 criminal code). In his own defense, Kraevsky argued that the basic information in question, including Alexander's remarks to a delegation of Old Believers in April 1863, had first appeared in duly-censored papers in Moscow and St Petersburg.

Agreeing that information previously approved by the censorship could not become the basis for prosecution (recognition of a form of privilege), the St Petersburg judges, on 14 January, 1866, ruled that the article expressed reasonable judgments on legally published material. Although the phrase about 'unthinking followers' abused officials, said the judges, Kraevsky's motive had been to further religious toleration in the empire. The court therefore acquitted Ostrikov and merely fined Kraevsky 200 rubles, a decision Nikitenko saw as a 'cruel defeat' for Valuev.[17]

The procurator appealed the acquittal to the next higher court, the First Department of the Senate, and there won a reversal on 27 May. The First Department sentenced Kraevsky to the guardhouse for two months and Ostrikov for three days.[18] Intervening events, however, must have influenced that decision; for on 4 April sometime-student Dmitry Karakozov had tried to kill the emperor and had raised grave fears of a wide revolutionary conspiracy. On 8 April, Alexander had appointed an investigating commission under M.N. Muraviev, and on 13 May, two weeks before Kraevsky's sentencing, a ukaz had appeared which implicated the press in attempts to subvert the state.

A shake-up of administrators also took place. Minister of Public Education Golovnin, a champion of the press, stepped down in favour of D.A. Tolstoy, until then procurator of the Holy Synod; Dolgorukov resigned as head of the Third Section and was replaced by P.A. Shuvalov, the energetic governor of the Baltic region; and in St Petersburg, where the post of governor-general was abolished, General F.F. Trepov, commander of the police in Warsaw during the suppression of the rebellion there, became the new head of the capital police.

Demonstrations of support for Alexander followed Karakozov's attack, but Valuev warned the emperor on 26 April that he should heed closely the dangerous discontent in Russia.[19] So far merchants, peasants, schismatics, and clergy were merely in 'ferment' over economic difficulties, said Valuev; but the press, educators, and a significant part of the official class were already in 'movement' to effect changes through publishing. To keep them in line, the minister vowed strict application of the new statute, helped by what he hoped would be 'appropriate co-operation' from the reformed courts (begun that month) and solidarity among the ministries.

III

At a conference on 28 April the emperor and Valuev heard Shuvalov call for reforming the police and educational systems as well as silencing dangerous commentary on government affairs in meetings of the gentry and zemstvos reported by the press. Taking aim at Valuev's press policy, the new head of the Third Section doubted that warnings and closings could restore control over disaffected writers; a new press law might well be necessary.[20] What could be done, for example, to discipline Michael Katkov?

The Moscow editor was in trouble for refusing to publish the warning issued to his *Moscow Bulletin* on 29 March, a defiance that Nikitenko called 'genuine constitutional opposition' to the government (that is, opposition by the press like that in constitutional states). The fracas had started when Katkov, in the lead article of *Moscow Bulletin* on 21 March, had charged that a 'party' of government officials was not taking a sufficiently tough stand towards the Baltic provinces. On 23 March, the Council of the Chief Administration had discussed Katkov's article and voted 4–2 against a warning, but Valuev had overruled them, mentioning that the emperor agreed with such a step. Katkov failed to publish the warning, paid a fine for that failure, and then maintained that the payment had ended his obligation to print the warning. Muraviev, head of the assassination inquiry, told Valuev that he must end the impasse, but not by 'stopping the paper, which is simply impossible.'[21] By mid-April, Valuev had decided not to proceed with a second warning to Katkov, only to come under fire from Shuvalov.

Valuev, responding to Shuvalov's criticism, issued a second warning to the *Bulletin* on 6 May and a third the next day, accompanied by an order suspending the paper for two months.[22] He charged Katkov with having repudiated government orders and having 'agitated' in a manner that could lead to 'inconvenient results.' When Katkov announced that he would not reopen his paper, the emperor intervened, lest the valued voice of Muscovite patriotism be lost. While in Moscow in the summer of 1866, Alexander met with Katkov and persuaded him to continue the *Bulletin*. No act could better have demonstrated that, through his publications, Katkov had become a powerful force in Russia.

Even as he acted against Katkov on the right, Valuev proceeded against publications on the left, a segment of the press especially vulnerable in the aftermath of the assassination attempt. On 2 May Valuev told Muraviev that certain journalists had created the 'social-literary environment in which the idea of regicide could develop.'[23] *Russian Word*, he wrote, had been the main source for 'communistic and materialistic ideas' (it was then under temporary suspension). Valuev also condemned two publishers (A.S. Suvorin and A.F. Golovachev) and three books: Bobrovsky's *All Sorts* (Valuev apparently did not yet know that Bobrovsky was a pseudonym for A.S. Suvorin), Nicholas Sokolov's *The Renegades*, and Ivan Sechenov's *Reflexes of the Brain*. Although Valuev directly linked no one with the assassination attempt, the Muraviev commission did arrest several persons close to the *Russian Word*, only to find no evidence of their being conspirators.

As support for his approach, Valuev welcomed, and perhaps even inspired, the ukaz issued on 13 May by the emperor in the name of the chairman of the Committee of Ministers, Prince P.P. Gagarin. Published in Valuev's *Northern Post*, the ukaz echoed Valuev's report to the commission. It accused schools, certain private persons, and the press of attempting to subvert the state. The Muraviev investigation, it said, had already laid bare the prevalent evil 'philosophizing' against such time-honoured Russian principles as religion, family life, property, authority, and, especially, the gentry, 'in whom the enemies of public order naturally see their immediate opponents.'[24]

On 23 May a special group of high officials, dubbed the 'Comité du salut public' by Valuev, met to plan a campaign against the radicals. When they argued for harsher measures against the press, Valuev responded that no set of regulations could tame unruly writers. 'It is impossible to cut out a pattern for the press like a uniform. Coercion and orders will not produce a good press and will not stop a bad one.'[25]

Then came an endorsement from the emperor for the Statute of 1865; and, on Alexander's orders, the Committee of Ministers on 28 May directed Valuev to draft the planned 'Supplement' to the statute and to delineate judicial procedures for press cases in the new courts just established. The same directive also announced the permanent closing of two journals of 'dangerous orientation' – *Russian Word* and *Contemporary*. These extraordinary closures by the Committee of Ministers (a by-passing of the authority given to the Senate by the Statute of 1865) and the earlier arrest and release of a number of journalists by the Muraviev commission were the main measures against the press immediately following the assassination attempt. Despite calls by Shuvalov and others for a new, stricter censorship statute, the system of press control identified with Valuev remained virtually intact.[26]

In his April report to the Muraviev commission, Valuev had cited three dangerous books, and, by June, court cases against two of them were under way. That summer the newly-created circuit court (*okruzhnyi sud*) in St Petersburg undertook its first press trial; and, on 18 August, its judges convicted a writer whom Valuev had cited as a dangerous publisher in his April report: A.S. Suvorin.

Through another publisher, Suvorin had had printed late that March a volume of his narrative essays, half of which had earlier appeared in the *St Petersburg Bulletin* with censorship approval. By adding enough material to total ten signatures, Suvorin had avoided submitting his book, *All Sorts*, to preliminary censorship under the new law; and he signed it, as he had the previously published parts, 'A. Bobrovsky.'

Publisher N. Tiblen gave a copy of the printed work to the censorship authority for the three-day holding period on the morning of 4 April, the very day of the assassination attempt. When Muraviev's investigation of that event began four days later, the censorship administration had already started judicial proceedings against *All Sorts* and used its special authority to confiscate it. As Suvorin later recalled, the Muraviev commission 'began arrests and strong measures against writers and journalists. I wanted to take my book back [from the censorship] and with that intention wrote to the Minister of the Interior P.A. Valuev.'[27]

In his letter of 12 April, Suvorin assured Valuev that he had written *All Sorts* to show the good and bad of the nihilist generation and of the gentry at the time of the emancipation.[28] He now planned to rewrite the second half or 'simply destroy it.' Suvorin added that he had no fear of a trial, however, for he could fully defend his essays there. Some staff member designated Suvorin's letter 'for the file,' and Valuev probably never saw it – or he would not have attributed Suvorin's book to Bobrovsky in his May 2 letter to Muraviev's commission. The chairman of the St Petersburg Censorship Committee learned 'Bobrovsky's' identity from a Third Section official, who roundly condemned *All Sorts* for its dangerous political stand and sympathy for state criminals.

An alleged sympathy for Chernyshevsky was central in the August trial to the arguments against Suvorin by the procurator, A.A. Stadolsky, who recommended destruction of the book and two months in jail for the author for violating articles 1035 and 1040 of the criminal code. Article 1035 prescribed up to sixteen months in jail or a fine of up to five hundred rubles for anyone convicted of the intention of eroding public confidence in laws and official institutions – the same charge Kraevsky had faced. Extenuating circumstances justified a short sentence, argued Stadolsky. Half the book, he pointed out, had already appeared with approval of the censors and, as another consideration, the destruction of the book would penalize Suvorin financially.[29]

In his 'sympathetic' portrayal of Chernyshevsky through the character of Samarsky, said the prosecutor, Suvorin had defended a state criminal. Through two other characters, Shchebynin and Ilmenev, Suvorin had contrasted a member of the gentry class with an agitator, to the discredit of the former. (Suvorin had had a forewarning of this argument during a pre-trial search of his study by an officer from the Muraviev commission. Arriving one morning at 3 a.m., just after Suvorin had returned home from work, the officer confided that he sought information relating to Chernyshevsky and the character like him in *All Sorts*. Of the materials seized, Suvorin later recovered everything but a letter from A.N. Pleshcheev describing his deposition to the Senate in the Chernyshevsky affair.)[30]

One trial judge admitted the difficulty of citing lines as evidence of criminal intent: 'Very frequently, the criminal character of a work is completely lost when one turns from the character of the whole and focuses attention on excerpts and parts of a book.'[31] But to speak of the criminality of the book as a whole amounted to ascribing to it a dangerous orientation, argued Suvorin's defense attorney, K.K. Arsenev, who pointed out that the regulations for periodicals had ruled out that charge as grounds for prosecution.

As for article 1040 (the second basis for prosecution in this case), its violation could bring fines of up to three hundred rubles and a jail sentence of up to three months as punishment for abusive comments about persons, private or official, and about official institutions or public societies. In Suvorin's defense, Arsenev disagreed that 'public societies' could mean the gentry, who lacked the corporate status of an organization. Arsenev also argued that the author of *All Sorts* 'recognized that agitation was attractive for the young' and 'wanted to show that they necessarily paid for this passing attraction with their tears.'[32] The prosecutor, he told the court, had misconstrued the ideas of Suvorin's heroes as the ideas of Suvorin.

Finding Suvorin guilty of all charges, the circuit court judges next decided Suvorin's degree of guilt and the fate of the book. Once again, the prosecutor urged the book's destruction and argued that the presentation of a printed book to the censorship committee was a 'completed' act of illegal publishing if a court found the book criminal. Arsenev countered that an act of publication was incomplete until the work had been distributed to the public, an act of 'completion' the censorship had prevented. Arsenev in turn paralleled Suvorin's position with that of an author who, under preliminary censorship, incurred no criminal responsibility when a censor found a work illegal and kept it from the public. Arsenev categorized the degree of Suvorin's offense as a 'preparation,' a degree not punished under imperial law except in cases of high crimes against the state.

The judges chose to convict Suvorin of an 'attempt' – a degree of guilt above a preparation but just below the completed crime charged by the prosecution. All the same, the circuit court on 16 August 1866 imposed the recommended penalty: two months in jail for Suvorin and destruction of all 1,500 copies of the book.[33] Suvorin appealed to the next higher court.

Suvorin's trial, like his appeal which was to come before the Court of Appeals in St Petersburg the next December, attracted wide attention, for it was, as Arsenev noted, the first time 'the new courts dealt with a new problem.'[34] Among the several publications extensively covering the case were the *St Petersburg Bulletin*, *Russian War Veteran*, *Voice*, and *Judicial Messenger* (*Iuridicheskii Vestnik*).

From the government's point of view, the circuit court had rightly applied the doctrine of responsibility in the new press law: even though a printed book adjudged criminal did not reach the public, the author was liable for his own criminal intentions and words, and, additionally, for 'attempting' a publishing crime. If the book had circulated, as it had in Bibikov's case, the prosecution would have had firm grounds for charging a completed crime, but the assassination attempt had caused the censorship administration to use its extraordinary power to seize Suvorin's book before it could circulate. (Similar powers of confiscation to prevent 'freed' periodicals from circulating criminal words did not exist.)

IV

By permanently closing *Contemporary* and *Russian Word* in May, the government had peremptorily silenced the most objectionable journals. Even before that decision, a two-part article in the February and March issues of *Contemporary* entitled 'The Question of the Younger Generation' had prompted a court case instead of a warning. In that article, Iu.G. Zhukovsky had criticized the gentry for exploiting peasants and for being 'social riff-raff, parasites, lickspittles, and wastrels' – strong words in the Russian press of the sixties, but part of the widespread journalistic criticism of the landed class.[35] The accusatory act (indictment) named Zhukovsky and editor A.N. Pypin.

Assistant procurator N.B. Jacoby charged violations of articles 1040 and 1039, which prohibited the publication of 'defaming circumstances' (facts published with slanderous intent). Jacoby asked for a three-month sentence for Pypin and three weeks for Zhukovsky. Arsenev again undertook the defense, this time on behalf of persons 'whom I sympathized with because they faced a completely groundless accusation.'

Arsenev argued that article 1040 protected the privacy of an individual, society, or institution and that none of these had suffered abuse from Zhukovsky. With respect to article 1039, Arsenev similarly held that the gentry were not a 'judicial person' (a body which could make or answer court charges) and therefore could not be defamed. He pleaded further that Zhukovsky had criticized practices of serfdom outlawed in

1861, that caustic criticism of the gentry was not new to Russian letters, and that strong language was justified in argumentative articles on 'social questions.'[36]

Agreeing with Arsenev, the circuit court on 25 August acquitted both Zhukovsky and Pypin, a verdict that prompted courtroom applause. Zhukovsky had written fair comment instructive to those gentry who had ignored the verdict of emancipation, declared the judges.[37] Given the press's right to discuss social questions under the 1865 statute, the judges accepted the strong language of Zhukovsky's article.

An appeal by the prosecution brought a relatively quick reversal by the Court of Appeals on 4 October, an action Arsenev saw as deliberately hurried. In the appeal, procurator N.O. Tiesenhausen introduced a new argument: that the 'renewal' of Russia required 'agreement and unity' and that every publication 'inclined to incite enmity and difference ... ought to be judged strictly from the viewpoint of the general state order.' In effect, Tiesenhausen was arguing that Zhukovsky had violated article 1036, which forbade inciting one class against another, a charge far more fitting than those originally cited. Arsenev vainly responded that in press cases, as in all others, the statutory law must prevail, and judgment must rest on the articles cited in the indictment.[38]

At the close of the proceedings on 4 October, the court again acquitted the two defendants of criminal abuse (article 1040) because the criminal code provided for social criticism.[39] But it found the accused guilty of one part of article 1040: Zhukovsky's strong language was defamatory in having offended public decency. The judges fined both men one hundred rubles and sent them to the guardhouse for three weeks.

Arsenev believed that the government had persisted in pursuing a guilty verdict in order to 'expose with full clarity the reprehensible character [of *Contemporary*] which had led to its closing.' The original decision by the circuit court had instead 'given partial rehabilitation to "ill-intentioned" people and dangerous tendencies.' Still, as Nikitenko observed, the mildness of the final penalty was a set-back for Valuev, who had hoped to convict the two men of abusing the gentry.[40]

Valuev's success in censoring the press through the courts in the twelve months through October 1866 was mixed, for the courts' judicial perspective differed from the administrator's. In the first case, Bibikov had been convicted of intending to undermine the family but had served only seven days in the guardhouse. Ostrikov's acquittal and the mere fining of Kraevsky for publishing the phrase 'blind followers of Ortho- doxy' had been reversed on government appeal to the First Department of the Senate; but Kraevsky's appeal to the emperor against his guard-house sentence was still pending. For showing sympathy for Cherny-shevsky in *All Sorts*, Suvorin had been convicted of 'attempting' to publish a criminal book (a lesser offence than that charged); but his appeal against that verdict and his sentence were also pending. For strong words against the gentry in the since-closed journal, *Contemporary*, Pypin and Zhukovsky had first been acquitted and then, upon government appeal, been convicted and lightly punished with a three-week jail sentence.

Still in preparation was the case against Nicholas V. Sokolov, whose government-confiscated book, like Suvorin's, had been submitted to censors for the three-day waiting period on the day of the assassination attempt. Unlike Suvorin, however, Sokolov was to face charges of attempting high crimes against the state, and the government was framing the indictment with care.

Meanwhile, in response to the Committee of Ministers' directive of 28 May, Valuev, Zamiatnin (the minister of justice), and Panin (the head of the Second Section) debated what supplementary rules should govern press trials. One dispute between Valuev and Zamiatnin was an old one: who should decide when prosecutions were justified. Just before the Statute of 1865 took effect, as described earlier, Valuev had informed Zamiatnin that the emperor had authorized the censorship administration to make that decision, albeit with provisions for arbitration of disagreements.

As before, Zamiatnin favoured granting more authority to the pro-curator. Only a legal expert, he argued, could decide when to prosecute, because an offense 'not falling under an accurate and literal sense of the criminal law cannot be successfully prosecuted before the court – and especially not before a public court.'[41] Requiring the procurator to rely solely on information from a censorship committee meant that the court could not verify facts as it could in its usual investigation before criminal trials.

Another question concerned the court level at which trials for press felonies should begin. Panin argued that all violations of articles 181, 189, 274, 1035–7, 1039, and 1040 (which forbade undermining the church, social order, state, family, property, or the honour of official or private persons) were serious crimes against the state and must be tried by the Court of Appeals as the court of first instance (the judicial reform of 1864 had specified that trials of high state crimes be initiated at that level). Panin expressed, as well, a distrust of juries and their possible use at the next lower level, the circuit court. Convictions for press crimes were imperative, he said, and the judges of the Court of Appeals had proved readiest to convict. In response, Zamiatnin objected that to eliminate a single judicial instance was to deprive the prosecution and defense of the full progression of appeals from the lowest to the highest courts.[42]

The proper court of first instance for press misdemeanours, or minor violations primarily related to publishing and inspection procedures, raised no disagreement. Although, in the criminal justice system as a whole, all misdemeanours were decided by the justice courts, Panin and Zamiatnin agreed with Valuev that the 'special character' of press misdemeanours justified assigning most of them to the next higher court of first instance, the circuit court.[43]

Only the misdemeanours in eleven articles were to be left to the justice court: seven proposed by Valuev (1010–13, 1015, 1017, and 1018) and four by Panin (1016, 1019, 1030, and 1032).[44] As a group, these eleven articles show the minutiae of controlling the printed word. For example, article 1010 required owners to report changes in printing equipment, while article 1016 required government approval for equipment sales; article 1015 required each printer to keep a record book of his work for the inspector; articles 1017–19 required approval for each new bookstore and forbade the storing, selling, or distributing of any books on the prohibited list.

By implication, the misdemeanours assigned to circuit court jurisdiction carried greater potential for mischief. While essentially technical, they involved important possible evasions, including operating a secret printing plant (1008); owning an unauthorized hand press (1009); falsifying the names of the editor, publisher, or printer (1014); selling (1020) or printing (1024) material requiring censorship before censors approved it; and selling Hebrew books printed in Poland or abroad which did not bear the official stamp of approval (1023).

With respect to the circulation of works pending trial, Panin proposed what was more an amendment than a supplement to the 1865 statute – that a court could, if it chose, confiscate a publication at the start of the pre-trial investigation and hold it while deciding its fate. In contrast, the regulations of 6 April, 1865 (sec. 4, art. 18, which became articles 1045 and 1046 of the criminal code) provided that a conviction must precede penalties. Only in exceptional cases (sec. 3, art. 1, para. 14) could the censorship administration confiscate a printed work before the court reached a verdict. What had been an 'extraordinary' measure of the censorship administration Panin now proposed as an 'ordinary' one for the court.

V

Having begun work on the supplementary rules to the Statute of 1865 in October 1866, the State Council issued them 12 December.[45] The supplement included almost everything that Valuev and Panin had asked for: the court's authority to confiscate an allegedly criminal work pending the outcome of the case against it; the censorship administration's authority to initiate prosecution by providing the evidence and directing the procurator to act on it (the minister of justice to settle disagreements); the assignment of most press misdemeanours to the jurisdiction of the circuit court; and the assignment of the felonies singled out by Valuev and Panin to the jurisdiction of the Court of Appeals. The one concession to Minister of Justice Zamiatnin was authorizing the procuracy alone to initiate prosecutions concerning the abuse through printed words of government offices, institutions, and officials (a private person who suffered abuse had to bring suit on his own).

For those serious crimes assigned to the Court of Appeals in the first instance, ruled the State Council, decisions reached without juries could be appealed to the First Department of the Senate; decisions by juries were final, or not subject to appeal. (This provision regarding jury trials already governed prosecutions in the imperial courts of justice generally.) Because both defense and prosecution had to agree to a jury trial, the council could safely assume that at least one of the parties would choose the right of appeal over a jury trial – an assumption subsequently proved true. Thus were juries virtually ruled out from politically sensitive press trials.

Fears of widespread conspiracy incited by the assassination attempt in the spring of 1866 had proved unfounded by that fall, and the State Council, in drafting the supplementary rules during October and November, saw no need to add severe restrictions to the original statute. They termed their rules, like the Statute of 1865, 'temporary' because a widening of limits on freedom of expression would 'take shape under the influence of a series of judicial decisions.'[46] They reaffirmed the government's commitment to a gradually freer press, first set forth in the Statute of 1865, and linked that change with the greater involvement of the court system, thus accepting the principle that Russia had embarked on a course of gradually evolving press rights.

As 1866 ended, then, the government once again emphasized judicious treatment of the press. In keeping with that emphasis, the Court of Appeals on 20 December upheld the conviction of Suvorin for 'attempting' to publish a criminal book but reduced his jail sentence from two months to three weeks.[47] That same day Alexander himself reduced the punishment meted out to Kraevsky in May from a three-month jail term to house arrest for the same period. Still pending was the trial of Sokolov.

11

Control of press freedom: warnings, court cases, and libel laws, 1867–89

Without question, the post-1865 system of press controls greatly eased the burden of censorship for most writers and publishers. Even the displaced staffs of *Contemporary* and *Russian Word* were to reach an accommodation with the censorship administration within a year of the closures of those journals and were to resume publishing activities. However reluctantly, the imperial government was granting the press more agreed-upon rights, defined by laws elaborated and enforced by the new Russian courts. Press 'rights' in themselves, however, primarily mattered to journalists and members of the legal profession; the censorship administration under the Ministry of the Interior continued to emphasize press responsibility to the state.

I

Among the 1866 provisions in the criminal code serving to define and even limit the rights of the press were four articles forbidding injurious words: 1035 (words intended by their author to undermine public confidence); 1039 (defamatory words); 1040 (abusive words); and 1535 (libelous words). The drafters of the censorship reform had introduced 'defamation' and 'abuse' as crimes under imperial law, and the supplementary rules of December 1866 included both as serious crimes against the state to be prosecuted at the Court of Appeals level.

As already shown in chapter one, the political value of keeping the good name of the state and government unsullied – in Russia, as in the West – had prompted the first laws against injurious words, whether written or spoken. Once publishing had begun, preliminary censorship kept most such words out of print; but, as governments abandoned censorship, new laws broadly banned injurious words as crimes against the state and against private persons. Thus, one more way in which the Russian press law of 1865 borrowed from the West was in delineating (in the words of legal scholar Boris Chicherin) 'protection of the state from erosion by political passions' and 'protection of persons from infamy and slander.'[1]

That slander in itself could undermine the existing order troubled imperial officials alert to the class tensions surrounding emancipation, especially as revealed in press attacks on the gentry. In January 1860, for example, Minister of Justice Panin had learned from the Moscow provincial prosecutor that government officials and 'social classes' (meaning the gentry) had frequent cause to base libel suits on attacks made in print. Panin had therefore informed the head of the Second [legal] Section that the emperor wanted such cases handled more expeditiously, and Alexander himself had charged the censorship authority to forbid slanderous articles and caricatures in periodicals. That December, at the request of the Ministry of Justice, the State Council named the Court of Appeals the court of first instance for suits against slander in published works and referred other related proposals to the Second Section which was then drafting the judicial reform.[2]

Drafters of the censorship reform were meanwhile independently framing articles which forbade abuse, defamation, and all words which undermined confidence in the established order – rough equivalents to what English courts termed 'seditious libel.' These provisions in the Statute of 1865 subsequently became articles 1040, 1039, and 1035 of the Criminal Code of 1866.

Article 1035 (initially sec. 4, art. 9, paras. 1, 16 of the Statute of 1865) forbade published words which injured governmental and social institutions by undermining public confidence in them, no matter how truthful those words might be. The government alone could bring suit for this crime, a power it had exercised since publishing had begun in Russia. The great difference after 1866, however, was that such cases were prosecuted by the new courts created by the judicial reform.

Article 1039 (initially sec. 4, art. 9, para. 10 of the Statute of 1865) forbade the publishing of 'defaming circumstances' which endangered the 'honour, reputation, or good name' of a private individual or state official, organization, society, or institution. Defamation (*diffamatsia*, or *opozorenie*) occurred only if the injurious words had been 'published' – a term which proved crucial. (The injured party then had access to the columns of an offending journal to refute words adjudged to be defamatory.)[3] Only when a journalist defamed government personnel for official acts could he use truth as a defense (he could present documentary proof but not summon witnesses). Although he might prove his charges about official acts true, the court could still convict him if it held that he conveyed an 'obvious intention to insult an official or institution.' The barring of truth as a defense in all other defamation cases brought repeated criticism from Russian legal experts; and as late as 1891 V. Goltsev, an editor of *Russian Messenger*, called the law 'extremely severe and one-sided and a detrimental form of censorship.'[4]

Article 1040 (initially sec. 4, art. 9, para. 11 of the Statute of 1865) forbade 'abuse or insult' (*oskorblenie*) through printed words directed against private and official persons, societies, or institutions. Whereas defamation involved 'facts,' abuse involved 'name-calling,' or scurrilous remarks. Like the French *injure*, abuse was a printed insult with no reference to actual circumstances.[5]

These three articles the government could and did use to suppress words which might help stir discontent or rebellion. But it also permitted private individuals to use articles 1039 and 1040 – apparently to benefit the gentry, the non-official group most often criticized by the press, and the class whose prestige and loyalty the government held essential to its own well-being. An anomaly resulted, however, for a private citizen could charge defamation when injurious words printed about him were true or were difficult or unpleasant to disprove; otherwise he could disprove the facts fully in court by charging libel under article 1535.

II

Violaters of articles 1035, 1039, and 1040 were always members of the press. In contrast, anyone could violate article 1535, incorporated into the 1866 criminal code from a long-standing law forbidding libel (*kleveta*), or false words spoken or written against another. The essence of libel was knowingly making a false charge against another to a third person. Like defamation, libel involved facts; but the central issue was whether or not the alleged facts were true. Plaintiffs in such cases, therefore, sought not only to punish the libeler but also to disprove the injurious words.[6]

Members of the press could be sued for defamation, abuse, or libel by individuals or by the state, but only in cases of libel could they meet the plaintiff on almost equal ground. Being charged and convicted under the defamation and abuse laws, because truth seldom was a defense and because intentions alone could be adjudged criminal, amounted to censorship. In fact, the reformers of the censorship statute had borrowed both laws from the French, who had invented them to contravene their 1814 charter's ban on preliminary censorship. Through them judges acquired broad powers to punish unacceptable commentary.

Thin-skinned officials were ready clients for defamation and abuse suits. The retired chief of police of Nizhnii Novgorod, Major General P.V. Starzhenetsky-Lapp, for example, saw himself lampooned in the September and October 1867 issues of *Notes of the Fatherland* and requested the St Petersburg prosecutor to charge editor A.A. Kraevsky and writer V. Krestovsky with defamation. Once in court, Krestovsky argued that the only details in his imaginary account applicable to the former police chief were one character's imposing features, talent for the mazurka, and matched pair of horses.[7] These were hardly defamatory. The judges took only ten minutes on 27 August 1869 to find both journalists innocent.

Defamation and abuse suits on behalf of individuals after 1865, whether through the procurator or private attorneys, little affected the mainstream press policies of Imperial Russia. But a few such cases during the remainder of the century did lead to a degree of 'privilege' for journalists, and two deserve mention. (Privilege with respect to the press came into being in England through the Parliamentary Papers Act of 1840.[8] This act permitted press reports on the official business of Parliament, and from it evolved the court-upheld doctrine that reasonable reports of official deliberations were immune from prosecution as injurious to the state or individuals. Information accorded immunity, for whatever reason, is 'privileged.' The doctrine surfaced in Russia in the second half of the century, although in a different form.)

As shown in an earlier chapter, A.A. Kraevsky, in December 1865, won an acquittal from the St Petersburg circuit court on the grounds that what he had published could not be prosecuted – that is, was 'privileged' material – because censors had previously approved its publication. Attorney S.A. Andreevsky similarly argued in 1886 that two clients' indicted words were privileged. The defendants, editor O.K. Notovich and writer I.F. Vasilevsky of the daily *News* (*Novosti*), had been charged with defaming a Major Doniko-Iordansky by repeating facts from his open trial for dereliction of duty. Andreevsky argued that the court had confirmed the major's misdeeds in public session and had therefore made the facts privileged to the press. He won the case.[9]

In 1893, Andreevsky was to use the same argument to win an acquittal for E. Markov of *New Times* (*Novoe Vremia*), who had been sued by a judicial investigator, A. Rodislavsky, for printing an official complaint spoken against him in open court. Andreevsky pointed out that the 'complaint is not a lie but a fact' and that 'a newspaper answers only for the truth of the news.'[10] Once again the court agreed that published facts made public through the courts' deliberations were immune from prosecution. Thus, in these two cases won by Andreevsky, the government's own policy of publicity, or *glasnost*, through open courtroom deliberations in turn provided 'privileged' facts for the press, a development parallel to one in the West.

III

Of all the cases involving the press, the autocracy felt the gravest concern over those involving threats to state security and tranquillity; and the trial of author N.V. Sokolov in 1867 for crimes against the state, as described below, proved the most crucial publishing case to that time. It, too, further defined the legal status of the press.

Sokolov wrote for the *Russian Word* from 1862 until he broke with the editor, Blagosvetlov, in 1865. Early in 1866 he read French writer Jules Valles's *Les Réfractaires*, arranged for printing a translation of it with publisher V.I. Golovin, but submitted instead (under Valles's title translated into Russian: *Otshchepentsy*) a text of his own drawn from a number of European radicals.[11] This work reached the censorship administration for the three-day pre-distribution waiting period on the day of the assassination attempt against Alexander and was immediately confiscated. On 28 April the Muraviev commission arrested Sokolov in its roundup of persons possibly connected with the assassination attempt, but his deposition to them on 26 May led to his exoneration and release on 11 July. Meanwhile St Petersburg prosecutor Tiesenhausen prepared his case against Sokolov and publisher Golovin and took it to court in the spring of 1867.

Among several charges, Tiesenhausen accused Sokolov of intending to undermine church and faith and the principle of property and to incite the public to resist authority.[12] He charged Golovin with manipulating the number of pages in the book to avoid preliminary censorship and with failing to submit the book to the ecclesiastical censor.

Regarding the book as extremely dangerous, the government took two extraordinary measures. One was to close court sessions to the public; and the other, to try the case in the Court of Appeals with class representatives, an option in trials for the highest crimes against the state. The court panel therefore included its president, three judges, the St Petersburg gentry marshal, the Tsarskoe Selo district marshal, the mayor of St Petersburg, and a township (*volost*) elder – all ex officio members of the bench in such cases.[13]

Defending themselves without counsel, both Sokolov and Golovin pleaded that they had followed what they thought were proper procedures. Sokolov testified that he had told Golovin to submit the book for ecclesiastical censorship if necessary; Golovin said he had relied on Sokolov's signature accepting responsibility for the book and did not concern himself with its contents. Because Sokolov had never changed his original order for Valles's book, said Golovin, the inspection book had remained as initially inscribed; and he had not known that Sokolov had omitted the designation 'translation' on the title page and had inserted his own name as 'author.'

The court found Golovin innocent and convicted Sokolov of only two of the crimes charged by the prosecution: undermining the legitimacy of private property (article 181) and undermining Christianity and the Orthodox church (article 1037). In a move possible within the Russian legal system, the court itself charged and convicted Sokolov of a third crime, that of inciting against the monarchy (article 252).

Of great importance to the press, the court found Sokolov's degree of guilt with respect to the never-circulated book not an 'attempt,' as charged, but rather the lesser, lowest degree of 'preparation.' (The only other author prosecuted for a book confiscated before it could circulate was Suvorin, who had faced the charge of a completed crime but had been convicted of the lesser charge of 'attempt.') Of the three violated articles, only article 252, because it concerned one of the highest crimes against the state, prescribed punishment for 'preparation,' the lowest degree of guilt. On that single count the court, on 2 June 1867, sent Sokolov to the fortress for sixteen months and ordered two thousand printed copies of his book destroyed.[14]

Sokolov's trial had set a crucial precedent: when the state withheld a criminal printed work from the public, its author or publisher was limited to a crime of 'preparation' – a degree of guilt penalized only in the very highest crimes against the state. Still, because a court could order a confiscated work destroyed or purged once it had ruled the contents criminal, seizure and trial gave the state one means to keep objectionable words from ever reaching the public.

As for words objectionable to the church, an author or publisher's responsibility to submit a work for ecclesiastical censorship was imprecisely set forth in article 1024. The court ruled Golovin innocent under that article because Sokolov's book was not religious, but further court tests of the applicability of article 1024 were pending.

In November 1866 the censorship administration had seized the second volume of Wundt's *Spirit of Men and Animals*, translated from the German and printed by the St Petersburg publisher, P. Haideburov. Haideburov had published the first volume in 1865 under the old preliminary censorship system. After the ecclesiastical censor, in December 1865, had rejected the request of another publisher to issue the second volume, Haideburov printed a shortened version and submitted the book to the civil censorship authority just before it was to circulate. The church censor, to whom it was next referred, declared the volume a religious work, found it unpublishable, and asked that Haideburov be prosecuted for violating article 1024. The indictment drafted on 8 November also advocated banning the book.

The trial of Haideburov took place in the spring of 1867. And because the felony forbidden by article 1024 was among the lesser ones assigned to the circuit court, the case was heard at that level in St Petersburg. Haideburov argued that the censorship committee was responsible for forwarding books for ecclesiastical censorship, but the court, on 11 April 1867, placed that responsibility on the author or publisher for works freed from preliminary censorship by civil law.[15]

Haideburov appealed his conviction to the St Petersburg Court of Appeals, which, on 14 July, upheld the lower court's verdict. As for proper procedure, these judges decided that an author or publisher of any work touching on religious matters must submit to the secular censor in manuscript form – prior to its printing – not just the relevant passages but the entire work; these censors would then decide what parts to refer for ecclesiastical censorship.[16]

Undaunted, Haideburov appealed next to the First Department of the Senate. That body, before the end of 1867, ruled in his favour by further clarifying procedure under article 1024: authors and publishers had to submit the religious parts of all 'mixed' books in manuscript form to the civil censorship authority, which would make any necessary referrals to the ecclesiastical censor; authors and publishers had to submit all wholly-religious manuscripts directly to the ecclesiastical censorship authority. The First Department informed the Court of Appeals that it had erred in ruling that Haideburov should have submitted the entire work in manuscript form to the censorship committee and directed the case back to that court for an acquittal ruling.[17] Confiscation of the book consequently ended. The First Department had acquitted Haideburov on a technicality even as it confirmed for the press a responsibility it had not had under the preliminary censorship system – that of deciding when content was religious.

In his overview of censorship developments in the first five years following the Statute of 1865, attorney K.K. Arsenev, who repeatedly championed the press both in and out of court, concluded that the First Department's failure to define 'religious' content forced writers and publishers to practise extreme caution.[18] Although Arsenev feared that the government might repeatedly base prosecutions on the religious issue to harass the press, there are no indications that this strategy was ever used by the government.

IV

Other court decisions in 1867 helped define the limits on printed commentary permitted by the 1865 law. Two cases in point – both dealing with newspapers – helped establish what constituted legitimate reporting by the press on public affairs.

The first was the trial of I.A. Arsenev, the editor of one of the early sensational papers, the *Petersburg Gazette*. At the request of the capital police, censorship authorities initiated through the procuracy a court case against Arsenev and one of his writers, D.E. Zvenigorodsky, for published commentary injurious to the government and to officials in violation of articles 1035, 1039, and 1040.[19]

At the trial before the Court of Appeals that September, Arsenev's attorney, A.V. Lokhvitsky, argued that defamation required the naming of specific persons or institutions whereas Arsenev had only generally criticised the judiciary and the procuracy (Zvenigorodsky had in fact named a judicial investigator in his article). Nor could anyone damage the honour of the St Petersburg police given the chief's well-known argument that officers would continue to take 'holiday money' (bribes) unless they got higher salaries.[20] The judges disagreed and on 25 September convicted and stiffly penalized both men, fining Arsenev five hundred rubles and sentencing him and Zvenigorodsky to five months in jail. The court also ordered the newspaper closed and barred Arsenev from assuming an editorship for one year. Both men appealed to the First Department of the Senate.

That December the First Department confirmed that Arsenev and, to a lesser degree, Zvenigorodsky, had violated all three articles as charged, but it lessened the penalties by quashing closure of the paper and the ban on the editor and reducing both jail sentences to three months' duration. The Senate prosecutor stressed that the press had the right to criticize arbitrariness and injustice, but in this case Arsenev had made his paper an instrument merely for 'spreading abuse.' (The convictions appear to have instilled caution into the staff of the *Gazette* for, as of 1905, when administrative penalties ended, the paper had incurred only four warnings and two temporary suspensions. In that same period, however, its street sales were banned ten times, suggesting the staff avoided serious violations but continued to irritate the government.)[21]

Through its case against the *Gazette*, the government in 1867 showed its readiness to deal by judicial means with provocative journalists who wished to test the limits of the press reform. The First Department, prepared to draw a line on published commentary, had at the same time softened the penalties of the lower court and decided that the paper could continue to appear and Arsenev to edit despite the offense of both against the government.

A second court decision in 1867 further defined the limits of printed commentary. It concerned a new daily newspaper, *National Voice* (*Narodnyi Golos*), begun by P.A. Iurkevich-Litvinov at the start of the year. Nationalistic in bent, Iurkevich supported the reformist policies of Alexander II but over-zealously set about exposing wrong-doing among officials and clergy. On 18 January the censorship administration issued *National Voice* its first warning and, late that month, confiscated issue number 25 and directed the procurator to draft criminal charges.[22] (The Statute of 1865 required submission of an uncensored newspaper for censorship review at the end of the press run; confiscation of a single issue did not halt subsequent issues.) After further warnings on 17 February and 16 June, the newspaper was temporarily suspended.

In an indictment filed that April, Procurator Tiesenhausen accused Iurkevich and one of his writers, A.G. Rotchev, of violating articles 1028, 1035, and 1039 by defaming the Moscow chief of police and the supervisor of the Vosnesensky Girls' Secondary School in St Petersburg. Rotchev had allegedly undermined public confidence in the judicial system by charging an unnamed investigator of the St Petersburg Court of Appeals with abusing his powers by jailing suspects for insufficient cause.[23] In urging convictions at the November 1867 trial, Tiesenhausen pointedly reminded the court that its decision would affect 'the extent to which freedom is allowed to the published word and ... show beyond what limits this freedom becomes abusive.'[24] In its decision on 25 November the court ruled that Iurkevich's slurs against the police chief were abusive and his information against the school official was defamatory because evidence had proved it false.[25] Rotchev was acquitted because his criticism of judicial investigations had not singled out any official by name.

Iurkevich's penalty, however, was light. Because censorship authorities had confiscated the issue of *National Voice* found most offensive, it had not reached the public. Following the conviction, the court had ordered all 3,647 copies destroyed. Iurkevich's penalty amounted to only three weeks' arrest and a fine of two hundred rubles.

The judicial results of the trial served to clarify the principles of the Statute of 1865, and helped show the independence of the courts from government influence. The court had not penalized Rotchev's general criticism of a state institution although the government had asked it to do so. To be sure, the court had ordered the destruction of a complete edition of *National Voice*, but only after establishing legal cause through a judicial proceeding. Finally, the courts continued to take a stand which the government found objectionable: persons responsible for criminal words printed but not circulated committed only a minor offense.

Warnings and prosecutions to silence unacceptable printed commentary were proving effective, and the government appeared to be confident that it could maintain limits on the press. One piece of evidence is the virtually automatic approval given new periodicals once a publisher had applied to the minister of the interior and had deposited with him either 5,000 rubles for a daily newspaper or 2,500 rubles for a journal. Further evidence is the government's willingness to permit the staffs of the peremptorily closed *Russian Word* and *Contemporary* to associate themselves with new publications within a year.

Alexander II had closed *Russian Word* in May 1866, and editor G.E. Blagosvetlov two months later received permission to launch a new journal, *Affairs* (*Delo*), albeit under the restriction of preliminary censorship. The first issue was to appear 20 August but was delayed until September. (As of 4 September censors had rejected twenty-two of the forty-eight signatures in type.) The head of the Council of the Chief Administration of Press Affairs, General M.R. Shidlovsky, had told Blagosvetlov that he would 'find existence of the journal possible' so long as 'the editorship would give its word that it would avoid questions about marriage, private property, and religion.' For his part, Blagosvetlov believed that preliminary censorship ensured the survival of *Affairs*. The journal would be 'honest, although colourless, at first,' he vowed.[26]

Affairs used the subscription list that *Russian Word* had built, and Blagosvetlov invited his former collaborators to join the new venture.

Among those who did were Nicholas Shelgunov, author in 1861 of the clandestine manifesto, 'To the Younger Generation,' and Dmitry Pisarev. Despite some difficulties with the censor, *Affairs* was a great success. By 1868 its subscribers numbered 3,500; by 1870, 4,000.[27] Blagosvetlov died in 1880, but his journal continued eight more years.

N.A. Nekrasov accomplished the continuation of *Contemporary* under a new masthead without being subjected to preliminary censorship, and he did so by arranging with A.A. Kraevsky to lease the prominent, long-standing monthly, *Notes of the Fatherland*. He became legal editor in December 1868 under an agreement with Kraevsky which would automatically end if the journal received two warnings. Nekrasov also agreed to pay any fines against the journal. As owner, Kraevsky retained the right to read what was to appear in each issue and to object to material that he thought would provoke an administrative warning.[28]

Nearly all the old writers for *Contemporary* took up their pens for *Notes*, even the few arrested by Muraviev and then cleared by the special court investigating the assassination attempt. They included G.Z. Eliseev, who took charge of the contemporary events section, D.D. Minaev, and V.A. Sleptsov. M.E. Saltykov-Shchedrin soon joined the journal as well. (Of the old *Contemporary* staff, only Antonovich, Zhukovsky, and Pypin – who had personal differences with Eliseev – failed to make the transition.) The journal differed from the old version, however, for it lacked the combative spirit and pronounced western orientation of *Contemporary* and tended more to reflect the ideas of Russian populism. That less-contentious tone undoubtedly eased relations with the censorship authority; but Skabichevsky says that Nekrasov also discreetly bribed two influential censorship officials: 'On Thursdays Nekrasov gathered just for them a circle of gamblers who lost to them appropriate sums.'[29]

V

One dilemma faced by the government in this same period involved Ivan Aksakov and his new daily newspaper, *Moscow*, begun on 1 January 1867. Only two years before Aksakov had been in trouble with the censorship authority for his newspaper, *Day*. Voluntarily closing the unprofitable *Day* at the end of 1865, Aksakov had suspended his editorial efforts throughout 1866. Then he began *Moscow*. Arsenev, the attorney who specialized in press cases, found it uniquely straightforward. Whereas the preliminary censorship system had taught the Russian press to 'express its ideas in very muted form,' Arsenev noted in 1869, *Moscow* from the start 'spoke loudly, decisively, and called things by their real names.'[30]

Aksakov was an ardent Russian nationalist who sharply criticized the government for any shortcoming he saw in it.

For such directness, *Moscow* received a warning in each of its first three months; and with the third, on 26 March 1867, came a three-month suspension. On the heels of its reopening in July came another warning and, following two more late in November, a four-month suspension. Unwilling to be idle, Aksakov renamed the paper the *Muscovite* and sent a friend to Valuev for permission to 'open' it. As he regularly did for new periodicals, Valuev agreed – only to discover the ruse and to close the daily on 13 February 1868, after some thirty-eight issues. Restarted again in April, *Moscow* provoked three more warnings over the next six months, its third suspension coming on 21 October. Valuev had resigned as minister the previous May, and that December his successor, A.E. Timashev, was urging the Senate, the highest court in the empire, to close *Moscow* permanently. After *Moscow*'s first suspension, said Timashev, Aksakov had thanked the government in print for giving him needed publicity and, following the second, had justified masquerading *Moscow* as the *Muscovite* 'as though to show the public that the government penalty imposed on *Moscow* was in essence without force.'[31]

On 29 January 1869, the First Department of the Senate pondered at length whether Aksakov's case was an administrative or judicial matter. All ten senators agreed that 'if it is impossible for the court to prosecute each printed article which contains some signs of violating the criminal code, then ... a whole series of such articles ... makes up a dangerous orientation which is subject, by law, to the application of administrative penalties.' Seven senators approved Timashev's administrative proposal to close *Moscow* permanently. Three opposed an administrative closure because, they argued, Aksakov had violated articles 1035, 1036, and 1040, which the Statute of 6 April had made grounds for prosecution in the courts.[32]

The General Assembly of the Senate on 7 February also disagreed whether the government should deal with Aksakov administratively or judicially. Twelve senators favoured the permanent closure of *Moscow*; eleven favoured judicial prosecution; three opposed either course. Without a decision by the required three-quarters majority, the Senate sought an opinion from the minister of justice. He replied on 7 March that because Aksakov had already suffered administrative penalties for all that had appeared in *Moscow*, a court case based on those same issues would constitute double jeopardy. But, the minister concluded, Aksakov did deserve further punishment.[33]

The Senate referred the Aksakov case to the State Council, whose combined civil and legal departments discussed it on 24 March. On 13 April, the General Assembly of the State Council overwhelmingly approved closure. Notably, the stand taken by the combined departments sounded like article 1035: 'It is obvious that Aksakov, advancing himself as true to the principle of autocracy, has constantly tried to undermine confidence in those organs through which the autocratic power acts ...'[34]

Persons who 'undermined confidence' were, by law, subject to the courts, but the combined departments had punished Aksakov administratively for that very charge. Anyone aware of the case could discern that the government had closed *Moscow* administratively because at no time could it find grounds for judicial prosecution. Moreover, although administrative penalties were to end when the new courts were fully established, *Moscow* provided proof for many officials that the transitional measures should continue. Administrative controls provided greater flexibility and surer penalties than did the courts.

Still, the lengthy processing of the *Moscow* case early in 1869 differed markedly from the peremptory editorial ban that Aksakov had suffered under Nicholas I. The Statute of 1865 had involved the Senate and State Council, and both bodies sought to act in accordance with law. They had had to decide a problem of jurisdiction. The law sanctioned Senate-approved closure any time a publication was under temporary suspension, but the Senate and State Council pondered if they should instead subject Aksakov to judicial proceedings. The majority at both levels of government favoured action of some kind, but not until the minister of justice ruled out prosecution did the State Council close *Moscow* and forbid Aksakov from editing another journal, a ban that lasted until 1880.

In April, the month of the decision on Aksakov, censorship critic K.K. Arsenev found reason to argue that the position of the Russian press to that time had, on balance, improved: 'The abolition of preliminary censorship, by lessening press dependence on arbitrary circumstances and personal whim, made possible the discussion of subjects that were previously banned to literature ... Analysis of government policies is even now not easy and without risk, but several years ago the press could not even consider it. Tutelage over the press exists, of course, but it has lost its trivial, capricious character: it ponders thought but does not hang as before on each separate word.'[35]

For the great bulk of Russian writers, editors, and publishers, censorship had become far less onerous, a fact which must be kept in mind.

Necessarily, this account centres on those who discomfited the government and made officials less and less willing to grant greater latitude to the press in the next decade.

Following the lead of Europe, Russia had introduced the judiciary into press affairs in 1865 and had ended preliminary censorship for many periodicals and books. The courts found themselves wrestling not only with questions of legislative intent in the law but also with the dangers to the body politic posed by this or that published statement.

By their decisions, the courts helped define the place of publishing in reformed Russia and, on the whole, gave more latitude to the printed word. For the first time, the courts provided writers, editors, and publishers with a defense against government interference and with several levels of appeal. In keeping with western judicial practices, the Russian criminal code of 1866 empowered courts to uphold generalized social criticism, as long as it did not libel specific men and institutions, and to permit reportage of facts in the public record. Such were the considerable gains in press rights by the end of the sixties.

12

Censorship repression and the emergence of a 'European' press, 1869–89

During the forty years the Statute of 1865 remained in force, the government repeatedly adjusted its policies on publishing, the better to control the uncensored press; for the press had readily seized opportunities opened to it under the 1865 regulations. From 1869 to 1890, the main developments in the censorship system rested on the consensus among officials that (1) the government could not reimpose preliminary censorship on works exempted by the Statute, and (2) the 'transitional' administrative powers in matters of publishing had to continue.

Although the administrative measures introduced during the two decades under discussion suggest a repressive hand over the Russian press, the government, in fact, used the new controls primarily against a small number of radical publications. During these same twenty years – a period almost equally divided between the reigns of Alexander II and Alexander III – the publishing industry in Russia modernized and developed broadly, asserted strong independence from the state, and became fully European in character and organization. Newspapers continued to grow and to overshadow the journals, as private firms responsive to popular tastes dominated publishing in St Petersburg and Moscow.

I

Alterations in the 1865 press regulations had evolved by 1868 through the court trials already discussed and through administrative rulings, the latter often instigated by the minister of the interior. For example, on 17 October 1866 a new rule favoured by Valuev stopped periodicals closed by the state from publishing and sending to their subscribers a miscellany of articles, as the staff of *Russian Word* had done after the closure of that journal. In turn, a ukaz of 13 June 1867 required the permission of local governors for any words printed about the 'decisions, reports, opinions, debates, and speeches' in 'zemstvo, gentry, city, public, and class meetings.' The 1865 statute had required permission solely about the 'resolutions' of these bodies. A year later, Valuev's successor, Timashev, received authority to ban street sales of a single issue of an uncensored periodical that seemed to him 'dangerous.'[1] In practice, however, Timashev and subsequent ministers of the interior were to prohibit street sales for extended periods – a severe penalty to newspapers. Kufaev lists fifty-three such prohibitions in seven years during the seventies: two in 1872, six in 1873, six in 1874, eleven in 1875, ten in 1876, nine in 1877, and nine in 1878. The censorship authority employed this penalty 218 times for all periodicals in the period to 1904. The editors of *Voice*, for example, calculated a loss of 150,000 rubles in revenue as a result of the prohibitions of street sales in the seventies involving 466 issues.[2]

In its efforts to control the press through the courts, the government had met its greatest set-back through the Sokolov trial; and, in February 1868, in the *Journal* of the Ministry of Justice, a jurist, N.I. Lange, took exception to the precedent set by that trial. 'Merely printing an illegal work not published [circulated],' wrote Lange, 'must be considered ... a fully completed crime.' Otherwise, he argued, persons could write and print works to express 'blasphemy, to mock the state power, to incite enmity among classes, to repudiate the principles of property [none of which were the very highest crimes against the state] and not be liable to penalty when a book is confiscated by the censorship department.'[3] Lange, of course, could do nothing to change the fact of law to which he objected.

The same month that Lange's article appeared Valuev sent his final report on censorship to Alexander, ending seven years as minister,[4] and criticized the courts' role in press cases. He stressed that the government must bolster rather than end the transitional administrative measures of the 1865 statute, for writers could comply with the criminal code while indirectly conveying meanings those same laws forbade. The government could act only 'against the peak' – that is, against blatant provocateurs – and its swiftest and surest means were administrative. For Valuev, the courts were too slow and too lenient.[5]

The last court of appeal in publishing trials, however, was the First Department of the Senate; and, finding good cause to ban words that complied merely with the letter of the law, that body in 1869 chose to overrule a lower court. It did so in considering the case against F.F.

Pavlenkov, publisher of 3,000 copies of the second volume of the collected works of Dmitry Pisarev, which the St Petersburg censorship committee had confiscated in 1866 when it initiated prosecution against the publisher.

The long-delayed trial before the St Petersburg Court of Appeals began in the spring of 1868. The government saw the trial as an opportunity to fill a loophole opened to publishers by the Suvorin case of 1866 when the court had decided that material approved by censors prior to the reform of 1865 was immune from prosecution. Several publishers had subsequently taken advantage of that decision to republish works previously approved and the courts had upheld their right to do so.

To counter that ruling, Prosecutor N.O. Tiesenhausen charged that two articles in the second volume of Pisarev's works, although published with censorship approval in 1862, violated articles 1035 and 1001 of the criminal code. Article 1001 concerned works subject to preliminary censorship and prohibited any which had the 'intent of corrupting morals' or which were 'clearly opposed to morality and decency.'[6] Tiesenhausen insisted that this article applied to the case even though the Pisarev volume, because of its length, was not subject to preliminary censorship. He argued that the courts should not permit the publication of articles containing criminal content simply because a censor had approved them several years before.

In his own defense, Pavlenkov pointed out that, as in the Suvorin case, persons were immune from prosecution for republishing works earlier approved by censors.[7] The Court of Appeals on 5 June 1868 (one day after Pisarev drowned in the Gulf of Riga) acquitted Pavlenkov of intending to undermine the government or morality and quashed the book's confiscation because article 1001 dealt only with works subject to preliminary censorship. Tiesenhausen appealed the decision to the First Department of the Senate.

In a public session of 14 March 1869 the Ober-Procurator of the Senate, M.E. Kovalevsky, argued that circumstances in 1869 made one of Pisarev's articles, 'Meager Russian Thought,' criminal. He urged that article 1001 could be applied by 'analogy' inasmuch as no other article in the criminal code more closely touched the case.[8]

In 'Meager Russian Thought,' Pisarev had described the influence of Peter the Great as minimal: 'The life of seventy millions who go under the general name of Russians indeed would not have changed in its ways if the young Peter had been murdered by Shaklovity.' (Theodore Shaklovity, commander of the palace guard and lover of the Tsarevna Sophia, led a revolt against Peter in 1689.) Kovalevsky held that Pisarev's glib references to regicide could 'disrupt the basic principles of government or confidence in the dignity of the emperor.' Lacking grounds in the letter of the law, Kovalevsky argued that the 'spirit of our legislation on the press' bars 'such expressions as those in the article.'[9]

K.K. Arsenev, defending Pavlenkov, disagreed that Pisarev's words condoned assassination. Their point had been that no single person could basically alter a people's evolution.[10] Even should the First Department rule those words criminal, continued Arsenev, the confiscation of the book had limited Pavlenkov to a mere 'preparation' to publish the article and exempted him from punishment.

On 14 March the First Department gave a mixed decision. On the one hand, it specified that Pisarev's article contained no criminal content, ruled article 1001 innapplicable, and upheld Pavlenkov's acquittal by the Court of Appeals. On the other, it ordered the article's destruction, 'since the tone and expression used by Pisarev were opposed to the general censorship rules and the wide distribution of such a work would have a dangerous influence.'[11] This suppression skirted the 1865 regulations (article 1045 of the criminal code) which permitted a court to act against a printed work only after it had ruled the contents criminal and had convicted those responsible. As the full Senate would do in dealing with *Moscow* in April, the First Department resorted to using its own authority to ban printed content it adjudged 'dangerous' because it lacked grounds under the law to rule it 'criminal.'

At the same time, in its general statement about the case, the First Department confirmed once again that printing without circulating a criminal work was merely a 'preparation' to commit a crime and unpunishable in all but the highest crimes against the state. (Arsenev hailed this statement as a victory for the press.) It held that 'there can be such cases in which a book turns out to be very dangerous [as in Pavlenkov's case] or even of criminal content, but the writer or publisher cannot be subject to penalty ... because he is guilty only in the sense of preparation to criminality.'[12]

Still the First Department had stretched the law to order the article's destruction, and the *Legal Messenger* (*Sudebnyi Vestnik*) would soon object to this expedient ruling.[13] But, although the First Department had destroyed threatening words, it had not undermined 'privilege' – as it would have had it found the articles, previously published with censorship approval, criminal.

The charges against Pavlenkov had proved exceedingly weak. Those levelled against P.V. Shchapov before the Court of Appeals in August

1869 were equally so; and that trial was even more delayed.[14] The work in question was a two-volume translation of Louis Blanc's *Letters from England*, which the St Petersburg Censorship Committee had confiscated during the three-day waiting period before initiating court action on 7 January 1867.

Blanc's 'letters' to various French newspapers from 1861 through 1863 described English life, politics, letters, and religion (the original book in French had earlier circulated in Russia with the approval of the Foreign Censorship Committee). Once again the prosecution urged imprisonment and a fine, despite the fact that the book had never circulated and the charges against it were less than the highest crimes against the state. In an unusually brief statement, Procurator Tiesenhausen charged that passages in the book made it subject to ecclesiastical censorship (article 1040) and that the 'intention of the author is obviously to shake confidence in monarchical authority wherever it exists' (article 1035).[15]

Defense attorney V.D. Spasovich confidently responded: 'Rarely has it fallen to me to begin a defense under such favourable circumstances.' Even should the court find that the book violated article 1035, he said, precedent had established that Shchapov should receive no penalty because the book had not circulated, just as the verdict on Haideburov in 1867 had established that publishers need not submit the manuscript of 'mixed' works for ecclesiastical censorship.[16] (Spasovich could ignore the ruling in the same case that religious sections of 'mixed' works had to undergo civil censorship, for the state had not raised that point.)

On 22 August the Court of Appeals acquitted Shchapov and ruled that Blanc's book could circulate, 'for between the topics prohibited in article 1035 and discussion about the English and French governments there is no analogy.'[17] Citing the 1865 statute and the Haideburov decision and categorizing Blanc's book as not 'completely' religious in content, the judges held that Shchapov had been under no obligation to refer his publication to the ecclesiastical censors.

Once again the procuracy appealed the decision by the Court of Appeals to the First Department of the Senate. Once again, as well, it extended the confiscation period of the book. But judicial precedents and weak legal grounds for charges were making press trials extremely difficult for the prosecution to win by the end of the sixties.

II

Three years had passed since the courts had undertaken publishing cases, a reasonable length of time for the 'transition' called for in the

Statute of 1865. Journalists had all the while chafed under and even spoken against the transitional administrative measures. In 1868, for example, K.K. Arsenev's *Messenger of Europe* (*Vestnik Evropy*) had analysed French censorship and scorned the warning system for preserving preliminary censorship 'without its hated name.'[18] In the second half of 1869, Alexander II chose to name a commission to take up the issue of permanent regulations once again; and he selected as chairman an official whose record and reputation signalled the likelihood of further reform.

That man was Prince S.N. Urusov (1816–83), whom Nikitenko described as a 'remarkable person among our high officials.'[19] Urusov had at one time been director of ecclesiastical education for the Holy Synod and the Synod's representative on the Chief Administration of the Censorship. As state secretary in 1865, he had helped the Grand Duke Constantine draft a plan to reform the State Council; he had next served as assistant minister of justice and briefly as acting minister; and he had defended press cases in the courts. At the time of his appointment, Urusov headed the Second Section and sat on the State Council. His credentials placed him among reformist officials.

As chairman, Urusov vainly called for volunteers to serve under him. He instead had to draft commission members from within the bureaucracy – a disappointment, he confided to Nikitenko, who noted in his diary: 'Prince Urusov has been set the task of finding the philosopher's stone, that is, of formulating press laws which will satisfy the government and society equally.'[20]

Alexander publicly announced the commission on 2 November and directed it to achieve some 'advantage' for the press but also to 'arm the administrative and judicial authority with the strength necessary to repel the dangers which are the result of the ungovernability and excesses of the printed word'; these words were duly quoted by Arsenev in *Messenger of Europe*. In the daily newspaper of the Ministry of Justice, *Legal Messenger*, and in the unofficial St Petersburg daily *Voice* there soon appeared six articles by A.D. Gradovsky, law professor at St Petersburg University, who advised the commission to lift the 'siege' against the press, that is, the warning system. That December, *Messenger of Europe* agreed that the transitional measures must give way to press controls exercised solely by the courts.[21]

Counter-arguments came from P.A. Shuvalov, head of the Third Section, and Minister of the Interior Timashev. Shuvalov used his year-end report for 1869 to condemn the press and censorship generally. He opposed, for example, the fact that the laws permitted the publishing of lawyers' courtroom speeches which often contained hostile ideas. On 20 November Timashev gave his assessment of press affairs to the Council of Ministers and, in it, complained about the brashness of the press, permissiveness of the courts, and weaknesses of the 1865 statute. In particular he cited the insubordination of Katkov and his *Moscow Bulletin*.[22]

Five days later, on 25 November, came the discovery of a body on the grounds of Moscow Agricultural Academy. Investigators found that the victim had been executed by a secret revolutionary society led by Sergei Nechaev, who soon escaped abroad. The sensational and fully publicized trial of Nechaev's followers a year-and-a-half later would have its affect on the draft proposals of the Urusov commission; but, in the closing months of 1869, the emperor appeared yet to favour proceeding, however gradually, towards subjecting the press solely to the courts.

During its first year of work, the commission found several problems with the existing controls over the press. It listed as shortcomings of the Statute of 1865, for example, that it (1) narrowly defined anti-religious content and opened the way to materialism and attacks on Christian doctrine; (2) narrowly defined sedition and provided no grounds to prosecute indirect attacks on the social and political order; (3) lacked specific directives for censors of foreign publications, who often approved works banned in the Russian language; (4) set no standards for juries which, although unused so far, could include 'illiterates ... or those persons who belong to the most ignorant classes of society'; (5) denied the procurator the necessary power to reject weak press cases brought by the censorship administration. It also saw loopholes: in the Pavlenko case, the First Department of the Senate had destroyed a publication but had acquitted the publisher; and publishers often inflated short books to a sufficient number of signatures to avoid preliminary censorship.[23]

With respect to the procurator's role, Procurator N.O. Tiesenhausen testified before the commission on 12 June 1870 that the censorship administration too often called for prosecutions on insufficient grounds.[24] Of the eighteen recommendations for prosecution to which Tiesenhausen referred, only eleven had proceeded to trial; and, of these, only four had resulted in convictions. Although he had apparently had his way in not prosecuting seven cases urged by censorship officials, the procurator must have obeyed higher authority in filing the very weak cases against Pavlenkov and Shchapov. Both of these two most recent prosecutions he had lost.

Tiesenhausen had met final defeat in the Shchapov case on 18 February 1870, when the First Department of the Senate upheld the acquittal verdict by the Court of Appeals. The First Department had, none the less, found Blanc's *Letters* a religious, not a 'mixed' book, and required Shchapov to obtain approval from the ecclesiastical censors to free *Letters* from confiscation.[25]

A full account of the trial of Shchapov before both the Court of Appeals and the First Department appeared, as then permitted by law, in *Stock Market Bulletin* in 1870. Freely quoting the lines of the book cited as 'dangerous' by the prosecution, *Bulletin* drew public attention to the very words which the procurator (but not the judges) saw as anti-monarchical. Officials angered by the account sent the Urusov commission strong arguments for limiting such reports of judicial proceedings.[26]

The acquittal of Shchapov by the First Department brought to an end the period of major press trials. None took place in 1871, the year the Urusov commission completed its work; but that same year came the trial which must have strongly influenced the commission's recommendations: the sensational open trial of the eighty-one 'Nechaevists' from July to September 1871. The press reported all testimony and evidence, including the fanatic 'Catechism of a Revolutionary' confiscated from a defendant. Instalments of Dostoevsky's novel, *The Possessed*, begun at this same time in *Russian Messenger*, provided a psychological study of the accused and made the threat of conspiracy the more dramatic. Despite the court's conviction of Nechaev (he was extradited the next year from Switzerland and served the rest of his life in prison), the government felt grave concern about revolutionary plotters still at large.

With his Third Section especially on alert as the trial ended, Shuvalov detected subversion in a book routinely released for distribution on 24 September by the St Petersburg Censorship Committee. By-passing the censorship administration, he convinced the emperor to take the extraordinary measure on 15 October of banning the *ABCs of the Social Sciences*, published anonymously but written by V.V. Bervi-Flerovsky, a member of the Chaikovsky circle. The book's sponsors, Shuvalov argued, had made the work long enough to avoid preliminary censorship and priced it at a mere two rubles per copy to attract student buyers. Its message about the 'bankruptcy of the existing order' was 'pernicious.'[27] Shuvalov linked the book to the activities of the 'Russian wing of the International,' whose recently discovered constitution called for propagandizing through legally published books on the social sciences.

Sponsors of *The ABCs* were a populist organization founded by a medical student, M.A. Natanson, in the late 1860s to take advantage of the greater publishing freedom granted by the reform of 1865. This circle, identified with N.V. Chaikovsky after Natanson's arrest in November 1871, made a project of *knizhnoe delo* ('the book business') – or the distribution of populist books. The Chaikovists, subsidized by radicals and sympathetic liberals, had their works printed and then sold them cheaply through bookstores or gave them away through a network of students and other agents. Before *The ABCs* was banned, they had, without incident, produced and distributed Peter Lavrov's *Historical Letters* (first serialized in the paper *Week* [*Nedelia*]) and Bervi-Flerovsky's *The Position of the Working Class in Russia*.

On 30 October Shuvalov persuaded Alexander II to order on his own authority the confiscation of all copies of *The ABCs* because radicals had continued to distribute them. Shuvalov objected that the Third Section was powerless to halt such books, that law suits to uphold confiscation had failed repeatedly, and that the light penalties for possessing banned books did not deter their circulation. On the margin of Shuvalov's report on imperial aide wrote that Prince Urusov had been advised that supplements to the press law must prevent any more such works reaching the public.[28]

Only a week later, on 7 November, the Urusov commission produced its draft proposals for improving the 1865 statute.[29] It had probably completed them by 30 October but could still have found time to ponder the issues raised by *The ABCs*. In any case, the commission at some time had drawn back from its initial stand that the judiciary should decide which press cases to try, for it recommended that the Chief Administration of Press Affairs retain that authority. The commission also included in its draft the regulation effected by the ukaz of 13 June 1867 to control news about zemstvo, gentry, and duma meetings; and it urged that the civil censorship administration absorb the ecclesiastical censorship agency. Finally, the Urusov commission proposed to limit full press coverage of open trials to juridical publications and periodicals given special permission by the censorship authority; all others would print judicial decisions as officially recorded.

Notably, the commission did not propose ending the administrative warning system, a change that had seemed possible before the trial of the 'Nechaevists.' Instead it put forward relatively minor changes for Minister of the Interior Timashev to consider.

Following the extraordinary confiscation of *The ABCs* by the emperor, the St Petersburg Censorship Committee, on 24 November, recommended prosecution of the book, but the procuracy successfully argued the absence of sufficient grounds.[30] Given this standoff, Shuvalov on 19 January 1872 included in his proposals to the State Council for altering the 1865 statute a change to empower the government to confiscate and ban a work that was not subject to prosecution.

On 4 February, Shuvalov also took part in turning down the Urusov commission's proposals (the five-man review committee named by Timashev included Shuvalov, Minister of Public Education Tolstoy, former minister of justice Panin, former censorship head M.R. Shidlovsky, and Urusov); and the very next day Timashev stood before the State Council endorsing Shuvalov's proposals to that body. This signal of a sterner press policy was followed that month by another: the four-month suspension of the popular and liberally inclined *Voice* – a decision protested by the Grand Duke Constantine.[31]

At this same time, the Chaikovsky circle was preparing to circulate a third Bervi book, *Investigations on Current Questions*. On 10 March, during the pre-distribution waiting period, the St Petersburg Censorship Committee confiscated the work but had to release it when the prosecutor would not initiate court action. In May the committee took the same steps with the same result against a second edition of Bervi's *The Position of the Working Class in Russia*; but, by this time, the State Council was about to end its long debate on the press regulations proposed by Shuvalov. It did so by approving them on 31 May.[32]

A ukaz of 7 June proclaimed the new press rules and authorized the censorship administration to confiscate uncensored books and periodicals (except daily papers) which were beyond acceptable bounds but also beyond the reach of the courts.[33] At the request of the minister of the interior, the Committee of Ministers could ban these works. Permanent confiscation would follow immediately. As before, the censorship administration was to initiate prosecution against any work violating the law, for the new rules were to buttress, not displace, established regulations. To ease the censors' burden, the pre-circulation waiting period was increased from three to seven days for books and from two days to four for journals.

Soviet scholar I.Ia. Aizenshtok, as the editor of Nikitenko's diary, concludes that the new rules 'withdrew the judiciary from press affairs, ... levelled the difference between preventive and post-publication censorship, ... and took back the not modest "attainment" of the law of 6 April 1865.' Arsenev more precisely describes the ukaz as a reasonable response to subversive books but one which ministers of the Interior sometimes wrongly used to avoid court cases.[34] Still, the exemptions from preliminary censorship granted by the 1865 law continued unchanged, and the Committee of Ministers used its 'exceptional' authority relatively infrequently: during the thirty-two years until 1904 that its authority lasted, the committee annually banned about six foreign and domestic printed works.[35]

Publishing figures suggest that the initial reaction of the book publishing industry to the June 7 rules was wariness. Although figures for 1870 and 1871 are missing, Kufaev shows that the number of Russian and foreign-language titles published in Russia in 1872 (2,191) and 1873 (2,668) fall about one-third below the yearly totals from 1866 through 1869, the four-year period following the 1865 statute. Totals increased again in 1873, and by 1877 the annual number of titles published in the empire (5,451) was more than twice that in 1872.[36] (See Govorov's figures, table 6.) The second half of the eighties was to show an even more dramatic expansion in book publishing.

III

One main reason for the great acceleration in the publishing of books and newspapers in Russia was the technological advances in printing. Most early nineteenth-century Russian printers toiled over a wooden or iron press powered by a single, hand-operated lever which lowered a platen to imprint one sheet of paper at a time; but in 1816 the Russian Bible Society imported Russia's first flat-bed printing press. This kind of press, still man-powered, imprinted much faster because a rotating drum bore successive sheets of paper to meet a 'flat-bed' of type.[37]

At the beginning of the sixties, the large printing establishments acquired the steam-powered, one-man platen press producing 1,000 impressions per hour. By this time, steam also powered the flat-bed presses which could print the large sheets necessary for newspapers and books at rates of up to 1,000 impressions per hour.[38] Although typesetting remained a hand-operation in Russia until the twentieth century, the use of machines for type-manufacturing, stereotyping, and printing had greatly cut costs and increased productivity by the seventies. (By the eighties, the largest publishing plants would be using rotary presses which could produce 10,000 copies of a newspaper per hour and, a decade later, 30,000 per hour.) Processes for printing colour, illustrations, and even photographs also improved, and from 1870 to 1888 twenty-eight new illustrated papers appeared in St Petersburg and ten in Moscow.

Orders by industries, mercantile enterprises, and railroads for business forms and advertisements made printing profitable, just as the expansion of schools added to already substantial markets for educational materials and, as readers increased, to the number of book buyers and periodical subscribers. As already pointed out, the press reform of 1865 had made state interference less of a problem for publishers. Finally, higher literacy rates in the principal urban areas help to explain the expansion and concentration of periodical publishing in the cities. By 1897 the literacy level for the population as a whole was only 21.1 per cent (males: 29.3 per cent; females: 13.1). But in the same year it was 55.1 per cent for adults of both sexes in St Petersburg province and 40.2 per cent in Moscow province. In the cities themselves, rates were higher still (60.7 in Moscow in 1897 and 70.5 in 1900 in St Petersburg, for inhabitants five years or older).[39]

These advances also made possible the cheap editions which troubled the government, and among the first works confiscated and banned under the new regulations of 7 June 1872 were Bervi's *Position of the Working Class in Russia* and *Investigations on Current Questions*, published for the Chaikovsky Circle. Other works seized, banned, and destroyed were Herbert Spencer's *Social Statics: On the Conditions Essential to Human Happiness*, Louis Blanc's *A History of the February 1848 Revolution*, and Alexander Radishchev's *Works*.[40]

In retrospect, 1871 – the year of the Nechaevist trial – had marked a turning point in press policy. That year M.N. Longinov had become the new head of the Chief Administration of Press Affairs under instructions to watch the press closely, a mandate he dutifully obeyed until his death in 1875. Longinov would not personally recommend the approval of new periodicals during the last three years of his tenure, although the council did permit a few to begin. When an applicant protested being turned down as a 'violation of law, a limitation of rights,' Longinov replied, 'This is a minister's rule. You can complain to the Senate.'[41]

The reluctance to permit new periodicals probably related to the Chief Administration's press survey which recorded 429 periodicals in 1872 (in contrast to 345 in 1868) along with an increase in the number exempt from preliminary censorship. (In 1872, 67 of the 143 periodicals in St Petersburg and 20 of the 38 in Moscow published on their own responsibility.) The Ministry of the Interior must also have used these figures to justify budget increases. For 1872 and several years before, the censorship authority had employed eighty-seven persons and spent 231,500 rubles; in 1873 its personnel increased to ninety-three and its expenditures to 266,300 rubles.[42]

On 16 June 1873 Minister Timashev gained another weapon against the press when the State Council authorized him 'in unusual and rare circumstances' to ban commentary on sensitive topics. Lemke recorded some 570 bans between 1873 and 1904 under such broad categories as the Jewish question, censorship, and famine. The minister could also suspend for up to three months any periodical which discussed banned topics, a penalty imposed twenty-three times during the thirty-one years the rule stood.[43]

Again at Timashev's urging, the Committee of Ministers on 19 April 1874 handed down a rule to prevent publishers from printing just a few copies of a book, submitting them to the censorship committee, and proceeding to print what they hoped to market only after the committee had released the book for circulation.[44] (Should the committee reject the book, the publisher could make changes to satisfy the committee or abandon the book without incurring any costs beyond type-setting. The government disapproved this practice because it made publishers less cautious about what they printed.) The committee consequently defined a book as 'printed' and ready for submission to the censorship committee only after all the planned copies had come from the press. Any book not meeting this standard was subject to preliminary censorship.

A new requirement for the press made on 4 February 1875 – this time by the State Council – stemmed from the arrest of more than one thousand youth involved in the 'go to the people' movement of 1874, an effort the government saw as seditious. With the trials of the young people pending, the State Council banned any pre-trial commentary on cases to be heard in closed court and limited reportage to official announcements from the courts.[45]

Upon Longinov's death in 1875, V.V. Grigoriev became head of the Council of the Chief Administration of Press Affairs. His greater receptivity to new periodicals brought a substantial expansion of journalistic publishing by the eighties, even as the government took exception to what many reporters were writing about the Russo-Turkish War and domestic turmoil in this same period.

One outspoken journalist who received repeated warnings, for example, was G.K. Gradovsky. In March 1876 he won approval for a new literary-political weekly newspaper dedicated to the full implementation of Alexander II's reforms. The first issue appeared 11 July, and his *Russian Review* (*Russkoe Obozrenie*) was soon self-supporting.[46] Within forty-five days the paper received it first warning, followed by a second on 16 November. Early in January 1877 a third warning brought a two-month suspension.

Blaming that suspension on his statements against the high costs and reactionary measures of war, Gradovsky reopened the *Review* and initially supported the Russo-Turkish war that began that April. But a stint as a war correspondent at the Danubian front got Gradovsky into trouble again. Disagreeing with Russian propaganda that the 'civilized ... the rich and the free' were aiding the 'poor and oppressed,' he reported on greater freedoms in Rumania and marvelled at Russian officers reading literature outlawed at home.[47] Such comments brought the *Review* three more warnings and a second suspension on 8 February 1878, only a week after a victorious Russia had signed an armistice with Turkey.

Two other crucial events coincided with the treaty. January 23 marked the end of the second mass political trial, or 'Trial of the 193,' which had banished to Siberia most of the youth prosecuted for going 'to the people' three years before (the 'Trial of the 50' had taken place a year earlier); and on 24 January, Vera Zasulich tried to assassinate St Petersburg military governor F.F. Trepov for ordering the flogging of a prisoner.

All three topics the press reported fully, a measure of how westernized journalism in Russia had become. So too, in June, Russian periodicals told how the Berlin Congress had forced Russia to relinquish the gains of the Treaty of San Stefano; and by then they had also revealed to the public how the imperial government had suffered yet another defeat in its public trial of Vera Zasulich.

In choosing immediate trial-by-jury in open court, the government had confidently expected to convict Zasulich and to stir the public against revolutionaries like her. Instead, Zasulich's defence attorney had used the trial to indict officialdom's inhumanity, and a sympathetic press had amplified that charge. Gradovsky, in *Voice*, for example, wrote that the imperial state, not Vera Zasulich, was on trial.[48] On 31 March 1878 the jury acquitted Zasulich and, although the government attempted to arrest her again, Zasulich escaped abroad, so that the Senate's overturning of her acquittal merely made her a criminal in exile.

To deter others from defying authority, Alexander designated an assortment of 'attacks' on officials as crimes – including acts of disobedience, resistance, abuse, and disrespect – and named a Special Conference of the Committee of Ministers under Valuev to study why so many people were restive. By June, the month of the Berlin Congress, the Special Conference had listed these causes: weakening police authority, higher educational institutions that had become 'conduits' for revolutionary propaganda, and a press that, under the guise of scholarly articles, was spreading subversive ideas.[49]

That August the Council of Ministers moved trials for crimes against the state or against officials to military courts and forbade trial-related publicity. When, this same month, terrorists assassinated a member of the Special Conference, General N.V. Mezentsov, the head of the Third Section, the government increased police powers, mounted special squads to handle mob demonstrations, and ordered the press to cease 'unfounded and systematic vilification of the police.'[50] On 1 September, the Council of Ministers approved a temporary measure permitting, merely with the approval of the head of the Third Section and the minister of the interior, the arrest and exile of persons accused of criminal acts against the state; and the evidence could be secret and unverified.

Early in February 1879 assassins shot the governor of Kharkov and, in mid-March, others tried to kill the new head of the Third Section. On 2 April a member of a revolutionary organization fired five shots at the emperor, but all missed. Two days later Minister of the Interior L.S. Makov called in twenty St Petersburg editors and warned them to meet his standards or face closure. That May the Special Conference insisted on stricter publishing controls along with positive moves by the government to win public support.

One such effort was the founding of semi-official (ofitsioznye) periodicals, which both Valuev and Mezentsov had favoured during meetings of the Special Conference. Valuev held that the government must no longer remain 'dumb' but must 'track the press ... and at each step oppose truth to untruth.' What resulted were two seemingly unofficial papers backed by secret government subsidies, the weekly Echoes (Otgoloski, 1879–81) and the daily Shore (Bereg, 1880). Neither was to attract a worthwhile public following, and members of the truly unofficial press were to discover and mock Shore's subsidy. At Shore's demise, Notes of the Fatherland would taunt officials for having openly demonstrated their inability to publish a successful paper.[51]

Another failed project, underscoring the haplessness of the government, resulted from Alexander II's appointment of the Grand Duke Constantine to head a group to consider including representatives of the gentry in the State Council. No agreement emerged, and the group ceased meeting in January 1880. On 5 February dynamite destroyed the banquet hall of the Winter Palace, but Alexander escaped injury. Grigoriev, as head of the censorship authority, summoned the principal editors of St Petersburg the next day for a cautionary warning.

One week later Alexander named a Supreme Executive Commission for the Preservation of National Order and Tranquillity, chaired by General Michael T. Loris-Melikov, esteemed for his leadership in the Russo-Turkish war. At the urging of Loris-Melikov, Alexander made administrative and ministerial changes, among them naming N.S. Abaza to head the Chief Administration of Press Affairs. To launch a reform program, Loris-Melikov abolished the Third Section and consolidated all police activities in the Ministry of the Interior, gave greater autonomy to the universities and a stronger voice to the zemstvos, and eased the censorship restrictions. Within a few months he advised Alexander that the Supreme Commission had served its purpose. Then, in assuming the post of Minister of the Interior on 6 August, Loris-Melikov virtually became prime minister of Imperial Russia.

Much like Golovnin two decades before, the new minister held a briefing for St Petersburg editors on 6 September about his plans to blend *zemstvos*, municipal councils, and courts with the institutions of the old order, 'modifying them as necessary.' According to *Notes of the Fatherland*, Loris-Melikov said that the press could discuss state 'measures, decisions, and orders' but could not propose that the public 'participate in legislation or in the government, whether in the form of a European-type representative assembly or in the form of our ancient *zemskii sobor*. There will be nothing of this kind.'[52]

Some press criticism appeared, and Loris-Melikov wrote the emperor that he had expected it. He also claimed that opposition from journalists had lessened, but alongside these words the emperor jotted: 'In my opinion, it is worse.'[53] Still, the government had made conciliatory concessions to journalists.

The Special Conference under Valuev, named earlier by the emperor, on 5 November asked a delegation of editors what measures the state should take. On their behalf, M.M. Stasiulevich argued that supplementary 'ministerial regulations' destroy even a good law and urged that only the 'law and the court' govern the press. S.A. Muromtsev, a Moscow law professor, made the same point in the October and December issues of *Judicial Messenger*.[54]

A majority of the Special Conference agreed and recommended in their report on 28 February 1881 that administrative penalties should end and fewer books be subject to preliminary censorship. Such censorship of periodicals, they held, should end in all cities, except for those publishers who wanted it. At the same time, they favoured stiffer penalties for criminal content, higher deposits for uncensored publications, and continued bans on sensitive topics.[55] From the whole report emerged a familiar pattern: concessions coupled with extra restraints on radical publications.

But the very next day, 1 March, a member of the People's Will mortally wounded the emperor and killed the plan for press reform. The assassination also ended another plan to add representatives to the State Council from the zemstvos, city dumas, and private citizenry. Yet, had Alexander II reigned longer, the autocratic government might not have approved the commission's proposals to end administrative controls over the press. The alternative – the use of the courts to limit the press – had proved inadequate in the sixties.

IV

Alexander III (1881–94), the new emperor, had for years favoured strong measures against dissidents and terrorists and opposed any hint of representative government. He did attend a debate by high officials about the plan of Loris-Melikov for State Council reform a week to the day after his father's death, but he heard nothing to change his mind.[56]

Within a few weeks, the advocates of compromise with the press disappeared from the highest levels of government: Loris-Melikov, Abaza, and Miliutin resigned and the Grand Duke Constantine stepped down as head of the Naval Ministry. As an appointee of Alexander III, the new minister of the interior, Count N.P. Ignatiev, proposed a Supreme Commission on Press Affairs independently empowered to open and close publications and to ban topics to press discussion, but such a plan did not win approval until 1882, when Count D.A. Tolstoy succeeded Ignatiev. It then became a 'temporary' measure, enacted by the emperor on 27 August.[57]

The Supreme Commission did not base its closures on the warning system and could bar a publisher or an editor from press activity for an indefinite period. In addition, the system of 27 August provided that any daily or weekly periodical suspended following three warnings could resume publishing only under preliminary censorship (a severe alteration of the 1865 statute) and had to submit a printed copy of each edition by 11:00 p.m. on the night before publication (an extreme hardship for a daily paper).

The Supreme Commission used its closure power almost exclusively in the eighties, and it acted first against the *Moscow Telegraph* (*Moskovskii Telegraf*), a liberal daily sympathetic to the peasants and to the zemstvos that had begun during Loris-Melikov's administration. According to Zaionchkovsky, the commission closed seven periodicals from 1881 through 1889; and, during these same years, eight thrice-warned papers chose to close rather than submit to preliminary censorship, among them the popular *Voice*. In figures for 1883 to 1904, Rozenberg cites a total of seventeen closures, some voluntary and some required by the Supreme Commission; and he lists ten additional closures by other authorities (for instance, the Senate and the governor-generals) during the longer span from 1866 to 1904.[58]

The high point for temporary suspensions and warnings, always imposed by the censorship administration, came in the second half of the seventies, rather than in the eighties. Taken together, these figures for closures, warnings, and suspensions suggest a certain constancy in the severity of press controls, but shifting means. (See table 8.)

One measure favoured by Tolstoy at the outset of his term as minister of the interior came to be known as the 'reptile fund,' for it encouraged servility by bribing papers to support the government. Finding the head of the Chief Administration, Prince P.P. Viazemsky, unsuited for the task, Tolstoy asked E.M. Feoktistov to administer the fund. Feoktistov refused because he disapproved of the government 'haggling' with journalists and acting covertly.[59] When Viazemsky fell ill and Feoktistov replaced him in December 1882, systematic bribes had not begun; they would within a year or two. In 1887, for example, an anti-reform, anti-Semitic weekly in St Petersburg, *The Citizen (Grazhdanin)*, would receive 100,000 rubles in government support.[60] Begun about the same time was the bribing of foreign publications by the Department of Police, a program similar to that undertaken by Bismarck.

Just after Feoktistov took office, in January 1883, the government made the first move against *Notes of the Fatherland*, the influential successor to *Contemporary*. The police arrested and sent into administrative exile the editor, Mikhailovsky, for a speech criticizing the government before the students at the St Petersburg Technical Institute. The police also knew of his connections with the People's Will organization since its founding early in 1879. Mikhailovsky still contributed to *Notes* anonymously from exile and continued to attack his rival, Katkov.

By mid-1883, both Katkov and K.P. Pobedonostsev, advisor to the emperor and procurator of the Holy Synod, were urging the closure of *Notes*, which had received a second warning earlier in the year. V.K. Plehve, the director of the Department of Police, arguing similarly in an unsigned memo to Tolstoy in August, linked the journal to a network of subversives who, he said, had taken control of the ten most widely-read St Petersburg periodicals. Citing this memo and several related letters, the Soviet scholar S.A. Makashin contends that the Department of Police, not the censorship administration, demanded the closure of *Notes*.[61]

Fearing adverse public reaction, the government proceeded very cautiously. *Notes* duly appeared in September, the month after Plehve's memo, with G.V. Plekhanov's first major article (unsigned) on Marxism in Russian, 'The Economic Theories of Karl Rodbertus.' In January 1884 the police arrested three more, though lesser, members of the *Notes* staff, S. Krivenko, A.E. Ertel, and M.A. Protopopov. The last issue of the journal appeared in April.

On 13 April the Supreme Commission approved both the closure of *Notes* and a carefully phrased public statement explaining why – an unusual step showing officials' uneasiness over public reaction. The emperor agreed to the closure on 19 April, and the order and explanation appeared in the *Government Messenger* the next day. 'The government,' read the explanation, 'cannot permit ... an organ of the press which not only opens its pages to the spread of dangerous ideas but even has as its closest collaborators people who belong to secret societies.'[62] It also charged that the responsible editor, Saltykov, had contributed articles to underground and foreign publications that could not have appeared legally in his own journal. Closure thus rested on the illegal activities of the staff and contributors apart from what they wrote for *Notes*, as well as on the actual content of the periodical.

Closure of *Notes* dealt a blow to the populists, but most of the staff moved to other journals – several to *Northern Messenger* (*Severnyi Vestnik*), begun in 1885. After returning from exile, Mikhailovsky joined them there in 1886 and in the nineties, like several others, became a leading contributor to two populist journals: *Russian Wealth* (*Russkoe Bogatstvo*) and *Russian Thought* (*Russkaia Mysl*).[63] Articles by Saltykov meanwhile appeared in the liberal journal, *Messenger of Europe*.

Tolstoy's administration proved difficult for journalists, but not impossible. In 1885, although the Supreme Commission closed three periodicals, the government permitted new journals to open and tolerated moderate criticism. When, for example, Katkov wrote in 1886 that, because it served no political parties, the Russian press was freer than the European, K.K. Arsenev could retort in print that the English, French, and Germans, but not the Russians, had the political rights essential to freedom. Not even the assassination attempt against Alexander III in 1887 by Lenin's brother Alexander and other students brought a generalized crack-down against the press. In the main, the government continued to act only against the most radical publications.

One example of the many periodicals that discussed sensitive issues, attracted loyal readerships, and did not severely antagonise the government is a newspaper founded in 1863 which achieved a circulation of 20,000 in the seventies: the *Russian Bulletin* (*Russkie Vedomosti*). It stands out for winning widespread respect through what one minister of the interior, I.N. Durnovo, described as a 'kind of cautious tone, which, while it does not disapprove of the government, does not sympathize with it either.'[65] Staff members considered the *Bulletin* to be the first genuine newspaper in Russia, that is, one owned and operated by journalists to provide balanced and objective coverage of news and opinion. Populists Saltykov and Mikhailovsky contributed articles, as did a number of writers with legal training, including G.A. Dzhanshiev, A.S. Posnikov, and V.A. Goltsev. The *Bulletin* had to pay fines and stop its street sales a number of times (while continuing to circulate to its subscribers), but during its long span of publishing to 1918 it suffered suspensions only in 1898 and 1901.[66]

Despite various forms of censorship harassment, many weekly and daily newspapers prospered during the political turmoil of the seventies and eighties. Closure of a periodical by the government was rare; and the beginnings of the age of mass readership, a period long since entered by the West, had come to Russia. Popular newspapers aimed at a wide cross-section of the population had displaced the journal, the traditional pulpit of the Russian intelligentsia, as the dominant Russian publication. In 1860 the number of unofficial general-content journals and papers published in the Russian language had been equal (at 15); in 1871 newspapers outnumbered journals better than two to one (36–14). By 1900 the 125 papers versus 36 journals made the ratio better than three to one. (See table 9.) Like the European papers they copied, the popular Russian periodicals catered to common tastes and gave Pobedonostsev cause to complain to Feoktistov: 'Think, what poison this is: by means of cheap new papers the filthiest corrupt French and English novels are penetrating the countryside.'[67]

V

Several trends stand out sharply in newspaper publishing during the twenty years under discussion.[68] First, respected major daily papers established themselves firmly in the capitals and there showed strong signs of journalistic independence. Second, newspapers of the kind offensive to Pobedonostsev also won mass readerships, especially in St Petersburg and Moscow. Third, despite the continuation of preliminary censorship in the provinces, regular newspapers became institutions in cities well beyond the capitals and there provided local, national, and even some international coverage. Fourth, the telegraph accelerated news coverage nationwide.

Names of newspapers in St Petersburg that would have been familiar even to an ordinary resident during the seventies and eighties included *Week* (*Nedelia*), *New Times* (*Novoe Vremia*), *News* (*Novosti*), *St Petersburg Bulletin*, and *Voice*. In Moscow, *Moscow Bulletin* and *Russian Bulletin* were the leading papers. These papers tended to favour a furthering of the reforms of Alexander II and, in general, circulated from 20,000 to 30,000 copies.

Newspapers that practised sensationalism flourished after 1870, although none equalled the enormous circulation of the contemporaneous *Daily Mail* in London, which was to exceed one million copies daily in 1900. They were usually illustrated and, like the French 'boulevard' paper, featured scandals, criminal trials, and bizarre happenings. Many people joined Pobedonostsev in criticizing them, one outburst coming from the St Petersburg weekly *Rumour* (*Molva*) in 1876 against their vying for 'not that public which our journalists used to have in mind – that is, the progressive, educated minority – but a pavement public which increases street sales and which seeks in a newspaper no more than scandal.'[69]

Typical of such papers was the weekly *Field* (*Niva*), published in St Petersburg by the enterprising book publisher, A.F. Marks. *Field* began in 1870 with a circulation of 9,000, reached 55,000 a decade later, 115,000 by 1890, and 235,000 by the turn of the century. Competitors included the *Petersburg Newssheet* (*Peterburgskii Listok*) and the *Petersburg Gazette* (*Peterburgskaia Gazeta*) (which the government had successfully prosecuted for abusive language in 1867 and for which Chekhov later wrote pseudonymously), both of which became dailies in the early 1880s. *Light* (*Svet*) was the most pro-government of the popular papers and attracted a strong circulation of 70,000.

Daily and weekly papers helped quicken commercial life throughout Russia, dependent as they were on private advertisements. In turn, as has been said before, newspapers' growth reflected the expansion in numbers of readers, for which even circulation figures do not provide a true measure. Because papers and journals were still relatively expensive, a single copy often reached several readers. It was common Russian practice, as well, for one person to read a copy of a paper aloud to several others. For this reason subscription figures provide an inadequate guide to readership size.

In the provinces, especially in the prosperous south and lower Volga region, more and more papers were appearing. Kiev acquired its second daily and a semi-weekly in the late seventies; Odessa, a daily in 1864 and a second one in 1880. Tiflis, the capital of Georgia, gained a daily in 1876, another two years later, and a third in 1884. The important *Volga Messenger* (*Volzhskii Vestnik*) of Kazan became a daily rather than a thrice-weekly in the mid-eighties. In Samara, the *Gazette* began daily publication in 1884 and attracted a wide following, in part because Maxim Gorky wrote for it. A weekly begun in Taganrog in 1882 to serve the Sea of Azov region became a daily twenty years later. Voronezh had two papers serving the Don region, both of which turned to daily publication in 1900.

Providing Russian papers faster access to world-wide happenings during the two decades under discussion was the first European-type news agency, founded in Russia in 1866 to distribute brief summaries of European political events and market information.[70] Before 1866, editors permitted to publish foreign news had to depend on bulletins from the Ministry of Foreign Affairs and whatever foreign news appeared in official papers, a painfully slow procedure and one especially difficult for the editors of provincial papers. Then, following the press reform of 1865, the editors of the St Petersburg papers petitioned for the right to receive and publish telegrams directly from outside Russia. The next year the government approved the organization of the privately owned Russian Telegraph Agency (RTA), with nominal supervision by a censor stationed at the agency. The RTA purchased dispatches from European agencies and distributed them to its Russian customers; before long, it began to send Russian news abroad.

In 1872, A.A. Kraevsky founded the competing International Telegraph Agency (ITA), associated with his paper *Voice*, and placed a greater emphasis on newsgathering in Russia than did the RTA. The ITA did not survive the closing of *Voice* in the eighties. The Northern Telegraph Agency provided a similar service from 1882 to 1894, and a revitalized RTA increased its international news bulletins after 1895.

The censorship measures imposed by the government in the seventies and eighties posed hardships for radically inclined publications, but figures for the years from 1864 to 1890 show that private printing and publishing enterprises multiplied no fewer than seven times (from 181 to 1,299). The rate slowed somewhat in the early 1900s, but growth was to continue. Expansion of the industry relied to a great extent on the improved mechanical equipment discussed earlier. In Moscow, for example, where the number of printing enterprises more than doubled from 21 to 48 between 1865 and 1880, the number of mechanical presses more than tripled (37 to 124), while hand presses dropped to about half their former number (114 to 66).[71]

To meet the demand for skilled operators of the new equipment, A.S. Suvorin opened a school for printers and machinists at his *New Times* plant in St Petersburg in 1884, and the Russian Technological Society founded a printers' school the same year. The growing complexity of the industry prompted publishers to organize the Russian Society of Booksellers and Book Publishers in the eighties to advance mutual interests and promote printing technology. The society began its own publication, *Book News* (*Knizhnyi Vestnik*).

VI

Russian publishers in the seventies and eighties who were bent on reaching the people through printed works were one aspect of a broad cultural trend – Russian populism – which influenced manners, pedagogy, painting, music, and thought. These publishers included such 'men of the sixties' as F.F. Pavlenkov, L.F. Panteleev, and A.S. Suvorin, who wanted to spread advanced scientific and social ideas from Europe and who suffered penalties for their efforts. But others like I.D. Sytin and M.O. Wolf chose to avoid sensitive subjects in publishing for the markets opened by the liberation of the serfs and the expansion of schools.[72]

Suvorin, Sytin, and Wolf exploited these new readerships to help build publishing empires which resembled trusts because they combined into a single corporate enterprise both publishing and marketing through their own outlets. (The profits to be gained in publishing also attracted entrepreneurs whose principal interests lay elsewhere, so that banker K.V. Trubnikov, for example, became a publisher.)[73] Sytin far and away proved to be the most successful in producing publications that appealed to the peasants, and initially he concentrated on simple prints and calendars, popular favourites since the seventeenth century.

First to produce such publications were peasant craftsmen using lime boards, wood chisels, hand presses, and home-made ink to imprint whatever other peasants would buy. Although many copied foreign-printed pictures and stories from the West, these folk printers began in the second half of the seventeenth century to develop their own styles, emulating icons and illustrated manuscripts. A typical picture was a line engraving of a heroic historical figure surrounded by smaller scenes from his life.[74] Among the regular and more daring publishers were the schismatics, those Old Believers who had cut their ties with the official church and who used printing to spread their ideas and to satirize the official church establishment and its secular masters, the tsars. Peter I was, for instance, a prominent target of schismatic publishing in the early eighteenth century, and he naturally attempted to halt such illegal and subversive printing through the Holy Synod. Peter also used the Academy of Sciences – which had other censorship functions in the eighteenth century, as noted in the first chapter – to control the second prominent form of publishing for the people: the calendar.[75] Peter granted the academy exclusive printing rights over calendars, which it held until just after the reform of censorship in 1865.

In the middle of the nineteenth century, a peasant serf named I.A. Golyshev became the first large-scale publisher of popular pictures.[76] On several hand-powered presses set up in Mstera, a village in Vladimir province and a centre for the crafting of inexpensive icons, Golyshev was soon producing each year a half-million pictures with religious motifs. A similar but more secular enterprise developed in a cluster of small print shops in Moscow around the Ilinsky Gate. Itinerant peddlers bought the pictures and carried them as wares to the far reaches of the empire.

It was near the Ilinsky Gate that Sytin, the son of a village scribe, learned the publishing business and its distribution system. As a young apprentice in the printing and book shop of a schismatic named Sharapov, Sytin dealt with peddlers, travelled to country fairs, and learned what would sell in the villages. (He also learned that popular pictures, especially those printed over and over again, were virtually ignored by the censor.)

Knowing the scorn of intellectuals for popular pictures (*lubochnye kartiny*), Sytin was to argue in his memoirs: 'Not only the completely illiterate but even the partly literate Russian found his "political information" in the packsack of the peddler. Newspapers were a little absurd and were published in a language that the people did not understand. A book was rare and was on sale only in the capitals. Whole regions of Russia had no bookstores, not a single printing plant.'[77]

In 1876 Sytin himself began to produce for the peasant market. Using a French lithograph press, he was able to publish bold drawings by professional artists in as many as seven bright colours – an enormous advance over the older lime-board engravings and the black and white prints daubed with home-made paints by peasant housewives. Sytin first realized a great commercial success in 1877 by printing battlefield scenes and maps of the Russo-Turkish War, and he expanded next to publish calendars which featured an artist's drawing in several colours on the front cover and included a second bright picture as a 'premium.' Eye-catching illustrations also enlivened the texts Sytin printed for the village schools. (Because they readily engaged the young and rarely posed problems of censorship, pictures, said Sytin, 'carried the book.') Through other books, Sytin capitalized on a broad movement to teach adult peasants to read. Well aware of the debate in the newly organized literacy societies about how best to reach the 'people,' and of the surveys by experts of peasants' reading habits, Sytin none the less designed his books for the village market by following his own instincts and customers' advice.[78]

Leo Tolstoy, who had his own ideas about books for the people, enlisted the help of Sytin, who understood the peddler system. Tolstoy proposed a cheap, simplified series that would reflect his moral teachings and not be copyrighted. Writers, editors, and artists were to contribute their services. Sytin agreed and, as intermediary between writers and readers, chose the name 'Mediator' (*Posrednik*) for the series. Tolstoy wrote and edited many of the volumes himself. Artists, including Ilia Repin and Nicholas Ge, contributed drawings. Peddlers sold the end product at one-and-a-half copecks per copy. By the late 1880s, Sytin had produced one hundred titles in more than twelve million copies for the Mediator series, the greatest effort of all to reach the peasants. Despite such projects, however, the peasants kept their preference for the old-time pictures and stories.[79]

Sytin could afford such philanthropic publishing because authors and artists gave their services and because his publishing business as a whole reaped impressive profits. As his business expanded during the eighties, Sytin reorganized his company and added stores in several cities. In 1893, he was to found a joint stock company and five years later reached a gross annual income of over a million-and-a-half rubles. In 1905 that annual figure would again more than double and, in 1915, with 11.5 per cent of all domestic publishing in Sytin's hands, would reach nearly eighteen million rubles.[80]

Important as his publishing house was, Sytin had no ties with the government and suffered his share of censorship trouble. For example, the peddlers who went out to the peasants came under close government control in 1881 because the emperor's advisor, Pobedonostsev, disapproved of the Tolstoyan character of the Mediator books. In addition, the government chose to impose restrictions on public libraries and reading rooms in the early nineties. In the latter case, Sytin organized a company section to advise libraries and reading rooms on the rules. Inevitably, some of his books failed to pass the censors, but given his ample resources, Sytin could always substitute something acceptable. Sytin faced several prosecutions in 1905, and although he won acquittals, the judges ordered the destruction of some brochures. Through it all, Sytin's company prospered.[81]

Although the censorship measures imposed during the two decades from 1870 to 1890 suggest a period of repression by the censorship authority in Russia, a wider view of the impact of the censorship system on all periodical publications and the publishing industry yields a different conclusion. The increased number of newspapers and popular periodicals and the spread of telegraph news services testify that the government continued to tolerate the development of a free publishing industry along the lines of those in Europe.

Like the governments of England after 1695, France after 1789, and Germany after 1874, the Russian imperial government after 1865 experimented with and adopted a variety of measures to control an unofficial press partly freed from preliminary censorship. These measures were largely designed to deal with radical writers and publishers rather than the press as a whole, and even the assassination of an emperor did not arrest the development of the trends discussed above.

13

The last years of the
administrative system, 1889–1906

Succeeding to the throne upon his father's death, Nicholas II (1894–1917) was to face a private publishing industry far larger and more influential than any of his predecessors had known. Its members, confident that they provided an essential service and buoyed by their commercial success in the overall industrial growth of the eighties and nineties, felt increasingly venturesome and proved more willing to organize for mutual assistance in many matters, including resistance to the censorship authority.

Censorship continued but with diminishing impact, as the government grudgingly and then resignedly withdrew its administrative controls over the unofficial press. During the last months of 1905, the press was to publish largely what it pleased, and in 1906 was to win from the emperor the complete withdrawal of preliminary censorship and the warning system. For all his insistence that the government have sufficient means to suppress printed words which sowed disorder, Nicholas II had as his only weapon against the radical press the force of law wielded by the judicial system.

I

The deaths of Ivan Aksakov in 1886 and Michael Katkov the next year had silenced two vocal and irascible Russian journalists during the calm concluding years of D.A. Tolstoy's term as minister of the interior and overseer of the censorship authority to 1889. Then, as always, writers grumbled about censors. In 1888, for example, Gleb Uspensky resigned from the *Northern Messenger* because, he said, the 'outrages of censorship' were warping his writing and the journal as well. According to

Alexander Kugel, a Moscow journalist, the censors were imposing a 'boring and flaccid' style on the press. On the other hand, the press conducted a lively debate throughout the second half of the eighties on the issue of local government, focusing in particular on Tolstoy's plans to reduce the authority of the zemstvos. Thoroughly involved were such publications as *Moscow Bulletin*, *Russian Wealth*, and *Russian Thought*.[1]

For critics of the censorship system, especially those within the juridical societies of Moscow and St Petersburg, the judicial reform of 1864 and the liberal features of the Statute of 1865 had set the right standards for controlling printed words. The Moscow society's monthly journal, *Judicial Messenger*, repeatedly took that stand. In 1887 an article opposed a project before the State Council to allow the minister of justice, not just the courts alone, to close trials to the public and the press. To ensure a 'truthful press,' *Messenger* in 1891 urged completion of the 1865 reform of censorship; and the next year it asked that the principle of publicity in the 1864 judicial reform be applied again to pre-trial criminal investigations and to political trials, as it had been before the late seventies.[2] For advocating these and other reforms, the journal was placed under preliminary censorship in 1892, but the editors instead ceased publication.

Journalists could see the value of the kind of professional solidarity binding the judicial societies; and in 1894, the year of a new emperor, *Russian Observer* proposed a society that could speak with one voice on behalf of the press. As the year ended, an ad hoc group of St Petersburg writers acted towards that end. Expressing the hope that the new emperor would grant the 'profession of journalists' that 'justice' of which he had spoken upon taking the throne, they drafted a petition, asking for an end to preliminary censorship, the warning system, and the bans placed on topics and on the street sales of newspapers. An accompanying explanatory note by G.K. Gradovsky traced the 'legal and illegal' means used by the government to subvert the principles of 1865.[3] Early in January 1895 seventy-eight St Petersburg writers and thirty-six from Moscow (a number were also attorneys and two had been on the staff of the *Judicial Messenger*) signed the petition, which went forward to Nicholas.[4]

Then came Nicholas's 'senseless dreams' remarks of 17 January telling zemstvo delegates to abandon hopes of participating in the central government. When, six weeks later, the journalists learned that their petition 'had not been acted upon,' Gradovsky appealed for help from Pobedonostsev, the procurator of the Holy Synod, because the press, he insisted, was the one institution capable of taking truthful stands on issues despite the follies of government or the crowd. Pobedonostsev made no reply.[5]

Not until two years later did St Petersburg writers actually found a society, the Union of Writers' Mutual Assistance, and, early in 1898, its fifteen-member judicial commission drafted another petition to Nicholas asking that administrative measures end.[6] On 24 April they sent the petition to Minister of the Interior I.L. Goremykin. Once again, the government made no response.

Three years were to pass before the government made its first move towards lifting administrative restrictions. It came on 4 June 1901, when the State Council approved the proposal of Minister of the Interior D.S. Sipiagin that a first warning (not followed by a second) be cancelled at the end of one year and that two warnings (not followed by a third) be cancelled at the end of two years.[7] No longer would the threat of preliminary censorship, automatically imposed after three warnings, hover indefinitely over a twice-warned periodical.

Complicating the question of press freedom in the meantime was the government's use of administrative, not judicial, means against the Social Democrats, or Marxists – proof, once again, that the courts alone could not adequately fight radical words.[8] Marxist periodicals had first become identifiable in the 1890s. From the fall of 1895 *Samara Messenger* (*Samarskii Vestnik*, founded in 1883) published articles – subject, one must note, to preliminary censorship – by all the leading Social Democrats. Those same writers, including Lenin, appeared in *Scholarly Review* (*Nauchnoe Obozrenie*, founded in January 1894, granted permission to broaden its program in 1896, and closed by the censorship authority in 1904). In 1896 Peter Struve became editor of *New Word* (*Novoe Slovo*) and made it a Marxist publication; it was the first such periodical to suffer a closure, that order coming from the Supreme Commission in 1897. Struve's next publication, *Beginning* (*Nachalo*), suffered the same fate and lasted only a few months in 1899. Other Marxist journals included *Life* (*Zhizn*, founded as a family journal in 1896 but closed by the government in 1901); *God's World* (*Mir Bozhii*, an extremely popular St Petersburg monthly for youth begun in 1892, recognizably a journal of the Social Democrats by the mid-nineties, and closed by the government in 1906); and *Truth* (*Pravda*, begun in January 1904 and closed in 1906).[9]

True to past practice, the government acted against these publications but not their staffs, who were left free to publish elsewhere. For their part, although they had ready access to émigré publications and to illegally published pamphlets, the Marxists (and other radical writers) used legal publishing channels with considerable care to keep a more socially acceptable outlet to a wider audience.

Troubled with such radicals, the government continued its debate over administrative versus judicial controls, a controversy that involved the broader question of the right relationship between the autocratic state and the people. An exchange in October 1902 between Minister of the Interior V.K. Plehve (Sipiagin had been assassinated in April) and Minister of Finance S.Iu. Witte (already ten years in that office) shows the main opposing positions within the government on fighting disaffection. Plehve was the quintessential tsarist loyalist who valued stern, commanding force; and Witte, the post-emancipation, modernist reformer who approved the autocracy as a Russian institution but favoured timely changes. Both were 'among the most illustrious and intelligent of Russian statesmen' of their time. Their debate took place informally, over dinner, and D.N. Liubimov, an official in Plehve's ministry, later recorded it from memory.[10]

In Liubimov's account, Witte held that the 'social movement' in Russia was too deep to yield to repressive police methods. The reforms of Alexander II had caused that movement by raising hopes of representation and individual rights, and the government should 'put itself at the head of it' by involving the educated classes in further reforms. Witte deplored that too many government leaders – he named Pobedonostsev, Count A.P. Ignatiev, and Senator A.A. Naryshkin – blindly rejected change.

Plehve agreed that the movement was deeper than many imagined – and he uttered 'many' in the muted tone he always used when speaking of the emperor, says Liubimov. Still the government should 'set limits on [disruption] in order to hold it back; there is no way to swim with the current, trying at all times to stay ahead of it.' As for the educated classes, continued Plehve, they were the revolutionaries. They wanted power, but any attempt by them to rule would unleash 'from the underground all the dangerous criminal elements with the Jews at their head' to ruin Russia. The educated elements might give advice, but the government alone had to decide when reforms were necessary. To this came Witte's reply: 'Most revolutions occur because the government does not satisfy ripened demands in time.'

Witte trusted the intelligentsia, which included the press, and believed that they would gladly support a reformist autocracy; Plehve thought the intelligentsia were foolishly bent on overturning the autocracy, which alone had the authority needed to rule Russia. In this exchange, three years before the revolution of 1905, both Witte and Plehve expected criticism of the government to intensify. Although neither mentioned the press, each was to try in 1902 to influence that institution in line with his views.

Witte and Plehve, it may be inferred, differed on who the intelligentsia were. Plehve, the police functionary, had in mind the traditional, rebellious, even radical members of the intelligentsia, so evident in the sixties and seventies, who used their periodicals, as Belinsky had earlier put it, as pulpits. They wished to stimulate a political movement against the autocracy, and some of them had connections with revolutionary organizations. These writers, from Chernyshevsky on, are even today synonymous with the Russian intelligentsia.

But in the eighties and nineties, along with the growth of the popular press, came the professional journalists, editors, and publishers, and these were among the intelligentsia Witte had in mind. (Few of them are given the place they deserve in Russian cultural history.) They sought to democratize the offerings of the Russian press and set about doing so by reporting news in a readable, colourful, and immediate fashion, as the great dailies of the West were doing. One of their main objectives was to show the 'human' side of events to ordinary readers, but another was to point out wrongs. Witte held that the new journalists were prepared to help improve and modernize Russia and its government peacefully. Their wish to publish unimpeded by arbitrary bureaucratic decisions lay behind their urging the government to return to the principles of its own legislation of 1865.

II

Still others Witte thought of as members of the intelligentsia were the many reform-minded lawyers and academicians. Two demonstrations of their support for press freedom took place not long after Witte's discussion with Plehve. The first was before the St Petersburg Juridical Society on 23 February 1903, when Senator A.F. Koni rose to salute V.D. Spasovich, prominent in the late sixties as defense counsel in press cases. Spasovich, said Koni, had clarified 'freedom of speech and its true limits' – a freedom, Koni implied, possible only when the courts exercised authority over the printed word.[11]

One day later, the divisions of Russian language and literature of the Russian Academy of Sciences petitioned the government for solely judicial controls over the press. The 'temporary regulations' should end, argued the academy petition, because censorship controls added since

1865 impeded education and scholarship. As proof the petitioners listed the many works, including major western ones, banned by censors; and they disagreed that a press controlled by the courts might endanger the state.[12]

On 26 February, however, the government wholly ignored censorship in its manifesto describing planned reforms. Rather, it promised religious toleration and financial aid to peasants and gentry, vowed to consider how citizens might take part in affairs of state and how peasants might leave communes, and pledged reforms to make provincial and local governments meet local needs.[13]

Despite this silence on press reform, some officials were all the while pondering how, not whether, to grant press freedom. Thus, about July 1904, on orders from Plehve, the Ministry of the Interior drafted a memorandum arguing that giving the press absolute freedom would wrongly permit subversive books to circulate, however briefly.[14] Agreeing that the government should end preliminary censorship and leave violations of the criminal code to the courts, the memorandum insisted on pre-circulation screenings to permit the seizure of criminal works before they went on the market.

When on 15 July, a terrorist killed Plehve, Prince Sviatopolk-Mirsky succeeded as minister of the interior, accepting the post on the understanding that the emperor favoured a reformist program, including a free press. Mirsky immediately attracted press support, but Nicholas bitterly remarked that reforms would merely placate the 'intelligentsia,' not, as Mirsky insisted, public opinion generally. Still, the emperor must have known from the outset Mirsky's plans to 'soften' autocracy – a term D.N. Liubimov says he heard the minister use many times.[15] Mirsky confidently included in his proposals to fellow ministers late in 1904 a plan for representation from the upper classes on the State Council.

Reference to the reform discussions under way was made on 19 November in a public meeting arranged by the St Petersburg Juridical Society to mark the fortieth anniversary of the judicial reform. K.K. Arsenev called for freedom of the press and cited the good years for publishing in the late sixties when courts had a degree of authority; and M.I. Sveshnikov deplored the piecemeal addition of press regulations since that time which had largely ended judicial involvement.[16]

Although, on 8 December, the emperor and his ministers accepted Mirsky's proposals, Nicholas had second thoughts and rejected the consultative assembly Mirsky so strongly advocated. The rest of Mirsky's program became the principles enunciated in Nicholas's decree of 12

December, published two days later in *Government Messenger*. Those principles were, in Count Witte's summation, meant 'to establish legality; extend freedom of speech, religious toleration, and the scope of local self-government [*zemstvos*]; to remove disabilities on national minorities; and to eliminate all manner of extraordinary laws.' Their implementation fell to the Committee of Ministers under Count Witte.[17]

In discussing press policy on 28 and 30 December, the committee had before it the memorandum from the Interior ministry of mid-year, the 1903 Academy of Sciences petition, and point eight of the December ukaz, which committed the government to ending needless restrictions on publishing and setting clear legal limits. The ministers recommended two new bodies: a Special Conference for the Drafting of a New Statute on the Press and a watch-dog agency over the Ministry of the Interior.[18]

On 9 January 1905, a week after the start of a general strike in St Petersburg, the tragic shooting of marching workers since known as 'Bloody Sunday' stirred widespread anger against the government. Three days later the censorship administration prohibited uncensored publications from reporting 'news on strikes and disorders without permission of the local police chiefs.'[19] By month's end two more rules banned 'inciting' articles on the worker question or published accounts of 'clashes' between the military and crowds or individuals. So volatile were events, Mirsky stepped down as minister of the interior to be succeeded on 20 January by A.G. Bulygin; but the modest beginnings towards censorship reform continued.

With Bulygin in their ranks, the Committee of Ministers on 21 January proposed changing several press regulations. They saw no need for the minister of the interior to prohibit advertisements in unofficial publications (as empowered by orders in 1863 and 1879) or to require the dismantling of typeforms for a book before its pre-circulation examination (as ordered in 1874). Only for specific prosecutions or for security needs, said the ministers, should the names of anonymous authors be demanded. Finally, the committee wanted not just the opinion of the minister of the interior, but of outside experts as well, before it banned a book – a modification of the order of 7 June 1872.[20]

Nicholas approved these proposals. Then, although he apparently had rejected the watch-dog agency over the Ministry of the Interior favoured before Mirsky's resignation by the ministers, the emperor on 26 January announced the chairman of a special conference to draft a new statute on publishing – D.F. Kobeko, director of the Imperial Library. Under Kobeko, twenty-four experts named from 'members of the Imperial

Academy of Sciences, honored academicians, ... eminent journalists and publicists, and representatives from responsible departments' were to complete the draft within two years.[21] They began work at once and voted 15 to 8 on 17 February to end the warning system and the authority of the minister of the interior to suspend periodicals.[22] Faced with an organized and insistent call for censorship reform and with public unrest, the government was moving again to end administrative censorship.

As drafting progressed, Minister of the Interior Bulygin proposed another reform: ending 'regular payments' to unofficial publications and giving more funds to government periodicals, particularly those not blatantly official. Nicholas disagreed, but Bulygin did win a larger budget for *Village Messenger* (*Selskii Vestnik*), published by the Ministry of the Interior for the peasants.[23] This newspaper was to reach a daily circulation of 115,000 later in 1905, all but 15,000 through paid subscriptions.

Another plan for government publishing reached the emperor about this time from the man named governor-general of St Petersburg following Bloody Sunday, former police chief D.F. Trepov. With D.P. Golitsyn, a member of the Kobeko conference, Trepov proposed a new 'unofficial' St Petersburg daily, *Russia* (*Rossiia*), to counter papers critical of the government. Nicholas gave his approval and agreed to transfer 100,000 rubles to Golitsyn in September for secret arrangements.[24] Reflecting the division within his own government on how to deal with the press, the emperor chose to use both open reforms and covert means to influence public opinion.

In the spring of 1905, Nicholas made two other decisions affecting the press. On 17 April he decreed religious toleration and ended all penalties against persons leaving the Russian Orthodox faith. Ecclesiastical censorship, the preventer of published heresy, lost its main reason for being – a development the Kobeko conference would have to deal with. In May Nicholas approved the State Council's decision to abolish the Supreme Commission and transfer its authority to close periodicals to the Senate, acting on the recommendation of the minister of the interior.[25] The minister, in turn, surrendered his power to suspend periodicals under preliminary censorship.

Beset with strikes, losses in the year-old war with Japan, and money shortages, Nicholas turned more and more to Count Witte as his advisor. Witte had plans of his own for dealing with the press based on his experience as finance minister from 1892 to 1903, when he had so successfully rallied public opinion behind railroad building and industrial development. Part of his success lay in cultivating the press – at home, through communiqués and personal contact; abroad, through agents and funds.[26]

Witte's agent in Paris, Arthur Rafalovich, for example, had warned the minister in 1901 that local bankers saw the criticism of Russia by the French press as a threat to the price of Russian bonds on the Paris bourse. Witte responded with some 160,000 francs to buy pro-Russian articles. As he explained to Nicholas, 'not one of our loans in France would have been realized without some influence on the press by the bankers floating the loan,' and those bankers were insisting that Russia help pay the bribes.[27]

Although Nicholas I had taken similar steps, the first concerted program to win support abroad had begun in 1884 under Alexander III, when P.I. Rachkovsky went to Paris to establish and head the Foreign Agency (unofficially tagged the *Zagranichnaia Okhrana*, or Foreign Okhrana) under the Department of Police then headed by Plehve in the ministry of the interior. From the Russian embassy in Paris, Rachkovsky dealt with agents in Europe and England and, by the end of the 1880s, was spending 90,000 rubles a year and enjoying close ties with the French secret police.[28] In March 1892 Rachkovsky reported that he had sent 2,000 copies of a brochure discrediting the Russian revolutionary movement to editors and officials in England, Europe, and even America.[29]

In 1902 Plehve moved up to become minister of the interior and sent to Paris as his agent an experienced intriguer. He was Ivan F. Manuilov-Manasevich, who was to boast about the 'very great sums entrusted to me.' After harsh articles had appeared in Europe against the so-called Kishinev massacre in Russia during Easter 1903, Manuilov received orders to correct 'misinformation' about the pogrom in English, French, and German papers. He directly subsidized *Figaro*, *L'Echo de Paris*, and *Gaulois*, one year spending 24,000 francs.[30]

Through 1903 these foreign bribes by the ministry of the interior were distinct from Witte's campaign to influence foreign opinion. Then, early in 1904, Witte set after his highest goal yet – approval from France for the sale there of Russian bonds worth 2.25 billion francs. Because efforts to win that loan required careful co-ordination, the Russian ambassador in Paris, Alexander Nelidov, early in 1904 assumed authority over all information released by government personnel abroad, even by Manuilov.[31] Rafalovich continued to disburse funds to influence the press only until March, when Plehve established a Section on the Foreign Press under the Chief Administration of Press Affairs and limited the Foreign Okhrana to intelligence matters.

Close connections between Plehve's new section and Count Witte's campaign for French funds are apparent in the transfer to the services of Plehve in 1904 of a distinguished Witte agent – S.S. Tatishchev, probably the most able and learned of the imperial propagandists. In the eighties, he had collaborated with Katkov on *Russian Messenger* and, following Katkov's death in 1887, conducted *Messenger*'s foreign politics section from 1889 to 1897, also working for Suvorin's *New Times* and writing four histories sympathetic to the autocracy.[32] Tatishchev joined Witte's Finance ministry in 1898 and served as the minister's agent in London until 1902.

By March 1904 Tatishchev had joined Plehve's new Section on the Foreign Press; for, in that month, Manuilov in Paris learned that he was to take orders from the section and that his controlling officer would be Tatishchev. Very soon Manuilov was arranging a June interview in the French capital between a Paris publisher and Tatishchev. Tatishchev must also have directed Manuilov's founding in 1904 of a small Paris journal to extol Russia, *La Revue Russe*, staffed solely by Frenchmen and located within the editorial offices of *Figaro* at a cost of 10,000 francs per month.[33]

En route to Paris in May, Tatishchev paused to recruit an agent for Plehve in Germany. While there, he reported to the minister that he had found in German papers an unremitting hostility towards Russia. He would, he said, propose counter-measures for the Russian embassy in Berlin and plans for reforming the Russian 'press bureau' when he returned to St Petersburg.[34]

What appeared in print about Russia during the bond negotiations during 1904 and 1905 mattered greatly, and in those two years the imperial government spent 2.5 million francs to influence the French press. The 'press bureau' in St Petersburg to which Tatishchev referred was also called upon to write articles throwing the best light on such recurring disruptions in Russia as strikes and pogroms. In the summer of 1905, for example, the bureau would try to minimize the Potemkin mutiny in the Russian Black Sea fleet.[35]

The purchase of favourable publicity attests to the government's mounting anxiety over public opinion. The emperor and high officials like Plehve and Witte had come to agree that to secure positive reportage abroad the government had to buy it. In supporting this practice and a similar one at home, the emperor followed policies like those of Germany during Bismarck's time.

III

With respect to the domestic press, the major challenge to the government in 1905 came not from genuinely radical writers, for their influence was slight, but from the increasingly-Europeanized press as a whole. Periodicals with mass circulations had the capacity to shape public opinion on a wide scale. Press controls that had earlier intimidated small journals had little effect on modern, fact-finding newspapers backed by considerable financial resources, supported by loyal readerships, and linked directly to the news wires of the world. Foremost among them was *Russian Word* (*Russkoe Slovo*), owned by I.D. Sytin, who was discussed earlier as the leading publisher of books for peasants and the schools.

When, before the turn of the century, his writer-friend Anton Chekhov had urged him to start a newspaper, Sytin had facetiously doubted that the government would grant permission to someone it regarded as a 'dirty liberal.'[36] Then in 1899, with government approval, he acquired *Russian Word*, a small, ailing Moscow paper noted for its ardent nationalism and kept alive by a government subsidy. Very gradually changing the staff and editorial policy, Sytin by 1902 had carried through his plan to transform the paper into a kind familiar in Europe but little known in Russia. He did it by concentrating on fast, arresting, accurate coverage of news events; by separating news from opinion; and by charging low subscription rates (his price of eight rubles per year was the lowest of any major daily in Russia).

Under Sytin, *Word* stressed 'progressive' and practical matters, and its editors felt free to print full reports on the government, including its errors. One principal writer described the paper's success in these words: 'The *Russian Word* did not try to play an influential role. All its strength was in its distribution.'[37] But that wide distribution and immense circulation depended in large part on the editors presenting in print material that attracted readers' attention.

Bent on striking an identity of interest between his staff and his readers, Sytin required that all editors be Russian and that news be 'filtered' through them (his writers included many nationalities). Vlas Doroshevich, *Word*'s popular and emulated author of *feuilletons*, set the standard for writing with his staccato style, 'galloping' thought, and regular play of opposites. Now virtually forgotten, Doroshevich at the turn of the century was a writer of stature second only to Chekhov himself, in the view of Leo Tolstoy.[38]

Sparing no costs, Sytin insisted on telegraphed and even telephoned reports from his correspondents in the provinces and his one-hundred-man bureau in St Petersburg. So much news flowed into the Moscow telegraph agency that Sytin, ever mindful of attracting attention, hired a rider and a white horse to relay dispatches to his news-room. In time, the agency moved next door to Sytin's operations and, finally, installed a wire directly into the news-room.

When the Russo-Japanese War broke out in 1904, reporters from *Word* at the front rushed news of that mounting military disaster back to Moscow, and *Word* spread their reports throughout Russia. (Rigid publishing deadlines ensured that daily editions made their way to the provinces on the earliest trains departing Moscow.) Profits and circulation soared. In 1903, the year before the war, *Word* grossed 422,700 rubles; in 1904, the gross was 943,400 rubles. The press run was just under 50,000 in 1903; it more than doubled in 1904 and more than tripled in 1905. By 1916 the paper's circulation of 750,000 was the largest ever achieved by a Russian daily newspaper.

Coverage of the Russo-Japanese War by *Word* and other papers had decided political effects, for in no small measure it undermined public trust in the imperial government and strengthened arguments for change. What one reader said of the daily *Russian Bulletin* applied generally: 'The failure of the war began to be discussed as the ruin of the old regime ... Persons who earlier did not want to hear about opinion expressed in *Russian Bulletin* began to speak about the need for a constitution.'[39] Moreover, the papers, in describing the war, had not violated censorship regulations. The new capacity of Russian papers to discover facts and to disclose them to a wide public audience very simply meant an end to the power of the autocracy, through censorship and other measures, to require that its rule always appear in the best light.

IV

Through the mounting unrest of 1905, the Kobeko conference met repeatedly. The enormous growth and influence of the press had virtually foreclosed the continuation of preliminary censorship and administrative restrictions. Still, the government had to decide precisely what its authority over the press would be. By its thirty-first session in the first week of

October, the conference had drafted proposals to abolish preliminary censorship and the warning system, give the courts sole authority over publishing crimes, and grant any law-abiding citizen of at least twenty-five years the right to open a periodical.[40]

On the restrictive side, the conference favoured retaining the censorship administration to inspect Russian and foreign periodicals before they circulated. As before, censors were to confiscate all works deemed criminal and to initiate prosecution against those published in Russia. The conference also proposed that judicial decisions appear in the press in official form only and opposed references to pre-trial investigations or charges.[41] Then, apparently having completed periodical regulations and being not yet ready to proceed to those for books, the conference recessed, very likely hampered by the mounting unrest in the capital.

Within the next week the St Petersburg Soviet of Workers' Deputies met and declared a general strike. Before another week had passed, Nicholas II issued on the pages of *Government Messenger* his October 17 Manifesto promising suffrage rights, an elective legislative body, and freedom of speech and assembly. Witte, the prime instigator and drafter of the manifesto, had high hopes for it. For one thing, it would help him draw the periodical press back from tending to undermine the government. As his first step, on the day the manifesto was issued, Witte invited the editors of thirty-three publications in St Petersburg for 'conversation' in his own apartment the next day at 11:00 a.m.

Whether Witte knew it or not, these same editors – with their publishers – had formed the Union for the Defense of Freedom of Speech just one day before. Having failed to organize in January to protest restrictions on reporting Bloody Sunday, they had now united in anger over restrictions relating to the escalating strike movement. (Some were already independently bypassing censorship when the printers joined the general strike and closed most publishing plants on 14 October.) The day-old union met three times on 17 October, its first session interrupted by the appearance of the manifesto early that evening.

After cheering the breakthrough, the union resolved that members were to comment freely on the manifesto in print. At Witte's meeting, too, they would freely speak their minds, although one designate would express the union's demands: freedom of the press and amnesty for those arrested for political acts during the year.[42]

The next day forty editors met with Witte and heard this extraordinary plea: 'I appeal to you as a Russian, as a citizen, and not as a courtier or minister. Help me to calm minds. This calming depends chiefly on you.

While disorders remain, nothing can be done.'[43] Witte was banking strongly that his candour and sincerity would win over his listeners.

New Times (Novoe Vremia) editor M.A. Suvorin responded first, insisting that 'political amnesty' for those arrested during 1905 took first priority in calming the country; and S.M. Propper of the Stock Market Bulletin repeated the demand as 'categorical' because the press in the capital had united in 'political agreement' about it. News (Novosti) representative K.I. Arabazhin expressed the other union demand: 'freedom of the printed word as declared in the manifesto.' A disconcerted Witte repeatedly protested against any demands from the press, and Prince Ukhtomsky, editor of St Petersburg Bulletin, described the session as 'depressing.'[44] Neither side promised anything or made a bid for conciliation.

Later that day Witte issued a public statement as president of the newly-formed Council of Ministers and leader of the government. In it he gave the guidelines for change as those already published in the ukaz of 12 December 1904, based on Sviatopolk-Mirsky's modest reform program. Freedom of the press would come, vowed Witte, before the start of the first State Duma. Two days later, Witte stressed to the public the need for restored order and for time to implement reforms.[45] On the next day, 21 October, when papers reappeared as the strike ended, most editors scorned Witte's meeting and largely criticized the manifesto.

Witte expressed in his memoirs his bitter disappointment over the October 18 meeting. The belligerent tone of the editors had convinced him not to depend on a press 'completely demoralized' except for those 'openly advocating an arch-democratic republic.' Witte also blamed the new Printers' Union and the 'pocket-book considerations' of publishers for causing 'almost all the papers' to be 'revolutionized.'[46]

To be sure, coercion by the printers was in evidence following a government decree issued on 19 October. Aimed at those bypassing censorship, the decree required periodicals to obey existing censorship rules until a new press statute appeared. The St Petersburg Soviet at once ordered the Printers' Union not to work for any publisher who complied. Publications submitted by any editor for inspection 'will be confiscated from the sellers and destroyed, printing plants and machinery will be damaged, and workers who do not submit to the order of the Soviet will be boycotted.'[47] During the 'days of freedom' in late October and early November, printers also refused to print what they disliked and required publishers to reprint articles from the Soviet's News (Izvestiia), plus manifestos and calls for strike support.

Along with the collapse of the censorship authority in October came the breakdown of the inspection system for printing plants and bookstores. As a consequence, the Social Democrats and Social Revolutionaries freely used regular publishing and distribution means to circulate more copies of their writings than would have been possible using only clandestine presses. The Bolsheviks' Forward Bookstore and the Social Revolutionaries' School and Library Bookstore are only two examples of legal bookstores which served as outlets for socialist literature. Publishers of illegal works also devised means to circumvent whatever inspections did take place. The Marxist publisher Maria Malykh, for example, would print more copies of a pamphlet than she noted in her record books. If the police arrived to confiscate a press run, she would surrender the number of copies recorded, having hidden the rest.[48]

In this same period Witte received Tatishchev's 'Project for the Organization of a Government Press,' which opposed secret subsidies and favoured the start of semi-official papers.[49] These papers, like the official ones, would openly use state funds and staff; but they would correct misinformation in the unofficial press, defend 'persons under attack who have a reasonable mode of thought,' and explain the government's 'general program.' Tatishchev gave highest priority to a semi-official daily in St Petersburg under the minister of the interior but closely connected with the president of the Council of Ministers (Witte). He also wanted the government to revitalize its seventy-five provincial bulletins.

Although Witte relayed the project to Trepov, the St Petersburg Governor-General was then helping to launch a capital daily of the kind Tatishchev opposed – the ostensibly-unofficial *Russia*, planned with Golitsyn and approved by Nicholas during the first half of the year. Under editor V. von Briskorn, *Russia* began in November and, during 1906, was to reach a press run of 30,000. On his own, in February 1906, Witte launched the kind of daily Tatishchev favoured, *The Russian State* (*Russkoe Gosurdarstvo*), and Tatishchev would have edited it but for his sudden death that winter.[50]

Witte's main objective in the post-manifesto period was to restore government authority and public order. To deal with the press, he wrote new rules to grant the freedom he had promised, although that freedom was to have limits. The proposals of the Kobeko conference, he said, 'partly served as material' but, with respect to freedom of the press, were cut 'in significant degree.'[51] The result was the statute of 24 November 1905, an attempt to strengthen press controls under the label of freedom of the press.

The new laws abolished for all periodicals (except in the provinces) whatever pre-circulation screening each had been subject to. Instead, a registered 'responsible editor' was to give a local 'press affairs' (not 'censorship') committee each issue as it began circulating. Upon discovering criminal content in a periodical, the committee could 'arrest,' or seize, all unsold copies, so long as the Court of Appeals had agreed to initiate prosecution; and because the periodicals would have circulated, those responsible could be convicted of completing a crime, not acquitted for merely preparing one. In addition, the rules ended ecclesiastical censorship 'in the cities [not defined] of Russia,' gave the courts sole jurisdiction over press crimes, and permitted any twenty-five-year-old citizen in good standing to start a periodical. Finally, Witte included a law forbidding periodicals to publish words which incited disorder.

Because common usage defined a 'free press' as one subject solely to the courts, Nicholas II could declare that he was granting 'one of the fundamental freedoms' through the ukaz of 24 November which decreed the new statute law. 'These regulations,' declared the emperor, 'remove all administrative rules in the area of the periodical press and restore decision making to the court in matters of criminal nature committed by the printed word.'[52] Rules for book publishing were yet to be written, but the Russian government, in eliminating administrative measures, had given up distinguishing 'dangerous' words from 'criminal' ones. The burden of policing the printed word would now fall on the procuracy and the courts.

A blizzard of prosecutions against the press was to follow in Russia beginning in late 1905, and critics of the new system would insist that the press had not secured real freedom because the Russian criminal code defined press crimes so loosely. But, strictly speaking, the Russian periodical press had been freed.

Meanwhile, to enhance his relations with the public and the press, Witte on 25 November acquired as a press emissary Alexei A. Spassky, an aide who favoured personal appeals to editors and who, in effect, became the first public relations officer or communications director for the government. Spassky approached several editors to argue that their support for Witte would help save the nation; and, when the semi-official daily *Russian State* began in February, Spassky was to serve editor N.A. Gurev as principal assistant and editorialist.[53]

In the general tumult, Witte had so far largely deferred taking action against law-breaking by the periodical press; but, on 2 December, eight St Petersburg dailies published a revolutionary 'Financial Manifesto' prepared by the local Soviet of Workers' Deputies and endorsed by four major radical groups. To bring the government to a 'full standstill,' the manifesto urged citizens to withdraw all savings in gold coins from the State Bank and to insist on gold or silver in transactions with banks – a desperate measure to keep opposition alive. Some papers printed the manifesto, one observer argues, 'partly because of pressure from printers who refused to release the paper unless [the manifesto] was carried on the front page.'[54] Ineffectual though it was, its appearance reflected badly on the government at a time when Witte was concluding negotiations for the sale of Russian bonds in France.

With the approval of the Council of Ministers, Witte closed the eight papers, filed suits against their publishers, and seized all issues carrying the financial manifesto. Although he had tolerated earlier manifestos, this one, in Witte's words, was 'revolutionary' and 'had as its aim the bankruptcy of the government.'[55] Without consulting his ministers, Witte on 3 December ordered the arrest of the executive committee and the council of the Soviet, about 250 persons in all. Such militant action made some ministers fear even greater disturbances. Scattered uprisings did occur in a number of cities, including Moscow, that December, but the government more and more reasserted its authority.

One means employed to regain control of the situation was the rash of court cases against the press. Publisher A.A. Suvorin of *Russia* (*Rus*), for example, faced charges both for the financial manifesto and for earlier notices and manifestos. Attorney S.A. Andreevsky argued in Suvorin's defence that papers should publish all news-worthy items because they 'stand on neutral ground like a Red Cross dressing station.'[56] Ruling that Suvorin had violated article 129 by intending to incite mutiny, the Court of Appeals on 7 January 1906 sentenced him to a year in jail.

A week later, the same court heard Andreevsky argue that publisher L.V. Khodsky of *Our Life* (*Nasha Zhizn*) had neither agreed with the financial manifesto published in his paper nor demonstrated 'practical activity' to incite mutiny, a proof the court had heretofore required for conviction under article 129. (Courts in 1905 had specifically rejected the printing of general propaganda as 'practical activity' in this sense, a stand the Senate had upheld – probably in recognition of the printers' coerciveness.) This time agreeing with Andreevsky, the court fined Khodsky five hundred rubles for violating the November regulation banning 'criminal content' in periodicals, but did not send him to jail for incitement.[57]

On the procurator's appeal, the Senate redefined 'practical activity.' Whether sharing the 'convictions expressed' or not, it ruled, the accused need know only that he was publishing content that could incite crimes.

As a warning to others not to bow to printers' demands, the Senate sentenced Khodsky to jail.[58]

Although figures are imprecise, the government closed well over fifty periodicals in the two months after the financial manifesto. One source lists the arrest of fifty-eight editors and closure of seventy-eight periodicals; another, the closure of sixty-three periodicals.[59] Russian editors, publishers, and writers paid a high personal and financial price for the elimination of censorship; but European precedents had already shown that the introduction of press freedom meant the government would use alternative measures to control the printed word.

V

Seeming loopholes in laws regulating the press caused the Council of Ministers to write its rules of 18 March 1906.[60] These new regulations set court-imposed fines of up to three hundred rubles for anyone publishing a periodical without holding an appropriate license or without identifying the publisher and printer. They forbade the publisher of a suspended paper to start another (a measure that proved ineffective) and authorized the government to seize stereotype plates of issues arrested by court order. To give the government time to lay charges and seize issues the moment they began to circulate, the ministers required satirical journals to submit illustrations to press affairs committees at least twenty-four hours before publication.

On 3 April came the heady news that Russia could sell bonds on the French market to raise 2.25 billion francs. Having accomplished that goal, Witte stepped down as president of the Council of Ministers; his successor, Goremykin stopped the publication of *Russian State*. That paper had appeared, Witte himself said, for 'one reader alone – his Majesty'; for Nicholas had scrutinized it closely. Spassky testified that Witte used its columns to test the emperor's reaction to tentative proposals.[61]

Witte's departure deprived the government of a leader skilled in public relations, and Goremykin made no efforts along these lines during his brief tenure until 9 July. His successor, P.A. Stolypin, was to make full use of *Russia*, the paper the emperor was funding; but he did so clumsily. Because many knew it was a government-run paper, a question about who financed *Russia* was later to come up during a Duma interpellation. Stolypin directed a deputy to describe the paper as a 'private publication,' and Witte took pains to record in his memoirs that the press thereafter regularly denigrated *Russia* as 'that private publication.'[62]

Witte had promised a free press before the first Duma, and on 26 April, with only one day to spare, a ukaz announced new rules set by the Council of Ministers for books, brochures, and pamphlets.[63] Complementing Witte's rules for periodicals of 24 November 1905, these regulations allowed most books to reach the public at the same time that they reached the local press affairs committees. Exceptions were short works: those up to sixteen pages were due at least two days before circulating and those of from seventeen to eighty pages (up to five signatures), at least seven days early. With such advance inspection, the government could seize and initiate prosecution of short works viewed as criminal the moment circulation began, so that very few reached the public.

These pre-circulation inspections dictated in the new law did somewhat circumscribe the 'free press' principle because the government could prevent some printed works from reaching readers.[64] But confiscations were permanent only for works found criminal by the courts; they were lifted for works the courts found legal.

Thus completed, the Statute of 1906 ended censorship (with only minor exceptions) in Russia. The courts alone could ban, in part or in full, legally printed works and alone could penalize those responsible. (Works printed illegally – that is, secretly on unlicensed presses – were at once criminal and subject to police seizure whenever and wherever they appeared; and these are outside the scope of this study.) Forty-one years after the Statute of 1865 had committed the government to move toward granting it, 'press freedom' was law. That freedom was to continue, with certain adjustments, for the remaining peaceful years of the imperial government – in other words until the outbreak of war in 1914 brought military censorship.

As for the frequency of prosecution of periodicals, one set of available figures for October 1905 through December 1906 shows 433 confiscations followed by prosecutions in St Petersburg alone. Of the 113 periodicals then in St Petersburg, just over half, or 59, suffered one prosecution each. Closures of periodicals throughout the empire totalled 371 in this same period; closures of printing plants totalled 97, with 607 fines or jail terms meted out to publishers, editors, and writers.[65]

Through prosecutions, the state continued to harass outspoken publications. It repeatedly prosecuted *Russian Bulletin*, for example, but won only two convictions. As for taking Marxists to court, there were 126 prosecutions against the Bolsheviks' *Truth* and its various incarnations over 416 issues, 130 prosecutions over 294 issues of the Mensheviks' *Beam* (*Luch*) and its offshoots. There were 46 prosecutions over 96 issues of the Socialist Revolutionary paper *Workers' Voice* (*Trudovoi Golos*).[66] And, in cases against what it termed 'radical papers,' the St Petersburg Press Affairs Committee credited the courts with an eighty-five per cent conviction rate.

Many officials would have preferred convictions in every case. Goremykin, for example, complained to the emperor in June 1906 about a 'revolutionary' segment of the press in the capital; he contended that 'judicial prosecutions are not attaining their objective' and that 'to count on the law alone is impossible.'[67]

Advantages to the government built into the press statute in turn became the target of publishers and booksellers at their first congress in 1909. 'The former censorship caused a mass of abuses for publishing,' they said, 'but it protected the editor and the bookseller from the annoyances of judicial prosecution.' By ending preliminary censorship, the government had granted 'more or less real freedom of the press.' But, they concluded, our 'criminal law remains on the old foundations' – that is, it favoured the state. One specific objection was the absence of a time limit on a book's liability to prosecution.[68]

The Statute of 1906 granting the press its 'freedom' is the end point of this study of the imperial administrative system of censorship begun in 1804. By western standards, the Russian government in 1906 had only belatedly freed its unofficial press. But, judged in the Russian historical setting, the creation and dismantling of a preliminary censorship system during the span of the nineteenth century accorded with the growth patterns of the Russian press and its readership and with the reform efforts of the autocracy. As in the West, the government eventually found censorship a political liability, abolished it, and introduced press freedom, in turn making greater use of judicial restraints on the printed word.

14

Autocracy and the press:
the historic conflict

This history of government censorship and the press in Imperial Russia bears out the statements by Nabokov and Solzhenitsyn (cited in the first chapter) that the autocracy granted extensive publishing freedom, governed by law, and did so to a degree far greater than westerners realize. The government had gone a long way towards western practices in dealing with an institution – the press – that had developed by copying western precedents. But this study also shows that the government fell far short in implementing the principles of the reform of 1865 and thereby itself contributed to the growth of opposition to the throne in the second half of the nineteenth and first few years of the twentieth centuries. Moreover, by the early twentieth century, the Imperial government faced a periodical press that could not be stopped from exposing the shortcomings of the autocracy.

The fight over what words should appear in print was and is universal, and the confrontation between the government and the privately owned press in Imperial Russia in many ways duplicated the European experience. There are marked differences, however, with respect to when and under what kind of rule the European press and the Russian press gradually won freedom from preliminary censorship. During all the years that publishing in Russia advanced from simple beginnings to the modern age of rapid printing and massive circulations, the absolutist government remained essentially unchanged.

The imperial government permitted privately owned presses only in the late 1700s, centuries after their beginnings in the West. Not until the second quarter of the nineteenth century could Russian editors and publishers, still under the tutelage of the state, sell their works in sufficient numbers to prosper commercially. Only during the reign of Alexander II, when that tutelage largely disappeared, did journalists begin to write about governmental issues from an independent point of view. From that time through the second half of the nineteenth century, publishers modernized quickly, and, despite continuing government restrictions, increased the influence of their periodicals and books through ever wider readerships. Their efforts amounted to an explosion in Russian printing, publishing, and journalism. At the same time, nowhere more than in Russia did modern journalism stand in such sharp contrast to a system of outmoded absolutistic controls. These partly effective controls, as Fouché and Von Vock had anticipated much earlier, stirred in writers an irritation against the state which they passed on to their readers.

By giving the press a position recognized in law in 1865, the imperial government did modify its paternalistic role over the printed word. Under the statute of that year, writers, editors, and publishers could for the first time in Russia defend before the courts the legality of what they had published and circulated. Such a modifying of the old preliminary censorship system gave all writers, radicals included, the opportunity to publicize their views both in print and in open courtrooms. As never before, 'dangerous' words could legally reach the Russian public.

At the same time, the new legal requirements for openness by the government in its dealings with the press proved to have a debilitating effect on the post-1865 censorship system. Prior to 1865, the decisions of the Russian censor were confidential. A censor might suggest to an author why a particular passage or work was unacceptable (as Nikitenko did in the late forties in refusing to permit the publication of Obodovsky's 'Bogdan Khmelnitsky'); but he did not make public his decision or the reasons for it.

All that changed once censors began to issue administrative warnings based on published writings. The reform of 1865 required not only that the censor state his reasons for warning a publication but also that the periodical publish that statement of warning. This practice, designed to chasten editors and writers and to make clear the limits on public discourse, served to place in full view of the public what often seemed to be vague and petty rulings by censors. In turn, such exposure could and did arouse public derision, as did some of the charges lodged by censorship officials against members of the press who were put on trial. In the wake of the 1865 reform, moreover, such new and obvious administrative measures as limits on street sales of papers and on private advertisements, along with bans on 'sensitive' topics, stirred in the reading public and the press a shared antagonism against seemingly trivial interventions by the government.

Public awareness of what and why censors censured inevitably accompanied the shift to post-publication censorship and open trials for persons accused of press-related crimes under the reform of 1865. To the discomfort of officials, conducting censorship in the public arena revealed the inconsistencies of the system more strongly than ever, gave guidance to those who wished to circumvent or undermine it, and focused public attention on words the government preferred to keep from the public altogether.

Whether the words of the amorphous 'press' tend more to reflect public opinion or to shape it was as insoluble a question then as it is today; but, invariably, the emperor accepted the power of the printed word to sway the reader. Imperial proclamations and sacred texts had long commanded the obedient trust and faith of Russian subjects and had thereby lent a certain mystique and strong authority to words imprinted on paper. Knowing that the simple and untutored all too readily believed anything in print, the government feared even more the proclivity of the educated young to receive as profound truth every published criticism of the established order. Aware of the role of the press in revolutions in the West, many nineteenth-century imperial officials shared the rationale of the Romantic Age on which Admiral Shishkov based the 'cast-iron statute' of 1826: words by and of themselves can subvert the existing order.

Conversely, many held that to follow the Miltonian tradition by expecting all readers to exercise their reason and to judge carefully whatever appeared in print was to foster another evil: scepticism, an attitude of mind that would itself undermine humble obedience to church and state. The plans of Golovnin and other liberal officials to promote vigorous public debate as an antidote to the poisonous ideas of the radicals consequently did not find widespread support within the government and held no appeal for the emperor. The government was unwilling to encourage Russians to think critically about its policies and the fundamental ideas which supported the political and social order.

Evidence that the autocracy greatly feared the effects of printed words on the reading public is its insistence as late as 1906 that the state retain pre-circulation inspection rights over printed words intended for a popular audience – a means to ensure immediate seizure of anything criminal the moment it went on the market. The autocracy by that time knew it had lost the allegiance of the intelligentsia; intent on keeping the masses loyal, it feared further losses in an open contest of ideas.

From 1804 to 1863, preliminary censorship in Imperial Russia operated under the Ministry of Public Education. This agency could and did show a certain paternalistic concern for Russian literature and recruited writers and academics to serve as censors. While it cautioned members of the press, closed certain periodicals, and banned unacceptable words prior to publication, it in no way penalized writers. (Authorities outside the ministry, including the emperor, periodically did so.) Overall, the main problem for the ministry was its wide but imprecise mandate: it was to forbid the appearance of 'dangerous words,' an entirely open category that was impossible to define.

The Ministry of the Interior assumed authority over censorship in 1863 under the same mandate but with quite different powers. Under this ministry, officials of the censorship system became responsible for imposing new administrative penalties, for deciding when a publication deserved a warning for a 'dangerous orientation,' and, under the Statute of 1865, for determining when the public prosecutor, an official of the Ministry of Justice, must initiate a prosecution against writers, editors, or publishers for violations of the criminal code.

With respect to the all-important Statute of 1865, the autocracy made its greatest mistake in granting responsibility before the law to members of the press while retaining administrative powers to deny that liberal concession. It gave statutory form to its double-edged policy: under a single legislative measure, overseers of the press in the Ministry of the Interior could choose to employ either administrative or judicial measures against persons whose published words they found intolerable. Among the reasons for this two-edged censorship 'reform' was the urgent need, widely perceived, for new, liberal measures to replace a preliminary system of censorship that did not work. But the need for change came at the very time the judicial reform had set in motion the dismantling of the old court system as the first step in establishing new courts. Given the disrupted state of the courts, those who favoured an immediate 'reform' of censorship saw no alternative to including supposedly temporary administrative measures. The double-edged reform also satisfied those opposed to granting the courts sole authority over the press, or what was commonly understood as 'freedom of the press.' The monority of officials who did favour unadulterated freedom for the press argued in vain for deferring the reform of censorship until the new courts were fully established. Their warnings that the transitional measures would undercut press freedom were to prove well-founded.

In the relatively few trials for alleged press crimes that went forward after 1865, judges had to decide the merit of cases set in motion by censorship officials in the Ministry of the Interior. Whether from ineptness, insufficient understanding of the judicial process, an inclination to prove the courts inadequate, or a determination to harass the press, those same censorship officials failed to make the essential distinction between merely 'dangerous' words and those that a court could rule 'illegal'; repeatedly they demanded prosecutions which were doomed to fail for insufficient grounds. Minister of the Interior Valuev, backed by the Third Section, in turn cited the outcome of those trials as proof that the courts could not adequately fight subversive words – a justification for bypassing the courts and using instead his administrative powers. That turnabout roused the opposition of journalists and lawyers, who persistently called for the freedom promised in 1865.

Western historians have praised the reorganization of the courts under the Statute of 1864 as the best of the reforms under Alexander II. But, for great numbers of pragmatic officials who had risen in government service under Nicholas I, this most westernized of the reforms set forth a process too slow, public, and uncertain in outcome to provide the government with adequate safeguards against published subversive ideas. The courts evidently would not bend their decisions to suit the government. For his part, Minister of the Interior Valuev argued that radicals within the press could manipulate the judicial system and that using only the courts against them would, in effect, leave the government defenseless against patently dangerous words. Valuev was also the principal shaper and effector of the censorship reform of 1865. From start to finish he showed that he was primarily concerned with fighting radical words. He wanted weapons in his own hands to silence journalists who were attempting to advance disruptive ideas.

Valuev had achieved a two-edged censorship reform, then, because the old preliminary system had proved outmoded, because the government recognized the necessity of some liberal concessions to the press, and because the potential political influence of radical journalists alarmed officials. A fourth factor, already touched upon, was the link between the reform of the censorship system and the reform of the judiciary. On the one hand, the judicial reform, with its rule of codified law to be enforced and interpreted equally for all citizens by jurists, provided the strongest possible argument for subjecting to due process persons accused of publishing-related crimes. On the other hand, as already mentioned, the inchoate state of the reformed court system provided the strongest possible argument for transitional administrative measures. The judicial reform must be seen as a contingent factor of immense importance in the development of censorship practices.

Under Valuev, who remained minister during the first three years of the 1865 statute, the two-edged system worked fairly well. But successive ministers, who served in years more troubled by radical elements in the press, over-used their powers. Even so, as late as 1881 Valuev (heading yet another committee to study censorship) favoured extending the legal rights of the press. The assassination of Alexander II in March 1881 made that move impossible as the autocracy defensively drew back from the promise of 1865 to grant the press, in due time, full responsibility before the courts. Alexander III and his advisors feared the demands of the unreasoning majority and the selfish ambitions of opportunists and subversives among the intelligentsia should the law guarantee them access to the public through the printed word.

But, despite its retention of administrative measures, the government could not satisfactorily regulate the periodical press. One main reason for this failure was that those measures had been tailored in 1865 for what were then the leading periodicals, the monthly journals. The government consequently dealt with them quite effectively, as it did with books, right up to 1905.

The provisions of the Statute of 1865 less effectively controlled dailies and weeklies, whose growing circulations made them the leading periodicals in the years after 1870. An end to time-consuming preliminary censorship, which had made strong, private daily newspapers virtually impossible, had enabled Russian publishers to undertake and master the rapid-fire news-gathering, composition, and printing techniques necessary for papers offering immediate news of the empire and the world. Publishers also learned to please the tastes of expanding readerships in the growing urban areas of European Russia through news, comment, pictures, and advertisements – far less tendentious fare than the monthly journals offered.

Because, after Alexander II, the government begrudged rather than blessed the general growth of private periodicals, many Russian publishers and editors justified as a rightful cause their circumvention of any and all official obstacles. Thus did I.D. Sytin, the most successful of the publishers, assume a vaguely radical cast by championing his readers, not the government. Sytin's vast financial resources enabled him to deal easily with the few official restrictions he met and to make his *Russian Word* the largest and best daily in Russia in the first years of the twentieth century.

By 1905, newspapers and publishing plants in the large Russian cities matched those in the West; and, during the revolution of that year, opponents of the government quickly seized upon the usefulness of readily available presses. Almost to a man, they used the printed word to spread their ideas, to publicize meetings, and to convince workers to strike. Besides issuing countless revolutionary pamphlets, they manipulated editors and publishers (through the newly organized printers' union) to disregard all government regulations and even to surrender their own editorial authority to their printers.

Editors and publishers organized as well; and, as the shapers of and spokesmen for public opinion, they determined to make demands on the foundering government, much as the republican editors of Paris had done in 1848. Then Count Witte, the president of the Council of Ministers, gave these same editors and publishers an even greater sense of power when he personally called them together and pleaded with them to support the beleaguered government.

This turnabout clearly shows that, whereas much had changed in the measures used by the government in the previous 125 years to control the printed word, much had also changed in the real power of journalists and of the private press. Novikov under Catherine II, Labzin under Alexander I, Bulgarin under Nicholas I, Chernyshevsky under Alexander II, Gradovsky under Alexander II, and Doroshevich under Nicholas II all attest to the rising authority and influence of Russian journalists during the period covered by this study.

Although, by the twentieth century, the tendentious quality of earlier Russian journalism had not entirely faded, the style and content of reportage had become modern: catholicity of subject matter, relative objectivity in the treatment of news, and writing that was crisp, vigorous, and concise. Most newspaper editors emulated *Russian Word* and sought to make the press a respected and responsible institution. They agreed that their role, aptly described by attorney Andreevsky, was 'to stand on neutral ground like a Red Cross dressing station.'

In the heated atmosphere immediately following the October manifesto, however, the editors and publishers summoned by Count Witte chose not to be neutral and crossed the line from objectivity to advocacy. Well aware of the weaknesses of the government, they contended that – on behalf of the people – they should direct Witte into correct action. These leading members of the press abruptly gave full vent to what earlier had been a resentful, impatient tendency. Witte, who had long appreciated and cultivated the press, had hoped for co-operation. His disillusionment after the press conference led directly to an all-out offensive by the government against its opposition, notably in the arrest of the St Petersburg Soviet and the stepping up of prosecutions against editors and publishers.

But neither Witte nor the government saw any alternative to using the court system as the last line of defense against the printed word. To restore order, the government had no choice but to grant to the press the freedom promised exactly four decades before in the Statute of 1865. Not unlike governments in the West in earlier years, the autocracy at last conceded that the press should become a free institution, responsible to courts alone, precisely because available alternate measures no longer worked.

APPENDICES

Regulations on the press:
The reign of the sovereign Alexander II,
April 1865*

No. 41988, 6 April
The Personal Imperial Decree handed down to the Senate – *Concerning the granting of certain [measures of] relief and convenience to the national press.*

Wishing to grant the national press all possible relief and convenience, we deem it right to make the following changes in and additions to the censorship decrees in force during the present temporary position of our judicial branch and henceforth until such time as subsequent instructions in the experiment are handed down:

I. The following are exempted from preliminary censorship:

a In both capitals:

(1) all periodical publications appearing to date whose publishers themselves announce their desire [for exemption];

(2) all original writings consisting of no fewer than 10 printed signatures; and

(3) all translations consisting of no fewer than 20 printed signatures.

b In all localities:

(1) all governmental publications;

(2) all publications of academies, universities, and educational organizations and establishments;

(3) all publications in ancient classical languages and translations from these languages;

(4) drafts, plans, and maps.

II. Those periodicals and other publications, writings and translations freed from preliminary censorship in which occur violations of the laws are subject

* A lengthy footnote on legislative technicalities has been omitted.

to judicial prosecution; furthermore, in the event that a dangerous orientation is discerned in periodical publications, they are subject to administrative penalty according to the laws especially established for this purpose.

III. The management of censorship and press affairs is generally concentrated in the Ministry of the Interior under the higher supervision of the minister in the newly-established Chief Administration for these affairs.

IV. The operations of the existing decree do not, at the present time, apply to:

a writings, translations and publications and portions thereof which are subject to Ecclesiastical Censorship according to the decrees and orders now in effect. These decrees and orders will continue to be carried out on presently existing principles, as will foreign censorship;

b periodical and other publications of prints, drawings, and other pictorial representations with or without texts which are subject to the operation of censorship regulations also [based] on existing principles.

Having affirmed along with these [regulations] those changes and additions which, in consequence of the above-stated measures, must be included in the details of the regulations now in effect concerning the press, we ask the Governing Senate to issue an order for the promulgation of this, Our Will, so that it would take effect as of September 1 of the current year.

No. 41990, 6 April

The imperially approved opinion of the Council of State. *Concerning certain changes in and additions to censorship regulation now in effect.* The Council of State in the Department of Laws and in General Meeting has examined the presentation of the Minister of the Interior concerning these changes in and additions to the details of the regulations now in effect concerning the press which are necessary to conform with the Imperial Will as revealed in the decree of 6 April of this year (41988), and *has proposed* the enactment of the following regulations:

I. Concerning the Chief Administration of Press Affairs.

1 The Chief Administration of Press Affairs consists of:

(1) the Head of the Chief Administration, and

(2) the Council of the Chief Administration.

2 To the Chief Administration are attached:

(1) the Office;

(2) special Censors of dramatic works; and

(3) clerks with special commissions.

3 The Head of the Chief Administration is appointed and dismissed by Imperial decree [handed down to] the Governing Senate upon recommendation of the Minister of the Interior.

4 The Council of the Chief Administration under the chairmanship of the Head of the Administration consists of the Chairmen of Censorship Committees on hand in St Petersburg and of members appointed and dismissed by Imperial decrees of the Governing Senate upon recommendation of the Minister of the Interior.

5 The Office of the Chief Administration is administered by the Managing Director assisted by aides under the direct supervision of the Head of the Chief Administration.

6 The Managing Director and his aides and the clerks with special commissions are hired and dismissed on the orders of the Minister of the Interior, but the office clerks and workers are hired and dismissed by the Managing Director of the Chief Administration on whose discretion depends their number and distribution of salary.

7 The concerns of the Chief Administration of Press Affairs are:

(1) supervision of the operations of the Censorship Committees and special Censors in both domestic and foreign censorship; settlement of their disagreements and questions and examination of complaints brought against them;

(2) supervision of works published by the press which come out without censorship permission; detection in them of violations of established regulations; institution of judicial prosecution when this was not done by subordinate authorities, and of matters concerning warnings to periodical publications exempted from preliminary censorship;

(3) matters concerning the openings of printing-houses, lithographies, etching works, and institutions producing and selling printing accessories, and supervision of these establishments as well as the book trade.

8 The Council of the Chief Administration of Press Affairs is subordinate to the general directives governing all Councils of the Ministries.

9 In the event that they discover violations of the regulations concerning press matters, all other administrative institutions apply to the Chief Administration through their superiors for prosecution of the guilty.

II. Concerning the periodical press.

1 The following are considered to be periodical publications:

(1) newspapers and magazines published in separate issues, folios, or pamphlets;

(2) collections or anthologies of new, original, or translated writings or articles of various authors published more than twice a year under one general title.

2 Supplements forming part of newspapers or magazines are considered as supplements only if they are not sold separately or in subscription or as separate pamphlets or numbers. Any publication having the character of a

separate magazine or newspaper and one which may be bought separately, on subscription, or as individual pamphlets or issues is not considered a supplement to another periodical publication even though it might bear the same title as the periodical, and that is why all conditions of publication established by present regulations must be observed by each of the two publications separately.

3 The following are not relevant to the collections mentioned in article 1:

(1) collections of previously printed writings and translations, for example, anthologies;

(2) collections of historical documents;

(3) all types of dictionaries.

4 Anyone wishing to publish a new periodical publication in the form of a newspaper, magazine, or collection is obliged, at the present time, to ask permission to do so from the Minister of the Interior on whom depends the permission for the release of such a publication either without censorship or on condition of preliminary censorship.

5 Petitions concerning permission are to be submitted to the Chief Administration of Press Affairs and must contain the following information:

(1) the name or title of the publication, the table of contents, date of publication, and price of subscription;

(2) the name and address of the publisher and editor-in-chief, and, if there are several of the above, the name and address of each of them;

(3) the printing-house in which the publication is to be printed.

6 To the petition must be appended the following:

(1) the identity papers of both the publisher and the editor-in-chief or, if there are several of the above, of each of them;

(2) a written and personally signed statement of the editor-in-chief that he assumes the responsibility for the supervision of the publication or a part thereof, signifying which part.

7 If the publisher and editor-in-chief are the same person, this must be mentioned in the petition.

8 If anyone undertakes to publish any periodical publication without obtaining lawful permission, or if anyone includes in his magazine an article which exceeds the limits of the program established for the publication (article 17, point 2), he is liable to a fine not exceeding 50 rubles for each number or article, even if the published numbers or articles do not contain any unlawful material.

9 Anyone who has obtained permission through proper channels to put out a periodical publication has the right to undertake its publication within a year of receiving permission. In the event that this time expires, the publication is considered ineligible and the permission granted is considered void.

10 Any periodical publication which has already appeared but which, for whatever reason, does not come out in the course of the year is considered discontinued and new permission is required to renew its publication.

11 In the event of the transfer of a periodical publication from one publisher to another, the Chief Administration must be informed of it in good time and the notification must be signed by both the former and present publishers. For a change of editor, permission must be obtained according to the procedure mentioned in articles 4–7. Those guilty of violations of these regulations are liable to a fine not exceeding 100 rubles; transfer of a publication or replacement of an editor are considered invalid if done without permission.

12 The responsible editor will forfeit his position:

(1) if he becomes subject to the loss or reduction of his rights of status or if he comes under police surveillance on orders of the court:

(2) if he loses his civil rights for any other reasons whatsoever;

(3) if he travels abroad without informing the Chief Administration or if he does not return at the summons of the Administration or some other authority.

13 The publisher must notify the Offices of the Governors General in the capitals and the Offices of the Provincial Governors in other localities concerning the transfer of a publication from one printing-house to another.

14 Permission for each periodical publication is issued by the Chief Administration in the form of certificates in duplicate. Without producing this certificate, no printing-house has the right to undertake the typesetting and printing of a periodical publication. One copy of the certificate remains in the printing-house for as long as the printing of a publication continues; if, however, a publication is subject to a deposit, the printing-house must demand a receipt when the deposit is paid before it begins typesetting and printing.

15 Publishers of periodical publications which are exempted from preliminary censorship measures are required to pay the deposit to the Chief Administration.

16 The deposit is paid according to the following scale:

(1) for a daily newspaper or a newspaper appearing not less than 6 times a week – 5,000 rubles;

(2) for all other periodical publications – 2,500 rubles.

17 The following are not required to pay a deposit:

(1) periodical publications appearing with the permission of preliminary censorship;

(2) publications the contents of which, in conformity with approved programs, are purely educational, economic, or technical;

(3) governmental publications and publications of academies, universities, and educational organizations and establishments.

18 The deposit is paid to the Chief Administrator of Press Affairs in accordance with the wishes of the publisher, either in cash, or in Russian government credit notes which are considered at their nominal value upon receipt, or in stocks and bonds which are acceptable as deposits in transactions involving government contracts and sales. The holder receives interest-bearing coupons on the dates prescribed for the issuance of such bonds.

19 The deposit covers fines imposed on a periodical publication. If the fine is not paid within the specified time, a corresponding sum is deducted from the deposit in cash or through the sale of credit notes at the going rate of exchange. In the latter case, ordinary expenses connected with the sale are also deducted from the deposit.

20 The part of the deposit deducted in payment for the prescribed fine must be repaid up to a fixed amount under threat of the discontinuation of the publication if this is not done.

21 Publications which appear more than twice a month are given two weeks from the date of the court decision to repay the deposit; regarding publications appearing less frequently, repayment must be made at least a day before the publication of the pamphlet due to appear after the fine is levied.

22 In the event that a publication is discontinued, the deposit is returned to the publisher not earlier than a year from the date of the appearance of the last number of the publication.

23 Each separately published number of a newspaper, each copy of a magazine, or each issue of a collection must bear the following information: the names of the publisher, editor-in-chief, and printing-house, and the price of subscription; if the publication has been examined by the censor ahead of time, the permission of the censor must also be printed. Those guilty of a violation of this regulation are liable to a fine not exceeding 25 rubles for each number, copy or issue.

24 Those guilty of falsifying the names of the publisher, editor-in-chief, subscription price, or censorship permission on a publication are subject to imprisonment for the term determined in vol. 15, part 1, article 42 [The Code of Law].

25 Periodical publications exempted from preliminary censorship are submitted by the publishers to the Censorship Committee at the following times:

(1) copies of each number of a newspaper or publication in general which appears not less than once a week are submitted at the time of the final printing of that number;

(2) copies of each issue of a publication appearing less frequently than once a week are submitted not later than two days before its distribution to subscribers or its release for sale.

In fulfilment of this regulation the publishers are issued notices indicating the stated times for the submission of their copies. Those guilty of not submitting their copies are liable to a fine not exceeding 100 rubles.

26 Any periodical publication is obliged to print without delay and free of charge an official refutation or correction of information appearing in the publication without change in or comment on the text and with no objections to the text itself.

27 If information concerning a private individual appears in a periodical publication, the said publication cannot refuse to accept refutations or corrections submitted by that individual.

28 A refutation or correction submitted by a private individual must be printed without delay in the same script and in the same section as the original information; in addition, no charge [is levied] if such refutations or corrections do not take up more space than twice the length of the article to which they are an answer. A refutation or correction must be signed by the individual submitting it in his defense.

29 The Minister of the Interior is granted the right to issue warnings to periodical publications with reference to the articles giving cause for such warnings. A third warning results in the suspension of the publication for a period which is determined by the Minister of the Interior at the time he issues the warning, but which does not exceed 6 months. This regulation is applied with equal force to periodical publications controlled by governmental or educational institutions.

30 If, after a third warning the Minister of the Interior deems it necessary to discontinue a publication irrespective of a preliminary suspension of a periodical publication for a specific time, he will submit a proposal concerning this action to the First Department of the Governing Senate.

31 A periodical publication receiving a warning is obliged to print it without changes or objections at the beginning of the first issue to appear after the warning has been issued.

32 A discontinued publication may not be reinstated without the personal permission of the Minister of the Interior.

33 For failure to print the following in a periodical publication: If the publisher fails to print a court decision or an administrative warning or refutations or corrections submitted by the Government or by private individuals within 3 days in a daily publication, and in the following number of a monthly publication, he is liable to a fine of 25 rubles for each number published after the fixed date when the publication appears more than once a month, and 100 rubles per number when it appears once a month or less often for as long as the submitted decision, warning, refutation, or correction

are not printed; and if the decision, warning, refutation, or correction are not printed within three months, the publications will be discontinued on the order of the Chief Administration of Press Affairs.

III. Concerning printing-houses, lithographic works, etching works, and establishments producing and selling printing equipment, and also concerning the book trade.

A *Concerning printing-houses, lithographies, and etching works.*

1 Under the control of the Chief Administration of Press Affairs, the supervision of printing-houses, lithographies, and etching works (and also of establishments producing and selling printing equipment and of the book trade) is undertaken in the capitals by special Inspectors attached to the Offices of the Governors General, and in the provinces by Clerks under special commission designated by the Governors.

2 Those wishing to set up printing-houses, lithographies, etching works, or other establishments for printing written and pictorial material must get permission for this from the Governors General in the capitals and from the provincial governor in other localities. At the same time they are obliged to:

(1) produce, in cases stipulated by the regulations governing taxation for the right to engage in trade and other business, a certificate prescribed by these regulations;

(2) indicate the number and size of the rapid printing machines and presses which they propose to have in their establishment.

3 The permission granted to open a printing-house or another establishment mentioned in the previous article remains in force for two years; if, however, the establishment is not brought into production by the end of that time, new permission is needed for it to open.

4 Transfer of a printing-house, lithography, or etching works from one individual to another is allowed only with the permission of the authority which is also responsible for granting permission for their opening.

5 Whoever inherits a printing-house, lithography, or etching works must either fulfill the demands of article 2 or turn over the establishment to someone else under the same conditions within 6 months.

6 Any printing-house, lithography, or etching works opened or taken over from another individual by anyone at all without permission of the responsible authority is considered clandestine, and those guilty of opening or maintaining such an establishment are liable to a fine not exceeding 300 rubles and detention of not more than 3 months, or to imprisonment for a term defined as not more than 3 months, or to imprisonment for a term defined by vol. 15, part 1, article 42, for the first and second degree of this type of punishment, or to one of these punishments at the discretion of the court.

7 Proprietors of establishments are obliged to report any changes in the number and size of their rapid printing machines and presses to the Office of the Governors General in the capitals and to the Offices of the provincial governors in other localities. Those who fail to do so are liable to a fine not exceeding 50 rubles.

8 Anyone wishing to possess a small, hand-operated printing press for personal use must ask permission to do so from the Governor General in the capitals and from the provincial governor in other localities. A violation of this condition puts the guilty party under the same liability as that which rests on those maintaining clandestine printing-houses.

9 Each printing-house, lithography, and etching works must have a ledger, each page of which is initialled by Inspectors of book printing in the capitals, and, in other localities, by clerks especially designated for this task by the provincial governors. In this ledger is noted any work intended for printing along with an explanation of whether it is being printed without preliminary submission to censorship or with the permission of the latter, and with evidence, in each case, of the number of copies and the format of the publication. Those guilty of non-fulfilment of this regulation are liable to a fine not exceeding 50 rubles.

10 Entries in the ledger as well as works already completed and those which are in production may be verified at any time by the individuals mentioned in the preceding article.

11 Offices which acquire hand-operated printing-presses for office needs must bring this to the attention of the individuals mentioned in article 9.

12 When the printing of any publication is finished and prior to the distribution of the publication, printing-houses, lithographies, and etching works are obliged to submit the number of copies designated by censorship Regulations to the local Censorship Committee which will then issue a receipt to this effect. The only exceptions to this regulation are office notices and writings which have as their subject community or domestic requirements, such as: wedding and various other invitations, visiting cards, matters of etiquette, price-lists, notices of sales of goods, or of change of address, etc. A printing house, lithographic works, or etching works is held accountable for the printing of such writings only in the event that their form conceals some other material foreign to these subjects.

13 A work printed or lithographed without preliminary censorship may be released for publication (with the exception mentioned in the preceding article) no sooner than three days after receiving notification that the Censorship Committee has received the required number of copies. Those guilty of not fulfilling this regulation are liable to a fine not exceeding 100 rubles specifically for a breach of this regulation.

14 In the extraordinary circumstance when, because of the seriousness of the harmful influence envisaged by the distribution of an illegal work or periodical publication, seizure cannot be postponed until a court verdict for it has been handed down, the Council of the Chief Administration and the Censorship Committee are given the right to suspend immediately the appearance of such a work, but they must have instituted court proceedings against the guilty party at the same time.

15 Each copy that is released by the printing house, lithographic works, or etching works must bear the name and address of the printer, lithographer, or etcher and, if the work was subject to preliminary censorship, the approval of the censor. Those guilty of non-fulfilment of this [regulation] are liable to a fine not exceeding 50 rubles.

16 Those guilty of falsifying the name of the printer, lithographer, or etcher are subject to imprisonment for the term defined in vol. 15, part 1, article 42.

17 Those guilty of printing a work subject to preliminary censorship without the permission of the censor are liable to a fine not exceeding 300 rubles and detention of not more than 3 months, even though the contents of the printed work contain nothing illegal.

18 Also subject to such punishment is the owner of a printing house who allows the printing of a periodical publication without getting from the publisher the certificate or receipt required by article 14 of the regulations governing periodical publications.

19 Whoever is guilty of reprinting a work forbidden by the court and entered in the catalogue of forbidden books is liable, in addition to the confiscation of the whole publication, to a fine not exceeding 300 rubles and to detention of not more than 3 months.

B *Concerning establishments producing and selling printing equipment.*

20 Permission to set up establishments for the production and sale of printing equipment is given to all individuals without discrimination who have the right to practise a trade or vocation. The permission is granted on the basis of the Regulations governing industries and factories and on the basis of the Regulations governing trade and vocation.

21 Every establishment producing or selling printing equipment must have a ledger, each page of which is initialled by clerks on whom falls the responsibility of dealing with printing-houses as stated in article 9. Into this ledger is entered any sale conducted in the factory or in a store along with a note of the name, rank, and address of the buyer. Those guilty of non-fulfilment of this (regulation) are liable to a fine not exceeding 50 rubles.

22 Within the Empire, printing-presses and types may be sold only to printers; furthermore, types may also be sold to individuals who have received

permission to possess a hand-operated printing-press. Those guilty of non-fulfilment of this regulation are liable to a fine not exceeding 100 rubles.

23 Verification of the ledger in factories and stores which produce and sell printing accessories is carried out on the basis of article 10.

24 In the event that presses, rapid printing-presses, and types are imported from abroad, customs officials must immediately inform the Offices of the Governors General if the goods are shipped to the capitals, and the Offices of the provincial governors if they are shipped to other places, along with information about the quantity of the shipment and the name of the receiver to whom the shipment is being sent through customs. This information is forwarded by the Offices to the individuals mentioned in article 9.

C *Concerning the book trade.*

25 Private individuals as well as joint-stock companies or associations are allowed to establish bookstores, shops, and reading-rooms according to the procedure set out for the opening of printing-houses, lithographies, and similar enterprises. Those guilty of non-fulfilment of this [regulation] are liable to a fine not exceeding 100 rubles.

26 Individuals who receive the right to establish a bookstore or shop or a reading-room are obliged to declare the exact locations of these establishments and the person running them in each case to the Offices of the Governors General in the capitals and to the Offices of the provincial governors in other localities.

27 Anyone without discrimination is allowed to sell or deliver approved books and various periodical publications in separate issues, not in shops, but on the streets and squares with the proviso that those wishing to sell or deliver [these materials] have the permission of the local police authorities to conduct such trade, in addition to the certificate prescribed for such trade by the current regulations. Those guilty of non-fulfilment of this [regulation] are liable to a fine not exceeding 25 rubles.

28 Bookstores, shops, and reading rooms have the right to keep in stock and sell or loan all approved publications printed in Russia in Russian or in foreign languages and, of those publications printed abroad in Russian or in foreign languages, all those which are not included in the general catalogue of forbidden books. This regulation also applies to those delivering books or selling them in the streets and squares.

29 If the proprietor of a bookstore, shop, or reading room, and this applies to street-sellers and book retailers [as well], keeps for sale and distribution such books or publications listed in the general catalogue of forbidden books or if these materials have been duly banned by the local police, he is liable to a fine not exceeding 250 rubles.

30 If a book which is initially permitted is subsequently banned, booksellers and proprietors of reading rooms are not held responsible for its distribution so long as it has not been entered in the general catalogue of forbidden books, or so long as the local police have not duly banned it.

D *Concerning the court in matters of the press*

1 Those held responsible for holding printed or lithographed works, prints, etc., may be: the author, the publisher, the typographer or lithographer, the bookseller, and the editor. The measure of responsibility of each of the above-mentioned individuals is determined by the court which examines the degree of complicity in the transgression on the precise basis of vol. 4, part 1, articles 13–17.

2 The individuals mentioned in the preceding article are called before the court in the following order:

(1) the author, in all cases in which he does not prove that his work was published without his knowledge or consent;

(2) the publisher, in the case in which the name or address of the author is unknown or if the latter lives abroad;

(3) the printer or lithographer, when neither the author nor the publisher is known or when their place of residence is not evident or when they live abroad;

(4) the bookseller, in the case in which the copy of the work does not bear the name and address of the printer or lithographer.

3 In the cases when publishers, printers, and booksellers abrogate their direct responsibility on the basis of the preceding article, they may be prosecuted as accessories to offenses and misdemeanours of the press, depending on the circumstances, if it is proved that they wittingly participated in the publication and distribution of the printed matter while being aware of the criminal intention of the chief offender.

4 In any case, responsibility for holding articles printed in periodical publications falls on the editor of the publication, as well as on the chief offender.

5 Violations of decrees concerning the press which are subject to prosecution (pending the enactment of the Court Decrees of November 20, 1864) are handled in the special Sessions of the Criminal Chamber which act as a lower court and which are organized for this purpose in St Petersburg and Moscow; these sentences can be appealed to the Governing Senate.

6 The special Sessions consist of the Chairman of the Criminal Chamber, two Colleagues of the Chairmen of the Criminal and Civil Chambers, and four Assessors of those chambers [all of whom] take turns according to a system determined among themselves in order that the Session should be a complement of two Assessors of the Criminal Chamber and one from each Department of the Civil Chamber.

7 The institution of judicial prosecution for violations, in accordance with the regulations governing the press, must commence within a year from the date of the perpetration of the violation.

8 In handing down punishment for offenses and misdemeanours of the press as fixed by vol. 15, part 1, the court is granted the right, depending on the circumstances, to reduce the severity of the punishment by one or several degrees, and even to reduce the verdict to the highest degree of the next lowest category of punishment.

9 Independent of the felonies and misdemeanours in matters of the press which are prosecuted under vol. 15, part 1, the following are also subject to judicial prosecution and punishment.

(1) Whoever prints insulting references to the laws operating in the Empire with the aim of undermining public confidence, or to established governmental or judicial decrees and orders, or who permits himself to call into question in the press the compulsory force of the laws and to approve or justify the acts forbidden by them with the aim of arousing disrespect for the laws is liable to imprisonment for the term indicated in vol. 15, part 1, article 42, or to detention from 4 days to 3 months or, finally, to a fine not exceeding 500 rubles.

(2) Whoever makes an appeal in the press which incites one segment of the population of the state to animosity against another, or one class against another is subject to incarceration in a detention centre or in a prison for the term defined in vol. 15, part 1, articles 40–42, or to detention from 4 days to 3 months, or to a fine not exceeding 500 rubles.

(3) If someone is guilty of directly calling into question or censuring the principles of property or the family unit in printed publications with the intention of undermining or weakening their foundations, even though there is no incitement to commit a crime, he will be liable to a fine not exceeding 300 rubles and to detention of not more than 6 weeks, or to only one of these punishments according to the discretion of the court.

(4) Those guilty of publishing and promulgating resolutions of assemblies of the *gentry* and urban and *zemstvo* assemblies without the permission of the Governors-General in the capitals and of the provincial governors in other cities are liable to a fine not exceeding 300 rubles and to detention of not more than 3 weeks, or to one of these punishments according to the discretion of the court.

10 If someone publishes about a private individual or official or society or institution in the press such circumstances which may damage their honour, reputation, or good name [i.e., defaming circumstances], he is liable to a fine not exceeding 500 rubles and to imprisonment for the term defined in vol. 15,

part 1, article 42, or to one of these punishments according to the discretion of the court.

11 If someone is guilty of an insulting reference in the press to a private individual or official or to a society or establishment, and if this reference expresses or implies abuse or insult without indication of specific defaming circumstances, he is liable to a fine not exceeding 300 rubles and to detention for a period defined in vol. 15, part 1, article 43, for first and second degree offenses, or to imprisonment of not more than 6 months.

12 Anyone who prints insults of one kind or another against private individuals is not, under any circumstances, granted the right to furnish evidence of their validity.

13 If the insult points to any defaming circumstances, and if it concerns the official or public activities of an individual holding a post by appointment of the Government or through election, then anyone who prints the insult is granted the right to present any written proofs he may have in his possession as confirmation of the truth of his testimony. Testimony of witnesses is not admissible in this case.

14 For his part, anyone who undertakes an action against a charge of defaming circumstances imputed to him in the press has the right to use any means, both to refute the validity of the proofs presented by the accused on the basis of the preceding article, and to present witnesses to confirm his moral qualities; however, the accused is forbidden to present witnesses to dispute the moral qualities of the plaintiff.

15 Anyone who proves the truth of a defaming circumstance on the basis of article 13 is free from punishment as understood in article 10; however, he may be liable to a fine under article 11 if the court discovers an obvious intention to insult an official or establishment in the form of the work being prosecuted or in the method of its distribution and other circumstances.

16 A discussion of individual laws and general legislation or of the publication of governmental decrees is not liable to criminal charge and is not subject to punishments provided that the published article does not contain an incitement to disobey the laws, does not dispute their obligatory force, and is not insulting to constituted authority.

17 In meting out punishment for offenses and misdemeanours of the press, the court may decide on the obliteration of a drawing, book, etc., or of only those sections of a work which contain a criminal trend of thought; the court may also decide to close down printing houses, lithographic works, or etching works.

18 In meting out punishment for offenses discovered in a periodical publication, the court is allowed:

(1) to order the suppression of such a periodical publication for a period it considers necessary, or its complete suppression;

(2) having decided to suspend or discontinue a periodical publication, at the same time to forbid the publisher and editor, or one of them if they have been proved guilty, to accept the title of publisher or editor of any periodical publication whatever for a certain period of time which, however, shall not exceed 5 years.

19 In handing down a verdict concerning a periodical publication, the court may decide that the next number of the publication should carry a notice of the aforesaid verdict provided that the publication has not been discontinued; it is forbidden to print an objection or refutation along with the notice.

E *Concerning dramatic presentations.*

1 Dramatic works are passed for presentation in theatres set aside for this purpose by special Censors attached to the Chief Administration of Press Affairs.

2 In addition to the permission of the domestic censor or special Censors, permission is required from local Governors-General for the presentation of dramatic works in a language other than Russian in theatres of the northern and south-western regions, in the Baltic and Odessa gubernias; the permission of the Vice-Regent is required for the presentation of all dramatic works in the theatres of the Caucasus and Trans-Caucasus regions.

3 All dramatic works scheduled for presentation in theatres are submitted to the Chief Administration in the form of neatly and legibly written manuscripts or in printed facsimiles in 2 copies.

4 The Head of the Chief Administration entrusts the examination of the submitted play to one of the Censors who puts his official imprimatur on it, passing it for theatrical presentation, and enters the title of the play in an alphabetical register set up in the Office of the Chief Administration. The manuscript or one printed facsimile remains with the Chief Administration.

5 If the Censor considers it necessary to make certain changes or deletions in the play before its presentation on stage, he marks these places in the manuscript or printed facsimile in red ink and submits all doubts arising from the examination to the Head of the Chief Administration.

6 If the Censor does not consider it possible to pass the play for presentation, he writes a report concerning this and including a detailed account of his reasons to the Head of the Chief Administration for Press Affairs for presentation with his opinions to the Minister of the Interior for a final examination.

7 A special register of forbidden plays is kept at the Office of the Chief Administration, and no theatre in the Empire is allowed to stage these plays under threat of certain penalty. The above-mentioned register exists for the information of the provincial governors.

8 Printed, alphabetized lists of plays passed for presentation with absolutely no changes and deletions are sent to all theatre managers by order of the Chief Administration through the agency of the provincial governors.

9 The lists mentioned in the preceding article and which serve as exclusive guides in the staging of plays and also in the authorization to print play-bills are updated on a yearly basis and more often if possible.

10 All plays which are not entered in the above-mentioned lists must be submitted by theatre managers to the Chief Administration of Press Affairs through the agency of the provincial governors for examination by the censor.

11 A theatre manager who stages a play which is entered in the register of forbidden plays is liable to a fine not exceeding 500 rubles and to detention of not more than 3 months, or to imprisonment for a term defined by vol. 15, part 1, article 42 for the third and second degree of this kind of punishment, or, at the discretion of the court, to one of these punishments. A theatre manager who stages a play without observing the changes or deletions indicated by the Censor is also liable to the same penalty.

Tables

TABLE 1
Russian periodicals published, 1801–25

Year	General content	Official	Learned, specialized	Total
1801	6	–	4	10
1806	16	2	12	30
1813	12	3	7	22
1815	21	3	11	35
1820	15	3	8	26
1825	17	6	19	42

SOURCE: N. Lisovsky, 'Periodicheskaia pechat v Rossii, 1703–1903 gg.,' *Sbornik statei po istorii i statistike russkoi periodicheskoi pechati, 1703–1903* (St Petersburg 1903), 15

TABLE 2
Russian periodicals under imperial censorship, 1833–60

Year	No.	Year	No.	Year	No.	Year	No.
1833	54	1840	54	1847	55	1854	103
1834	48	1841	54	1848	56	1855	104
1835	51	1842	61	1849	56	1856	110
1836	46	1843	56	1850	56	1857	122
1837	48	1844	56	1851	102*	1858	165
1838	51	1845	60	1852	103	1859	199
1839	53	1846	62	1853	104	1860	230

SOURCE: *Zhurnal Ministerstva Narodnogo Prosveshcheniia* 142, nos. 1–3 (1862), table following p. 47
* In 1851, the government began to censor the unofficial sections of provincial bulletins (*vedomosti*), which are included in this figure. About forty such bulletins were first published in 1838.

TABLE 3
Number of book titles approved by imperial censorship and published, 1837–54

Year	Total approved*	Min. Ed.	Synod	Other depts.	Poland
1837	1,147	838	162	147	127
1838	1,082	842	167	73	138
1839	1,028	832	161	35	–
1840	1,028	813	167	48	–
1841	878	727	106	45	–
1842	967	732	172	63	–
1843	945	747	148	49	–
1844	1,038	824	138	76	133
1845	981	804	142	35	233
1846	1,009	810	148	51	141
1847	1,122	862	201	59	148
1848	1,097	823	230	44	77
1849	1,113	809	254	50	84
1850	995	640	310	45	85
1851	1,004	765	149	90	208
1852	1,215	947	161	107	148
1853	1,230	920	225	94	225
1854	1,354	1,059	201	94	235
Total	19,242	14,795	3,242	1,205	1,972

SOURCE: N.N. Ablov, 'K stoletiiu pervoi popytki "ofitsialnoi" registratsii pechati v Rossii (1837–1855),' *Sovetskaia Bibliografiia*, no. 1 (1937), 104
* Estonia, Latvia, Lithuania included.

TABLE 4
Number of book signatures approved by imperial censorship annually, 1833–60*

Year	No.	Year	No.	Year	No.
1833	10,659	1843	7,925	1852	10,483
1834	10,242	1844	10,107	1853	9,959
1835	10,106	1845	8,964	1854	10,465
1836	11,006	1846	9,034	1855	9,961
1837	9,677	1847	9,762	1856	12,328
1838	10,918	1848	9,261	1857	13,936
1839	9,024	1849	8,186	1858	16,168
1840	8,477	1850	6,799	1859	16,136
1841	8,316	1851	8,973	1860	17,999
1842	7,873				

SOURCE: *Zhurnal Ministerstva Narodnogo Prosveshcheniia* 142, nos. 1–3 (1862), table
following p. 47
* Each signature represents sixteen pages.

TABLE 5
Warnings to journals and newspapers, September 1865 to February 1870

Publications	1st warning	2nd warning	3rd warning
*Contemporary**	10 Nov 1865	4 Dec 1865[†]	−
*Judicial Messenger**	25 Nov 1869	−	−
Moscow	17 Jan 1867	20 Feb 1867	26 Mar 1867[‡]
Moscow Bulletin	29 Mar 1866	6 May 1866	7 May 1866[‡]
National Voice	18 Jan 1867	17 Feb 1867	16 Jun 1867[‡]
New Times	27 Nov 1868	14 Mar 1869	−
News	13 Jan 1866	11 Oct 1866	−
Russo-Slavic Echo	18 Jun 1868	28 Jun 1868	12 Jul 1868[‡]
*Russian Word**	20 Dec 1865	8 Jan 1866	16 Feb 1866[†‡]
St Petersburg Bulletin	20 Sep 1865	13 Apr 1866	2 Sep 1866[‡]
St Petersburg Leaflet	4 Jan 1867	24 Mar 1868	−
St Petersburger Zeitung	3 Oct 1868	25 Jul 1869	−
Stock Exchange Bulletin	6 Sep 1867	−	−
Universal Gazette	15 Dec 1869	3 Feb 1870	−
Voice	1 Dec 1865	7 May 1866	5 Dec 1869[‡]
Week	27 Apr 1868	6 Mar 1869	5 May 1869[‡]

Warnings to newspapers following first temporary suspension			
Moscow	4 Jul 1867	22 Nov 1867	29 Nov 1867[‡]
Moscow Bulletin	8 Jan 1870	−	−
St Petersburg Bulletin	1 Mar 1867	−	−
Voice	21 Oct 1867	1 Nov 1867	−

Warnings to Moscow following second temporary suspension			
Moscow	11 Apr 1868	28 Apr 1868	21 Oct 1868[‡§]

SOURCE: *Materialy*, 2: 117–63. This information was gathered for the Urusov Commission.
* Journals
† Closed permanently by imperial order, 28 May 1866.
‡ Temporarily suspended on day of third warning.
§ Closed permanently by State Council, 13 April 1869.

TABLE 6
Growth in the book trade in Imperial Russia, 1855–94

Year	Printing plants	Book titles	Bookstores
1855	150	1,020	40*
1864	276	1,836	63*
1874	800	4,274	611
1883–84	899	5,430	1,377
1893–94	1,315	10,230	1,725

SOURCE: A.A. Govorov, *Istoriia knizhnoi torgovli v SSSR* (Moscow 1976), 178

* These figures seem low in light of Gary Marker's estimate that there were fifty or more persons selling books in St Petersburg and Moscow by the end of the eighteenth century; see Gary Jon Marker, 'Publishing and the Formation of a Reading Public in Eighteenth-Century Russia' (unpublished PHD dissertation, University of California, Berkeley 1977).

TABLE 7
Periodicals published in Imperial Russia, 1871–1900

Year	Russian journals	Russian papers	Periodicals in all languages			
			General	Official	Specialized	Total
1871	14	36	71	148	134	353
1872	13	42	75	155	148	378
1874	9	40	68	164	159	391
1875	9	41	72	171	183	426
1876	12	46	83	174	173	430
1878	19	57	104	180	174	458
1879	20	62	109	179	174	462
1880	22	62	112	187	184	483
1881	35	83	153	184	194	531
1882	30	86	154	192	208	554
1883	26	80	141	198	218	557
1885	27	81	146	203	257	606
1888	24	72	138	206	293	637
1890	29	79	149	214	334	697
1892	35	80	153	226	366	745
1893	28	85	156	227	380	763
1895	36	93	171	243	427	841
1898	39	123	208	267	470	945
1900	36	125	212	282	508	1002

SOURCE: N. Lisovsky, 'Periodicheskaia pechat v Rossii, 1703–1903 gg.,' *Sbornik statei po istorii i statistike russkoi periodicheskoi pechati, 1703–1903* (St Petersburg 1903), 22, 24

TABLE 8
Temporary suspensions by five-year periods, 1865–1904

| | Uncensored periodicals | | | |
	After three warnings	For comment on topics under prohibition	Censored periodicals	Totals
1865–69	10	–	–	10
1870–74	13	1	–	14
1875–79	18	9	3*	30
1880–84	8	6	5	19
1885–89	4	4	7	15
1890–94	1	–	9	10
1895–99	7	–	22	29
1900–04	3	3	20	26

SOURCE: V. Rozenberg and V. Iakushkin, *Russkaia pechat i tsenzura v proshlom i nastoiashchem* (Moscow 1905), 140

* In the second half of the 1870s, the government began the practice of suspending periodicals under preliminary censorship. The minister of the interior turned to the authority given him 12 May 1862, which had not been incorporated into the 1865 law (V. Rozenberg, 'Pressa, tsenzura i obshchestvo,' in Rozenberg and Iakushkin, *Russkaia pechat i tsenzura*, 115–16).

TABLE 9
Growth of periodical publications
between 1888 and 1896*

Publication schedule	1888	1896
Daily	98	117
Several times weekly	81	106
Weekly	210	235
Several times monthly	87	107
Monthly	132	196
Several times yearly	36	70
Yearly	1	–
Irregularly	20	30
	665	861

SOURCE: L.N. Pavlenkov, 'Knizhnoe delo i periodicheskaia izdaniia v Rossii v 1888 godu,' *IV* 36 (1889): 490; 66 (1896): 713

* The ratio of censored to uncensored periodicals remained fairly constant during these three years at about two to one.

Notes

Archives
GBL Otdel rukopisei Gosudarstvennoi Biblioteki im. V.I. Lenina (Moscow)
GIM Gosudarstvennyi Istoricheskii Muzei (Moscow)
GPB Otdel rukopisei Gosudarstvennoi Publichnoi Biblioteki im. M.E. Salty-
kova-Shchedrina (Leningrad)
PD Pushkinskii Dom (Leningrad)
TSGAOR Tsentralnyi Gosudarstvennyi Arkhiv Oktiabrskoi Revoliutsii (Moscow)
TSGIA Tsentralnyi Gosudarstvennyi Istoricheskii Arkhiv (Leningrad)

Books
LN Literaturnoe Nasledstvo
PSS Polnoe sobranie sochinenii

Journals
GM Golos Minuvshego
IV Istoricheskii Vestnik
KA Krasnyi Arkhiv
OZ Otechestvennye Zapiski
RA Russkii Arkhiv
RB Russkoe Bogatstvo
RS Russkaia Starina
VE Vestnik Evropy

Law Code
PSZ Polnoe Sobranie Zakonov Rossiskoi Imperii

Published Documents
SIRIO Sbornik Imperatorskogo Russkogo Istoricheskogo Obshchestva

CHAPTER 1

1 See Solzhenitsyn's BBC interview with Michael Charlton published in *The Listener* (4 March 1976, 260) and *The Oak and the Calf: Sketches of Literary Life in the Soviet Union*, trans. Harry Willetts (New York: Harper and Row 1980), 2. The question of the extent of press freedom in pre-revolutionary Russia also bears on the debate between Solzhenitsyn and 'his critics' about the meaning of Russian history and its relationship to the Soviet state (see *Foreign Affairs*, spring and summer issues, 1980). See Nabokov to Wilson, 23 February 1948, in Simon Karlinsky, ed., *The Nabokov-Wilson Letters, 1940–1971* (New York: Harper and Row 1979), 195–6.

2 From the eleventh century manorial courts had tried as personal libel those cases involving assault to individuals or injury to their property. In 1275, through *De Scandalis Magnatum* Edward I forbade seditious libel, or false news and tales which would create discord between the king and his subjects, and gave jurisdiction of the law to judges of the common courts. A law from Richard II in 1389 meted punishment to 'every deviser of ... false lies of ... nobles and great men of the realm.' See Peter F. Carter-Ruck, *Libel and Slander* (London: Faber and Faber [1972]), 37.

3 Edward G. Hudon, 'Anglo-Saxon Law against Seditious Libel,' in John Phelan, ed., *Communications Control: Readings in the Motives and Structures of Censorship* (New York: Sheed and Ward 1969), 173

4 'Prohibiting Erroneous Books and Bible Translations,' 22 June 1530, in Paul L. Hughes and James F. Larkin, eds., *Tudor Royal Proclamations: The Early Tudors (1485–1553)*, 3 vols. (New Haven: Yale University Press 1964), 1: 194–5

5 'Prohibiting Unlicensed Printing of Scripture ...,' 16 November 1583, in *Tudor Royal Proclamations*, 271–2

6 J.R. Tanner, *Tudor Constitutional Documents, A.D. 1485–1603, with an Historical Commentary* (Cambridge: Cambridge University Press 1922), 245

7 William M. Clyde, *The Struggle for the Freedom of the Press from Caxton to Cromwell* (London: Oxford University Press 1934; reprint ed., 1970), 3

8 Hudon, 'Anglo-Saxon Law,' 173–4; Sir James Fitzjames Stephen, *A History of the Criminal Law of England*, 3 vols. (London 1883), 2:302–3

9 Carter-Ruck, *Libel and Slander*, 38

10 Clyde, *The Struggle for the Freedom of the Press*, 40–5

11 William Riley Parker, *Milton: A Biography*, 2 vols. (Oxford: Oxford University Press 1968), 1:241

12 Donald Thomas, *A Long Time Burning: The History of Literary Censorship in England* (London: Routledge and Kegan Paul 1969), 14, 32

13 Gareth Jones, ed., *The Sovereignty of the Law: Selections from Blackstone's Commentaries on the Laws of England* (Toronto: University of Toronto Press 1973), pp. 204–5

14 *The Speeches of the Hon. Thomas Erskine ... on Subjects Connected with the Liberty of the Press*, 4 vols. (London 1810; reprint ed., 1974), 2:95–6

15 Audrey Williamson, *Thomas Paine, His Life, Work, and Times* (London: Allen and Unwin 1973), 191

16 Carter-Ruck, *Libel and Slander*, 47

17 David Tribe, *Questions of Censorship* (London: Allen and Unwin 1973), 69

18 'Decree on the Press, March 29, 1793,' in Frank M. Anderson, ed., *The Constitutions and Other Select Documents Illustrative of the History of France, 1789–1907*, 2nd ed. (Minneapolis: The H.R. Wilson Co. 1908; reprint ed., 1967), 159; 'The Decree on Printing and Bookselling, February 5, 1810,' in Anderson, *The Constitutions*, 433–5; 'The Constitutional Charter, 4 June, 1814,' in G.A. Kertesz, ed., *Documents in the Political History of the European Continent, 1815–1939* (Oxford: Oxford University Press 1968), 45

19 Irene Collins, *The Government and the Newspaper Press in France, 1814–1881* (London: Oxford University Press 1959), 22–4

20 'Law on the Press, March 17, 1822,' in Anderson, *The Constitutions*, 488–9

21 'Royal Ordinance on the Press, June 24, 1827,' in Anderson, *The Constitutions*, 489; 'The July Decree of Charles X, July 25, 1830,' in Kertesz, *Documents*, 51

22 Collins, *The Government and the Newspaper Press*, 84

23 Natalie Isser, *The Second Empire and the Press: A Study of Government-Inspired Brochures on French Foreign Policy in Their Propaganda Milieu* (The Hague: M. Nijhoff 1974), 6

24 Isser, *The Second Empire*, 14

25 Collins, *The Government and the Newspaper Press*, 118–35

26 Collins, *The Government and the Newspaper Press*, 181

27 Kertesz, *Documents*, 108

28 Ernst Rudolf Huber, ed., *Dokumente zur Deutschen Verfassungsgeschichte*, 3 vols. (Stuttgart: W. Kohlhammer Verlag [1961–66]), 2:65–7. For a discussion of the decree of 1 June 1863, see Huber, *Deutsche Verfassungsgeschichte seit 1789*, 5 vols. (Stuttgart: W. Kohlhammer Verlag 1957–69), 3:318–19.

29 Montague Shearman and O.T. Rayner, eds., *The Press Laws of Foreign Countries* (London 1926), 104. The press law is dated 7 May 1874.

30 Hans-Wolfgang Wetzel, *Presseinnenpolitik im Bismarckreich (1874–1890): Das Problem der Repression oppositioneller Zeitungen* (Bern: Herbert Lang 1975), 299

31 Huber, *Deutsche Verfassungsgeschichte seit 1789*, 3:371

32 Stewart A. Stehlin, *Bismarck and the Guelph Problem, 1866–1890: A Study in Particularist Opposition to National Unity* (The Hague: M. Nijhoff 1973), see especially chapter 8; Fritz Stern, *Gold and Iron: Bismarck, Bleichröder, and the Building of the German Empire* (New York: Alfred A. Knopf 1977), 265–6

33 'Law against the Publicly Dangerous Endeavours of Social Democracy,' in Vernon D. Lidtke, *The Outlawed Party: Social Democracy in Germany, 1878–1890* (Princeton: Princeton University Press 1966), 341–3

34 *The Press Laws of Foreign Countries*, 57–60, 266–85

35 A. Pokrovsky, 'K istorii gazety v Rossii,' *Vedomosti vremeni Petra Velikogo*, 2 vols. (Moscow 1906), 2:28

36 O. Notovich, *Istoricheskii ocherk nashego zakonodatelstva o pechati* (St Petersburg 1873), 28

37 Alexander V. Muller, ed., *The Spiritual Regulation of Peter the Great* (Seattle: University of Washington Press 1972), 52

38 Notovich, *Istoricheskii ocherk*, 30–4

39 Sumarokov to Shuvalov, quoted in K.A. Papmehl, *Freedom of Expression in Eighteenth Century Russia* (The Hague: M. Nijhoff 1971), 26

40 W.F. Reddaway, ed., *Documents of Catherine the Great* (Cambridge: Cambridge University Press 1931), 287–8

41 Hans Rogger, *National Consciousness in Eighteenth Century Russia* (Cambridge, Mass.: Harvard University Press 1960), 240

42 *SIRIO*, ser. 2, no. 4, 43 (1885), 373

43 *SIRIO*, ser. 2, no. 4, 43 (1885), 302

44 A.M. Skabichevsky, *Ocherki istorii russkoi tsenzury* (St Petersburg 1892), 36, 37; S.P. Dolgova, 'O pervykh vladeltsakh chastnykh tipografii v Rossii (I.M. Gartung i I.K. Shnor),' *Kniga: Issledovaniia i materialy*, 32 (1976), 179

45 I.M. Pekarsky, 'Izdaniia pri Senate,' *Istoriia Pravitelstvuiushchego Senata iz dvesti let, 1711–1911*, 5 vols. (St Petersburg 1911), 5:78

46 *PSZ*, ser. 1, 21, no. 15.634 (15 Jan. 1783), 792

47 Papmehl, *Freedom of Expression*, 77; A.N. Pypin, *Russkoe masonstvo* (Petrograd 1916), 182

48 A.G. Dementev et al., eds., *Russkaia periodicheskaia pechat (1702–1894): Spravochnik* (Moscow 1959), 70

49 Papmehl, *Freedom of Expression*, 97–9. She wrote thus in a personal edict to Count Ia. A. Bruce, the military governor of Moscow.
50 *SIRIO*, ser. 2, no. 4, 27 (23 Jan. 1786), 363–4; Skabichevsky, *Ocherki*, 47; *PSZ*, ser. 1, 22, no. 16.556 (27 July 1787), 875–6
51 Quoted in Roderick Page Thaler, 'Introduction' to A.N. Radishchev, *A Journey from St. Petersburg to Moscow* (Cambridge, Mass.: Harvard University Press 1958), 6
52 D.S. Babkin, *A.N. Radishchev: Literaturno-obshchestvennaia deiatelnost* (Moscow 1966), 150; S.S. Kononovich, 'Tipografshchik Selivanovsky,' *Kniga: Issledovaniia i materialy*, 23 (1972), 101
53 Radishchev, *A Journey*, 167, 199–200
54 Radishchev, *A Journey*, 239
55 D.S. Babkin, *Protsess A.N. Radishcheva* (Moscow 1952), 167–73
56 Babkin, *Protsess*, 276–7
57 V. Bogoliubov, *N.I. Novikov i ego vremia* (Moscow 1916), 418; *SIRIO*, ser. 2, no. 4, 2 (17 May 1792), 123–30
58 *PSZ*, ser. 1, 23, no. 17.508 (16 Sept. 1796), 933–4. The Senate described the offices in a separate ukaz, *PSZ*, ser. 1, 23, no. 17.523 (22 Oct. 1796), 960–1.
59 'O tsenzure v Rossii,' *OZ* 160 (1865): 59
60 *PSZ*, ser. 1, 25, no. 18.524 (17 May 1799), 247–8
61 *PSZ*, ser. 1, 26, no. 19.386 (17 April 1800), 133; no. 19.387 (18 April 1800), 133; no. 19.388 (18 April 1800), 133

CHAPTER 2

1 M.K. Lemke, 'Propushchennyi iubilei: Stoletie pervogo russkogo ustava o tsenzure, 1804, 9 iiulia – 1904,' *Russkaia Mysl*, 9 (1904): 44
2 *PSZ*, ser. 1, 26, no. 19.807 (31 March 1801), 599
3 *PSZ*, ser. 1, 27, no. 20.139 (9 Feb. 1802), 39
4 Sergei V. Rozhdestvensky, *Istoricheskii obzor deiatelnosti Ministerstva Narodnogo Prosveshcheniia, 1802–1902* (St Petersburg 1902), 39
5 Rozhdestvensky, *Istoricheskii obzor*, 38–9
6 M. Sukhomlinov lists members of the Chief Administration of Schools for the entire reign in *Zhurnal Ministerstva Narodnogo Prosveshcheniia*, 128, sec. 2 (1865): 151–2.
7 M. Sukhomlinov, *Issledovaniia i stati po russkoi literature i prosveshcheniiu*, 2 vols. (St Petersburg 1889): 1:407
8 Sukhomlinov, *Issledovaniia i stati*, 1:409–13
9 *PSZ*, ser. 1, 28, no. 21.388 (9 July 1804), 439–44
10 Lemke develops this theme in 'Propushchennyi iubilei,' 34–62.

11 With the new law, the Universities of Moscow, Vilna, and Dorpat continued already authorized censorship functions. The emperor signed the statutes founding the universities of Kazan and Kharkov, which chartered them to perform censorship duties. See N.N. Bulich, *Iz pervykh let Kazanskogo universiteta (1805–1819)*, pt. 1 (St Petersburg 1904), 15

12 *PSZ*, ser. 1, 28, no. 21.388 (9 July 1804), 441

13 Ibid.

14 Kant so argued in 'What Is Enlightenment?' in 1784. The essay is in Immanuel Kant, *The Philosophy of Kant: Moral and Political Writings*, ed. Carl J. Friedrich (New York: Random House 1949), 134–9.

15 M.N. Kufaev, *Istoriia russkoi knigi v XIX veke* (Leningrad 1927), 50

16 Ibid., 49–50

17 *PSZ*, ser. 1, 29, no. 22.579 (5 Aug. 1807), 1230

18 A.E. Stanko, *Russkie gazety pervoi poloviny XIX veka* (Rostov 1969), 7–8

19 I have based this estimate on the list in A.G. Dementev et al., eds., *Russkaia periodicheskaia pechat (1702–1894): Spravochnik* (Moscow 1959), 102–89.

20 Kufaev quotes segments from I.P. Pnin's 1805 essay, 'Truth,' in *Istoriia russkoi knigi*, 57

21 I.I. Zamotin, 'Ocherk istorii zhurnalistiki za pervuiu polovinu XIX veka,' in D.N. Ovsianiko-Kulikovsky, ed., *Istoriia russkoi literatury XIX v.*, 5 vols. (St Petersburg 1908), 2:383; N.K. Piksanov, 'Publitsistika Aleksandrovskoi epokhi,' in Ovsianiko-Kulikovsky, *Istoriia russkoi literatury XIX v.*, 1:47–8

22 *Ocherki po istorii russkoi zhurnalistiki i kritiki: XVIII vek i pervaia polovina XIX veka*, 2 vols. (Leningrad 1950), 1:161

23 Ministerstvo Narodnogo Prosveshcheniia, *Istoricheskie svedeniia o tsenzure v Rossii* (St Petersburg 1862), 10–11

24 N.N. Bulich, *Ocherki po istorii russkoi literatury i prosveshcheniia s nachala XIX v.*, 2 vols. (St Petersburg 1902), 1:96

25 Stanko, *Russkie gazety*, 10

26 Ibid., 12

27 P.N. Sakulin, 'Literaturnye techeniia v Aleksandrovskuiu epokhu,' in Ovsianiko-Kulikovsky, *Istoriia russkoi literatury*, 1:104. Some changes in the first edition must have been made; otherwise it could have bypassed censorship, according to the Statute of 1804. The book aroused considerable public interest, however, which may have alerted the censorship authorities.

28 Sukhomlinov, *Issledovaniia i stati*, 451

29 M.A. Dmitriev, ed., 'A.F. Labzin: Literaturno-biograficheskii ocherk,' *RA*, no. 6 (1866), 817–59. See also Bulich, *Ocherki*, 359–61.

30 N.F. Dubrovin, 'Nashi mistiki-sektanty,' *RS* 84 (1894): 74

31 Dementev, *Russkaia periodicheskaia pechat,* 121

32 Dubrovin, 'Nashi mistiki-sektanty,' 83; Labzin's bibliography is in *RA,* no. 6 (1866), 826–30.

33 Zamotin, 'Ocherk istorii zhurnalistiki,' 385, 386

34 P.S. Squire, *The Third Department: The Political Police under Nicholas I* (Cambridge, Eng.: Cambridge University Press 1968), 25; *PSZ,* ser. 1, 29, no. 22.425 (13 Jan. 1807), 983–4

35 *PSZ,* ser. 1, 31, no. 24.687 (25 June 1811), 726. The Ministry of Police secured authority to distribute lists of approved domestic and foreign books to governors for use of booksellers on 17 October 1814 (N. D., ed. [N.F. Dubrovin], 'K istorii russkoi tsenzury [1814–1820],' *RS* 104 [1900]: 646).

36 F.F. Vigel, *Zapiski,* ed. S.Ia. Shtraikh, 2 vols. (Moscow 1928; reprint ed., 1974), 1:316. Vigel (1786–1856) at this time was an official in the Ministry of the Interior. Although never in a high position, he knew many of the leading figures in the government in the first half of the nineteenth century. His memoirs are a useful source for the reigns of Alexander I and Nicholas I.

37 Prince Adam Czartoryski, *Memoirs,* ed. Adam Gielgud, 2 vols. (London 1888; reprint ed., 1971), 1:179–80

38 Vigel, *Zapiski,* 321

39 Judith C. Zacek, 'The Russian Bible Society and the Russian Orthodox Church,' *Church History* 35, no. 4 (December, 1966): 414

40 A.N. Pypin, 'Russkoe bibleiskoe obshchestvo,' *VE* 8 (1868): 698; Zacek, 'The Russian Bible Society,' 418

41 N.K. Piksanov, 'Publitsistika Aleksandrovskoi epokhi,' 50

42 A.S. Shishkov, 'Mneniia ... o rassmatrivanii knig, ili o tsenzure,' *RA* 10–11 (1878), col. 1346. Shishkov explains his memorandum in *Zapiski, mneniia i perepiska,* ed. N. Kiselev and Iu. Samarin, 2 vols. (Berlin 1870), 1:43.

43 Dubrovin, 'Nashi mistiki-sektanty,' 121

44 Ibid., 127

45 Rozhdestvensky, *Istoricheskii obzor,* 109

46 V.V. Zakharov, 'Svedeniia o nekotorykh peterburgskikh tipografiiakh (1810–1830-e gody),' *Kniga: Issledovaniia i materialy* 26 (1973), 65–71

47 Ibid., 71–5

CHAPTER 3

1 Cited in Maurice Paleologue, *The Enigmatic Tsar: The Life of Alexander I of Russia,* trans. E. and W. Muir (London 1938), 260.

2 N.K. Schilder, *Imperator Aleksandr Pervyi, ego zhizn i tsarstvovanie*, 4 vols. (St Petersburg 1898), 4:302

3 Sukhomlinov lists the members of Golitsyn's Chief Administration in *Zhurnal Ministerstva Narodnogo Prosveshcheniia* 128, sec. 2 (1865): 152. Sturdza, a Moldavian noble, became a lay defender of the Russian Orthodox church. In 1816, he wrote a book, *Considerations on the Doctrine and Spirit of the Orthodox Church*, proposing that the Orthodox church provide spiritual guidance to the Holy Alliance.

4 Dubrovin, 'Nashi mistiki-sektanty,' *RS* 85 (1895): 87

5 A.S. Sturdza, 'Iz zapisok: O sudbe pravoslavnoi tserkvi russkoi v tsarstvovanie Imperatora Aleksandra I,' ed. N.I. Barsov, *RS* 15 (1876): 276; Dubrovin, 'Nashi mistiki-sektanty,' 77

6 Dubrovin, 'Nashi mistiki-sektanty,' 35–6, 47–8

7 I. Ostroglazov, 'Istoriia odnoi redkoi i zamechatelnoi knigi,' *Bibliograficheskie Zapiski* 5 (1892), 340

8 A. Kotovich, *Dukhovnaia tsenzura v Rossii (1799–1855)* (St Petersburg 1909), 111

9 Ibid., 113; M.Ia. Moroshkin, ed., 'K istorii bibleiskikh obshchestv,' *RA* 6 (1868), col. 945. (A letter from Innokenty in Penza to Photius, the cleric who was to be involved in the fight against Golitsyn, reaffirms their spiritual ties.)

10 Kotovich, *Dukhovnaia tsenzura*, 114–22

11 Ostroglazov, 'Istoriia odnoi,' 3 (1892), 185–6

12 Sturdza, 'Iz zapisok,' 280

13 N.I. Grech, *Zapiski o moei zhizni* (St Petersburg 1886), 314–15

14 N.D., comp. [N.F. Dubrovin], 'K istorii russkoi tsenzury (1814–1820), *RS* 104 (1900): 663

15 N.N. Bulich, *Ocherki po istorii russkoi literatury i prosveshcheniia s nachala XIX v.*, ed. N. Kiselev and Iu. Savarin, 2 vols. (St Petersburg 1902), 2:296; A.S. Shishkov, *Zapiski mneniia i perepiska*, 2 vols. (Berlin 1870), 2:179, fn. 2

16 [M. Ia. Moroshkin, comp.], 'Zapiska o kramolakh vragov Rossii, s obiasnitelnym vvedeniem i primechaniem ottsa M.Ia. Moroshkina,' *RA* 6 (1868), cols. 1389–90

17 I.A. Chistovich, *Rukovodiashchie deiateli dukhovnogo prosveshcheniia v Rossii v pervoi polovine tekushchego stoletiia* (St Petersburg 1894), 214

18 Schilder, *Imperator Aleksandr Pervyi*, 248, 251; Photius, 'Avtobiografiia Iurevskogo Arkhimandrita Fotiia,' *RS* 83 (March 1895): 178

19 N.D., comp. [N.F. Dubrovin], 'K istorii russkoi literatury: Popytki bratev A.A. i M.A. Bestuzhevykh izdavat zhurnal (1818–1823),' *RS* 103 (1900): 392, 399–400

20 Sukhomlinov, *Issledovaniia i stati po russkoi literature i prosveshcheniiu*, 2 vols. (St Petersburg 1889), 1:439, 444–6

21 Ibid., 1:463–4. The Magnitsky project is also in A.P. Piatkovsky, 'Tsenzurnyi proekt Magnitskogo,' *Iz istorii nashego literaturnogo i obshchestvennogo razvitiia*, 2 vols. (St Petersburg 1889), 1:237–64.

22 Sukhomlinov, *Issledovaniia i stati*, 1:474

23 Moroshkin, 'K istorii bibleiskikh obshchestv,' col. 950

24 Photius, 'Avtobiografiia,' 87 (August, 1896): 425

25 Grech, *Zapiski*, 315–19. Although his plant had published pietistic books, Grech says he quickly recognized that agreeing to print the Gosner volume was a mistake. He blames the commitment to do so on Bezak. Grech, in a later interview with the police, declared that the censor of the book bore no guilt for the approval because he hadn't read it. 'He signed it at the direction of superiors, Prince Golitsyn, Runich, and others.'

26 Chistovich, *Rukovodiashchie deiateli*, 229 (an official of the Holy Synod, A.A. Pavlov, was a source of information for the plotters, and he probably leaked the news of the *Commentary*); Grech, *Zapiski*, 316

27 Serafim made the decision to visit the emperor on the same day he walked out of a meeting of the St Petersburg Bible Society. He went with some reluctance. According to Moroshkin, the prelate got into his carriage three different times before Arakcheev and others made certain that he stayed there and ordered the driver to proceed to the Winter Palace. According to Peter Bartenev, publisher of *Russkii Arkhiv*, Magnitsky followed Serafim's carriage to make certain that it went directly to the Palace (Moroshkin, 'Zapiski o kramolakh,' col. 1390).

28 Ostroglazov, 'Istoriia odnoi,' no. 3, 189; A.N. Pypin, 'Russkoe bibleiskoe obshchestvo,' *VE* 11 (1868): 283; Chistovich, *Rukovodiashchie deiateli*, 230

29 Ostroglazov, 'Istoriia odnoi,' no. 5, 340–1

30 Photius, 'Avtobiografiia,' 84 (December 1895): 195–203

31 Photius to Arkhimandrite Gerasim, 20 August 1824, in Moroshkin, 'K istorii bibleiskikh obshchestv,' 944; Judith Zacek, 'The Russian Bible Society and the Russian Orthodox Church,' *Church History* 35, no. 4 (December 1966): 433

32 Shishkov, *Zapiski*, 205; Ostroglazov, 'Istoriia odnoi,' no. 4, 270

33 Chistovich, *Rukovodiashchie deiateli*, 241. The police confiscated 3,000 copies of the book and burned them. Three copies, two of them complete, somehow survived, and one was acquired by Ostroglazov in later years. He describes the condition, annotations, and location of each in his article in *Bibliografichskie Zapiski*, cited above.

34 Shishkov, *Zapiski*, 247; F.F. Vigel, *Zapiski*, ed. S.Ia. Shtraikh, 2 vols. (Moscow 1928; reprint ed., 1974), 2:122

35 Shishkov, *Zapiski*, 247. Photius continued to press for the closing of the Bible Society, claiming that secret organizations were using it to forward

plans for destroying the church and state. He wrote to the emperor to this effect on 14 June 1824. His letter is in Photius, 'Avtobiografiia,' 87 (August 1896): 426–7.

36 Pushkin to L.S. Pushkin, 13 June 1824, *The Letters of Alexander Pushkin,* trans. J. Thomas Shaw, 3 vols. (Bloomington, Ind.: University of Indiana Press 1963), 1:160. Grech, in an unflattering portrait, declares that the 'muddle-headed Shishkov, who had lost his faculties, was given Golitsyn's position because of an absurd critique of ... Gosner's book' (Grech, *Zapiski,* 314).

37 Shishkov, *Zapiski,* 168

38 Shishkov, *Zapiski,* 176, 249. Another item of early business was Stanevich's book. On Shishkov's recommendation, it appeared in 1825 as a 'second edition' approved by the ecclesiastical censorship.

39 A.V. Nikitenko, *Dnevnik,* ed. I.Ia. Aizenshtok, 3 vols. (Moscow 1955), 2:553

40 Ostroglazov, 'Istoriia odnoi,' no. 4, 540. The lengthy delay of the Popov trial was probably caused by a devastating flood of St Petersburg by the Neva River in November 1824. The clean-up and reconstruction program preoccupied the imperial government for months. See also N. Dubrovin, ed. *Pisma glavneishikh deiatelei v tsarstvovanie Imp. Aleksandra I s 1807–1829 god* (St Petersburg 1883), 243.

41 Ostroglazov, 'Istoriia odnoi,' no. 8, 543; Grech (*Zapiski,* 315) and Shishkov (*Zapiski,* 173), both self-interested witnesses, claim that Popov translated whole chapters of the book.

42 Ostroglazov, 'Istoriia odnoi,' no. 4, 543, 554

43 Shishkov, *Zapiski,* 241; Ostroglazov, 'Istoriia odnoi,' no. 8, 547; Grech, *Zapiski,* 321

44 Shishkov, *Zapiski,* 279

45 Alexander I by ukaz created a special chancellery in the Post Office Department and named Popov its director on Golitsyn's recommendation (*PSZ,* ser. 1, 39, no. 29.916 [16 May 1824], 320). Popov served until early in Nicholas's reign.

46 Moroshkin, 'K istorii bibleiskikh obshchestv,' cols. 947–8

47 Pypin, 'Russkoe bibleiskoe obshchestvo,' no. 12, 728; Moroshkin, 'K istorii bibleiskikh obshchestv,' col. 943

48 The Bible Society had, in its twenty-year span, published 876,106 volumes (Pypin, 'Russkoe bibleiskoe obshchestvo,' 741).

49 Moroshkin published the memorandum, 'Zapiski o kramolakh,' in *RA* 6 (1868), cols. 1329–91, having obtained a copy from A.A. Popov, who had served under the Holy Synod procurator Prince Meshchersky and who evidently leaked information to Golitsyn's opposition. Moroshkin con-

cludes that P.A. Shirinsky-Shikhmatov had written the memorandum, or most of it. That Shikhmatov wrote for Shishkov is confirmed by the editor of Shishkov's memoirs. A comparison shows that the memorandum is based on Shishkov's statement to the Committee of Ministers on Gosner's book (Shishkov, *Zapiski*, 205).

CHAPTER 4

1 [V.V. Stasov, comp.], 'Tsenzura v tsarstvovanie Imp. Nikolaia I,' *RS* 107 (1901): 396, 397; S. Glinka, 'Moe tsenzorstvo,' *Sovremennik* 110, no. 9 (1865): 220; M.K. Lemke, *Ocherki po istorii russkoi tsenzury i zhurnalistiki XIX stoletiia* (St Petersburg 1904), 382

2 *PSZ*, ser. 2, 1, no. 403 (10 June 1826), 550–71

3 *PSZ*, ser. 2, 1, no. 403 (10 June 1826), 551–3

4 A. Kotovich, *Dukhovnaia tsenzura v Rossii (1799–1855)* (St Petersburg 1909), 135

5 Ministerstvo Narodnogo Prosveshcheniia, *Istoricheskie svedeniia o tsenzure v Rossii* (St Petersburg 1862), 44; 'Peterburgskoe obshchestvo pri vosshestvii na prestol Imperatora Nikolaia po doneseniiaem M.Ia. Foka – A.Kh. Benkendorfu,' comp. P.M. Doragon, *RS* 32 (1881): 583

6 A.S. Shishkov, *Zapiski mneniia i perepiska*, ed. N. Kiselev and Iu. Samarin, 2 vols. (Berlin 1870), 2:284–5 and 287–8

7 Ibid., 2:284–5

8 The Lievens were very highly placed. Karl's mother had been governess to the young Nicholas; Karl's brother, ambassador to England; and his sister, the wife of Benckendorff and an intimate of a number of leading statesmen of the era (she left important letters and a diary).

9 *PSZ*, ser. 2, 3, no. 1979 (22 April 1828), 459–78. A.V. Nikitenko was a defender of the new law. It produced, he said, a 'convulsive shock' in the bureaucracy because officials thought it allowed too much freedom, and he doubted that his superior M.K. Borozdin, the superintendent of the St Petersburg education district, had the strength of will to champion it (A.V. Nikitenko, *Dnevnik*, ed. I.Ia. Aizenshtok, 3 vols. [Moscow 1955], 1:82, 86, 89).

10 *PSZ*, ser. 2, 3, no. 1979 (22 April 1828), 463. Under the 1804 statute, the Ministry of Public Education had approved new printing plants, a power transferred to the Ministry of the Interior under the 1826 law. The drafters of the 1828 statute failed to assign this power in their law, and on 28 February 1829 an imperial ukaz gave it to the Ministry of the Interior (*PSZ*, ser. 2, 4, no. 2702 [28 Feb. 1829], 133–4).

11 A. Yarmolinsky, 'A Note on the Censorship of Foreign Books in Russia under Nicholas I,' *New York Public Library Bulletin* 38 (1934): 907–10

12 *PSZ*, ser. 2, 3, no. 1980 (22 April 1828), 478–80. Pushkin had high praise for the new law: Pushkin to Baron A.G. Barante, 16 December 1836, *The Letters of Alexander Pushkin*, trans. J. Thomas Shaw, 3 vols. (Bloomington, Ind.: University of Indiana Press 1963), 3:809–10.

13 M.N. Rozanov, 'Kniga i liudi v XIX veke,' *Russkaia kniga deviatnadtsatogo veka*, ed. V. Ia. Adariukov and A.A. Sidorov, 2 vols. (Moscow, 1924–25; reprint ed., 1966), 2:473

14 As quoted in T. Grits, V. Trenin, M. Nikitin, *Slovesnost i kommertsiia (Knizhnaia lavka A.F. Smirdina)*, ed. V.B. Shklovsky and B.M. Eikhenbaum (Moscow [1929]), 242.

15 Glinka, 'Moe tsenzorstvo,' 223

16 V.F. Odoevsky, 'Iz bumag,' *RA* 2 (1874), cols. 16, 30

17 M. Polievktov, *Nikolai I: Biografiia i obzor tsarstvovaniia* (Moscow 1918), 80

18 M.K. Lemke, *Nikolaevskie zhandarmy i literatura, 1826–1855* (St Petersburg 1909), 39, and Lemke, 'Trete otdelenie i tsenzura, 1826–1855,' *RB* 9 (1905): 208. Another important study is Sidney Monas, *The Third Section: Police and Society under Nicholas I* (Cambridge, Mass: Harvard University Press 1961). See especially the chapter on Pushkin and censorship. I have been greatly influenced by this important book.

19 *PSZ*, ser. 2, 3, no. 1981 (22 April 1828), 480–9

20 Prince Richard Metternich, ed., *Memoirs of Prince Metternich, 1773–1815*, trans. Mrs. Alexander Napier, 5 vols. (New York 1880–82), 2:225

21 P.S. Squire, *The Third Department: The Establishment and Practices of the Political Police in the Russia of Nicholas I* (Cambridge: Cambridge University Press 1968), 30, 39 (Russian officials, including the emperor, admired Fouché's Ministry of the Police and appear to have modelled the Russian counterpart of 1811 on it. Von Vock became Director of the Special Chancellery of the Ministry, a secret police agency resembling the special section of Fouché). See also Donald E. Emerson, *Metternich and the Political Police: Security and Subversion in the Hapsburg Monarchy, 1815–1830* (The Hague: M. Nijhoff 1968), 137, and François Guizot, *Memoirs to Illustrate the History of My Time*, trans. J.W. Cole, 8 vols. (London 1858–67; reprint ed., 1974), 3:201–4.

22 'Peterburgskoe obshchestvo,' 550–1

23 A.Kh. Benckendorff, 'Graf Benkendorf o Rossii v 1827–1832 gg.,' ed. A. Sergeev, *KA* 37 (1929): 138–74; 38 (1930): 109–47; 46 (1931): 133–59

24 'Graf Benkendorf o Rossii,' 37 (1929): 150–3

25 'Graf Benkendorf o Rossii,' 38 (1930): 127

26 Ibid., 156–63

27 Ibid., 109–32; *PSZ*, ser. 2, 4, no. 3192 (25 Sept. 1829), 682

28 'Graf Benkendorf o Rossii,' 38 (1930): 133–47. The writers were A. Voei-kov, publisher of The *Slav* (*Slavianin*), for printing Viazemsky's satirical verse, 'The Censor,' and Grech and Bulgarin for their attack on Zagoskin's historical novel *Yury Miloslavsky*. The first arrest was ordered by Nicholas and the second and third by Benckendorff.

29 'Graf Benkendorf o Rossii,' 38 (1930): 139, 141. By the Organic Statute, signed 26 February 1832, following the rebellion, Nicholas confirmed some but not all features of the Polish Constitution granted by Alexander I in 1815. Poland kept its own system of law, administration, and budget, but its Council of State was no longer to take part in lawmaking. The emperor henceforth issued the laws by decree from St Petersburg (R.F. Leslie, *Polish Politics and the Revolution of 1830* [London: Athlone Press 1956], 262).

30 'Tsenzura v tsarstvovanie,' 113 (1903): 306–7; *Istoricheskie svedeniia o tsen-zure*, 58. Even editors tried to make their own arrangements for improved censorship. Nicholas Polevoi, editor and publisher of *Moscow Telegraph*, wrote General Volkov, who headed the Moscow district of the Corps of Gendarmes (the regular imperial police), and with whom he was on friendly terms, to request that he personally approve the journal, serving as its censor. Polevoi evidently hoped to win higher support against a troublesome Moscow censorship. Nicholas I approved the request and ordered that Volkov read Polevoi's articles 'prior to the Moscow censor' (Lemke, 'Trete otdelenie i tsenzura,' 214).

31 Polievktov, *Nikolai I*, 113

32 'Tsenzura v tsarstvovanie,' 107 (1901): 662; A.I. Delvig, *Polveka russkoi zhizni: Vospominaniia, 1820–1870* (Moscow-Leningrad 1930), 154. Delvig says a new regulation had forbidden any mention of the July revolution, but the editors knew nothing about it.

33 Aleksandr I. Koshelev, *Zapiski, 1812–1833* (Berlin 1884), 31–2; 'Tsenzura v tsarstvovanie,' 107 (1901): 663

34 Nikitenko, *Dnevnik*, 1: 95, 99

35 'Tsenzura v tsarstvovanie,' 107 (1901): 666

36 Ibid., 666–7

37 Ibid., 113 (1903): 311

38 On Bulgarin, see *Russkii biograficheskii slovar* (St Petersburg 1908), s.v. 'Bulgarin, Faddei Venediktovich.'

39 N.D. [N.F. Dubrovin], 'K istorii russkoi literatury: F.V. Bulgarin i N.I. Grech (Kak izdateli zhurnalov),' *RS* 103 (1900): 577–9; Lemke, *Ocherki po istorii russkoi tsenzury*, 378–81

40 A.S. Shishkov, 'Mnenie o tsenzure i knigopechatanii v Rossii 1826 g.,' *RS* 109 (1904): 205

41 M. Sukhomlinov, 'Polemicheskie stati Pushkina; po neizdannym dokumentam,' *IV* 15 (1884): 487. Benckendorff had ready access to the columns of Bulgarin's *Bee*. On 11 August 1836 he asked M.N. Zagoskin for an account of Nicholas I's visit to the Uspensky Cathedral 'for publication in the paper the *Northern Bee*.' Zagoskin and the *Bee* complied (M.N. Zagoskin, 'Iz zapisok,' ed. I.A. Bychkov, *RS* 111 [1902]: 86–7). Benckendorff also controlled a Polish-language paper, *The Weekly* (*Tygodnik*), established in St Petersburg in 1829, From 1832 it became the 'Official Newspaper of the Kingdom of Poland' (until its closing in 1858) and an outlet for official declarations (O.A. Przhetslavsky, 'Iosafat Ogryzko i ego polskaia gazeta Slovo ...,' *RA* 5 [1872], cols. 1032–3).

42 *Russkii biograficheskii slovar*, s.v. 'Bulgarin.' Bulgarin objected to the expense of co-operating with the Third Section. He said that Grech recruited someone abroad to send 'reports from the papers and various written tittle-tattle,' but that the *Northern Bee* had to pay the agent 1,000 rubles silver ('Pismo Bulgarina k K.P. Liprandi,' 23 March 1855, *RA* 9 [1869], col. 1557).

43 Sukhomlinov, 'Polemicheskie stati Pushkina,' 490

44 Sukhomlinov, 'Polemicheskie stati Pushkina,' 482–3. Pushkin's piece appeared on 6 April 1830, and the feud continued. *Bee* panned Pushkin's *Onegin* and Pushkin ridiculed Bulgarin's novel, *Ivan Vyzhigin*.

45 Bulgarin gave this formula for successful publishing to his editor, Pavel Usov, in 1852: 'The majority of the public loves light things. [So] there are no politics in the *Bee*; there is no place for great literary articles, so please put on the back page small, good, and important literary items and add a whole column of miscellany' (P. Usov, 'F.B. Bulgarin v poslednee desiatiletie ego zhizni,' *IV* 13 [1883]: 302–3).

CHARTER 5

1 Ivan Kireevsky, 'Deviatnadtsatyi vek,' *PSS*, ed. M. Gershenzon, 2 vols. (Moscow 1911), 2: 85–108. Abbott Gleason discusses this article in *European and Muscovite: Ivan Kireevsky and the Origins of Slavophilism* (Cambridge, Mass.: Harvard University Press 1972), 104–15.

2 M.K. Lemke, *Nikolaevskie zhandarmy i literatura, 1826–1855* (St Petersburg 1909), 73

3 Ibid., 76

4 Ibid., 77

5 M.K. Lemke, *Ocherki po istorii russkoi tsenzury i zhurnalistiki XIX stoletiia* (St Petersburg 1904), 188

6 Lemke, *Nikolaevskie zhandarmy*, 85

7 [V.V. Stasov, comp.], 'Tsenzura v tsarstvovanie Imp. Nikolaia I,' *RS* 113 (1903): 586–9

8 M.N. Sukhomlinov, 'N.A. Polevoi i ego zhurnal "Moskovskii Telegraf,"' *Issledovaniia i stati po russkoi literature i prosveshcheniiu*, 2 vols. (St Petersburg 1889), 2:403

9 A.N. Pypin, *Kharakteristiki literaturnykh mnenii ot dvadtsatykh do piatidesiatykh godov*, 3d ed. (St Petersburg 1906), 486; Sukhomlinov, 'N.A. Polevoi,' 409

10 Nikitenko, *Dnevnik*, ed. I.Ia. Aizenshtok, 3 vols. (Moscow 1955), 1:188. As so often happened, someone outside the censorship administration and the police (F.F. Vigel) protested the article (to the Metropolitan Serafim, who in turn complained by letter to Benckendorff). The documents are in M.Ia. Moroshkin, ed., 'Donos ego [F.F. Vigel] mitropolitu Serafimu o state Chaadaeva ...,' *RS* 1 (1870): 574–8.

11 Lemke, *Nikolaevskie zhandarmy*, 414. These penalties were soon relaxed to enable Chaadaev to take daily walks, Nadezhdin to return within a year from exile, and Boldyrev to regain his pension rights (Raymond T. McNally, *Chaadayev and His Friends: An Intellectual History of Peter Chaadayev and His Contemporaries* [Tallahassee: Diplomatic Press 1971], 45).

12 P.A. Viazemsky, 'Proekt pisma k S.S. Uvarovu,' *PSS*, 12 vols. (St Petersburg 1879), 2:211–26. In 1822, Pushkin had written a poem dedicated to his censor arguing that publishing appropriate for London is premature for Moscow (A.S. Pushkin, 'Poslanie tsenzoru,' *PSS*, ed. M.A. Tsiavlovsky, 6 vols. (Moscow-Leningrad 1936), 1:335–8.

13 E. Tarle, ed., 'Doneseniia Iakova Tolstogo iz Parizha v III otdelenie ...,' *LN*, nos. 31–32 (1937), 572

14 A.Kh. Benckendorff, 'Zapiski,' IV 91 (1903): 53–4

15 Tarle, 'Doneseniia Iakova Tolstogo,' 567, 572, 574; Lemke, *Nikolaevskie zhandarmy*, 108

16 Lemke, *Nikolaevskie zhandarmy*, 143

17 Ibid., 148. The German version of the pamphlet appeared in Heidelberg in 1844 and the French in Paris the same year, both under Grech's name. A refutation of Custine by Tolstoy, under the pseudonym of J. Yakovlev, also appeared in 1844 in German in Leipzig and in French in Paris. Yet another pamphlet, written by a Russian diplomat of Polish origin, Xavier Labenski, who was in the Foreign Ministry in St Petersburg, appeared

anonymously in a French version and an English translation in 1844. All this George Kennan describes in detail in *The Marquis de Custine and His 'Russia in 1839'* (Princeton: Princeton University Press 1971), 93–105.

18 T. Grits, V. Trenin, M. Nikitin, *Slovesnost i kommertsiia (Knizhnaia lavka A.F. Smirdina)*, ed. V.B. Shklovsky and B.M. Eikhenbaum (Moscow [1929]), 227–55

19 I.E. Barenbaum, E.L. Nemirovsky, A.G. Shitsgal, 'Knigopechatanie i knigoizdatelstvo v Peterburge pervoi poloviny XIX v.,' *Russkoe knigopechatanie do 1917 goda, 1564–1917*, ed. A.A. Sidorov (Moscow 1964), 267–8; N.M. Lisovsky, *Kratkii ocherk stoletnei deiatelnosti tipografii Glazunovykh v sviazi s razvitiem ikh knigoizdatelstva, 1803–1903* (St Petersburg 1903), 64–5

20 Smirdin also may have come to use the process of galvanizing (soon called electrotyping) discovered by a German on the faculty of the Russian Academy of Sciences, M.N. Jacoby (Iakobi), by which an electrochemical process made a raised copper engraving suitable for use on a printing press. B.M. Nevezhina, 'Litografiia,' *Ocherki po istorii i mekhanike graviury* (Moscow 1941), 77–86. Lithography ('stone printing') involves lines drawn on limestone in ink containing fat and fixed by chemical means. Printers ink rolled on the image is transferred to paper by means of a printing press. Although Russians first disdained lithography as a vulgarization of art, the technique spread rapidly after 1820, the year the press of the General Staff issued the first handbook in Russian on the subject. The German inventor, Aloysius Senefelder, sold the world's finest limestone for lithography from his quarries in Bavaria and made exports to Russia. And because the French were the European leaders in lithography, Frenchmen proved central in the Lithographic Institute founded in Russia with an imperial subsidy in 1844. Lithography became fairly widely used by Russian publishers in the 1830s and 1840s.

21 *Russkii biograficheskii slovar* (St Petersburg 1904), s.v. 'Senkovsky, Osip Ivanovich'

22 A.A. Starchevsky, 'Vospominaniia starogo literatora,' *IV* 45 (1891): 312; L.Ia. Ginzburg, '"Biblioteka dlia Chteniia" v 1830–kh godakh. O.I. Senkovsky,' *Ocherki po istorii russkoi zhurnalistiki i kritiki; XVIII veka i pervaia polovina XIX veka*, 2 vols. (Leningrad 1950), 1:326

23 As quoted in Grits et al., *Slovesnost*, 310–11.

24 A European parallel was the Paris *Presse*, begun by Emile de Girardin in 1836 to appeal to a wider audience than that of the traditional French paper dependent on the government or a political party for support. By offering colourful journalism, gossip, fashions, and serialized novels, Girardin won a readership which attracted enough advertising revenue to

rule out the need for political funding. The *Bee*, of course, welcomed government favours.

25 Grits et al., *Slovesnost*, 338–48

26 Ibid., 352–4

27 V.G. Belinsky, *PSS*, 13 vols. (Moscow 1953–59), 4:482

28 D.S. Mirsky, *A History of Russian Literature*, ed. and abr. Francis J. Whitfield (New York: Alfred A. Knopf 1955), 120

29 Lenore O'Boyle, 'The Image of the Journalist in France, Germany, and England, 1815–1848,' *Comparative Studies in Society and History* 10 (1967–68): 290–1. The nineteenth-century French journalist as a parvenu exploiter of the public's tastes is captured in Guy de Maupassant's *Bel-Ami* and Honoré de Balzac's *Lost Illusions*.

30 *Russkii biograficheskii slovar* (St Petersburg 1904), s.v. 'Polevoi, Nikolai Alekseevich,' 'Nadezhdin, Nikolai Ivanovich'

31 A.S. Pushkin [zametki o russkikh zhurnalakh], *PSS*, 5: 341, 535–6

32 Nikolai V. Gogol, 'O dvizhenii zhurnalnoi literatury v 1834 i 1835 godu,' *Khrestomatiia po istorii russkoi zhurnalistiki XIX veka*, ed. A.V. Zapadov (Moscow 1969), 105

33 Belinsky to V.P. Botkin, 28 February 1847, in V.G. Belinsky, *PSS*, 13 vols. (Moscow 1956), 12:340; P.V. Annenkov, *The Extraordinary Decade: Literary Memoirs*, ed. Arthur P. Mendel (Ann Arbor: University of Michigan Press 1968), 133

34 Among those who helped make *Notes* the outstanding periodical of the forties were Alexander Herzen, Ivan Turgenev, Michael Lermontov, M.E. Saltykov-Shchedrin, V.P. Botkin, I.I. Panaev, and V.F. Odoevsky; I.I. Panaev, 'Zametki novogo poeta: Ocherk peterburgskogo promyshlennika,' *Sovremennik* 66 (1857): 268; Starchevsky, 'Vospominaniia,' *IV* 34 (1888): 123

35 A.G. Dementev, '"Otechestvennye Zapiski" 1840–kh godov,' *Ocherki po istorii russkoi zhurnalistiki i kritiki*, 1:525–29

36 Belinsky to Botkin, 16 April 1840, in Belinsky, *PSS*, 11:505; Belinsky to Botkin, 19 February 1840, in Belinsky, *PSS*, 11:453

37 Belinsky was already ill when he joined *Contemporary* and there failed to get on well with either Panaev or Nekrasov. Early in 1847 he despaired: 'My repugnance for literature and journalism *as a trade* grows from day to day, and I do not know what will finally come of it' (Belinsky to Botkin, 6 February 1847, *PSS*, 12:321). Belinsky to Botkin, 5 November 1847, in Belinsky, *PSS*, 12:406. Belinsky died of tuberculosis in 1848.

38 Pypin, *Kharakteristiki literaturnykh mnenii*, 489

39 Nikolai Barsukov, *Zhizn i trudy M.P. Pogodina*, 22 vols. (St Petersburg 1888–1910), 6:23, 27

40 A.G. Dementev, 'Moskvitianin,' *Ocherki po istorii russkoi zhurnalistiki*, 1:488
41 Barsukov, *Zhizn i trudy*, 8:24–5
42 Nikitenko, *Dnevnik*, 1:133
43 Ibid., 1:161
44 Ibid., 1:180
45 Ibid., 1:301

CHAPTER 6

1 M.K. Lemke, *Nikolaevskie zhandarmy i literatura, 1826–1855* (St Petersburg 1909), 175–6
2 M.A. Korf, 'O zakrytii komiteta vysochaishe uchrezhdennogo 2 aprelia, 1848,' December 1855, TSGIA, 772/1/3757, sheet 5; A.V. Nikitenko, *Dnevnik*, ed. I.Ia. Aizenshtok, 3 vols. (Moscow 1955), 1:311; K.S. Veselovsky, 'Otgoloski staroi pamiati,' *RS* 100 (1899): 10
3 M.A. Korf, 'Iz zapisok,' *RS* 101 (1900): 572; Korf, 'Zapiska stat sekretaria barona Modesta Korfa, podannaia Nasledniku Tsesarevichu,' in V. Semevsky, ed., 'Materialy po istorii tsenzury v Rossii (1848),' *GM*, no. 3 (1913), 221
4 Korf, 'Iz zapisok,' 572; Semevsky, 'Materialy po istorii tsenzury,' 219; Korf, 'Spisok ...,' December 1855, TSGIA 772/1/3757, sheet 4
5 N. Barsukov, *Zhizn i trudy M.P. Pogodina*, 22 vols. (St Petersburg 1888–1910), 9:282
6 M.K. Lemke, *Ocherki po istorii russkoi tsenzury i zhurnalistiki XIX stoletiia* (St Petersburg 1904), 199–200
7 'Ob ustroistve komiteta dlia peresmotra tsenzurnogo ustava,' 3 April 1848–19 September 1849, TSGIA 772/1/2097, pt. 1, sheet 1
8 'Ob ustroistve,' sheet 7. Viazemsky's *PSS* (St Petersburg 1876–1887) omits this memorandum on censorship but includes two others about it written in 1836 and 1857.
9 'Ob ustroistve,' sheet 13
10 V.E. Evgenev-Maksimov, *'Sovremennik' v 40–50 gg. ot Belinskogo do Chernyshevskogo* (Leningrad 1934), 243–4
11 Evgenev-Maksimov, *'Sovremennik' v 40–50 gg.*, 246
12 Lemke, *Nikolaevskie zhandarmy*, 193–4
13 F. Bulgarin, 'Zapiska ... o tsenzure i kommunizme v Rossii,' in Semevsky, 'Materialy po istorii tsenzury,' 222–5
14 Korf, 'Spisok,' sheet 11; 'Iz zapisok,' 573; D.P. Buturlin, 'O dostavlenii v publichnuiu biblioteku iz tipografii mesiachnykh vedomostei ...,' 17 April 1848–19 December 1855, TSGIA, 772/1/2096, sheet 1

15 Lemke, *Ocherki po istorii russkoi tsenzury*, 207; [V.V. Stasov, comp.], 'Tsenzura v tsarstvovanie Imp. Nikolaia ı,' *RS* 115 (1903): 410; O.A. Przhetslavsky, 'Vospominaniia ... tsenzura, 1830–1865,' *RS* 14 (1875): 160

16 Nikitenko, *Dnevnik*, 1:311–12; Barsukov, *Zhizn i trudy*, 9:303

17 A.F. Koni, 'M.N. Zagoskin i tsenzura,' *Ocherki i vospominaniia: (Publichnye chteniia, rechi, stati, i zametki)* (St Petersburg 1906), 866

18 'Tsenzura v tsarstvovanie,' 115 (1903): 148–9

19 Ibid., 152; 'Po proektu ustava o tsenzure,' 19 January 1849, *Materialy, sobrannye osoboiu komissieiu vysochaishe uchrezhdennoi 2 noiabria 1869 g. dlia peresmotra deistvuiushchikh postanovlenii o tsenzure i pechati*, 5 vols. (St Petersburg 1870), 1:279–83

20 Lemke, *Ocherki po istorii russkoi tsenzury*, 241; 'Po proektu ustava o tsenzure,' 310–11

21 Shikhmatov had served in the Ministry of Public Education since 1824 when Admiral Shishkov had named the former naval officer director of his chancellery. Shikhmatov, like Golitsyn and Shishkov, attempted to base education and censorship on divine precepts (*Russkii biograficheskii slovar* [St Petersburg 1911], s.v. 'Shirinsky-Shikhmatov, kniaz Platon Aleksandrovich'). 'Tsenzura v tsarstvovanie,' 115 (1903): 425; 116 (1903): 173, 175

22 'Tsenzura v tsarstvovanie,' 115 (1903): 663; 116 (1903): 689–92

23 The censorship history of the *Sketches* is recounted in I.S. Turgenev, *Sochineniia*, 15 vols. (Moscow 1963), 4:500–6, 522–5. Documents on the case are in Iu.G. Oksman, *Ot 'Kapitanskoi dochki' k 'Zapiskam okhotnika'* (Saratov 1959; reprint ed., 1966), 246–303. *Sketches* passed under another cloud when an unauthorized French edition in Paris in 1854 included a denunciation of the Russian social system at the beginning of the Crimean War. The imperial censorship administration permitted a second Russian edition only after the government had opened the peasant question to discussion in the press in the next reign.

24 Lemke, *Nikolaevskie zhandarmy*, 204–13. Turgenev received so many friends in his room that the jailers put a stop to visits. A lady friend did continue to provide his dinner, lovingly prepared in her own kitchen.

25 V. Evgenev-Maksimov, 'Tsenzurnaia praktika v gody krymskoi voiny,' *GM*, nos. 11–12 (1917), 262

26 Nikitenko, *Dnevnik*, 1:386; 'Tsenzura v tsarstvovanie,' 117 (1904): 221–2

27 L.V. Dubbelt, 'Zapiska ... chitannye v zasedanii Glavnogo Upravleniia po Tsenzure po povodu izdaniia v svet polnogo sobraniia sochinenii Gogolia (1885 g.),' *RS* 29 (1880): 1001

28 Evgenev-Maksimov, 'Tsenzurnaia praktika,' 264

29 *Naval Miscellany* published monthly lists of persons wounded in the Crimean War, but no other periodical was permitted to reprint them. The *Miscellany* had a privileged position as the periodical issued by the Naval Ministry, headed by the Grand Duke Constantine Nikolaevich. Only in 1858 was it required to undergo regular censorship scrutiny. See E.D. Dneprov, '*Morskoi sbornik* v obshchestvennom dvizhenii perioda pervoi revoliutsionnoi situatsii v Rossii,' *Revoliutsionnaia situatsiia v Rossii v 1859–1861 gg.*, ed. M.V. Nechkina (Moscow 1965), 245–6.

30 Nekrasov to M.V. Belinskaia, 26 April 1854, N.A. Nekrasov, *Polnoe sobranie sochinenii i pisem*, ed. V.E. Evgenev-Maksimov, A.M. Egolin, and K.I. Chukovsky, 12 vols. (Moscow 1948–53), 10:203 (hereafter cited as *PSS*).

31 Evgenev-Maksimov, 'Tsenzurnaia praktika,' 251. 'Sevastopol in August' appeared in January 1856.

32 Anthony G. Netting compares population and circulation figures for western Europe and Russia in 'Russian Liberalism: The Years of Promise, 1842–1855' (unpublished PHD dissertation, Columbia University). The *Edinburgh* and the *Quarterly* each had more than 10,000 subscribers by 1825 but dropped off by mid-century. The *Westminister Review* had 1,200 in 1840 and 650 in 1853; the *Revue des deux mondes*, 1,000 in 1834, 2,500 in 1848, and 8,600 in 1856.

33 N.N. Ablov, 'K stoletiiu pervoi popytki "ofitsialnoi" registratsii pechati v Rossii (1837–1855),' *Sovetskaia Bibliografiia* 1 (1937), 105–8

34 A.A. Kraevsky, *Bumagi A.A. Kraevskogo*, ed. I.A. Bychkov (St Petersburg 1893), 119; A.G. Dementev, *Ocherki po istorii russkoi zhurnalistiki, 1840–1850 gg.* (Moscow 1951), 173; Nekrasov to M.V. Avdeev, 17 June 1852, in Nekrasov, *PSS*, 10:175; Netting, 'Russian Liberalism,' 110

35 Dementev, *Ocherki po istorii russkoi zhurnalistiki*, 78; Nekrasov to Turgenev, 27 March 1849, *PSS*, 10:127–28

36 Dementev, *Ocherki po istorii russkoi zhurnalistiki*, 216, 231

CHAPTER 7

1 A.V. Nikitenko, *Dnevnik*, ed. I.Ia. Aizenshtok, 3 vols. (Moscow 1955), 1:413

2 I.E. Barenbaum, 'Narodnye zhurnaly A.F. Pogosskogo v gody revoliutsionnoi situatsii,' *Revoliutsionnaia situatsiia v Rossii v 1859–1861 gg.*, ed. M.V. Nechkina (Moscow 1970), 202. A.F. Pogossky, a retired major, edited *Soldiers' Conversation.* He next founded *Popular Conversation* (*Narodnaia Beseda*, 1862–7), as the organ of the Sunday Schools (reading schools for commoners taught by volunteers). Pogossky insinuated liberal politi-

cal ideas into his journals to such an extent that he came to fear police arrest in 1863 and fled abroad.

3 A.G. Dementev et al., eds., *Russkaia periodicheskaia pechat (1702–1894): Spravochnik* (Moscow 1959), 339–40

4 Nikitenko, *Dnevnik*, 1:415

5 A.M. Skabichevsky, *Ocherki istorii russkoi tsenzury* (St Petersburg 1892), 417 (On the peasant in literature see Donald Fanger, 'The Peasant in Literature,' in *The Peasant in Nineteenth Century Russia*, ed. Wayne S. Vucinich [Stanford: Stanford University Press 1968], 231–62.); K.D. Kavelin, *Sochineniia*, 2 vols. (Moscow 1897), 2:104

6 S.M. Seredonin, *K stoletiiu komiteta ministrov, 1802–1902: Istoricheskii obzor deiatelnosti komiteta ministrov*, 5 vols. (St Petersburg 1902), 3, pt. 1:5–6. I have elaborated on the censorship and the peasant question in 'Censorship and the Peasant Question: The Contingencies of Reform under Alexander II,' *California Slavic Studies* 5 (1970), 137–67.

7 Of the several versions of the emperor's remarks, all contain words to the effect that Alexander had no intention of acting at once unilaterally. One example: 'I know, gentlemen, that among you rumours have circulated about my intentions to abolish serfdom ... I consider it necessary to explain to you that I have no intention of doing such a thing now' (quoted in R., 'Na zare krestianskoi svobody: Materialy kharakteristiki obshchestva, 1857–1861,' *RS* 92 [1897]: 8–9). Cf. A. Levshin, 'Dostopamiatnye minuty v moei zhizni,' *RA* 8 (1885), 476–77, and with A.Z. Popelnitsky, 'Rech Aleksandra II, skazannaia 30 marta 1856 g. moskovskim predvoditeliam dvorianstva,' *GM* 5–6 (1916), 393. Popelnitsky shows that Alexander himself edited this version.

8 S.S. Tatishchev, *Imperator Aleksandr II, ego zhizn i tsarstvovanie*, 2 vols. (St Petersburg 1903), 1:303

9 A.S. Pavlov, 'V.I. Nazimov: Ocherki iz noveishei letopisi severozapadnoi Rossii,' *RS* 45 (1885): 575–8; Levshin, 'Dostopamiatnye minuty,' 486

10 So named in P.I. Liashchenko's monograph, *Poslednii sekretnyi komitet po krestianskomu delu* (St Petersburg 1911). This book covers the period from the opening of the Secret Committee to its transformation into the Main Committee.

11 Levshin takes principal credit for this *zapiska* (Levshin, 'Dostopamiatnye minuty,' 490–2).

12 Liashchenko, *Poslednii sekretnyi komitet*, 11–13. Any such categorizing can only be an approximation. A summary of what the members of the Secret Committee wrote themselves on various aspects of the settlement for peasants is in Popelnitsky, 'Rech Aleksandra II,' 66–70.

13 Levshin, 'Dostopamiatnye minuty,' 492
14 Arkhiv Gosudarstvennogo Soveta, *Zhurnaly sekretnogo i glavnogo komitetov po krestianskomu delu, 1857–1861*, 2 vols. (Petrograd 1915), 1:3; M.N. Pokrovsky, 'Krestianskaia reforma,' *Istoriia Rossi v XIX veke*, 9 vols. (St Petersburg, n.d.), 3:91
15 M.M. Sikorsky, *Zhurnal 'Sovremennik' i krestianskaia reforma 1861 g.* (Moscow 1957), 44, 54
16 A.S. Norov to State Secretary V.P. Butkov, 7 January 1858, TSGIA, 772/1/4293, sheet 8
17 A.P. Zablotsky-Desiatovsky, *Graf P.D. Kiselev i ego vremia*, 4 vols. (St Petersburg 1882), 3:31; Liashchenko, *Poslednii sekretnyi komitet*, 28. Levshin says he contributed much to the *zapiska* of 26 July 1857, and he quotes it in full in 'Dostopamiatnye minuty,' 503–9.
18 A.V. Golovnin, 'Zapiska,' 3 vols., TSGIA, 851/1/4–5, 2:223. The emperor's statement is in Popelnitsky, 'Rech Aleksandra II,' 132.
19 Levshin, 'Dostopamiatnye minuty,' 528. The discussions in Lithuania are described in N.N. Ulashchik, 'Iz istorii reskripta 20 noiabria 1857 goda,' *Istoricheskie Zapiski* 28 (1949), 164–81
20 [D.P. Khrushchov, comp.], *Materialy dlia istorii uprazdneniia krepostnogo sostoianiia pomeshchichikh krestian v Rossii v tsarstvovanie imperatora Aleksandra II*, 3 vols. (Berlin 1860–62), 2:140–1
21 Ibid., 2: 139–40
22 Ibid., 2: 143, 145, 146, 147
23 Levshin, 'Dostopamiatnye minuty,' 535 (his italics)
24 *Zhurnaly sekretnogo i glavnogo komitetov*, no. 9 (5 Dec. 1857)
25 *Materialy dlia istorii uprazdneniia*, 2:169
26 That the emperor had approved this venture is indicated by the letter from Butkov to Norov on the subject of publishing the rescripts and the reasons for it (Butkov to Norov, 14 December 1857, 'Po otnosheniiu ... o dozvolenii pomeshchat v periodicheskikh izdaniiakh Vysochaishie reskripty ...,' TSGIA, 772/1/4293, sheets 1,3). Norov's order is referred to in retrospect in *Zhurnaly sekretnogo i glavnogo komitetov*, no. 14 (12 Jan. 1858). Norov to the superintendent of the St Petersburg education district, 15 December 1857, TSGIA, 772/1/4293, sheet 3
27 A summary of the principal speeches in in *Materialy dlia istorii uprazdneniia*, 2:182–203. The emperor and a number of officials recognized that the acclamations, as thinly-disguised commentary on the peasant question, exceeded government limits on what could appear in print. Norov reprimanded the censor who had permitted an account of the dinner in *Russian Messenger* (N., 'Moskovskii obed 28-go dekabria 1857 g. i ego posledstviia,' *RS* 93 [1898]: 49–72, 297–326).

28 *Zhurnaly sekretnogo i glavnogo komitetov*, no. 14 (12 Jan. 1858). Levshin, 'Dostopamiatnye minuty,' 540. Levshin credits the Grand Duke with a persuasive role and says the decision was probably reached at the end of a tiring meeting in deference to the views of Constantine. Levshin viewed the action as hasty and ill-conceived. No 'plan' was prepared to govern the press discussion.

29 Norov to Butkov, 7 January 1858, 'Po otnosheniiu Gosudarstvennogo Sekretaria Butkova ...,' TSGIA, 772/7/4316, sheet 6

30 The rules of 16 January 1858 are printed in *Prilozheniia k zapiske ... Berte i Iankevicha* (n.p., 1862), 3–4. This printed document was not published and was for internal use only. There is a copy in GBL.

31 Nikitenko, *Dnevnik*, 2: 9 (Viazemsky and Ivan Goncharov, a censor, assisted in the preparation of Norov's statement). The ministers were irritated in part because the censors had failed to halt an outbreak of 'accusatory literature,' satirical journals aimed at pompous officials. *Spark* (*Iskra*), the first and best of these journals, appeared in St Petersburg in 1859. Although the three and even four censors who screened it sometimes withheld as much as a third of the material for an issue, *Spark* survived and was to continue until the early seventies – to the irritation of many officials at whom it aimed its critical shafts (See I.Ia. Iampolsky, *Satiricheskaia zhurnalistika 1860–kh godov: Zhurnal revoliutsionnoi satiry 'Iskra' [1859–1873]* [Moscow 1964]).

32 In response to that supposition, Seredonin, the historian of the Committee of Ministers, observed: 'This principle was new because previously the government had not called for such co-operation' (Seredonin, *K stoletiiu komiteta ministrov*, 3, pt. 2:196–7).

33 *Prilozheniia k zapiske*, 5

34 Viazemsky's statement is evidently the document on censorship for 1858 which appears in his collected works (P.A. Viazemsky, *PSS*, 12 vols. [St Petersburg 1876–87], 8:48–51).

35 N.P. Barsukov, *Zhizn i trudy M.P. Pogodina*, 22 vols. (St Petersburg 1888–1910), 16:405

36 *Russkii biograficheskii slovar* (St Petersburg 1903), s.v. 'Evgraf Petrovich Kovalevsky'

37 N.G. Chernyshevsky, 'O novykh usloviiakh selskogo byta,' pt. 1, *PSS*, ed. V.I. Kirpotin et al., 16 vols. (Moscow 1939–50), 5: 65–107; pt. 2, 108–36. See K. Zhuravlev's notes on the article in Chernyshevsky, *PSS*, 5: 923–24.

38 'Zapiski ob osvobozhdenii krepostnykh krestian,' Chernyshevsky, *PSS*, 5:137–43

39 Ministerstvo Narodnogo Prosveshcheniia, *Sbornik postanovlenii i rasporiazhenii po tsenzure s 1720 po 1862 g.* (St Petersburg 1862), 421; Levshin,

'Dostopamiatnye minuty,' 541. Most journals championed the peasants, and landowners resented the one-sided press discussion. A. Zheltukhin had cited that problem even before the change in censorship about the peasant question when he proposed publishing the *Landowners' Journal* in late December 1857 (Zheltukhin to N.A. Mukhanov, 30 December 1857, GIM, 117/73/A113, sheets 70–73). From its beginning early in 1858, Zheltukhin's journal spoke for the opinion of a decided minority among the periodicals.

40 *Sbornik*, 428; Skabichevsky, *Ocherki*, 422

41 I. Ivaniukov, *Padenie krepostnogo prava v Rossii* (St Petersburg 1882), 94. Historians disagree on how much the press influenced the emancipation principles finally enacted. Daniel Field notes the effect of Herzen's émigré *Bell* on Rostovtsev and, therefore, on the final settlement (*The End of Serfdom: Nobility and Bureaucracy in Russia, 1855–1861* [Cambridge, Mass.: Harvard University Press 1976], 159–72). A. Kornilov sees Herzen, Katkov, and the slavophiles as more practical than Chernyshevsky and therefore more influential (*Obshchestvennoe dvizhenie pri Aleksandre II* [Moscow 1909], 78). Jerome Blum asserts that *Contemporary* was the most influential of the domestic journals but that *Bell* was the most influential of all (*Lord and Peasant in Russia from the Ninth to the Nineteenth Century* [Princeton: Princeton University Press 1961], 586). William F. Woerhlin credits an already sympathetic government with permitting Chernyshevsky to champion the peasants' rights (*Chernyshevskii: The Man and the Journalist* [Cambridge, Mass.: Harvard University Press 1971], 192–3).

42 Nikitenko, *Dnevnik*, 2: 17, 34, 37

43 Ibid., 2: 39

44 'Delo ob uchrezhdenii komiteta po delam knigopechataniia ...,' TSGIA, 772/1/4723 (26 Jan. 1859–3 March 1860), sheet 6

45 The committee was assisted by four functionaries and also hired readers to scan publications for unacceptable material. Nikitenko advised a former student who had been approached by Mukhanov not to accept such 'dark' work (Nikitenko, *Dnevnik*, 2:52).

46 Barsukov, *Zhizn i trudy*, 16: 312, 332

47 Nikitenko, *Dnevnik*, 2:56. 'We are not as distant from the reign of Nicholas Pavlovich as we like to think,' observed Nikitenko.

48 Barsukov, *Zhizn i trudy*, 16: 346–48; *Sbornik*, 440–1; Skabichevsky, *Ocherki*, 425

49 'Delo ob uchrezhdenii,' sheet 57. Count Alexei Tolstoy and his two cousins, the Zhemchuzhnikovs, parodied this committee in 'Project for the Introduction of Uniformity of Thought in Russia,' written under the

pseudonym Kozma Prutkov in 1859 but not published until 1863 (Kozma Prutkov [Aleksei Tolstoy et al.], 'Proekt o vvedenii edinomysliia v Rossii,' *PSS* [n.p., 1949], 128). M.K. Lemke, *Ocherki po istorii russkoi tsenzury i zhurnalistiki XIX stoletiia* (St Petersburg 1904), 343

50 Nikitenko, *Dnevnik*, 2:56–60

51 *Prilozheniia k zapiske*, 12

52 A.G. Troinitsky, 'Iz bumag: Zapiska ego ob uchastii periodicheskoi literatury v obsuzhdenii i razreshenii krestianskogo voprosa,' *RA* 7 (1896), 420

53 Nikitenko, *Dnevnik*, 2: 93–4, 96–8; 'Ob izmeneniiakh ustroistva komiteta po delam knigopechataniia i tsenzury,' 26 October 1859, TSGIA, 772/8.1/5033, sheets 23–9

54 Skabichevsky, *Ocherki*, 444–5; Ministerstvo Narodnogo Prosveshcheniia, *Proekt tsenzurnogo ustava … E.P. Kovalevskim v 1859 godu* (n.p., n.d.), 5–6 (GBL has a copy of this internal document). Lemke, *Ocherki po istorii russkoi tsenzury*, 363

55 Nikitenko, *Dnevnik*, 2: 103

56 Ibid.

57 'O nesostoiavshemsia ministerstve tsenzury: Pisma barona M.A. Korfa k A.G. Troinitskomu,' *RA* 6 (1896), 297–301; 'Proekt ukaza pravitelstvuiushchemu Senatu ob uchrezdenii Glavnogo upravleniia po delam knigopechataniia …,' GPB, 380/83, sheets 17–28; [N?] Smirnov to N.A. Ramazanov, 'O proekte M.A. Korfa sozdat ministerstvo tsenzury,' GIM, 457/15, sheets 31–2

58 Skabichevsky, *Ocherki*, 446

59 *Prilozheniia k zapiske*, 13–14. The emperor's order expressly prohibited articles on the question of the gentry's 'right to meet on public and governmental affairs in gentry assemblies.' It also cautioned editors to make certain the articles ostensibly forwarded by government officials be checked for authenticity.

60 Nikitenko, *Dnevnik*, 1:465

61 Zablotsky-Desiatovsky, *Graf P.D. Kiselev*, 2:345–7

62 Nikitenko, *Dnevnik*, 2: 184, 185. This committee, appointed in April 1861 under S.G. Stroganov, was actually the second one (the first was named under P.G. Oldenbourg just one year before). Rodzevich found the report of this committee and the views of Kovalevsky on the student problem very much alike and concludes that the minister left office for other reasons (N.N. Rodzevich, 'Otstavka E.P. Kovalevskogo [Po dokumentam arkhiva departamenta narodnogo prosveshcheniia],' *Istoricheskii Vestnik* 99 [January 1905], 98–129).

63 Kornilov, *Obshchestvennoe dvizhenie*, 123

64 'N.G. Chernyshevsky v doneseniiakh III otdeleniia (1861–1862), *KA* 14, no. 1 (1926): 83

65 A.A. Kornilov, *Modern Russian History*, 2 vols. (New York 1948), 2:67

66 M.K. Lemke, *Epokha tsenzurnykh reform, 1859–1865 gg.* (St Petersburg 1904), 53–4, 56

67 Ibid., 82. Katkov was principal drafter.

68 A.V. Nikitenko, 'Zapiska o napravlenii zhurnala *Russkoe Slovo*, 11 November 1861,' *RA* 1 (1895), 227

69 Skabichevsky, *Ocherki*, 473. For Fuchs's views on the Kovalevsky censorship reform, see *Zapiska o tsenzure ... Fuksa* (n.p., 1862). GBL has a copy of this printed document, which was prepared for internal use. In time a leading censorship official, Fuchs became a member of the committee to reform the censorship system (Obolensky committee) in 1863 and a charter member of Valuev's Council on Press Affairs in 1865. He helped prepare a new censorship statute for Poland and, in 1872, became head of the Warsaw Censorship Committee. See also *Zapiska o tsenzure ... Fridberga* (n.p., 1862).

70 *Zapiska predsedatelia dlia peresmotra tsenzurnogo ustava ... Berte i ... Iankevicha* (n.p., 1862), 34, 50. GBL has a copy of this document printed for internal use.

CHAPTER 8

1 I have discussed Golovnin in more detail in 'A.V. Golovnin and Liberal Russian Censorship, January-June, 1862,' *Slavonic and East European Review* 50, no. 119 (1972): 198–219.

2 'N.G. Chernyshevsky v doneseniiakh III otdelenia (1861–62),' *KA* 14, no. 1 (1926): 108. *Mneniia raznykh lits o preobrazovanii tsenzury* is a ninety-five page work that also includes briefs from several censors. Of the two shorter briefs from the press, one was by the publisher of *Russian Word*, Count A.G. Kushelev-Bezborodko. The other was by sixteen unnamed writers under the leadership of A.A. Kraevsky, although his name does not appear.

3 K.N. Zhuravlev has shown that Chernyshevsky wrote the document and his colleagues Nekrasov and Panaev approved the text (K.N. Zhuravlev, 'K voprosu ob avtore zapiski redaktsii zhurnala *Sovremennika* o preobrazovanii tsenzury,' *Istoricheskie Zapiski* 37 [1951]: 215–51). Zhuravlev argues that the brief of *Contemporary* was to persuade the censorship to treat this journal more generously. Evgenev-Maksimov suspects a 'compromise' between the journal and Golovnin (V.E. Evgenev-Maksimov,

'*Sovremennik*' *v 40–50 gg. ot Belinskogo do Chernyshevskogo* [Leningrad 1934], 509). Gerasimova gives recognition to Golovnin's 'manoeuvring,' as he attempted to win popularity with the press and to demonstrate new political techniques to old-guard bureaucrats (Iu.I. Gerasimova, *Iz istorii russkoi pechati v periode revoliutsionnoi situatsii kontsa 1850–kh – nachala 1860–kh gg.* [Moscow 1964], 124). In a recent study, Iaroslavtsev accepts the suggestion of Evgenev-Maksimov that Golovnin and Chernyshevsky had an advance 'agreement' on the content of the brief (Ia.A. Iaroslavtsev, 'A.V. Golovnin i N.G. Chernyshevsky,' *Chernyshevsky i ego epokha. Revoliutsionnaia situatsiia v Rossii v 1859–1861 gg.* [Moscow 1979], 126).

4 *Mneniia raznykh lits*, 88, 91–2
5 One article was by Chernyshevsky, 'Frantsuzskie zakony po delam knigopechataniia,' *Sovremennik* 92 (March 1862), 140–76. The other was the anonymous 'Letter' on censorship reform, pp. 59–64.
6 'Zapiska ob izmenenii nyneshnikh tsenzurnykh postanovlenii,' *Mneniia raznykh lits*, 58–73. The following publications were listed at the close of the brief: *Notes of the Fatherland, Russian Word, Time, Northern Bee, Russian War Veteran, Economist, Dawn (Rassvet), Illustrated Newssheet (Illiustrirovannyi Listok)*, and *Encyclopedic Dictionary (Entsiklopedicheskii Slovar)*.
7 'Zapiska ob izmenenii,' 69–73
8 I have drawn much of the information for this section on newspapers from V.G. Berezina, 'Gazety,' *Ocherki po istorii russkoi zhurnalistiki i kritiki; Vtoraia polovina XIX veka*, 2 vols. (Leningrad 1965), 2:30–59.
9 I have borrowed the term from Richard Altick, who has studied the spread of reading in nineteenth-century England to those outside the traditional educated groups. The spread of reading in England Altick shows to be one of the major causes of political and social reform in that country; reading promoted political alertness (Richard D. Altick, *The English Common Reader: A Social History of the Mass Reading Public, 1800–1900* [Chicago 1957]).
10 The first of such papers was *Field (Niva)*, begun in 1870.
11 Effie Ambler, *Russian Journalism and Politics: The Career of Aleksei S. Suvorin, 1861–1881* (Detroit: Wayne State University Press 1972), 57. On Katkov, see the study by Martin Katz, *Mikhail N. Katkov: A Political Biography, 1818–1887* (The Hague: Mouton 1966).
12 N. Lisovsky, 'Periodicheskaia pechat v Rossii, 1703–1903 gg.,' *Sbornik statei po istorii i statistike russkoi periodicheskoi pechati, 1703–1903* (St Petersburg 1903), 22
13 P.A. Valuev, *Dnevnik*, ed. P.A. Zaionchkovsky, 2 vols. (Moscow 1961), 1:375
14 Ibid., 1:140, 379

15 *Severnaia Pochta* 17 Jan. 1862), 49–50
16 Valuev, *Dnevnik*, 1:378
17 A. Kornilov, *Obshchestvennoe dvizhenie pri Aleksandre II* (Moscow 1909), 114. At the time Lobanov-Rostovsky was envoy to Constantinople. He served later as a provincial governor, as vice-minister of the interior, and as foreign minister.
18 A full discussion of this and related events is in Terence Emmons, *The Russian Landed Gentry* (Cambridge: Cambridge University Press 1968), 334–49. Valuev, *Dnevnik*, 1:145, 380
19 Valuev, *Dnevnik*, 1:145–6. For Panin's role in the affair see N. Barsukov, *Zhizn i trudy M.P. Pogodina*, 22 vols. (St Petersburg 1888–1910), 19:31–5.
20 P.A. Valuev, 'Doklad Aleksandru II po delu o zaiavlenii mirovykh posrednikov Tverskoi gub. napravlennykh protiv Polozheniia 19 fev. 1861,' 12 February 1862, GBL 169/40/4, 51–3
21 Valuev, *Dnevnik*, 1:148; 'Konstitutsionnye proekty tsarstvovaniia Aleksandra II,' ed. K.L. Bermansky, *Vestnik Prava* 35 (1905): 228. One specialist argues that Valuev proposed the assembly to preserve national unity in the face of a 'zemstvo-based federative constitutional movement' (S. Frederick Starr, *Decentralization and Self-government in Russia, 1830–1870* [Princeton: Princeton University Press 1972], 275).
22 P.A. Valuev, 'O vnutrennem sostoianii Rossii,' 22 June 1862, ed. V.V. Garmiza, *Istoricheskii Arkhiv*, no. 1 (1958), 143
23 No evidence establishes that Valuev knew of 'Letters without an Address'; but, given his close ties with the Third Section and the surveillance of Chernyshevsky, he very likely did – especially because the 'Letters' concerned the gentry.
24 N.G. Chernyshevsky, 'Pisma bez adresa,' *PSS*, ed. V.I. Kirpotin et al., 16 vols. (Moscow 1939–50), 10:101
25 Having completed his project on censorship, Golovnin arranged to discuss it with the emperor (Golovnin to Alexander II, 25 February 1862, GPB, 208/98, sheet 78.) The project is dated the next day (A.V. Golovnin, 'Doklad Aleksandru II o polozhenii russkoi literatury i neobkhodimosti reorganizatsii tsenzury,' 26 February 1862, TSGIA, 772/1/5977, 38 sheets).
26 Golovnin to Valuev, 7 December 1863, V. Binshtok, comp., 'Materialy po istorii russkoi tsenzury,' *RS* 89 (1897): 585
27 The Council of Ministers discussed Golovnin's report on 8 March and issued new rules to censors in a Senate ukaz on 10 March 1862 (Gerasimova, *Iz istorii russkoi pechati*, 125). The regulations of 10 March are in *PSZ*, ser. 2, 37, sec. 1, no. 38040 (10 March 1862), 182–3. The regulations plus supplementary instructions to the censors are in Ministerstvo Narod-

nogo Prosveshcheniia, *Sbornik postanovlenii i rasporiazhenii po tsenzure s 1720 po 1862 god* (St Petersburg 1862), 466–82.

28 The Ministry of the Interior was to notify the civil censorship authority or the department issuing an official publication or the ecclesiastical censorship office, depending on which was responsible for a publication (*Sbornik postanovlenii i rasporiazhenii*, 466). For Lemke, the step was Golovnin's 'surrender of command' over censorship (M.K. Lemke, *Epokha tsenzurnykh reform, 1859–1865 gg.* [St Petersburg], 131).

29 *Sbornik postanovlenii i rasporiazhenii*, 472–4

30 A.V. Golovnin, 'Vsepoddanneishie dokladnye zapiski ... s ianvaria po mai 1862 g.,' GPB, 208/98, sheet 141

31 Ministerstvo Narodnogo Prosveshcheniia, *Zhurnal ... dlia peresmotra, dopolneniia i izmeneniia postanovlenii po delam knigopechataniia*, 19 March 1862 (St Petersburg 1862), 3–4, 10–11

32 K. Veselovsky, 'Vospominaniia: Vremia prezidentstva grafa D.N. Bludova v Akademii Nauk, 1855–1865,' *RS* 108 (1901): 517–18

33 V.E. Rudakov, 'Poslednie dni tsenzury v Ministerstve Narodnogo Prosveshcheniia,' *IV* 125 (1911): 523

34 A.V. Nikitenko, *Dnevnik*, ed. I.Ia. Aizenshtok, 3 vols. (Moscow 1955), 2:268

35 A.M. Skabichevsky, *Ocherki istorii russkoi tsenzury* (St Petersburg 1892), 477; A.V. Golovnin, 'Predpisanie ...,' *LN* 63 (1956), 683, 685

36 *PSZ*, ser. 2, 37, sec. 1, no. 38270 (12 May 1862), 430–1. Also see Lemke, *Epokha*, 167–9. The emperor approved the new rules on 12 May and Golovnin sent them to his censors on 17 May. Five days after their publication on 14 June, Golovnin and Valuev used them to suspend *Contemporary* and *Russian Word* (M.V. Lvova, 'Kak podgotovilos zakrytie Sovremennika v 1862,' *Istoricheskie Zapiski* 46 [1954]:307).

37 *PSZ*, ser. 2, 38, sec. 1, no. 39613 (12 May 1863), 440

38 Lemke, *Epokha*, 167; Skabichevsky, *Ocherki*, 476; A.V. Golovnin, 'Vsepoddanneishye dokladnye zapiski,' sheet 171; Golovnin to the Grand Duke Constantine, 30 May 1862, GPB, 208/44, sheet 1

39 Golovnin to Valuev, 1 August 1862, TSGIA, 773/1/377, sheets 117, 122

40 *PSZ*, ser. 2, 37, sec. 1, no. 38276 (14 May 1862), 434–7

41 Valuev, *Dnevnik*, 1:175

42 Chernyshevsky to Nekrasov, 19 June 1862, *Literaturnoe nasledie: Pisma*, ed. N.A. Alekseev and A.P. Skaftymov, 3 vols. (Moscow 1928–30), 2:354–5

43 Documents on this case are in M.K. Lemke, *Politicheskie protsessy v Rossii 1860–kh gg.* (Moscow 1923), 161–502. Herzen published a notice in the *Bell* on 15 July 1862, that he was prepared to publish *Day*, *Contemporary*, and *Russian Word* at his own expense in London, a proposal that very

likely adversely affected their relations with the imperial government. Chernyshevsky mentioned Golovnin's offer in a written appeal to A.A. Suvorov, the governor-general of St Petersburg, dated 20 November 1862 (Lemke, *Politicheskie protsessy*, 229). Apparently expecting arrest, Chernyshevsky believed that a trial would show him innocent of crimes because censors had approved all his published works (Iaroslavtsev, 'A.V. Golovnin i N.G. Chernyshevsky,' 132).

44 Golovnin to the Moscow governor-general, 4 July 1862, TSGIA, 773/1/1043, sheet 85; Golovnin to the Moscow governor-general, sheet 86

45 P.A. Valuev, 'O vnutrennem sostoianii Rossii,' 142. Valuev introduced a resolution calling for the tightening of censorship at the meeting of the Council of Ministers of 5 July 1862. According to Valuev, the resolution embarrassed Golovnin, who consequently tried to appear a proponent of stricter censorship (Valuev, *Dnevnik*, 1:183). Golovnin to the emperor, 30 May 1862, GPB, 208/98, sheet 91

46 Golovnin to Tsee, 27 July 1862, *LN* 63 (1956), 685–6. The Moscow publisher had met Golovnin in April and had disliked him from the first (Veselovsky, 'Vospominaniia,' 523).

47 Samarin to Golovnin, 12 July 1862, GPB, 208/100, sheets 149–50; Golovnin to Samarin, n.d., GPB, 208/100, sheets 153–54

48 Golovnin to the emperor, 1 July 1862, GPB, 208/100, sheet 122; Golovnin to Shcherbinin, 17 and 22 July 1862, TSGIA, 773/1/377, sheets 108 and 110; Rudakov, 'Poslednie dni,' 532

49 Rudakov, 'Poslednie dni,' 528. That critical press commentary damaged the cause of censorship reform had been made clear to Aksakov months before by Obolensky, just as his commission was beginning its work. On 9 May he had written Aksakov: 'Golovnin is right when he says that you are endangering literature and hindering my commission. You are hindering me because you serve as living proof that without censorship the most loyal people will begin to write audaciously ... You are hindering me because you yourself are an honest man to whom is known all the problems of the present transitional era [but] who, under the banner of Orthodoxy, cannot find a single word of reconciliation' (quoted in Gerasimova, *Iz istorii russkoi pechati*, 163).

50 Golovnin to Tsee, 16 August 1862, TSGIA, 833/358, sheet 50; Golovnin to the emperor, 17 August 1862, GPB 208/100, sheet 237

51 Golovnin to Obolensky, 14 and 19 September 1862, TSGIA, 773/1/3, sheets 61–3

52 Tsee to Golovnin, 26 November 1862, GPB, 208/102, sheets 96–8. Golovnin had forwarded to Alexander a letter from Tsee.

53 [A.V. Golovnin], 'Vsepoddaneishii doklad o rezultatakh raboty komissii ...,' GPB, 833/48, sheet 2. This document appears to be the draft of the December 10 report by Golovnin. The final version was published in 1862.

54 Ministerstvo Narodnogo Prosveshcheniia, *Proekt ustava o knigopechatanii, vvedenie, obshchie polozheniia i tri pervykh razdela* (St Petersburg 1862), 17

55 *Proekt ustava*, 69

56 Nikitenko, *Dnevnik*, 2:307. Nikitenko provides a different interpretation of these events.

57 'Vsepoddaneishii doklad o rezultatakh raboty komissii,' sheet 2

58 Lemke, *Epokha*, 441

59 [P.I. Kapnist], *Kratkoe obozrenie napravleniia periodicheskikh izdanii i gazet i otzyvov ikh po vazhneishim pravitelstvennym i drugim voprosam za 1862 g.* (St Petersburg 1862), 2, 8. The *Kratkoe obozrenie* appears in Kapnist's *Sochineniia*, 2 vols. (Moscow 1901), 2:428–509. This publication was part of the campaign to show the emperor the efficacy of Golovnin's policies.

60 Binshtok, 'Materialy,' 593; Golovnin to the emperor, 14 December 1862, GPB, 208/100, sheet 182; I.S. Aksakov, *Sochineniia*, 4 vols. (Moscow 1888–96), 4:389. Although he was then still suspended from editing *Day*, Aksakov did not hesitate to criticize the government. Golovnin had in the meantime decided to grant Aksakov full control of the daily in January 1863, and wrote the emperor that he did not want to risk Aksakov's closing a publication that was useful to the government (Gerasimova, *Iz istorii russkoi pechati*, 174).

61 Binshtok, 'Materialy,' 594; Valuev, *Dnevnik*, 1:198

62 Valuev, *Dnevnik*, 1:199. Valuev notes this fact on 30 December (S.M. Seredonin, *K stoletiiu komiteta ministrov, 1802–1902: Istoricheskii obzor deiatelnosti komiteta ministrov*, 5 vols. (St Petersburg 1902), 3, pt. 2, 202). Golovnin's hopes for future relations between his ministry and writers appear in 'Ob otnosheniakh Min. Nar. Prosveshcheniia k literature,' GPB 208/100, sheets 4–9.

63 A.V. Golovnin, 'Zapiska,' 3, TSGIA, 851/1/5, sheet 377

64 Golovnin to Tsee, after 20 December 1862, GPB, 833/395, sheets 69–71

65 Rudakov, 'Poslednie dni,' 528; Shcheglov to Tsee, January 1863, *LN* 63 (1956), 689; Nikitenko, *Dnevnik*, 2:335–6

CHAPTER 9

1 V.E. Evgenev [Maksimov], comp., 'I.A. Goncharov o *Moskovskikh Vedomostiakh* Katkova,' *RS* 169 (1917): 40

2 V.E. Evgenev-Maksimov, 'Evoliutsiia obshchestvennykh vzgliadov Goncharova v 60–e gody,' *Zvezda* 5 (1925), 190–1, 192. Chernyshevsky wrote the novel between 14 December 1862 and 4 April 1863; publication had therefore begun before he finished the novel. Questions remain about why the censors approved *What Is To Be Done?* (following its publication in 1863, the government banned it until 1905). Because the novel appeared in three parts, the censors could have interrupted its publication midway. The account by O.A. Przhetslavsky of the Council for Publishing Affairs has wide acceptance (except for his mistaken assertion that Chernyshevsky published part one before entering prison). According to Przhetslavsky, Prince A.F. Golitsyn, who headed the investigating commission in the Chernyshevsky case, found nothing politically damaging in the novel and gave his approval. 'The censor [V.N. Beketov], having examined *Contemporary* after approval of the manuscript by Prince Golitsyn, was unable to stop its printing' (O.A. Przhetslavsky, 'Vospominaniia ... tsenzura, 1830–1865,' *RS* 14 (1875): 154). A recent Soviet scholar thinks Minister Golovnin had something to do with the publication of the novel to ease the guilt he felt for his part in the government's handling of Chernyshevsky (Ia.A. Iaroslavtsev, 'A.V. Golovnin i N.G. Chernyshevsky,' *Chernyshevsky i ego epokha. Revoliutsionnaia situatsiia v Rossii v 1859–1861 gg.* [Moscow 1959], 133).

3 'I.A. Goncharov o *Moskovskikh Vedomostiakh* Katkova,' 36–8

4 S. Nevedensky [I.S. Aksakov], *Katkov i ego vremia* (St Petersburg 1888), 233; Golovnin admits the pamphlet was a mistake but says he felt obliged to defend the Grand Duke, his benefactor for ten years. The mistake lay in offending the 'spirit of nationalism,' with which, said Golovnin, he did not sympathize (A.V. Golovnin, Zapiska, 3, TSGIA, sheets 478–9).

5 'I.A. Goncharov o *Moskovskikh Vedomostiakh* Katkova,' 31. In 1863 Golovnin had tried to be 'useful' to Katkov by offering to arrange a reduction in the publisher's mailing fees. Katkov refused. The minister then told Katkov that, if he would open a 'pedagogical section' in his newspaper, the ministry would buy 2,500 subscriptions for educational institutions (Nevedensky, 224–6) Golovnin to Katkov, 7 June 1863, GBL, 19 (Katkov fond), 45

6 A.V. Nikitenko, *Dnevnik*, ed. I.Ia. Aizenshtok, 3 vols. (Moscow 1955), 2:463–4, 467–8; [V.P. Butkov] to Golovnin, 11 September 1864, GPB, 208/225, sheets 1–2

7 'I.A. Goncharov o *Moskovskikh Vedomostiakh* Katkova,' 31; Nikitenko, *Dnevnik*, 2:640

8 'I.A. Goncharov o *Moskovskikh Vedomostiakh* Katkova,' 32; Nikitenko, *Dnevnik*, 2:641

9 Nikitenko, *Dnevnik*, 2:492; 'I.A. Goncharov o *Moskovskikh Vedomostiakh* Katkova,' 36

10 Ministerstvo Vnutrennikh Del, *Zhurnaly ... komissii dlia rasmotreniia proekta ustava o knigopechatanii*, 19 February 1863 (St Petersburg 1863), 9; Ministerstvo Vnutrennikh Del, *Proekt ustava o knigopechatanii* (St Petersburg 1863), sec. 1, para. 87–9

11 *Proekt ustava o knigopechatanii*, sec. 4, pt. 1, para. 1–2

12 V. Binshtok, comp., 'Materialy po istorii russkoi tsenzury,' *RS* 89 (1897): 585

13 Ibid., 90 (1897): 184, 197

14 [D.M. Zamiatnin], 'Otzyv ministra iustitsii ot 13 marta 1864 ...,' *Materialy sobrannye osoboiu komissieiu vysochaishe uchrezhdennoi 2 noiabria 1869 g. dlia peresmotra deistvuiushchikh postanovlenii o tsenzure i pechati*, 5 vols. (St Petersburg 1870), 1:113–14

15 [V.N. Panin], 'Otzyv grafa Panina, ot 19 sentiabria 1864,' *Materialy*, 1:117–27

16 Ministerstvo Vnutrennikh Del, 'Predstavlenie min. vnu. del gosudarstvennomu sovetu ot 17 noiabria 1864,' *Proekt ustava o knigopechatanii* (St Petersburg 1863), 5–38 (supplement). It is unclear why Valuev's presentation, dated in 1864, appears in a printed work with a publication date of 1863.

17 'Po proektu shtata ustanovlenii po delam knigopechataniia,' *Materialy*, 1:565–72; 'Proekt polozheniia o shtempelnom sbore s povremennykh izdanii i broshiur,' 26 May 1864–2 November 1866, TSGIA, 1405/62/4207b, sheets 477–8

18 [D.N. Zamiatnin], 'Spisok s otnosheniia min. ius. k gosudarstvennomu sekretariu, ot 14 ianvaria 1865 ...,' *Materialy*, 1:355

19 Ibid., 357, 359

20 P.A. Valuev, *Dnevnik*, ed. P.A. Zaionchkovsky, 2 vols. (Moscow 1961),2:17

21 A.V. Nikitenko, *Dnevnik*, 3 vols. (Moscow 1955), 2:496

22 [D.N. Miliutin], 'Zamechaniia chlenov obshchego sobraniia Gos. Soveta na proekty ... po delam pechati, Voennogo ministra,' *Materialy*, 1:478–83

23 'Zhurnal departamenta zakonov Gos. Soveta 16, 20, 21 i 23 ianvaria 1865 goda ... po proektu ustava o knigopechatanii,' *Materialy*, 1:390

24 [V.N. Panin], 'Zamechaniia II otdeleniia ... po delam pechati,' *Materialy*, 1:369. This undated memorandum was very likely submitted in January 1865.

25 Valuev, *Dnevnik*, 2:17

26 'Zhurnal soedinennykh departamentov gos. ekonomii i zakonov Gosu-darstvennogo Soveta, 27 ianvaria i 15 fevralia 1865 ...,' *Materialy*, 1:580–7; 'Proekt polozheniia o shtempelnom sbore,' sheets 477–8. Valuev had in mind a forty-six copeck tax on each copy sold over the counter. He argued that the tax would be borne by readers, pose no hardship for pub-lications, and would pay for hiring more censors. Reutern told him that taxation was not a censorship device. Tolstoy refused the extra work and opposed the 'obvious consequences': a cutback in subscribers, publica-tions, and educational benefits (Tolstoy to Valuev, 9 March 1865, GBL, 86/10 [Stoianovsky *fond*], sheet 3).

27 'Zhurnal departamenta zakonov Gos. Soveta, 10 i 13 marta, 1865 g. Po proektam zakonopolozhenii o pechati,' *Materialy*, 1:512–27

28 'Zhurnal departamenta zakonov Gos. Soveta 10 i 13 marta,' 515, 516

29 Valuev, *Dnevnik*, 2:29

30 'Vysochaishe utverzhdennoe, 11 aprelia 1865 g. mnenie ...,' *Materialy*, 1:586–7. Also see excerpts from State Council journal of 24 March (1:545–8). Valuev to Troinitsky, 24 March 1865, *RS* 99 (1899): 697

31 Dmitry Pisarev, 'Ocherki iz istorii pechati vo Frantsii,' *Sochineniia*, 6 vols. (St Petersburg 1909–13), 2: 427–502. N.G. Chernyshevsky, 'Frantsuzskie zakony po delam knigopechataniia,' *PSS*, ed. V.I. Kirpotin et al., 16 vols. (Moscow 1939–50), 10:136–8. (The article appeared in March 1862. Pavel S. Usov, the editor of *Son of the Fatherland*, said the ministers of the inte-rior and of public education saw the article as putting 'in an unfavourable light' the purposes of the government in preparing a new press statute [Chernyshevsky, *PSS*, 10:1021]. Chernyshevsky published several other articles on the censorship issue.) The Dostoevskys: 'Zakony pechati vo Frantsii,' and 'Zakony o pechati,' *Vremia* (May, June, 1862), 159–82, 284–304. I.S. Aksakov, 'Literatura dolzhna podlezhat zakonu, a ne administra-tivnomu proizvolu,' *Den* (22 December 1862), *Sochineniia*, 4 vols. (Moscow 1888–96), 4:394. V. Skariatin, 'Ob izmenenii tsenzurnogo ustava,' *OZ* 141, no. 4 (1862): 205–16. Katkov: 'Po povodu peremen predstoiashchikh nash-emu zakonodatelstvu o knizhnoi pechati,' *Moskovskie Vedomosti* (25 and 26 April 1862), 721

32 Chernyshevsky, 'Frantsuzskie zakony,' 138–9; 'Zakony o pechati,' 295; 'Po povodu peremen,' 721; Pisarev, 'Ocherki iz istorii,' 502; Aksakov *Den* (12 May 1862), *Sochineniia*, 4:361–6; D. Puzanov, 'Po predmetu svobody mysli i slova,' *Biblioteka dlia Chteniia* 171 (1862): 17; Skariatin, 'Ob izmenenii,' 213; A. Gieroglifov, 'Ob otnosheniiakh pravitelstva k literature ...,' *Russkii Mir* 20 (26 May 1862), 411–14

33 Aksakov, *Den* (12 May 1862), *Sochineniia*, 4:366; 'Zakony o pechati,' 302–3; Skariatin, 'Ob izmenenii,' 206; 'Po povodu peremen,' 720; E. Zarin, 'Pechatnye lgoty po proektu ustava o knigopechatanii,' *Biblioteka dlia Chteniia* 175 (1863): 82; S.Ch. Nelishchev, 'O preobrazovanii tsenzurnogo upravleniia,' *Biblioteka dlia Chteniia* 170 (1862): 95

34 D.F. Shcheglov, 'Vremennye pravila po delam knigopechataniia,' *Biblioteka dlia Chteniia* 171 (1862): 227; Zarin, 'Pechatnye lgoty,' 71–2, 91; N. [N.G. Chernyshevsky], 'Po delu preobrazovanii tsenzury,' *Sovremennik* 92 (1862): 59–65

35 *PSZ*, ser. 2, 40, no. 41990 (6 April 1865), 397–406; Ibid., no. 41988 (15 April 1865), 396. These decrees appear in the Appendix to this study.

36 I.S. Aksakov, 'O novykh pravilakh tsenzury po ukazu ...,' *Den* (24 April 1865), *Sochineniia*, 4:424

CHAPTER 10

1 M.K. Lemke, *Epokha tsenzurnykh reform, 1859–1865 gg.* (St Petersburg 1904), 406–9; 'Vysochaishee povelenie ... ministerstvom iustitsii, 29 avgusta 1865 g. za no. 1893,' *Materialy sobrannye osoboiu komissieiu vysochaishe uchrezhdennoi 2 noiabria 1869 g. dlia peresmotra deistvuiushchikh postanovlenii o tsenzure i pechati*, 5 vols. (St Petersburg 1870), 1:612

2 A.V. Nikitenko, *Dnevnik*, ed. I.Ia. Aizenshtok, 3 vols. (Moscow 1955), 2:514–15; V. Rozenberg, 'V mire sluchainosti,' Rozenberg and V. Iakushkin, *Russkaia pechat i tsenzura v proshlom i nastoiashchem* (Moscow 1905), 120

3 Of the old council, Goncharov and N.V. Varadinov, but not Nikitenko and Przhetslavsky, received appointments to the new Council of the Chief Administration. Both bodies had six members (P.A. Valuev, *Dnevnik*, ed. P.A. Zaionchkovsky, 2 vols. [Moscow 1961], 2:454); 'Pervoe predosterezhenie "S.-Peterburgskim Vedomostiam",' *Materialy*, 2:117

4 'Pervoe ... "Sovremenniku,"' *Materialy*, 2:118–19

5 K. Voensky, ed., 'Goncharov – tsenzor: Neizdannye materialy dlia ego biografii,' *RV* 10 (1906), 590–1; V.E. Evgenev-Maksimov, *I.A. Goncharov: Zhizn, lichnost, tvorchestvo* (Moscow 1925), 132; 'Vtoroe predosterezhenie zhurnalu "Sovremennik,"' *Materialy*, 2:120–2

6 'Pervoe ... gazete "Golos,"' *Materialy*, 2:119–20

7 I.A. Goncharov, 'Po dokladu,' in Voensky, 'Goncharov – tsenzor,' 579–83

8 'Vtoroe predosterezhenie zhurnalu "Russkoe Slovo,"' *Materialy*, 2:123; V.E. Evgenev [Maksimov], 'N.A. Goncharov kak chlen soveta glavnogo upravleniia po delam pechati,' *GM* 11 (1916), 146

9 *PSZ*, ser. 2, 45, no. 41990 (6 April 1865), 397; 'Vysochaishee povelenie ... ministerstvom iustitsii, 29 avgusta 1865 g. za no. 1893,' *Materialy*, 1:612–14

10 'Po otnosheniiu min. vnu. del po proektu knigopechataniia,' TSGIA, 1405/62/4207a, sheets 174–93

11 'O knige "Kriticheskie etiudy P.A. Bibikova, 1859–1865,"' *Materialy*, 3, pt. 1:5–12

12 Ibid., 5

13 *Svod zamechanii na proekt ustava sudoproizvodstva grazhdanskogo* ([St Petersburg] 1864), 299; *Sudebnye ustavy 20 noiabria 1864 goda ...* (St Petersburg 1870), 17, 25, 150

14 Generally, the accused and his attorney took no part in the preliminary investigation that, under Russian law, preceded the actual court trial in criminal cases; but the presiding magistrate could permit them to attend the hearing of witnesses (*Sudebnye ustavy*, 23).

15 'O knige "Kriticheskie etiudy,"' 9

16 'O napechatannoi v no. 333 gazety "Golos" za 1865 god stati g. Ostrikova ...,' *Materialy*, 3, pt. 1:12–14

17 Nikitenko, *Dnevnik*, 3:14

18 'O napechatannoi,' 64

19 P.A. Valuev, 'O politicheskikh nastroeniiakh razlichnykh grup russkogo obshchestva i sredstvakh ukrepleniia pravitelstvennoi vlasti, 26 aprel 1866,' in V.V. Garmiza, ed., 'Predlozheniia i proekty,' *Istoricheskii Arkhiv*, no. 1 (1958), 149–52

20 Valuev, *Dnevnik*, 2:121. From Valuev's description, Shuvalov's 'Zapiska' is surely the one published by P. Gurevich ('Nezabvennye mysli nezabvennykh liudei,' *Byloe* 1–4 [1907]: 236–46; see especially p. 238).

21 Nikitenko, *Dnevnik*, 3: 29, 32; Valuev, *Dnevnik*, 2:112; 'Zhurnal Soveta,' 23 March 1866, *Materialy*, 2:126–7

22 'Zhurnal Soveta,' 23 March 1866, 128–9

23 B. Naumov, comp., 'Russkaia literatura 60-kh godov v otsenke ministerstva vnutrennikh del P.A. Valueva,' *LN* 25–6 (1936), 681

24 Quoted in S.S. Tatishchev, *Imperator Aleksandr II ego zhizn i tsarstvovanie*, 2 vols. (St Petersburg 1903), 2:8–10.

25 Valuev, *Dnevnik*, 2:127

26 'Vysochaishee povelenie 28 maia 1866 g., o dopolnenii zakonopolozhenii o pechati 6 aprelia 1865 g.,' *Materialy*, 1:646–7. The May 28 order included directives to Valuev to enforce regulations that periodicals publish each warning received; to oversee more closely the book trade, printing plants, and three satirical publications (*Spark, Alarm Clock* [*Budilnik*], and *Diver-*

sion [*Razvlechenie*]); and, with the minister of public education, to halt the publication of dangerous text books. These refinements were all well within the spirit of the April 6 statute.

27 B.B. Glinsky, 'Aleksandr Sergeevich Suvorin: Biograficheskii ocherk,' *IV* 129 (1912): 23

28 Suvorin to Valuev, 12 April 1866, *Shestidesiatye gody: Materialy po istorii literatury i obshchestvennomu dvizheniiu*, ed. N.K. Piksanov (Moscow 1940), 406–7

29 'Delo po knige Suvorina "Vsiakie: Ocherki sovremennoi zhizni A. Bobrovskogo,"' *Materialy*, 3, pt. 1:70

30 Ibid., 66; Glinsky, 'Suvorin,' 24–5

31 K.K. Arsenev, 'Russkie zakony o pechati,' *VE* 16, pt. 1 (1869): 801

32 'Delo po knige Suvorina,' 74–5

33 Ibid., 81

34 K.K. Arsenev, 'Iz vospominanii,' *GM*, no. 2 (1915), 121

35 'Delo o ... Iulie Zhukovskom i ... Aleksandre Pypine, obviniaemykh v oskorblenii chesti i dostoinstva vsego dvorianskogo zemlevladelcheskogo sosloviia v state "vopros molodogo pokoleniia ...,"' *Materialy*, 3, pt. 1:130–1

36 Arsenev, 'Iz vospominanii,' 123; 'Delo o Zhukovskom,' 148

37 'Delo o Zhukovskom,' 160–1

38 Arsenev, 'Iz vospominanii,' 123–5. Arsenev remarked that the government could far better have based its case on article 1036. 'Delo o Zhukovskom,' 168, 171

39 'Delo o Zhukovskom,' 186

40 Arsenev, 'Iz vospominanii,' 125; Nikitenko, *Dnevnik*, 3:49–50

41 'Zapiska ... ministrom iustitsii ..., 28 oktiabria 1866 ...,' *Materialy*, 1:625–34

42 Arsenev later observed, with respect to the acquittal of Zhukovsky by the circuit court and the reversal of the decision upon the prosecutor's appeal in the Court of Appeals: 'In theory, of course, it was clear to all that the right of acquittal was available to the court in the same measure as the right of conviction; but, in practice, this did not exclude the likelihood of the court's having an obligation to adapt itself – especially in trials of a political character – to the interests and "views" of the government. The Court of Appeals reversed the decision of the circuit court; from this came an increased faith in it and a decline in faith in the other' (Arsenev, 'Iz vospominanii,' 125). 'Zapiska ministrom iustitsii,' 631

43 'Proekt iziatii iz obshchego poriadka ugolovnogo sudoproizvodstva,' 4 July 1866, *Materialy*, 1:598–609

44 'Otzyv ... ot 2 oktiabria 1866 goda,' *Materialy*, 1:615–24

45 'Vysochaishe utverzhdennoe, 12 dekabria 1866 g., ... po delam pechati,'
   Materialy, 1:640–2
46 'Zhurnal ... 29 oktiabria 1866 g.' *Materialy*, 1:636
47 The court confirmed the order to destroy the book and based that reduction in penalty on the minimal degree of the crime: an 'attempt' to commit a criminal act ('Delo po knige Suvorina,' 122–5).

CHAPTER 11

1 B. Chicherin, *Kurs gosudarstvennoi nauki*, 2 vols. (Moscow 1894), 1:220
2 'Ob oskorblenii chesti chastnykh lits pechatnym obrazom v kakikh-libo
   sochineniiakh: Delo Ministerstva Iustitsii,' 23 Jan. 1860–8 Jan. 1861, TSGIA,
   1405/58/2103, sheets 12, 31; *PSZ*, ser. 2, 25, no. 36456 (26 Dec. 1860), 516
3 L.S. Belogrits-Kotliarevsky, *Uchebnik russkogo ugolovnogo prava* (Kiev 1903),
   389. For example, a married Moscow merchant responded to an item in
   Voice about his frequenting taverns, squandering his money, and consort-
   ing with unseemly women by charging the editor with defamation. Publisher and editor Kraevsky was fined fifty rubles under article 1039 ('Delo
   ob oskorblenii v gazete "Golos," moskovskogo kuptsa Khludova,' *Materialy sobrannye osoboiu Komissieiu vysochaishe uchrezhdennoi 2 noiabria 1869
   g. dlia peresmotra deistvuiushchikh postanovlenii o tsenzure i pechati*, 5 vols.
   (St Petersburg 1870), 3, pt. 2: 791–2; *PSZ*, ser. 2, 40, no. 41990 (6 April
   1865), 400
4 *PSZ*, ser. 2, 40, no. 41990 (6 April 1865), 405; V. Goltsev, 'Sud i pechat
   (Zakon o pechati v pervuiu chetvert sushchestvovaniia sudebnykh ustavov 1864),' *Iuridicheskii Vestnik* 9 (1891): 321
5 Andres Davila, *Libel Law and the Press* (Zurich: International Press Institute 1971), 28
6 V. Spasovich, *Za mnogo let, 1857–1861* (St Petersburg 1872), 60. To disprove published allegations that he was in the pay of the government and
   the Jews, an editor in 1882 chose to sue a rival editor for libel rather than
   defamation (V. Spasovich, *Sochineniia*, 10 vols. [St. Petersburg 1894,
   1889–1902], 6:342–78).
7 'Po delu o redaktore zhurnala "Otechestvennye Zapiski" ... v narushenii
   zakonov o pechati,' *Materialy*, 3, pt. 2:1232–44
8 Peter F. Carter-Ruck, *Libel and Slander* (London: Faber and Faber [1972]), 44
9 S.A. Andreevsky, *Zashchititelnye rechi* (St Petersburg 1909), 384–5
10 Andreevsky, *Zashchititelnye rechi*, 447
11 B. Kozmin, 'N.V. Sokolov: Ego zhizn i literaturnaia deiatelnost,' *Literatura
   i istoriia: Sbornik statei* (Moscow 1969), 375

12 'O knige N. Sokolova "Otshchepentsy,"' *Materialy* 3, pt. 1:240. The indictment cited articles 181, 245, 251, 274, 1001, 1024, 1035, 1037, and 1041. The closed trial may have encouraged Tiesenhausen to make such sweeping charges.

13 Ibid., 239–40

14 'O knige Sokolova,' 258. Sokolov completed his sentence on 1 November 1868, but was immediately exiled to Archangel by administrative order through an arrangement by the procurator of the Court of Appeals, the minister of the interior, and the head of the Third Section. He escaped abroad in October 1872 'with the help of revolutionary circles known as the Chaikovtsy.' Kozmin further explains that the reason for the administrative exile was the authorities' belief that Sokolov was too dangerous to release (Kozmin, 'N.V. Sokolov,' 402–3). The Chaikovtsy issued a 'second' edition of Sokolov's book in Zurich in 1872 (L.M. Dobrovolsky, *Zapreshchennaia kniga v Rossii, 1825–1904* [Moscow 1962], 56).

15 'O knige Vundta "Dusha cheloveka i zhivotnykh,' tom II, izdannoi vremennym kuptsom P. Gaideburovym,' *Materialy*, 3, pt. 1:354–5

16 Ibid., 371

17 Ibid., 390

18 K.K. Arsenev, *Zakonodatelstvo o pechati* (St Petersburg 1903), 65–6

19 'Po delu o ... Areseneve i ... Zvenigorodskom, obviniaemykh v narushenii postanovlenii o pechati,' *Materialy*, 3, pt. 2: 806–7

20 'Po delu o Areseneve,' 825. Lokhvitsky was a specialist on the subject of defamation. In the early 1860s he conducted a press debate with V.D. Spasovich on the subject.

21 'Po delu o Areseneve,' 866

22 'O napechatannoi v no. 25 gazety "Narodnyi Golos" state,' *Materialy*, 3, pt. 1:400

23 'O napechatannoi v no. 25 gazety "Narodnyi Golos" state,' 431–2. Article 1028 was a catch-all provision which established a fifty-ruble fine for each issue or article of a paper found to include commentary outside the publication's prescribed program.

24 Ibid., 401

25 Ibid., 437–8

26 N. Shelgunov, 'Biograficheskii ocherk,' in G.E. Blagosvetlov, *Sochineniia* (St Petersburg 1882), x, xii, xiv

27 A.G. Dementev et al., eds., *Russkaia periodicheskaia pechat (1702–1894): Spravochnik,* (Moscow 1959), 473

28 V. Evgenev [Maksimov], 'Nekrasov i Eliseev v dele vossozdanii "Otechestvennykh Zapisok" Kraevskogo (Po neizdannym vospominaniiam G. Zakh.

i Ek. Pavl. Eliseevykh,' *GM* 2 (1916), 12, 27–8. The journal received its
first warning in 1872, a second in 1879, and a third in 1884, when it was
closed. Nekrasov died in 1877.

29 A.M. Skabichevsky, *Literaturnye vospominaniia* (Moscow 1928), 255, 260,
333. The banker and publisher N. Tiblen about the same time opened a
new journal and hired several writers formerly with *Contemporary*. His
monthly, *Contemporary Review* (*Sovremennoe Obozrenie*), produced six
issues in 1868.

30 K.K. Arsenev, 'Russkie zakony o pechati,' *VE* (April 1869), 806. Aksakov,
on 12 January 1866, married Anna Tiutchev, daughter of the poet F.I.
Tiutchev. Anna was lady-in-waiting to the Empress Maria and governess
to the imperial couple's daughter, the Grand Duchess Maria. Anna had to
secure the empress's permission in order to marry. This link to the throne
seems not to have helped Aksakov solve later difficulties with the censorship. See editorial notes in *Ivan Sergeevich Aksakov v ego pismakh*, 4 vols.
(St Petersburg 1896), 4:179.

31 'Raport min. vnu. del. v pravitelstvuiushchii senat, ot 18 dekabria 1868 ...
o prekrashchenii izdaniia gazety "Moskva,"' *Materialy*, 2:11

32 'Mneniia senatorov 1-go departamenta prav. senata po delu o prekrashchenii izdaniia gazety "Moskva,"' *Materialy*, 2: 68, 71

33 'Predlozhenie min. Iustitsii ...,' *Materialy*, 2:93

34 'Zhurnal obshchego sobraniia Gosudarstvennogo Soveta, ot 7 aprelia 1869
goda ...,' *Materialy*, 2:100–3; 'Zhurnal soedinennykh departamentov ...,'
Materialy, 2:98

35 Arsenev, 'Russkie zakony o pechati,' 810

CHAPTER 12

1 *PSZ*, ser. 2, 41, sec. 2, no. 43747 (17 Oct. 1866), 146–7; *PSZ*, ser. 2, 42, sec.
2, no. 44691 (13 June 1867), 898–9; *PSZ*, ser. 2, 43, sec. 1, no. 45973 (14
June 1868), 805

2 M.N. Kufaev, *Istoriia russkoi knigi XIX veke* (Leningrad 1927), 182; *Piat-
nadtsatiletie gazety 'Golos'* (St Petersburg 1878), lii

3 N. Lange, 'O polozhenii na prestupleniia po delam pechati,' *Zhurnal Ministerstva Iustitsii* (February 1868), 185–6

4 Such proponents of tougher measures against radicalism as the head of the
Third Section, Shuvalov, and the heir to the throne, Alexander, appear to
have influenced the emperor to replace Valuev with A.E. Timashev. Part of
the campaign to discredit Valuev were accusations in the press that he
had failed to prepare adequately against famine in two Russian provinces.

See the biographical outline on Valuev by P.A. Zaionchkovsky in Valuev's *Dnevnik*, 2 vols. (Moscow 1961), 1:43–4.

5 P.A. Valuev, 'Vsepoddanneishiye doklady Aleksandru II po delam pechati,' 8 February 1868, PD 559/21, sheet 57

6 The articles were 'The Russian Don Quixote' and 'Meager Russian Thought' ('Delo po izdannoi F. Pavlenkovym knige "Sochineniia D.I. Pisareva; chast vtoraia St. Petersburg, 1866,"' *Materialy sobrannye osoboiu komissieiu vysochaishe uchrezhdennoi 2 noiabria 1869 g. dlia peresmotra deistvuiushchikh postanovlenii o tsenzure i pechati*, 5 vols. [St Petersburg 1870], 3, pt. 1:259–334).

7 'Delo po izdannoi F. Pavlenkovym,' 270

8 Ibid., 304

9 'Delo po izdannoi F. Pavlenkovym,' 308, 319, 323

10 Ibid., 313

11 Ibid., 333

12 K.K. Arsenev, 'Iz vospominanii,' *GM* 2 (1915), 122; 'Delo po izdannoi F. Pavlenkovym,' 333

13 *Materialy*, 4:349

14 'Delo o ... Shchapove, obviniaemom v narushenii postanovlenii o pechati,' *Materialy*, 3, pt. 1:439–92

15 Ibid., 443

16 Ibid., 435, 444. Also see V. Spasovich, *Sochineniia*, 10 vols. (St Petersburg 1894, 1889–1902), 5:101–21

17 Ibid., 473

18 K.K. Arsenev, 'Novyi zakon o pechati vo Frantsii,' *VE* (April 1868), 905

19 A.V. Nikitenko, *Dnevnik*, ed. I.Ia. Aizenshtok, 3 vols. (Moscow 1955), 3:137–8

20 Ibid., 3:160

21 [K.K. Arsenev], 'Komissiia dlia peresmotra postanovlenii o pechati,' *VE* (December 1869), 905–6. Gradovsky's articles on censorship are collected in Prof. A. Gradovsky, *O svobode russkoi pechati; posmertnoe izdanie* (St Petersburg, n.d.).

22 I.V. Orzhekhovsky, *Administratsiia i pechat mezhdu dvumia revoliutsionnymi situatsiiami (1866–1878 gg.)* (Gorky 1973), 56–9, 65–6

23 *Materialy*, 3, pt. 2:1275

24 'Delo ... osoboi komissii dlia peresmotra deistvuiushchikh postanovlenii o tsenzure i pechati,' 12 June 1870, TSGIA, 776/28/1, sheets 203–17

25 'Delo o ... Shchapove,' 492

26 *Birzhevye Vedomosti* (1870), nos. 267, 271. The complaints about press reporting of open trials were wide-ranging. One member of the gentry, for example, objected to publishing an attorney's defense of an unhappy

husband's attempt to kill himself and his mistress so that they would be 'joined in heaven' ('Delo ... osoboi komissii,' sheet 27).

27 O.V. Aptekman, *Vasily Vasilevich Bervi-Flerovsky po materialam III otdeleniia i D.G.P.* (Leningrad 1925), 58–9

28 Ibid., 62–3

29 'Delo ... osoboi komissii,' sheets 351–404

30 L.M. Dobrovolsky, *Zapreshchennaia kniga v Rossii, 1825–1904* (Moscow 1962), 80

31 'O dopolnenii i izmenenii nekotorykh iz deistvuiushchikh postanovlenii po delam pechati,' Gosudarstvennyi Sovet v Departamente Zakonov, 5 February 1872, TSGIA, 1149/10 sheets 6–9; Nikitenko, *Dnevnik*, 3:227–8

32 Dobrovolsky, *Zapreshchennaia kniga*, 88, 93

33 *PSZ*, ser. 2, 47, sec. 1, no. 50958 (7 June 1872), 815–17

34 Nikitenko, *Dnevnik*, 3:454; K.K. Arsenev, *Zakonodatelstvo o pechati* (St Petersburg 1903), 90–1

35 These figures are based on the information in Dobrovolsky, *Zapreshchennaia kniga*. Lemke, who first compiled a list of the banned books and periodicals under this ukaz, recorded 180 domestic titles (in Russian) banned by the Committee of Ministers between 1872 and 1904, only 7 of which were individual numbers of periodical publications. Dobrovolsky, who had access to more complete archives, added to and corrected Lemke's list; and he cites 187 banned titles. Lemke's list is in M. Lemke, 'Rasporiazhenie komiteta ministrov ob unichtozhenii proizvedenii pechati za 1872–1904,' *Vestnik Prava* (April 1905), 124–34.

36 Kufaev, *Istoriia russkoi knigi*, 173, 309

37 I.E. Barenbaum, E.L. Nemirovsky, and A.G. Shitsgal, 'Knigopechatanie i knigoizdatelstvo v Peterburge pervoi poloviny XIX veka,' *Russkoe knigopechatanie do 1917 goda, 1564–1917*, 2 vols. (Moscow 1974), 2:267–82

38 Information on the state of the printing industry in the second half of the nineteenth century is drawn from two articles in *Russkoe knigopechatanie*: E.L. Nemirovsky, B.P. Orlov, and A.G. Shitsgal, 'Knigopechatanie i poligraficheskaia promyshlennost vtoroi poloviny XIX v.,' 364–5, and I.E. Barenbaum, 'Knigoizdatelstvo v Peterburge, 1861–1895,' 376–94.

39 A.G. Rashin, 'Gramotnost i narodnoe obrazovanie v Rossii v XIX i nachale XX v.,' *Istoricheskie Zapiski* 37 (1951): 41, 42, 48

40 These works and others are listed in Dobrovolsky, *Zapreshchennaia kniga*, along with censors' critiques.

41 G.K. Gradovsky, 'Istoriia "Russkogo Obozreniia",' *Itogi 1862–1907* (Kiev 1908), 267. Dementev's list of new periodicals in A.G. Dementev et al., eds., *Russkaia periodicheskaia pechat (1702–1894): Spravochnik* (Moscow 1959) for the first half of the seventies shows these years to have been

bleak. Most new publications were either provincial in location or non-political in character.

42 Orzhekhovsky, *Administratsiia i pechat*, 79, 80. (See Lisovsky's somewhat lower figures, table 7.)

43 *PSZ*, ser. 2, 48, no. 52395 (16 June 1873), 859–60; M. Lemke, 'V mire usmotreniia st. 140 i 156 ustava o tsenzure i pechati,' *Vestnik Prava* (July 1905), 97–106. Arsenev takes the position that this regulation had a certain justification, but successive ministers of the interior applied it to all manner of topics (Arsenev, *Zakonodatelstvo o pechati*, 91–3).

44 *PSZ*, ser. 2, 49, sec. 1, no. 53398 (19 April 1874), 667–8

45 *PSZ*, ser. 2, 50, sec. 1, no. 54353 (4 Feb. 1875), 114

46 Gradovsky, 'Istoriia "Russkogo Obozreniia,"' 272

47 Ibid., 295. The Russo-Turkish War was the first Russian war covered in the Russian press by unofficial Russian correspondents. Gradovsky first reported from Asia Minor in 1877 and then from the Danubian region. He was at Plevna and Adrianople during the Russian campaign and was the only Russian correspondent at San Stefano for the signing of the peace treaty. The government probably permitted this unprecedented coverage because it expected victory. The coverage of the war excited avid interest, as the figures on street sales of St Petersburg papers bear out: 5,950 in 1867; 9,227 in 1876; 12,716 in 1877; and 23,980 in 1880 (B.I. Esin, 'Materialy k istorii gazetnogo dela v Rossii,' *Vestnik Moskovskogo universiteta: zhurnalistika* 4 [1967], 85–6).

48 Gradovsky, *Itogi*, 430–6

49 P.A. Zaionchkovsky, *Krizis samoderzhaviia na rubezhe 1870–1880 godov* (Moscow 1964), 61–6

50 Zaionchkovsky, *Krizis*, 75

51 N.P. Emelianov, 'Iz istorii russkikh ofitsiozov, 1879–1880 gg.,' *Voprosy zhurnalistiki* 2 (1960): 73–80

52 Loris-Melikov's words were summarized by G.E. Eliseev, 'Sovremennoe obozrenie,' *OZ* 252 (1880): 140–2.

53 'Gr. Loris-Melikov i Imp. Aleksandr II o polozhenii Rossii v sentiabre 1880 g.,' *Byloe* 4 (26) (1917), 33–7

54 [M.M. Stasiulevich], *M.M. Stasiulevich i ego sovremenniki* (St Petersburg 1911), 546–7; Zaionchkovsky, *Krizis*, 237

55 Zaionchkovsky, *Krizis*, 267–8

56 Hans Heilbronner, 'Alexander III and the Reform Plan of Loris-Melikov,' *Journal of Modern History* 33 (1961): 384–97

57 *PSZ*, ser. 3, 2, no. 1072 (27 Aug. 1882), 390–1. The members of the Supreme Commission were the ministers of public education, of interior, and of justice and the procurator of the Holy Synod.

58 P.A. Zaionchkovsky, *Rossiiskoe samoderzhavie v kontse XIX stoletiia* (Moscow 1970), 281; V. Rozenberg, 'V mire sluchainosti,' Rozenberg and V. Iakushkin, *Russkaia pechat i tsenzura v proshlom i nastoiashchem* (Moscow 1905), 141–2

59 E.M. Feoktistov, *Vospominaniia za kulisami politiki i literatury 1848–1896*, ed. Iu.G. Oksman (Leningrad 1929), 214. Viazemsky was the son of the famous poet and friend of Pushkin.

60 The source is Gen. A.A. Kireev, quoted in Zaionchkovsky, *Rossiiskoe samoderzhavie*, 79.

61 Makashin has published the unsigned and untitled memorandum under its archival title. See '[Zapiska o napravlenii periodicheskoi pressy v sviazi s obshchestvennym dvizheniem v Rossii],' *LN* 87 (1977), 446–60.

62 A.D. Eikengolts, *Khrestomatiia po istorii russkoi knigi, 1564–1917* (Moscow 1965), 215–17

63 B.I. Esin, 'Zakrytie zhurnala "Otechestvennye Zapiski" i sudba ego sotrudnikov posle 1884 g.,' *Iz istorii russkoi zhurnalistiki*, ed. A.V. Zapadov (Moscow 1964), 44–61

64 B.B. Glinsky, 'Period tverdoi vlasti (Istoricheskie ocherki),' *IV* 129 (1912): 227

65 Quoted in Zaionchkovsky, *Rossiiskoe samoderzhavie*, 276.

66 The full record of measures against the *Bulletin* is in *Russkie Vedomosti, 1863–1913 (Sbornik statei)* (Moscow 1913), 304–8. See also V. Rozenberg, *Iz istorii russkoi pechati: Organizatsiia obshchestvennogo mneniia Rossii i nezavisimaia bespartiinaia gazeta 'Russkie Vedomosti' (1863–1918)* (Prague 1924).

67 Pobedonostsev to Feoktistov, 14 October 1891, *LN* 22–4 (1935), 547

68 For this summary of the development of newspapers in the seventies and eighties, I have drawn from the following sources: *Entsiklopedicheskii slovar* (St Petersburg 1892), s.v. 'Gazeta'; P.S. Karasev, 'Obshchii obzor gazetnoi periodiki,' *Ocherki po istorii russkoi zhurnalistiki i kritiki: Vtoraia polovina XIX veka*, 2 vols. (Leningrad 1965), 2:449–61; and A.V. Zapadov, ed., *Istoriia russkoi zhurnalistiki XVIII–XIX vekov* (Moscow 1973), 486–95.

69 Quoted in Karasev, 'Obshchii obzor gazetnoi periodiki,' 2:450.

70 B.I. Esin, 'K istorii telegrafnykh agentsv v Rossii XIX veka,' *Vestnik Moskovskogo universiteta: filologiia, zhurnalistika* 1 (1960), 61–7

71 Kufaev, *Istoriia russkoi knigi*, 211, 318; B.P. Orlov, *Poligraficheskaia promyshlennost Moskvy: Ocherk razvitiia do 1917 goda* (Moscow 1953), table following p. 149

72 See A.S. Suvorin, *Dnevnik*, ed. M. Krichevsky (Moscow 1923); L.F. Panteleev, *Vospominaniia*, intro. S.A. Reiser ([Moscow] 1958); N.A. Rubakin, 'Iz istorii borby za prava knigi ... Florentii Fedorovich Pavlenkova,' *Kniga: Issledovaniia i materialy*, bk. 9 (Moscow 1964), 207–40.

73 For a survey of Russian publishing in the nineteenth century, see M.N. Rozanov, 'Kniga i liudi v XIX veke,' *Russkaia kniga deviatnadtsatogo veka*, ed. V.Ia. Adariukov and A.A. Sidorov, 2 vols. (Moscow 1924–5), 2:442–80. Sytin will be discussed below. M.M. Wolf (1825–83) was the son of a Warsaw doctor who, says Rozanov, even as a child dreamed of 'flooding the country with a huge mass of books which would cover his name with glory as a benefactor of mankind' (p. 464). Wolf worked in bookstores in Paris, Leipzig, Lvov, and Cracow and returned to Russia, where, in 1853, he opened his own store and began a publishing business. The Wolf firm turned out around 5,000 titles and specialized in children's and illustrated books.

74 N.V. Chekhov, 'Lubochnye knigi,' *Polveka dlia knigi, 1866–1916: Literaturno-khudozhestvennyi sbornik, posviashchennyi piatidesiatiletiiu izdatelskoi deiatelnosti I.D. Sytina* (Moscow 1914), 152

75 A. Gusev, 'Kalendar,' *Polveka dlia knigi*, 436

76 I.A. Golyshev, 'Golyshev – osnovatel i vladelets litografii v Slobode Mstera,' *RS* 49 (1886): 679–726

77 I.D. Sytin, *Zhizn dlia knigi* (Moscow 1960), 36–7

78 Sytin, *Zhizn dlia knigi*, 32, 44

79 Paul Birukoff, *The Life of Tolstoy* (London 1911), 103; A. Kalmykova, 'Russkie lubochnye kartiny v ikh prosvetitelnom znachenii dlia naroda ...,' *Polveka dlia knigi*, 168

80 Orlov, *Poligraficheskaia promyshlennost Moskvy*, 250

81 S. Varshavsky, 'Pravovoe polozhenie izdatelskogo dela v Rossii,' *Polveka dlia knigi*, 297–9

CHAPTER 13

1 Gl. Uspensky, 'Pisma o tsenzure,' *Golos Minuvshego iz Chuzhoi Storony* 14, no. 1 (1926): 134; Aleksandr R. Kugel, *Literaturnye vospominaniia, 1882–1896* (Petrograd 1923), 95; L.G. Manulova, 'Zemskii vopros v russkoi periodicheskoi pechati epokhi kontrreform,' *Vestnik Moskovskogo Universiteta*, ser. 9, *Istoriia*, no. 2 (Jan.–Feb. 1966), 57–68

2 G. Dzhanshiev, 'Ogranichenie glasnosti v sude,' *Iuridicheskii Vestnik* 1 (1887): 108–14, 502–08; V. Goltsev, 'Sud i pechat: Zakony o pechati v pervuiu chetvert sushchestvovaniia sudebnykh ustavov 1864 goda,' *Iuridicheskii Vestnik* 9 (1891): 317–25; Sergei Viktorsky, 'Glasnost v ugolovnykh sudakh sovremennoi Rossii,' *Iuridicheskii Vestnik* 10 (1892): 547–67

3 K.K. Arsenev, 'Soslovie zhurnalistov,' *Za chetvert veka, 1871–1914: Sbornik statei* (Petrograd 1915), 570–1; *Khodataistvo russkikh literatorov ob oblegchenii tsenzury* (London 1895). (Issued under the auspices of the Russian

Free Press Fund, this publication contains an introduction, the petition, and an explanatory note.)

4 The names of 113 signatories appear in *Samoderzhavie i pechat* (St Petersburg 1908).

5 *Khodataistvo*, 9; Gradovsky to Pobedonostsev, 29 June 1896, *Itogi*, 313–19; see ibid., 300–13, for the explanatory note accompanying the petition. Gradovsky helped organize the petition in company with Arsenev, Koni, and several others. He frequently promoted literary dinners, helped found the Writers' Mutual Assistance Fund, and served as fund president in the nineties. His literary and journalistic memoirs were published as 'Iz minuvshego: Vospominaniia i vpechateleniia literatora, 1865–1897,' *RS* 133 (1908): 77–86, 323–30, 148–57; 134: 293–302; 136: 57–74, 553–62; 137 (1909): 528–35.

6 'Khodataistvo soiuza vzaimopomoshchi pisatelei pri russkom literaturnom obshchestve ... 24 aprelia 1898,' *Materialy vysochaishe uchrezhdennogo osobogo soveshchaniia dlia sostavleniia novogo ustava o pechati* [St Petersburg 1905], 7. The report of the judicial commission is entitled 'Doklad o nuzhdakh russkoi pechati.'

7 *PSZ*, ser. 3, 21, sec. 1, no. 20234 (4 June 1901), 435

8 Fedor Elenev, a member of the Council of the Chief Administration of Press Affairs, also argued that the courts alone could not fight radical words, and his essay to that effect was published abroad by the Union of Social Democrats in *Materialy dlia kharakteristiki polozheniia russkoi pechati*, vol. 2 [Geneva 1898], to show the attitude of a Russian official they held partly at fault for the 'disgraceful conditions' in Russia.

9 A new regulation on 28 March 1897 was surely a response to the Marxists' acquiring journals and changing them. In it, the Committee of Ministers forbade the transfer of the title of a periodical from one publisher to another without the permission of the minister of the interior (*PSZ*, ser. 3, 17, sec. 1, no. 13902 [28 March 1897], 144. The Statute of 1865 required permission from the Chief Administration of Press Affairs. Beginning in 1905, the number of legal socialist periodicals in Russia increased greatly. A full listing appears in L. Polianskaia, ed., 'Arkhivnyi fond glavnogo upravleniia po delam pechati,' *LN* 22–4 (1935), 618, 623 [reprint, 1963].

10 D.N. Liubimov, 'Russkaia smuta nachala deviatisotykh godov, 1902–1906; Po vospominaniiam, lichnym zapiskam i dokumentam,' Columbia University Archives, 48–54. Liubimov had entered the service in 1887 in the Ministry of State Domains; in 1902 he became head of the chancellery of the Ministry of the Interior and, in 1906, governor of Vilna province.

11 A.F. Koni, 'Vladimir Danilovich Spasovich (Rech v godovom sobranii S. Pet. Iuridicheskogo obshchestva, 23 fev., 1903),' *Ocherki i vospominaniia (Publichnye chteniia, stati, i zametki)* (St Petersburg 1906), 776

12 'Vypiska iz protokola ... Imperatorskoi Akademii Nauk ot 24 fevralia 1903 goda,' *Materialy ... dlia sostavleniia novogo ustava o pechati*, 6

13 A.A. Kizevetter, *Na rubezhe dvukh stoletii: Vospominaniia (1881–1914)* (Prague 1929), 345–6. On 22 March 1903 a new edition of the criminal code introduced penalties for printed words which incited to criminal action or stirred discord among social classes. Article 129, which became the grounds for cases against many periodicals, is discussed in Sergei Ordinsky, 'Pechat i sud,' in V. Nabokov et al., *Svoboda pechati pri obnovlennom stroe* (St Petersburg 1912), 122–52.

14 *Moscow Bulletin*, which published the document in no. 220 in 1905 as 'K istorii russkoi tsenzury,' 4, noted, 'The present article is a reproduction of a memorandum prepared under the orders and direction of V.K. Plehve, given not long before 15 July 1904.' The Plehve document is probably the 'failed' petition of the Minister of the Interior referred to in 1905 by the secretary of the Special Conference (under Kobeko) for censorship reform (*Protokoly, zhurnaly, Osoboe Soveshchanie dlia sostavleniia novogo ustava o pechati* [St Petersburg 1906], 6).

15 The views of Mirsky are summarized by his wife in E.A. Sviatopolk-Mirskaia, 'Dnevnik,' *Istoricheskie Zapiski* 77 (1965): 258. S.Iu. Witte, *Vospominaniia*, 3 vols. (Moscow 1960), 2: 328. (V.M. Kokovtsov, a lawyer and State Secretary who became prime minister in 1911, explains that Mirsky's press support angered many high bureaucrats; see *Iz moego proshlogo: Vospominaniia, 1903–1919 gg.*, 2 vols. [Paris 1933], 1: 48.) Liubimov, 'Russkaia smuta,' 218

16 'Protokol zasedaniia administrativnogo otdeleniia iuridicheskogo obshchestva,' 19 November 1904, *Vestnik Prava* (June 1905), 74

17 Witte, *Vospominaniia*, 2: 334, 354

18 *PSZ*, ser. 3, 24, sec. 1, no. 25495 (12 Dec. 1904), 1198; 'Osobyi zhurnal Komiteta Ministrov 28 i 31 dekabria, 1904,' *Materialy ... dlia sostavleniia novogo ustava o pechati*, 5

19 'Tsarizm v borbe s revoliutsionnoi pechatiu v 1905 g.,' *KA* 2 (105) (1941): 143

20 *PSZ*, ser. 3, 25, sec. 1, no. 25703 (21 Jan. 1905), 52–3. The Academy of Sciences was later to reject the proposal that it provide consulting experts to the censorship authority (S. Harcave, *First Blood: The Russian Revolution of 1905* [New York: The Macmillan Company 1964], 133).

21 *PSZ*, ser. 3, 25, sec. 1, no. 25703 (21 Jan. 1905), 52. The conference included such influential 'liberals' as Arsenev, Koni, Stasiulevich, the historian V.O. Kliuchevsky, and several Ministry of Justice officials.

22 *Protokoly, Osoboe Soveshchanie dlia sostavleniia novogo ustava o pechati*, 21. In mid-February, the conference received a petition from fourteen St Petersburg periodicals requesting just such reforms and echoing the petition of 1895 (V. Nabokov, 'K istorii ... zakonodatelstva o pechati,' in Nabokov, *Svoboda pechati pri obnovlennom stroe*, 4–5). The beginning of the Kobeko conference inspired an article by V. Sirkov in *Court Observer* (*Sudebnoe Obozrenie*) in May and June 1905 (nos. 11, 20, 23, 25). Sirkov explicated the principal western European censorship laws and pointed the way to a reformed Russian law. The state could be secure without preliminary censorship, he held, by incorporating into the criminal law injunctions against incitement to crimes and against published articles which made criminal activity 'attractive.' The Sirkov discussion foreshadowed the reform that followed in 1905–6.

23 Bulygin's memo of 10 March 1905 is in *KA* 2 (105) (1941): 144–5. S.I. Stykalin, 'Russkoe samoderzhavie i legalnaia pechat 1905 goda (k voprosu o proektakh sozdaniia ofitsioznoi pressy),' in B.I. Esin, ed., *Iz istorii russkoi zhurnalistiki kontsa XIX nachala XX v.* (Moscow 1973), 84–5

24 Ibid., 87–8

25 *PSZ*, ser. 3, 25, sec. 1, no. 26125 (17 April 1905), 257–8; ibid., no. 26263 (23 May 1905), 355–6

26 Witte became an official in the Odessa Government Railroad and maintained contacts with the local press; he knew well journalist S.T. Gerts-Vinogradsky. Later, in Kiev, as Director of the Southwestern Railroad, Witte was close to editor D.I. Pikhno of the *Kievan* (*Kievlianin*), in time a member of the Kobeko conference, and to editor-publisher A.Ia. Antonovich of the *Kievan Word* (*Kievskoe Slovo*). Witte inspired many articles on railroad and financial affairs. As minister of finance in St Petersburg, Witte was on friendly terms with M.N. Katkov, A.S. Suvorin, and V.P. Meshchersky – all important conservative publishers (A.E. Kaufman, 'Cherty iz zhizni S.Iu. Witte,' *IV* 140 [1915]: 220–31). See also Theodore H. von Laue, *Sergei Witte and the Industrialization of Russia* (New York: Columbia University Press 1963), 117–18.

27 A. Raffalovitch, '... *L'Abominable Vénalité de la Presse* ...' (Paris 1931), 2–6; S.Iu. Witte, 'Frantsuzskaia pressa i russkie zaimy,' *KA* 3 (10) (1925): 40. Witte's letter to the emperor appears to be a direct response to Rafalovich's letter of 13 October 1901.

28 Born into the hereditary gentry, Rachkovsky had a desultory career until he was accused of complicity in the assassination attempt on General Drenteln. While clearing himself, he expressed the wish to help the police fight revolutionaries; he later became a police agent. After the assassination of Alexander II, he joined the Holy Brotherhood, an anti-Semitic organization pledged to revenge the tsar's death. In 1883 he became an agent for the Department of Police under Plehve and the next year went abroad to establish the Foreign Okhrana. Norman Cohn has deduced that Rachkovsky directed the preparation of the notorious anti-Semitic document, 'Protocols of the Elders of Zion' (Norman Cohn, *Warrant for Genocide: The Myth of the Jewish World-Conspiracy and the Protocols of the Elders of Zion* [London: Eyre and Spottiswoode 1967], 86–8, 106–7). 'Karera P.I. Rachkovskogo: Dokumenty,' *Byloe*, n.s. [30], no. 2 (February 1918): 79

29 Frenchmen in Rachkovsky's pay included Jules Hansen, a government official who wrote for *L'Echo de Paris* and other publications; Calmette of *Figaro*; and Maure of *Petit Parisien*. Paid 500 francs per month as an advisor was Raymond Recouli (code name 'Ratmir') of *Le Temps* and later *Figaro* (V.K. Agafonov, *Zagranichnaia okhranka: Sostavleno po sekretnym dokumentam zagranichnoi agentury i Departamenta politsii* [Petrograd 1918], 369).

30 Manuilov was by all accounts a questionable character and the documents about him read like a picaresque novel ('Prikliucheniia I.F. Manuilova: Po arkhivnym materialam,' *Byloe*, n.s. [27/28], nos. 5–6 [November 1917], [236]–286). See also Okhrana Archives, Hoover Institution, IXb 2A, and Agafonov, *Zagranichnaia okhranka*, 61.

31 James William Long, 'Russian Manipulation of the French Press,' *Slavic Review* 31, no. 2 (1972): 347–8

32 Witte, *Vospominaniia*, 3: 316. Tatishchev's principal books, published in Russian, were *The Foreign Policy of Nicholas I* (1887); *The Emperor Nicholas I and Foreign Courts* (1889); *The Emperor Alexander II and His Reign*, 2 vols. (1903). Tatishchev also published articles in French periodicals.

33 Okhrana Archives, IXb 2A, B; Agafonov, *Zagranichnaia okhranka*, 61

34 E. Tarle, ed., 'Doneseniia iz Berlina S.S. Tatishcheva V.K. Pleve v 1904,' *KA* 4 (17) (1926): 186–92

35 Long, 'Russian Manipulation,'.354; Okhrana Archives, XIIIc (3), 18

36 V. Doroshevich, 'Russkoe Slovo,' *Polveka dlia knigi*, 394

37 Doroshevich, 'Russkoe Slovo,' 420

38 Kugel, *Literaturnye vospominaniia*, 102; Mirsky, *A History of Russian Literature*, 406

39 *Russkie Vedomosti, 1863–1913*, 137
40 The conference's proposed statute is in 'Vysochaishe uchrezhdennoe Osoboe Soveshchanie dlia sostavleniia novogo ustava o pechati,' *Proekt ustava o pechati* [St Petersburg 1905], 2.
41 *Proekt ustava o pechati*, 3–8
42 M. Ganfman, 'Iavochnyi period svobody stolichnoi pechati,' in Nabokov, *Svoboda pechati pri obnovlennom stroe*, 48–50
43 'Interviu S.Iu. Witte s predstaviteliami pechati,' *KA* 11–12 (1925): 99–105
44 Liubimov, 'Russkaia smuta,' 339
45 Witte's statement appeared in *Government Messenger*. Harcave quotes it in full in *First Blood*, 289–92. See also Howard D. Mehlinger and John M. Thompson, *Count Witte and the Tsarist Government in the 1905 Revolution* (Bloomington, Ind.: Indiana University Press 1972), 74.
46 Witte, *Vospominaniia*, 3: 63–4
47 Ganfman, 'Iavochnyi period,' 53
48 B. Doroshevsky, 'Knizhnoe delo v epokhu pervoi russkoi revoliutsii (1905–1907),' *Katorga i ssylka* 1 (1931), 170; A.Z. Dun, 'Izdatelstvo Marii Malykh [1901–1909],' *Kniga: Issledovaniia i materialy* 6 (1962), 189
49 Stykalin, 'Russkoe samoderzhavie,' 91. Stykalin credits S.P. Tatishchev with this project but surely S.S. Tatishchev initiated it. Both Witte and Spassky credit S.S. Tatishchev with conceiving a new kind of government newspaper, and Tatishchev had informed Plehve that he intended a new project for the 'press bureau.'
50 Stykalin, 'Russkoe samoderzhavie,' 88; Witte, *Vospominaniia*, 3: 316
51 Witte, *Vospominaniia*, 2: 358. The conference made one important change. Initially it had favoured a waiting period for censorship review between the printing of a work and its distribution. After 17 October, the conference agreed to the submission of a work to the censorship authority at the same time as its distribution (Nabokov, 'K istorii,' 41).
52 *PSZ*, ser. 3, 25, sec. 1, no. 26962 (24 Nov. 1905), 837
53 Aleksei Aleksandrovich Spassky, 'Vospominaniia,' Columbia University Archives, 213
54 M.L. Goldstein, *Pechat pered sudom: Rechi po delam 'Rusi,' 'Nashei Zhizni' i 'Syna Otechestva'* (St Petersburg 1906), 24; W.S. Woytinsky, *Stormy Passage: A Personal History through Two Russian Revolutions to Democracy and Freedom, 1905–1960* (New York: The Vanguard Press [1961]), 87
55 Witte, 'Vospominaniia,' 3: 65
56 Goldstein, *Pechat pered sudom*, 21
57 Ibid., 24, 32
58 Ordinsky, 'Pechat i sud,' 140

59 E.A. Valle-de-Barr, 'Svoboda' russkoi pechati (posle 17-go oktiabria, 1905) (Samara 1906), 24; Liubimov, 'Russkaia smuta,' 364

60 Otchet po deloproizvodstvu Gos. Soveta za sessiiu 1905–06 gg. (St Petersburg 1906), 637–44; PSZ, ser. 3, 26 sec. 1, no. 27574 (18 March 1906), 281–3

61 Spassky, 'Vospominaniia,' 213

62 Witte, Vospominaniia, 3: 317

63 PSZ, ser. 3, 26, sec. 1, no. 27815 (26 April 1906), 481–3

64 S. Varshavsky, 'Pravovoe polozhenie izdatelskogo dela v Rossii,' Polveka dlia knigi, 279–80

65 S.R. Mintslov, '14 mesiatsev "svobody pechati,"' Byloe 3 (March 1907), 123–46. Valle-de-Barr lists all the government actions against the press from 21 October 1905 to 14 June 1906 ('Svoboda' russkoi pechati, 33–182).

66 Jacob Walkin, 'Government Controls over the Press in Russia, 1905–1914,' Russian Review 13, no. 3 (1954): 206–7

67 Goremykin to Nicholas II, 4 June 1906, KA 2 (1922): 280

68 M. Lemke, ed., Trudy pervogo vserossiiskogo sezda izdatelei i knigoprodavtsev, 30 iiunia-5 iiulia 1909 goda v S. Petersburge (St Petersburg 1901), 261

Bibliography

Author's Note: I have limited the list of sources consulted to archives and principal imperial printed documents on the censorship administration. My main other sources appear in the chapter notes. I have benefitted from many other sources, especially works of scholarship in Russian history that do not appear either among the works consulted or in the notes. Scholars wishing to obtain my complete record of consulted works can write to me through the University of Toronto Press.

ARCHIVAL COLLECTIONS

Archive of Russian and East European History and Culture, Columbia University
Golitsyn, Prince A.D., 'Vospominaniia'
Liubimov, D.N., 'Russkaia smuta nachala deviatisotykh godov, 1902–1906: Po vospominaniiam, lichnym zapiskam i dokumentam'
Shlippe, F.V., 'Vospominaniia'
Spassky, A.A., 'Vospominaniia'

Archive of the Hoover Institution on War, Revolution, and Peace, Stanford University
Grand Duke Constantine Nikolaevich
Okhrana

Arkhiv Instituta Literatury. Pushkinskii Dom (PD)
Golovnin, A.V.
Kavelin, K.D.
Nikitenko, A.V.
Vestnik Evropy
Dolgorukov, P.V. (93)
Pletnev, P.A. (234)

Russkaia Starina (265)
Golos (584)
Valuev, P.A. (559)

Gosudarstvennyi Istoricheskii Muzei v Moskve (GIM)
Korf, M.A. (83)
Mukhanov, N.A. (177)

Tsentral'nyi Gosudarstvennyi Arkhiv Oktiabrskoi Revoliutsii (TSGAOR)
Alexander II (678)
Third Section (109)
Valuev, P.A. (544)
Marble Palace (722)
Winter Palace (728)
Grand Duke Constantine Nikolaevich (661) (678)

Tsentral'nyi Gosudarstvennyi Istoricheskii Arkhiv SSSR (TSGIA)
Chief Administration of the Censorship, Ministry of Public Education (772)
Special Chancellery of the Ministry of Public Education (773)
Council of the Ministry of the Interior for Press Affairs (774)
Central Administration of the Censorship, Ministry of the Interior (775)
Chief Administration of Press Affairs, Ministry of the Interior (776)
Petersburg Committee of Press Affairs under the Chief Administration for Press
    Affairs (777)
Censorship Office of the Third Section of His Majesty's Own Chancellery (780)
Golovnin, A.V. (851)
Valuev, P.A. (908)
Department of Law of the State Council (1149)
Department on the Economy of the State Council (1152)
Main Committee on Peasant Affairs (1180)
Files and Papers of the Chairmen and Members of the State Council (1250)
Second Section of His Majesty's Own Chancellery (1261)
Council of Ministers (1275) (1276)
Chief Administration on Local Economy, Ministry of the Interior (1288)
Documents from the Cancelled Files of the Senate and Ministry of Justice (1400)
Ministry of Justice (1405)

Otdel rukopisei Gosudarstvennoi Biblioteki im. V.I. Lenina v Moskve (GBL)
Katkov, M.N. (19)
Cherkassky / I (57)

Stoianovsky, N.I. (86)
Kiselëv (129)
Miliutin (169)

Otdel ruskopisei Gosudarstvennoi Publichnoi Biblioteki im. M.E. Saltykova-Shchedrina (GPB)
Valuev, P.A. (126)
Golovnin, A.V. (208)
Goncharov, I.A. (209)
Korf, M.A. (380)
Norov, A.S. (531)

LAWS, STATUTES, OFFICIAL PUBLICATIONS

[Golovnin, A.V.]. *Vsepoddanneishii doklad Min. Nar. Pros. po proektu ustava o knigopechatanii, chitannyi v Sovete Ministrov 10 Ian. 1863 g.* ... St Petersburg 1863
Glavnoe Upravlenie po Delam Pechati. *Sbornik postanovlenii i rasporiazhenii po delam pechati 1865 goda.* St Petersburg 1865
[Kapnist, P.I.]. *Kratkoe obozrenie napravleniia periodicheskikh izdanii i gazet i otzyvov ikh po vazhneishim pravitel'stvennym i drugim voprosam za 1862 g.* St Petersburg 1862
Materialy, sobrannye osoboiu komissieiu vysochaishe uchrezhdënnoiu 2 noiabria 1869 g. dlia peresmotra deistvuiushchikh postanovlenii o tsenzure i pechati. 5 vols. St Petersburg 1870
Materialy vysochaishe uchrezhdënnogo osobogo soveshchaniia dlia sostavleniia novogo ustava o pechati [St Petersburg 1905]
Ministerstvo Narodnogo Prosveshcheniia. *Mneniia raznykh lits o preobrazovanii tsenzury.* St Petersburg 1862
Ministerstvo Narodnogo Prosveshcheniia. *Ob'iasnitel'naia zapiska k proektu novogo ustava o tsenzure 1859 goda.* St Petersburg n.d.
Ministerstvo Narodnogo Prosveshcheniia. *Sbornik postanovlenii i rasporiazhenii po tsenzure s 1720 po 1862 god.* St Petersburg 1862
Ministerstvo Vnutrennikh Del. *Sbornik rasporiazhenii po delam pechati (s 1863 po 1-e sentiabria 1865 g.).* St Petersburg 1865
Ministerstvo Vnutrennikh Del. *Sobranie materialov o napravlenii razlichnykh otraslei russkoi slovesnosti za poslednee desiatiletie i obshchestvennoi zhurnalistiki za 1863 i 1864 g.* St Petersburg 1865
Otchët po deloproizvodstvu Gosudarstvennogo Soveta za sessiiu 1905–1906 gg. St Petersburg 1906
Pervonachal'nyi proekt Ustava o knigopechatanii, sost. komissieiu ... pri Ministerstve Narodnogo Prosveshcheniia. St Petersburg 1862

Prilozheniia k zapiske predsedatelia komiteta dlia peresmotra tsenzurnogo ustava, deistvitel'nogo statskogo sovetnika Berte, i chlena sego komiteta, statskogo sovetnika Iankevicha. St Petersburg 1862

Proekt tsenzurnogo ustava ... E.P. Kovalevskim, 1859 (n.p., n.d.)

Proekt ustava o knigopechatanii: Vvedenie, obshchee polozhenie i tri pervye razdela. St Petersburg 1862

Proekt ustava o knigopechatanii: Razdely chetvërtyi, piatyi i shestoi i proekt shtata ustanovlenii po delam knigopechataniia s ob'iasnitel'noiu zapiskoiu. St Petersburg 1862

Proekt ustava o knigopechatanii. St Petersburg 1863

Proekt ustava o pechati i'tsenzure. St Petersburg 1870

Proekty iz'iatii iz obshchego poriadka ugolovnogo sudoproizvodstva dlia del pechati ... St Petersburg 1866

Protokoly vysoch. uchrezhdënnogo pod pred. deistv. tainogo sovetnika Kobeko Osobogo Soveshchaniia dlia sostavleniia novogo ustava o pechati (10 fevr. – 4 dek. 1905). St Petersburg 1917

Svod Zakonov Rossiiskoi Imperii. Vol. 14. St Petersburg 1890

Svod Zakonov Ugolovnykh; kniga pervaia: Ulozhenie o nakazaniiakh ugolovnykh i ispravitel'nykh. St Petersburg 1866

Svod zamechanii na proekt Ustava sudoproizvodstva grazhdanskogo [1864?]

[Valuev, P.A.]. *Predstavlenie min. vnu. del po proektu ustava o knigopechatanii s sleduiushchimi k nemu prilozheniiami.* St Petersburg 1864

Vysochaishe uchrezhdënnoe Osoboe Soveshchanie dlia sostavleniia novogo ustava o pechati. *Proekt ustava o pechati* [St Petersburg 1905]

Zhurnal vysochaishe uchrezhdënnoi komissii dlia peresmotra, dopolneniia i izmeneniia postanovlenii po delam knigopechataniia, 19 March 1862. St Petersburg 1862

Zhurnal ... komissii dlia rassmotreniia proekta ustava o knigopechatanii. St Petersburg 1863

Zhurnaly osoboi komissii ... 2-go noiabria 1869 g. dlia peresmotra deistvuiushchikh postanovlenii o tsenzure i pechati. 8 November 1869–19 December 1870 (n.p., n.d.)

Index